HERE IS THE WAY IT WAS

on the coral atolls and in the island jungles that made up the Pacific Theater in World War II.

Some of these reports are written by trained war correspondents like John Hersey, Robert Sherrod and Hanson Baldwin, some are taken from the personal accounts of marines who waded into withering enemy fire on the beachheads.

In addition, there are maps, and a running commentary which establishes the background and the chronology of the war in the Pacific, and sets each report in its context.

The introduction is by a man who served as a reporter for YANK, The Army Weekly, in the Central Pacific.

This is a companion volume to COMBAT: EUROPEAN THEATER.

COMBAT
PACIFIC THEATER

WORLD WAR II

Edited by DON CONGDON
Introduction by MERLE MILLER

A DELL FIRST EDITION
an original volume

Published by
DELL PUBLISHING CO., INC.
750 Third Avenue
New York 17, New York

Designed and produced by
Western Printing & Lithographing Company

Cover painting by Robert Shulz

COPYRIGHT NOTICES AND ACKNOWLEDGMENTS

"Pearl Harbor," copyright, 1944, by the Marine Corps Association. Reprinted from the Marine Corps Gazette and *The Marine Corps Reader,* published by G. P. Putnam's Sons, N.Y.C.

"Death March on Bataan," copyright, 1944, by Marajen Stevick Dyess. From *The Dyess Story,* published by G. P. Putnam's Sons, N.Y.C., and reprinted by permission of the publisher.

"Action in the Sunda Strait," copyright, 1953, by Ronald McKie, from *The Survivors,* used by special permission of the publisher, The Bobbs-Merrill Company, Inc., Indianapolis, and the Australian publisher, Angus & Robertson, Ltd., Sydney.

"The Battle of Midway," copyright, 1949, by The Curtis Publishing Company. Reprinted from *The Saturday Evening Post* where it appeared under the title "Never a Battle Like Midway." Used by permission of the author's agent, Brandt & Brandt.

"Fighting Back in New Guinea," copyright, 1943, by George H. Johnston, from *The Toughest Fighting in the World,* used by permission of the publisher, Duell, Sloan and Pearce, Inc., N.Y.C., and the Australian publisher, Angus & Robertson, Ltd., Sydney.

"Guadalcanal: The Turning Point," copyright, 1947, by Major Frank Hough. From *The Island War,* published by J. B. Lippincott Company, Philadelphia, and used by permission of the publisher.

First printing—December, 1958

Printed in U.S.A.

Contents

INTRODUCTION

If I were to introduce a stranger to a friend of mine, my friend might reasonably ask, "What kind of guy is he?" and it would be up to me to tell my friend as candidly as I was able.

The same is true of a man who has taken on the responsibility of introducing a book. It is his duty to say what kind of book it is as frankly as he can.

Well, in the first place there are no heroics in these pages. There are courage and heroism, but those are quite different. Let me use a personal experience to illustrate the kind of thing I mean:

In mid-December, 1944, I attended a press conference at the headquarters of the First U.S. Army Division, then close to the Roer Valley. General Clarence Huebner, commander of the division, said a few words about the hundred and eighty-two fighting days his men had been through since they had landed at Easy Red Beach on D-Day. Then the general added, "At a time like this . . . it is fitting that a fighting soldier should be here. . . ."

And he told us about the young man who had been quietly sitting at his side; this sergeant, the general said, had been awarded the Congressional Medal of Honor, a Silver Star and a Bronze Star with clusters.

"Sergeant Ehlers is a platoon leader," General Huebner went on. "He did things that it is unbelievable that any man could do and live. It is not merely the doing of such deeds, magnificent as they are, that makes this great division, but that other men live up to the doing."

There is not time to tell here all of the courageous things that Sergeant Ehlers had done, but they had begun a few minutes after he had landed in Normandy on D-Day when he wiped out seven Germans in a single hedgerow, and had continued all the way until the time of a street fight in Stolberg, Germany, when, though wounded, he had done single-handed battle with a German tank, finally putting it out of action.

Now one of the correspondents at this conference, a fellow who flinched mightily every time a shell jiggled the map on the wall, leaned toward Sergeant Ehlers, who was twenty-two and before the war had worked on his father's farm in Kansas.

"Ehlers, do you really hate the Germans so much that you *like* killing them?" this individual demanded. At first, the sergeant appeared not to hear the question, but it was repeated, three times, as I recall, and then Ehlers, a very thin man with dark hair, looked at the correspondent, and, giving it thought as he went along, he answered the question to the best of his ability:

"Sir, I don't hate anybody, and I don't like to kill anybody. But if somebody gets in my way when I have a job to do so I have to kill him so I can get on with it, why then I kill him, and that's all there is to it."

The ruthlessly honest quality of what Sergeant Ehlers said is the quality that is in this book. This is a book which is concerned with men who from the time of Pearl Harbor until the last tunnel was cleared on Iwo Jima did what they had to do when somebody got in their way.

These accounts were written by men who were either there at the time or know what it was like to have been there and have the ability to tell about it accurately. There is, for instance, a sketch by a Marine First Sergeant telling what happened to him and to the detachment he headed on the *U.S.S. Tennessee* at the time of the Japanese attack on Pearl Harbor. He tells about the surprise and the fear and the killing and the destruction and about the awful silence that followed the departure of the enemy planes. He tells what he saw when he went topside on the *Tennessee*, the sight of the burning *West Virginia* and the *Arizona*, the bombed *Maryland*, the listing, smoking *California*, and the *Nevada*, which was sinking.

"One had a none too cheerful feeling at the thought that five of our eight battleships had been sunk or badly damaged in the attack," he wrote.

Sergeant Emmons jotted down his account of what he saw

at Pearl Harbor on that December morning shortly after the attack. He did not have time for frills of language, and that is true of all fourteen of the men whose contributions are here, and it is true of the men who set down what it was like in Europe for the companion volume, *Combat: European Theater—World War II*. J. Bryan, III wrote his detailed story of what happened during the Battle of Midway seven years after it occurred, but the effect is the same. It is the same in the story of what the Marines did on Iwo Jima, which was written by five of the combat correspondents who were members of the Marine Corps during the Second World War. At one point, they are describing the death of Sergeant Reid Chamberlain, a respected figure in the Corps who had been involved in many courageous exploits, including a hitch as a guerrilla in the Philippines.

"There is nothing you can say or do when a good friend is suddenly killed in battle," the Marines write. "You feel stunned, angry, and sad and somewhat frustrated. We could have fired point-blank for the rest of the day at those holes. The Japs would only have laughed at us. In an instant they had claimed one of our best men. Chamberlain's wonderful war record had ended abruptly. After so many heroic deeds, it seemed an added tragedy that he was killed while doing nothing but walking. There was nothing anybody could do about it."

It was the same on Eniwetok when Sergeant John Bushemi was killed by a Japanese knee-mortar while he and I were doing nothing but walking. It had no meaning; it was obscene waste, and there was nothing anybody could do about it. There is that quality of verisimilitude in each of the accounts of battle in this book.

Let me mention another quality this book has. It evokes a past about which most of us do a lot of thinking, and it does so vividly.

Nowadays on almost any given evening in any given bar and in a great many living rooms, if there are present two or more men who were in the Second World War, one or the other is likely to be reminded of something that happened to him while he was in the Army. Or the Marine Corps or Navy or Coast Guard or Ambulance Corps or Red

Cross. A number of ex-airraid wardens try to get into the act, but it has been my experience that they have just about as little to contribute as a retired scout master.

But the veteran whose memory has been stirred—and it usually takes so little—absolutely has to tell you how he felt when he was getting into an LST that would take him to the beachhead in Sicily. Or what it was like manning a gun on the *Enterprise* during the Battle of Midway. Or possibly the highly interesting thoughts that went through his mind while he was waiting for the ferry that would take him to Governor's Island where he spent the entire war, and, by God, don't think they had it so easy over there at Fort Jay. There was this one chicken colonel in charge of advanced calisthenics who . . .

If the veteran stops his narrative long enough to inhale or take another swallow of his whisky, someone else will move right in, describing what happened to him when he got back to Oran from the desert, or possibly the psychic trauma he suffered while waiting to get into the post exchange at the Roney Plaza Hotel in Miami Beach.

I'm not sure why we are all so fond of recalling those far-off days, but we are. Partly, I suppose, it is that we were young then, and, given a choice, it is better to be young. Partly it is that we did not have to worry about the payments on the house, or about the discouraging fact that the car which is not quite paid for has completely disintegrated. Partly it is because memory is short, and memory is kind. We tend to forget the bad moments and remember the good.

But there is something else, I think, which is particularly true of men who were in combat. There are moments in combat when most of us were a little better than we knew we could be or, very probably, have been since. In combat a man would give you his last cigarette or his last bar of chocolate or his last dry pair of socks, and maybe ten minutes later he would be dead, but maybe he is still alive, and maybe he is you. If he is, you will look back on that time with an aching longing.

There are many instances of such selflessness in the fourteen pieces which follow. But three brief examples will show you what it was.

The first is from the companion volume about the European Theater; it is by Sergeant Mack Morriss, who continued to think like an infantryman after he had been transferred to *Yank*, which is one reason he was able to write as he did of the Huertgen Forest:

". . . The forest will bear the scars of our advance long after our scars have healed, and the Infantry has scars that will never heal.

"For Huertgen was agony, and there was no glory in it except the glory of courageous men—the MP whose testicles were hit by shrapnel and who said, 'Okay, doc, I can take it'; the man who walked forward, firing Tommy guns with both hands until an arm was blown off and then kept on firing the other Tommy gun until he disappeared in a mortar burst."

In this present volume T/Sgt. Asa Bordages describes a bitter encounter with the Japanese which took place in New Britain. It was one which was probably not mentioned in the dispatches, but it will be remembered by the handful who were there and by all those who read Bordages's piece, "Suicide Creek."

You will be unable to forget it partly because of what Bordages wrote about a Marine Corps First Lieutenant with the wonderful name of Elisha Atkins. Lieutenant Atkins was understandably called Tommy Harvard; he had just graduated from that university, and he had played football there, too. A sergeant said that Atkins was "very quiet and polite as hell."

Sergeant Bordages describes the many tortuous attempts to get across that creek, which had no name except the one the Marines had given it; it was only twenty feet across at its widest, but many men were killed in the attempts to get across, and always the rest were driven back. Bordages writes of an enemy charge and a dive bombing which followed and which was all the more unendurable because there was no way of hitting back. "You can't describe hell," says Bordages. "You can only go through it."

A little later about half of Lieutenant Atkins's platoon did get across the creek, and then the Japanese opened up. There was no panic, but there was some dying. Some of the platoon got back to the place they had started out from; others, alive and wounded, lay in the cold water, including Tommy Harvard.

Private First Class Luther J. Raschke says:

"I tried to help him along, but he wouldn't come. He'd been hit three times. A slug had smashed his shoulder. He was losing blood pretty fast. But he wouldn't leave. He was trying to see that everybody got out first. He told me, 'Go on. Go on!' He wouldn't let anybody stop for him. He said, 'Keep the line moving.' He made us leave him there."

Raschke and his party finally made it out, but they couldn't forget Tommy Harvard. Raschke said, "I guess everybody else is out."

" 'Yeah,' said Corporal Alexander Caldwell of Nashville, Tennessee.

" 'Well . . .'

" 'Yeah,' said Corporal Caldwell.

"Raschke lay down on the edge of the creek, his nose practically in the water, and he softly called, 'Tommy Harvard . . . Tommy Harvard.'

"A voice said, 'I'm down here.'

" 'It sounded weak,' says Raschke, 'but we figured it might be a trap. So I said, "What's your real name?" '

"The voice said, 'Elisha Atkins.' So we knew it was him. We crawled down and pulled him out. He said, 'God! Am I glad to see you!'

"He was shaking from hours in the chill water, weak from loss of blood, but still calmly Harvard as they carried him to the rear."

I don't know what ever happened to Atkins. I wish I did. He is the kind of man one would want to know, and so are Private Raschke and Corporal Caldwell and the other two who volunteered to go back to look for Tommy Harvard.

Having said some of the things this book does do, let me finish off by putting down what to its great credit it does not do: it does not romanticize the war. Many movies have done that, and so have some writers. Memory being as unreliable as it is, I suspect we are all a little guilty of romanticizing, each in his own way.

One day last summer on Madison Avenue in New York I

met a man who had been a platoon leader with the First Division in Europe. Harry and I met many times during the war; he had joined the outfit in North Africa late in 1942, somewhat before the terrible battle for Hill 109. He went the full way in Europe, from Easy Red on, getting only a piece of shrapnel in his shoulder. He was given a battlefield commission because he was a very good soldier.

In those days Harry had talked about being a forest ranger after the war. He knew exactly the kind of place he wanted to be stationed. First, you took a two-day train ride, and then you had a two-day mule ride, away from the nearest railway station, after which you got off and walked into the woods for another two days. Once he got into those woods, Harry said, he never intended to come out; when he ran out of food, he would subsist on nuts and berries. Partly he was kidding, but mostly he was not. He really did want to be a forest ranger.

Well, when I saw Harry in New York last summer, he dismissed the forest ranger notion. In fact, he rather hurriedly said, "I don't ever remember saying anything so foolish." He was working for the Bell Telephone Company, and he lived in Levittown, and I must come out and meet the wife and three kids. Meantime, how about a drink?

We all know there is no such thing as one drink. Along about the third or fourth, Harry was saying things like, "We had it rough once in a while, sure, but, by God, we had our good times, too."

And he spoke of a couple of leaves he had had in London and of one in Oran, and of an overnight spent largely on and around the Champs Élysées, and he told the waiter we would both have another of the same.

"No, sir, by God," Harry said. "It wasn't so bad. I'm not saying I want my kid to go over and fight for Chancre Jack or anything like that, but you got to admit we had some high old times."

That night before I went to sleep I remembered something Harry had said many years before, at the time of the Ardennes. Harry was telling me about a night just before the breakout from St. Lô. The outfit was dug in at a cemetery, Harry said, and it was a warm day, and there were the graves that had been opened by the shells, and there were many recent dead about, ours and theirs and French civilians and one cow, killed two days before.

Remembering that warm night, Harry had said to me in the Ardennes, "I kept thinking at the time that I wished you could bottle that smell. I kept wishing you could bottle about ten thousand bottles of that smell, and along about twenty years from now when they start getting us ready for the next one, it could be unbottled a little at a time. Nobody that ever smelled that smell would ever go to another war."

Harry had forgotten that smell; all he remembered was the whiff of a whore's perfume on a Paris boulevard.

Maybe we have to do that; maybe if we remembered, life could not be endured.

I do not know. I do know that the events recorded in this book have recorded only the truth. There is a letter quoted in John Hersey's piece called *Survival.* The letter was written at a time when it looked as if Lieutenant John F. Kennedy and the other two officers and all ten enlisted men on Kennedy's PT boat had been killed. The author of the letter was another officer in the PT squadron and he wrote to his mother, "George Ross lost his life for a cause that he believed in stronger than any one of us, because he was an idealist in the purest sense. Jack Kennedy, the Ambassador's son, was on the same boat and also lost his life. The man that said the cream of a nation is lost in war can never be accused of making an overstatement of a very cruel fact."

Jack Kennedy, now a U.S. Senator from Massachusetts, and Ross were not dead, but the fact remains, and it is a cruel one.

Finally, a letter by a Lieutenant Timmermann, about whom you may read in *Combat: European Theater:* To his wife, this unlettered man wrote, "La Vera, there's no glory in war. Maybe those who have never been in battle find that certain glory and glamour that doesn't exist. Perhaps they get it from the movies or the comic strips."

MERLE MILLER
Brewster, New York

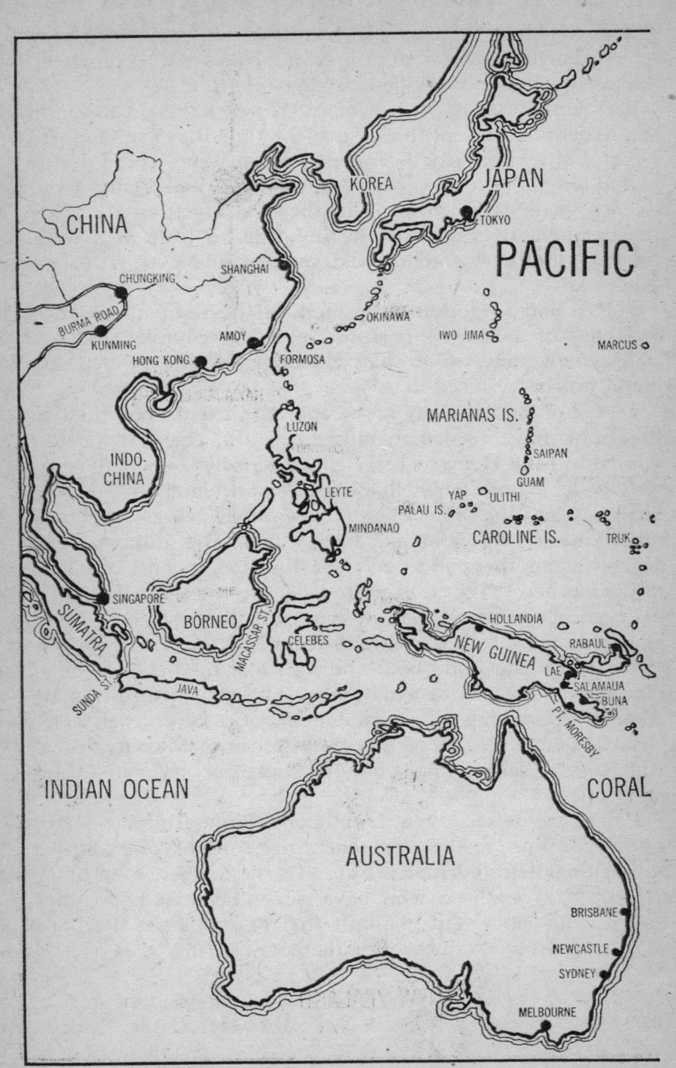
KOREA
JAPAN
TOKYO
CHINA
PACIFIC
SHANGHAI
CHUNGKING
BURMA ROAD
OKINAWA
KUNMING
AMOY
IWO JIMA
MARCUS
HONG KONG
FORMOSA
MARIANAS IS.
LUZON
INDO-CHINA
SAIPAN
GUAM
LEYTE
YAP
ULITHI
PALAU IS.
MINDANAO
CAROLINE IS.
TRUK
SINGAPORE
HOLLANDIA
SUMATRA
BORNEO
MACASSAR ST.
CELEBES
NEW GUINEA
RABAUL
LAE
SALAMAUA
BUNA
SUNDA ST.
JAVA
PT. MORESBY
INDIAN OCEAN
CORAL
AUSTRALIA
BRISBANE
NEWCASTLE
SYDNEY
MELBOURNE

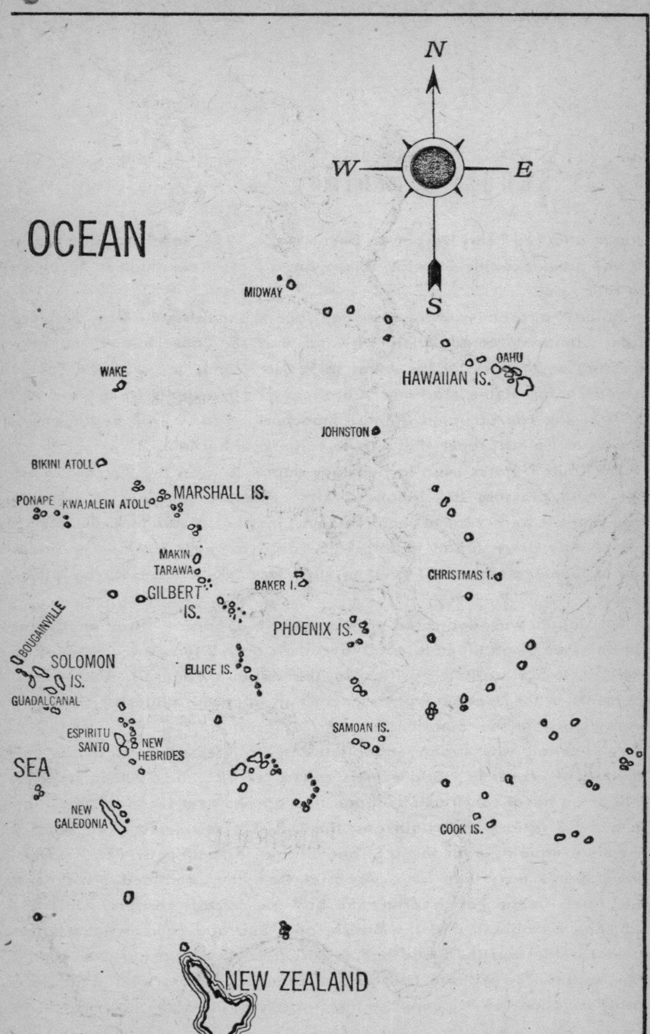
N
W
E
S
OCEAN
MIDWAY
OAHU
HAWAIIAN IS.
WAKE
JOHNSTON
BIKINI ATOLL
MARSHALL IS.
PONAPE
KWAJALEIN ATOLL
MAKIN
TARAWA
BAKER I.
CHRISTMAS I.
GILBERT
IS.
PHOENIX IS.
BOUGAINVILLE
SOLOMON
IS.
ELLICE IS.
GUADALCANAL
SAMOAN IS.
ESPIRITU
SANTO
NEW
HEBRIDES
SEA
NEW
CALEDONIA
COOK IS.
NEW ZEALAND

Sunday Morning

Japan attacked Pearl Harbor on December 7, 1941. For the United States it was a catastrophic surprise; for Japan, a logical next step in her drive to rule Asia.

In half a century of aggression, Japan had already won Formosa from China, defeated Russia on land and sea, absorbed Korea and, fighting on the side of the Allies in World War I, had won the Pacific island chains of the Marianas, Carolines and Marshalls from Germany; in 1931 she had occupied Chinese Manchuria, and in 1937 began an invasion of China proper that was to last through 1945.

The United States tried to persuade Japan to drop the war on China; she could pressure the Japanese with economic sanctions (U.S. scrap iron and oil were vital to their war machine) but it was feared that this would only drive Japan to attack the oil-rich Dutch East Indies (Indonesia). She therefore first tried to stop Japanese aggression by diplomacy.

But Japan was dedicated to war. Many Japanese traditionally regarded war as an ultimate good, and their army's past successes helped raise it to an exalted position in the nation's counsels. There were elements in the Japanese government that opposed militarism, but they were clearly in the minority.

And Japan was strong enough to ignore Western protests. In the naval conferences of world powers called in 1921 and 1930 to fix limitations on naval construction, Japan had agreed to a secondary position in a 5-5-3 ratio with Britain and the U.S. But secretly she worked for complete equality with the U.S. and Britain, or better. By Pearl Harbor day Japan's navy was more powerful than the combined British and U.S. fleets in the Pacific area. She had ten aircraft carriers, while the U.S. had only three and the British, one. She had constructed the two largest battleships the world had ever seen, both displacing over 60,000 tons, and armed with 18.1-inch guns. Even more important, Japan was the first nation to fully embrace the strategy of using the aircraft carrier as an offensive weapon (heretofore carriers had been used only to protect big battleships).

Diplomacy didn't succeed in persuading Japan to change her ways. Early in 1938 the U.S. began adopting economic sanctions against her piecemeal, until, in July 1941, trade with Japan was severed and her assets in the U.S. were frozen. A calculated risk had been taken that Japan would not strike at the East Indies before the U.S. was strong enough to deter her. But the American people weren't ready to take the risk of war seriously, and Congress was in no mood to appropriate the sums needed to expand the armed services. With only limited means, Gen. Marshall and Adm. Stark, the heads of the army and navy, now set about relocating their small forces, strengthening wherever possible the commitments the U.S. had assumed in the Pacific. Elements of the 4th Marine Division stationed in Shanghai were to be withdrawn to the Philippines (orders were not delivered in time to prevent their capture by the Japanese in December), an infantry division in training was scheduled to go to the Philippines (war began before they could be sent), and the navy was alerted to the possibilities of imminent war with Japan. In the meantime, the State Department and President Roosevelt were negotiating with the Japanese, for if nothing else could be accomplished time had to be gained for the nation to build up its strength.

But Japan had no time to waste. Suspension of trade with the U.S. caught her with little more than a year's supply of oil on hand. In September 1941, the Japanese military leaders gave their government six weeks to reinstate oil imports from the U.S.; otherwise they would invade the East Indies, accepting the full implications of possible war with the U.S. and European powers, most of whom were too involved in the war with Germany to fight Japan in the Pacific.

By early October the diplomats were still bogged down over the issue of Japan's withdrawal from China. The Japanese army now took over full control of the government, with Gen. Tojo as premier. Early in November Tojo's cabinet, now committed to hostilities, ordered the Japanese fleet to prepare for aggressive operations against the East Indies and the Philippines, and called for a carrier attack on Pearl Harbor. There was to be no declaration of war (as there had been none in Germany's earlier invasions), but a total surprise attack.* The Pearl Harbor

* Official negotiations would continue until the very hour news was flashed to Washington that Pearl Harbor was attacked.

striking force would consist of six carriers, two battleships, two cruisers, nine destroyers, and twenty-seven submarines. The fleet left Japan on November 26th, scheduled to strike Hawaii around December 8th, if all went well. To achieve surprise, a course was charted north to the Aleutians, and then south, coming in north of Hawaii. The Japanese naval commander had instructions to abandon his attack if discovered, but because of overcast weather, and because of failures in U.S. reconnaissance at Hawaii on the morning of December 7th, the attack would achieve its purpose—complete and disastrous surprise.

At a point 275 miles north of Pearl Harbor, the Japanese carriers turned into the wind, and launched their planes. But of 423 jammed into the carriers, 353 would see action that day. At 0750 they would find 70 combat ships of the U.S. Pacific Fleet in Pearl Harbor, and only one would be under way when the Japs arrived. Here is an eyewitness report of what happened.

PEARL HARBOR

by 1st Sgt. Roger Emmons

At 7:55 a.m. on 7 December, 1941 (as all the world now knows), the Japanese made a surprise aerial attack on the U.S. Pacific Fleet in Pearl Harbor, Territory of Hawaii. The sole object of the attack was to annihilate the American fleet—battleships in particular.

The *U.S.S. Tennessee,* Captain C. E. Reordan commanding, was one of eight battleships which participated in the battle. On that occasion the *California, Maryland, Tennessee, Arizona,* and *Nevada,* respectively, were moored in single file at Ford Island in the middle of Pearl Harbor. The *Oklahoma* was berthed alongside the *Maryland,* while the *West Virginia* was beside the *Tennessee.* The eighth battleship, *Pennsylvania,* was in drydock at the Navy Yard. Other warships of various types were also present in the harbor.

It was a beautiful morning with fleecy clouds in the sky, and the visibility was good. Aboard the *Tennessee* the usual Sunday schedule prevailed. Many of the officers had gone ashore over the week end. The Marine Detachment was drawn up on the fantail for morning Colors, mess tables were being cleared away, some of the men were getting dressed preparatory to going on liberty, while others "bat-ted-the-breeze" over their after-breakfast smoke. In its beginning the day was just another peaceful Sunday at the United States' largest naval base.

A few minutes before 7:55 a.m., several squadrons of mustard-yellow planes flew over the Hawaiian island of Oahu from the southwest, but this caused no alarm as military planes overhead were the usual thing. When those squadrons approached Pearl Harbor, they maneuvered into attack formations at low altitude over Merry's Point. At 7:55 a.m. wave after wave of those warplanes streamed across the harbor and hurled their deadly missiles upon the unsuspecting battle fleet. Every plane seemed to have its objective selected in advance, for they separated into groups and each group concentrated on a specific ship.

When the first wave of attacking planes came over, I was in the Marine Detachment office on the second deck of the *Tennessee*. Pfc George W. Dinning, the clerk, was seated at the desk making out the Morning Report. Suddenly we felt a violent bump which gave us the feeling that the ship had been pushed bodily sideways, and as I did not hear any explosion I remarked that some ship had run into us.

Immediately after that the alarm gongs sounded "General Quarters." I was so surprised that I could hardly believe my ears, but the noise of explosions through the open ports forced it upon me. George never did finish that Morning Report; he jumped seemingly sideways through the door and was gone like the wind. Snatching a detachment roster from the desk, I dashed after him.

My battle station was on the 5-inch broadside guns where I could see what actually was happening around us. I had a hurried look round from the casemates on the starboard side and then went over to the port side. The sky was dotted with black puffs of antiaircraft fire. A plane, trailing a plume of smoke, was plunging earthward over Ford Island. Off in the direction of Schofield Barracks, there was a vast cloud of black smoke. At the same time, two billowing pillars of smoke arose from the Navy Yard and Hickam Field area. The sky was full of planes bearing the Rising Sun emblem of Japan. Overhead droned a flight of horizontal bombers at an altitude of about 10,000 feet. Some sixty enemy planes were diving at our ships.

Then a great many things happened in a very short time. The Japanese planes struck time and time again to get in the killing blows. First came aerial torpedoes, then heavy bombers and dive bombers. Within a few minutes of the commencement of the attack, we were hit direct two times by bombs.

One bomb bursting on the forward turret disabled one gun, and a fragment from it penetrated the shield on the bridge above, killing a sailor and severely wounding Ensign Donald M. Kable. The commander of the *West Virginia,* Captain Mervyn S. Bennion, was mortally wounded by a portion of this bomb when he emerged from the conning tower to the bridge of his ship. The second, a 15- or 16-inch projectile, which the enemy was using as a bomb, hit the aft turret, but fortunately, it did not explode, but pierced the top, killing two men under the point of impact.

At about 8:00 a.m., a terrific explosion in the *Arizona,* astern of us, fairly lifted us in the water. She blew up in an enormous flame and a cloud of black smoke when her forward magazine exploded after a Japanese bomb had literally dropped down her funnel. Her back broken by the explosion, the entire forward portion of the ship canted away from the aft portion as the ship began to settle on the bottom.

It was a scene which cannot easily be forgotten—the *Arizona* was a mass of fire from bow to foremast, on deck and between decks, and the surface of the water for a large distance round was a mass of flaming oil from millions of gallons of fuel oil. Over a thousand dead men lay in her twisted wreck. Among those who perished were Rear Admiral Isaac C. Kidd and Captain Franklin Van Valkenburgh.

A few moments after this disaster, our attention was absorbed in the *Oklahoma.* Stabbed several times in her port side by torpedoes, she heeled very gently over, and capsized within nine minutes. The water was dotted with the heads of men. Some swam ashore, covered from head to foot with thick, oily scum, but hundreds of men trapped in the vessel's hull were drowned.

We had only been in the attack a few minutes when the *West Virginia,* about 20 feet on our port beam, began slowly to settle by the bow, and then took a heavy list to the port. She had been badly hit by several torpedoes in the opening attack. Incendiary bombs started fires which filled her decks and superstructure with flame and smoke.

In the midst of all this turmoil, the *Nevada,* the next ship astern of the blazing *Arizona,* got under way and headed for the channel. As she moved down stream, the vessel was a target of many enemy planes until badly crippled by a torpedo, and after that she ran aground to prevent sinking.

The next picture was a destroyer, name unknown, leaving the harbor under a withering fire from Japanese planes.

But to return to the *Tennessee.* The real story of this ship lies in the splendid manner in which the officers and men on board arose to the emergency. When "General Quarters" was sounded, all hands dashed to their battle stations. There was no panic. The shock found each and every man ready for his job. Antiaircraft and machine guns were quickly manned, the first gun getting into action in less than three minutes after the alarm.

For the next forty minutes, the *Tennessee* was the center of a whirlwind of bombs and bullets. The Japanese planes bombed our ship and then bombed again. They opened up with machine guns in low flying attacks. The ship's gun crews fought with utmost gallantry, and in a most tenacious and determined manner. They had no other thought than to keep the guns going and thereby annihilate those "slant-eyed sons-of-bitches" from the land of the Rising Sun. Hostile planes swooping down on what they thought an easy prey were greeted with volleys from our antiaircraft and machine guns. After such a warm reception, the Japanese airmen gave the *Tennessee* a wide berth.

So terrific was the noise of the explosions and our own antiaircraft guns that one could not hear himself speak and had to shout in anybody's ear. The air seemed to be full of fragments and flying pieces. In the general din, there was a *whoosh*, followed by a dull *whoomph* of huge explosives which struck so close to the ship that she shivered from end to end.

The Marines were stationed on the 5-inch broadside guns numbers 6, 7, 8, 9, and 10. They had nothing active to do at the beginning of the action—any firing by the broadside batteries was absolutely out of the question as the port guns trained on the adjacent *West Virginia*, while the starboard guns aimed at Ford Island. They had simply to stand by under a heavy aerial assault unable to reply; or to put it in the vernacular of the Marines in casemate No. 10, "We felt like bastards at a family reunion."

Captain Chevey S. White, in command of the Marines, seeing that it was no use keeping the Marines on the broadside batteries, sent a volunteer crew to man the 3-inch guns on the starboard side of the quarter-deck, and the surplus were given a chance to fight it out with ancient Lewis machine guns placed in advantageous positions about the ship.

There was an interval of comparative calm, which seemed a good opportunity to ascertain the casualties suffered by the Marines and make a report to Captain White. Accordingly, I began a tour of the assumed battle stations, checking the men by that roster which I had brought with me. I counted 76; there had been 81.

My next job then was to take a look round the ship for the men missing. Naturally, my first thought was to see if they were among the wounded. Went below to second deck, where sick bay was located. The passageway outside the ward was covered with men lying on mattresses or on cots. Stepping carefully between the rows of maimed, burned and bleeding, I groped my way to the surgeon's office. A hospital corpsman informed me that no Marines appeared on the casualty list.

Then I crossed over to the Marine office on the port side, and found the lock had been knocked off the door by a working party detailed to secure all battle ports. Thought it would be just as well to gather up our service record books in case it was necessary to quickly abandon ship, so I put the records in my pillowcase and carried them up to casemate No. 10.

Coming on deck again, I met Lieutenant Hugh J. Chapman, who had recently joined the detachment. He was occupied in organizing ammunition supply parties. Throughout the attack, he rendered invaluable service, directing the distribution of ammunition to guns requiring it.

Someone told me there were a few Marines manning the main-top, some 70 or 80 feet above the deck, access to which could be gained by ascending a series of iron ladders running up the interior of the mast. Deciding to have a look there for the missing men, I clambered up the ladders, past the first landing, through a belt of hot, acid, funnel smoke, and was halfway to the top when enemy planes suddenly reappeared and soon we were in the thick of a bombing and strafing attack.

Appreciating that I might momentarily expect to be blown or shot off the mast, I thought for a few seconds, "Should I go up or down," and decided on the former. I didn't waste much time in climbing up the ladder into the top through the "lubber's hole." When I stepped on the platform, my feet slipped out from under me and it was nothing short of a miracle that I didn't fall down the hole and get mashed up. Looked around to see what the trouble was, and discovered the source to be an overturned bucket of aluminum paint. Corporal C. Westover afterwards told me that he was painting there when the blitz started.

It is difficult to write clearly of the details of this attack for the whole thing outdid the most imaginative picture of a battle. The Japs dive-bombed our ships again and again, while low-flying planes, no more than 100 feet above the water, strafed the gun crews. They flew to the end of the bay, made a turn, and came back. For about twenty minutes the strafing attack kept up, the planes going continuously up and down, spraying the low row of battleships with machine gun bullets.

In the general din, I could hear the staccato bark of the pom-poms on the *Maryland* just ahead of us. There was something tremendously heartening about the sound of them, and the very noise was inspiring. After what seemed ages to me, some of the raiders left and the sky was clearer.

On the main-top I found four of the missing Marines, where also were Lieutenant Ernest C. Fusan and Gunnery Sergeant Porter W. Stark. They were craning their necks at the yardarm which had been struck by a bomb.

A terrible scene of destruction was revealed to me as I took a general look round. The *West Virginia* just abeam of us was flaming furiously. Only the bottom of the *Oklahoma* was visible. The *Arizona* was an inferno now, emitting dense volumes of oily smoke which hung over the harbor like a funeral pall. Our next ahead, *Maryland,* was hit by a large bomb on the forecastle which penetrated the deck and made an ugly hole in her port bow. An armor-piercing bomb had exploded in one of the casemates on the *Pennsylvania.* Looking toward the *California,* I noticed that she had a heavy list to the port side, and smoke appeared to be coming from her. The *Nevada* had been run hard ashore, in a sinking condition.

One had a none too cheerful feeling at the thought that five of our eight battleships had been sunk or badly damaged in the attack. In addition to these, three destroyers and a mine layer were sunk. The old target ship, *Utah,* moored at the place usually occupied by the aircraft carrier *Lexington,* had capsized as a result of being torpedoed.

My attention was called by Sergeant Stark to the bridge of the *West Virginia* below us. Her captain was lying there mortally wounded. Rescue parties could not reach him because the bridge was wreathed in fire and smoke. Still capable of movement, he was trying to roll away from the choking fumes and blistering heat.

Sergeant Stark said that during the first attack a low-flying torpedo-carrying plane coming in astern of us was blown into infinitesimal pieces by a direct hit from our antiaircraft batteries. It happened, literally speaking, in a flash; one moment there was an attacking plane; the next moment it was a puff of smoke. When this cleared, there was nothing to be seen save dust settling on the water.

I then got down from the tops and made another tour of

the battle stations, and at each found the same picture. The men were cool and in fine spirit. Everyone was doing his utmost, and the things that we had been training for for many months were being achieved. The men had set up machine guns on temporary mounts and were blazing away at the attackers.

Corporal Flood's volunteer crew on the quarter-deck worked the 3-inch gun with the precision and certainty of a well-regulated machine. They might have been at drill for all the excitement they displayed. A Jap plane flew over; the gun flamed, it roared, it leaped to the rear, it slid to the front; the gun was loaded; another target appeared, the gun was fired again, and the projectile screamed skyward. I thought these men performed their duties in a most efficient manner despite the fact that they had no previous experience in the use of that particular type gun. The members of the gun crew were Cpl. Warren K. Flood. Pfc George W. Dinning, Pvts. Robert H. Stinecipher, Jr., George H. Tarver, and Benjamin F. Williams, Jr.

Sergeant Frederick E. Frank (Xenia, Ohio) was in charge of a detail handling the 3-inch ammunition. In constant danger of being blown to bits, the men in this party carried ammunition from aft magazine to the gun with much enthusiasm and energy.

Went up on the bridge and located the last two of the missing Marines. They were manning a .50-caliber machine gun which Field Cook Clay H. Gee had carried to the bridge and set up in the face of severe enemy bombing and strafing. Other Marines on this gun were Pfc Delbert W. Johnson, Pfc Ralph F. Haws, and Pvt. Roy D. Kelly. While there I came upon the body of a sailor who had been killed by bomb fragments which penetrated the bridge shield as if it was tissue paper. He was propped in a sitting position and still wore head phones.

I was astonished to find that the only casualty among the Marines was Sergeant Walter Holland, injured in the right foot by flying debris or bomb fragment while operating with Group I, Machine Guns, but despite his injury, he continued to work at the guns.

Then I went in search of Captain White and found him

standing coolly on the quarter-deck, occupied in estimating the situation, giving orders, and receiving reports. I reported to him and then continued touring the battle stations to see how things were faring.

On one of my expeditions I was surprised to find a soldier at a battle station. He had come aboard that morning to visit Pfc Coy R. Tyson, and when "General Quarters" sounded, he was ordered by Sergeant Stark to go along with Tyson to his action station.

Very early in the action an incident occurred which history may record as the first hand-to-hand encounter of the American-Japanese War. A Nipponese plane crashed on Ford Island near us, and the uninjured pilot started running toward a nearby clump of trees when a Marine sentry with a bayoneted rifle intervened. The flier took out his pistol and attempted to shoot the Marine, but the latter plunged his bayonet into the Jap until he was dead. I personally did not see this, but some of the ship's company were witnesses.

Eventually the attackers gradually flew away, and toward 10:15 a.m., I saw one solitary Jap plane disappear beyond the mountain in back of Pearl Harbor. The action for us was ended although we did not think so at the time. The exact number of enemy planes disposed of could not be ascertained with any certainty, but my impression was that it was not very large. We, of course, did not know where the attackers came from, but thought they came from land bases as well as from aircraft carriers.

Most disappointing on this occasion was the total absence of our own aircraft. During the attack on Pearl Harbor itself, there was not one American plane to be seen in the sky. Those who participated in the battle had one thought, one question: "Where in hell is our air force?"

I have said little about the navy personnel in this narrative for I was fully occupied during the action with the Marines and had little time to observe the sailors, except the antiaircraft crews on which the brunt of the fighting fell. They were perfect. Their lot was the hardest, for it takes rugged men to stick to their guns as dive bombers come screaming at them, and low-flying planes spray the decks with machine gun bullets. Ignoring the bombs and strafing, these navy gunners pumped a hail of metal above the harbor just as coolly as if they were at target practice, and accounted for several raiders. No praise can be too high for them.

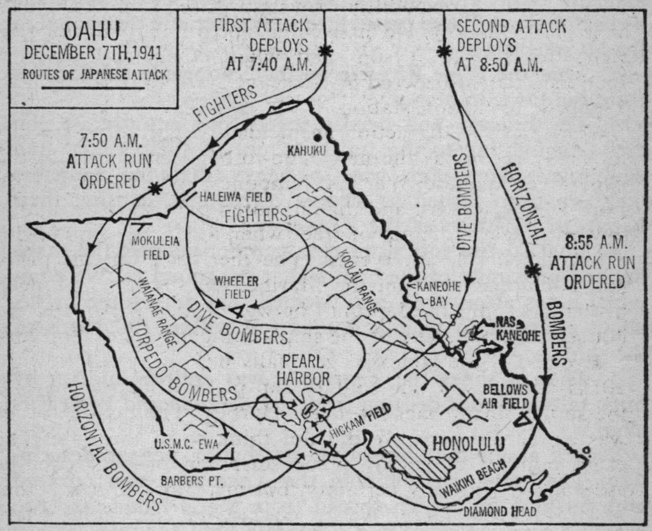

It might be mentioned here that the *Tennessee*'s casualties were only 6 men killed or died of wounds, 1 officer and 36 men wounded, and 1 man missing, which was really an astonishingly light number considering the total casualties in the attack.

The most vivid impression of the battle left to all of us was the suddenness and unexpectedness of the whole incident. Although the powers that be may have known that something more than usual was in the wind, the men were certainly unaware that anything was likely to happen. The first inkling we received that there was something doing was when the Japanese planes streamed across the harbor and hurled their torpedoes into our warships.

It will never cease to be a source of wonder to me that we

did not share the fate of the *Arizona.* One may attribute our comparative immunity to the following:

1. The Grace of God—for an armor-piercing bomb, deflected by the yardarm, struck the roof of the aft turret a glancing blow. Had the yardarm not been in its path, the projectile would have penetrated the turret and detonated in the aft magazine.

2. That the *West Virginia* berthed alongside shielded us from the torpedo planes.

3. The bravery and persistency of our antiaircraft gun crews in fighting to the fullest extent of their ability and equipment. Their fire was so heavy that the Japanese bombers were forced to swerve off course, causing their bombs to fall short of the *Tennessee.*

4. That so few hits were obtained considering the number and proximity of the bombs that fell round us. We compared notes afterwards, and decided that during the battle, about eighteen to twenty bombs fell within 100 yards of the ship.

5. That at times the *Tennessee* was entirely hidden by huge smoke clouds drifting from the *Arizona* and *West Virginia.*

Scenes about the ship, after the battle, beggar description. The water surrounding the *Tennessee* was covered with burning oil, which spread from the *Arizona,* and fire brigades were engaged in a desperate fight for two days to save the ship. During this time, damage control parties fought for many hours to extinguish a large fire that had started aft in the officers' quarters.

In the meanwhile casualties and survivors from other ships began to arrive. That afternoon ten survivors of the *Arizona* Marine Detachment were received on board. Among them was Captain John H. Earle, Jr., who had assumed command on the previous day. Prior to his transfer on the 6th of December, Captain Earle had been detachment officer on the *Tennessee* and we were thankful to see him turn up alive. It was a great shock to us when he informed us that of the eighty-seven Marines who formed the *Arizona* detachment, only thirteen were able to escape.

Most of the survivors had been in the main-top when the

ship blew up and in some miraculous way, in spite of the intense heat and choking smoke, they climbed down the mast, jumped overboard, and swam ashore through patches of oil burning on the water. The only injury received by the swimmers was "sore guts" caused by shock of bombs exploding in the water.

Among those who perished was the First Sergeant of the *Arizona*—Sergeant John Duveene. The survivors told us that after coming up on deck, Sergeant Duveene suddenly went back into the ship with the object of recovering the detachment's vital records. Presently he staggered on deck again, badly burnt all over, his clothing on fire, but carrying the records. He leaped overboard and was never seen again.

During the rest of the night nothing further happened, except that all this time the *Arizona* had been burning fiercely, lighting up the harbor for a great distance, and, much to our discomfort, we were visible for miles round. She burned for two days.

Philippine Defeat

The Japanese had won a stunning victory at Pearl Harbor—and we had helped them. The state of mind of the naval commanders in Hawaii explains much. They underestimated Japan's offensive power; they couldn't imagine the possibility of an attack at such long range, and a few hints from the U.S. command weren't enough to convince them. (After all, it took the Pearl Harbor trauma to shock a whole nation into action.) President Roosevelt and Secretary of State Hull had warned the military leaders of possible attack from Japan, but they had the advantage of the latest developments on diplomatic and economic fronts, as well as military; without this background, the local commanders in Hawaii couldn't appreciate the seriousness of the warnings they received.

And at Pearl Harbor (as in the Philippines), there was tactical failure in reconnaissance; when signs of unknown ships and planes were picked up, observers on the spot failed to appreciate their significance. When, for instance, planes were noted on a radar screen, still 125 miles away to the north, and duly reported to an officer, nothing was done about it because a flight of U.S. planes was expected from approximately the same direction. (For similar reasons, surprise through air attack was accomplished many times later in the war; in Doolittle's B-25 raid on Tokyo, the Japanese received prior warnings of enemy ships approaching offshore, but paid no attention.)

Japan gained enormously by crippling the American Pacific Fleet, but she was very much mistaken in thinking she had thereby crippled the United States. The surprise attack was "a low blow" that would arouse the American nation, as surely as smoke from a fire arouses a hornets' nest. The people of the United States were suddenly knit together in common purpose. But this in itself did not produce weapons for defense, let alone counterattack. There would be more defeats, tragic for those called to sacrifice themselves so the country could gain the time necessary to gird for battle.

The Philippines were next on the Jap schedule. The islands did not offer many economic advantages to Japan, but to secure their lines of communication for the attack on the East Indies, the Philippines had to be neutralized. Again the initiative was entirely Japan's; the U.S. had waited too long to reinforce the islands.

News of the Pearl Harbor attack had been flashed to the American commanders in the Philippines several hours before Clark and Nichols airfields were attacked on Luzon. The Japs intended to reduce the airfields quickly so that their invasion landings would have unopposed fighter support. The first raid alert in the Manila area found American planes in the air ready to do battle, but no Jap planes appeared; later in the day a real bombing strike, for which no warning had been issued, caught many planes on the ground, destroying a third of the fighters and half of the bombers.

After that the Japs bombed and strafed army and navy installations almost at will. Small invasion forces were put ashore on Luzon almost daily until December 22nd, when the main amphibious operation hit the beaches of Lingayen Gulf. All forces were consolidated for the drive south to Manila, forcing the U.S. 11th and 21st Infantry Divisions under Gen. Wainwright to retreat before them; on December 27th, Gen. MacArthur, over-all commander of the Philippines, decided Manila could not be properly defended, and withdrew his troops into the Bataan Peninsula. Supplies and reinforcements could not be got through the Jap naval and air blockade, and, with rations growing scarce, defeat for the defenders of Bataan was inevitable. During February and March, 1942, Gen. MacArthur and other top personnel were taken off the peninsula. On April 8th, Gen. Wainwright, now in command, transferred naval personnel and the Filipino scouts to Corregidor, and on April 9th, surrendered the troops left in the southern extremity of Bataan. Prisoners were herded together for the infamous Death March back up the peninsula. A moving account of this ordeal is found in the next selection.

DEATH MARCH ON BATAAN

by Lt. Col. William Dyess

North of our narrow flying field stood Mount Bataan, its jagged crater rising 4,600 feet above us into the clear, cool sky. From these upper reaches came the drone of Jap dive bombers, circling endlessly. To the south, smoke still was rising from the rubble which a few days before had been Mariveles.

Three miles away, across the harbor's blue-green waters, the rocky eminence of Corregidor stood unconquered, still guarding the sea approaches to a Manila that had fallen. Grayish smoke puffs blossomed along the sides and pinnacles of the Rock as high-flying Jap bombers dropped their loads.

The dust that enveloped Mariveles field was being stirred up by the wheels of trucks and gun carriages. Jap artillery was preparing to open fire on Corregidor from the sunken rice paddies and near-by ridges. From the pall of smoke and dust new prisoners—American and Filipino soldiers—emerged in lines and groups to join those of us already there, awaiting the pleasure of the Imperial Japanese army.

The first thing I heard after our arrival was an urgent whispering which came to us from all sides. "Get rid of your Jap stuff, quick!"

"What Jap stuff?" we whispered back.

"Everything; money, souvenirs. Get rid of it!" We did so without delay—and just in time. Jap noncommissioned officers and three-star privates were moving among us ordering that packs be opened and spread out. They searched our persons, then went through the other stuff, confiscating personal articles now and then.

I noticed that the Japs, who up to now had treated us

with an air of cool suspicion, were beginning to get rough. I saw men shoved, cuffed, and boxed. This angered and mystified us. It was uncalled for. We were not resisting. A few ranks away a Jap jumped up from a pack he had been inspecting. In his hand was a small shaving mirror.

"Nippon?" he asked the owner. The glass was stamped: "Made in Japan." The soldier nodded. The Jap stepped back, then lunged, driving his rifle butt into the American's face. "Yaah!" he yelled, and lunged again. The Yank went down. The raging Jap stood over him, driving crushing blows to the face until the prisoner lay insensible.

A little way off a Jap was smashing his fists into the face of another American soldier who went to his knees and received a thudding kick in the groin. He, too, it seemed, had been caught with some Japanese trifle.

We were shocked. This treatment of war prisoners was beyond our understanding. I still didn't get it, even after someone explained to me that the Japs assumed the contraband articles had been taken from the bodies of their dead. I was totally unprepared for the appalling deed that came next.

I was too far off to witness it personally, but I saw the victim afterward. We had known him. A comrade who had stood close by told me later in shocking detail what had taken place.

The victim, an air force captain, was being searched by a three-star private. Standing by was a Jap commissioned officer, hand on sword hilt. These men were nothing like the toothy, bespectacled runts whose photographs are familiar to most newspaper readers. They were cruel of face, stalwart, and tall.

"This officer looked like a giant beside the Jap private," said my informant, who must be nameless because he still is a prisoner of war. "The big man's face was as black as mahogany. He didn't seem to be paying much attention. There was no expression in his eyes, only a sort of unseeing glare.

"The private, a little squirt, was going through the captain's pockets. All at once he stopped and sucked in his breath with a hissing sound. He had found some Jap yen.

"He held these out, ducking his head and sucking in his breath to attract notice. The big Jap looked at the money. Without a word he grabbed the captain by the shoulder and shoved him down to his knees. He pulled the sword out of the scabbard and raised it high over his head, holding it with both hands. The private skipped to one side.

"Before we could grasp what was happening, the black-faced giant had swung his sword. I remember how the sun flashed on it. There was a swish and a kind of chopping thud, like a cleaver going through beef.

"The captain's head seemed to jump off his shoulders. It hit the ground in front of him and went rolling crazily from side to side between the lines of prisoners.

"The body fell forward. I have seen wounds, but never such a gush of blood as this. The heart continued to pump for a few seconds and at each beat there was another great spurt of blood. The white dust around our feet was turned into crimson mud. I saw that the hands were opening and closing spasmodically. Then I looked away.

"When I looked again the big Jap had put up his sword and was strolling off. The runt who had found the yen was putting them into his pocket. He helped himself to the captain's possessions."

This was the first murder. In the year to come there would be enough killing of American and Filipino soldier prisoners to rear a mountain of dead.

Our Jap guards now threw off all restraint. They beat and slugged prisoners, robbing them of watches, fountain pens, money, and toilet articles. Now, as never before, I wanted to kill Japs for the pleasure of it.

The thing that almost drove me crazy was the certainty that the officer who had just been murdered couldn't have taken those yen from a dead Jap. He had been in charge of an observation post far behind the lines. I doubt that he ever had seen a dead Jap.

Gradually I got control of myself. By going berserk now I would only lose my own life without hope of ever helping to even the score.

The score just now was far from being in our favor. The 160 officers and men who remained of the 21st Pursuit

Squadron were assembled with about 500 other American and Filipino soldiers of all grades and ranks. They were dirty, ragged, unshaven, and exhausted. Many were half starved.

Swirling chalky dust had whitened sweat-soaked beards, adding grotesquerie to the scene. It would not have been hard to believe these were tottering veterans of 1898, returned to the battlegrounds of their youth.

We stood for more than an hour in the scalding heat while the search, with its beating and sluggings, was completed. Then the Jap guards began pulling some of the huskiest of our number out of line. These were assembled into labor gangs, to remain in the area.

I doubt that many of them survived the hail of steel Corregidor's guns later laid down on the beaches and foothills of Bataan. These were men who for months had faced American iron, thrown at them by Jap guns.

Now, it appeared, they were to die under American iron thrown into their midst by American guns. As the remainder of us were marched off the field our places were taken by other hundreds of prisoners who were to follow us on the Death March from Bataan.

We turned eastward on the national highway, which crosses the southern tip of Bataan to Cabcaben and Bataan airfield, then veers northward through Lamao, Balanga, and Orani. From there it runs northeastward to San Fernando, the rail junction and banking town in Pampanga province.

Ordinarily, the trip from Mariveles to Cabcaben field is a beautiful one with the grandeur of high greenclad mountains on the north and a view of the sea on the right. The white of the road contrasts pleasantly with the deep green of the tropical growth on either side.

But on this day there was no beauty. Coming toward us were seemingly interminable columns of Jap infantry, truck trains, and horse-drawn artillery, all moving into Bataan for a concentrated assault on Corregidor. They stirred up clouds of blinding dust in which all shape and form were lost.

Every few yards Jap noncoms materialized like gargoyles from the grayish white pall and snatched Americans out of line to be searched and beaten. Before we had gone two miles we had been stripped of practically all our personal possessions.

The Japs made no move to feed us. Few of us had had anything to eat since the morning of April 9. Many had tasted no food in four days. We had a little tepid water in our canteens, but nothing else.

The ditches on either side of the road were filled with overturned and wrecked American army trucks, fire-gutted tanks, and artillery our forces had rendered unusable. At intervals we saw mounds of captured food, bearing familiar trademarks. These had fallen almost undamaged into Jap hands.

As we marched along I rounded up the 110 officers and men of the 21st Pursuit. I didn't know yet what the score was, but I felt we would be in a better position to help one another and keep up morale if we were together.

We hadn't walked far when the rumor factory opened up. In a few minutes it was in mass production. There were all kinds of reports: We were going to Manila and Old Bilibid prison. We were going to San Fernando and entrain for a distant concentration camp. Trucks were waiting just ahead to pick us up. We doubted the last rumor, but hoped it was true.

The sun was nearing the zenith now. The penetrating heat seemed to search out and dissipate the small stores of strength remaining within us. The road, which until this moment had been fairly level, rose sharply in a zigzag grade. We were nearing Little Baguio.

I was marching with head down and eyes squinted for the dual purpose of protecting myself as much as possible from the dust and glare and keeping watch on the Jap guards who walked beside and among us. Halfway up the hill we reached a level stretch where a Japanese senior officer and his staff were seated at a camp table upon which were spread maps and dispatches.

As I came abreast he saw me and shouted something that sounded like, "Yoy!" He extended his hand, palm downward, and opened and closed the fingers rapidly. This meant I was to approach him. I pretended I didn't see him. He shouted again as I kept on walking. His third "Yoy!" vibrated with anger. The next I knew a soldier snatched me out of line and shoved me toward the table.

"Name!" shouted the officer. He was staring at the wings and my uniform. "You fly?"

I told him my name without mentioning my rank and said I had been a pilot.

"Where you planes?"

"All shot down." I made a downward, spinning motion with my hand.

"No at Cebu? No at Mindanao?"

"No Cebu. No Mindanao."

"Yaah. Lie! We know you got planes. We see. Sometimes one . . . two . . . sometimes three, four, five. Where you airfields?"

I shook my head again and made the spinning motion with my hand. But I located the airfields for him on his map. I pointed to Cabcaben, Bataan, and Mariveles. He knew about these, of course. He made an impatient gesture.

"One more. Secret field!"

"Nope. No secret field."

"True?"

"Yes. True."

"Where are tunnel? Where are underwater tunnel from Mariveles to Corregidor? Where are tunnels on Corregidor Rock?" He held the map toward me.

"I don't know of any tunnels. No tunnels; no place. I never was on Corregidor. I was only at Nichols field and Bataan."

"You flying officer and you never at Corregidor Rock!" His eyes were slits. His staff officers were angry, too. "LIE!" he shrieked and jumped up.

He was powerfully built, as are most Jap officers. He seized my shoulder and whirled me around with a quick twist that almost dislocated my arm. Then came a violent shove that sent me staggering toward the line. I expected a bullet to follow the push, but I didn't dare look back. This would have been inviting them to shoot. As I reached the marching line, the officer shouted something else. The guards shoved me and motioned that I should catch up with my group.

I wanted to be with them, but the double quick up the hill in the scalding heat and dust almost finished me. I had the thought, too, that the guards I passed might get the idea I was trying to escape. My bullet expectancy was so high it made my backside tingle from scalp to heels. I caught up as we were passing through Little Baguio. In a short time we were abreast the blackened ruins of Hospital No. 1, which had been bombed heavily a couple of days before.

Among the charred debris, sick and wounded American soldiers were walking dazedly about. There was no place for them to go.

Their only clothes were hospital pajama suits and kimonos. Here and there a man was stumping about on one leg and a crutch. Some had lost one or both arms. All were in need of fresh dressings. And all obviously were suffering from the shock of the bombing.

They looked wonderingly at the column of prisoners. When the Jap officers saw them, these shattered Americans were rounded up and shoved into the marching line. All of them tried to walk, but only a few were able to keep it up. Those who fell were kicked aside by the Japs.

The Japs forbade us to help these men. Those who tried it were kicked, slugged, or jabbed with bayonet points by the guards who stalked with us in twos and threes.

For more than a mile these bomb-shocked cripples stumbled along with us. Their shoulders were bent and the sweat streamed from their faces. I can never forget the hopelessness in their eyes.

Eventually their strength ebbed and they began falling back through the marching ranks. I don't know what became of them.

About a mile east of the hospital we encountered a major traffic jam. On either side of the congested road hundreds of Jap soldiers were unloading ammunition and equipment.

Our contingent of more than 600 American and Filipino prisoners filtered through, giving the Japs as wide a berth as the limited space permitted. This was to avoid being searched, slugged, or pressed into duty as cargadores [burden carriers].

Through the swirling dust we could see a long line of trucks, standing bumper to bumper. There were hundreds of them. And every last one was an American make. I saw Fords—which predominated—Chevrolets, GMCs, and others.

These were not captured trucks. They bore Jap army insignia and had been landed from the ships of the invasion fleet. It is hard to describe what we felt at seeing these familiar American machines, filled with jeering, snarling Japs. It was a sort of super-sinking feeling. We had become accustomed to having American iron thrown at us by the Japs, but this was a little too much.

Eventually the road became so crowded we were marched into a clearing. Here, for two hours, we had our first taste of the oriental sun treatment, which drains the stamina and weakens the spirit.

The Japs seated us on the scorching ground, exposed to the full glare of the sun. Many of the Americans and Filipinos had no covering to protect their heads. I was beside a small bush, but it cast no shade because the sun was almost directly above us. Many of the men around me were ill.

When I thought I could stand the penetrating heat no longer, I was determined to have a sip of the tepid water in my canteen. I had no more than unscrewed the top when the aluminum flask was snatched from my hands. The Jap who had crept up behind me poured the water into a horse's nosebag, then threw down the canteen. He walked on among the prisoners, taking away their water and pouring it into the bag. When he had enough he gave it to his horse.

Whether by accident or design we had been put just across the road from a pile of canned and boxed food. We were famished, but it seemed worse than useless to ask the Japs for anything. An elderly American colonel did, however. He crossed the road and after pointing to the food and to the drooping prisoners, he went through the motions of eating.

A squat Jap officer grinned at him and picked up a can of salmon. Then he smashed it against the colonel's head, opening the American's cheek from eye to jawbone. The officer staggered and turned back toward us, wiping the blood off.

It seemed as though the Japs had been waiting for just such a brutal display to end the scene. They ordered us to our feet and herded us back into the road.

We knew now the Japs would respect neither age nor rank. Their ferocity grew as we marched on into the afternoon. They no longer were content with mauling stragglers or pricking them with bayonet points. The thrusts were intended to kill.

We had marched about a mile after the sun treatment when I stumbled over a man writhing in the hot dust of the road. He was a Filipino soldier who had been bayoneted through the stomach. Within a quarter of a mile I walked past another. This soldier prisoner had been rolled into the path of the trucks and crushed beneath the heavy wheels.

The huddled and smashed figures beside the road eventually became commonplace to us. The human mind has an amazing faculty of adjusting itself to shock. In this case it may have been that heat and misery had numbed our senses. We remained keenly aware, however, that these murders might well be precursors of our own, if we should falter or lag.

As we straggled past Hospital No. 2 the Japs were setting up artillery and training it on Corregidor. The thick jungle hid the hospital itself, but we could see that guns were all around it. The Japs regarded this as master strategy; the Rock would not dare return their fire. I wondered what the concussion of the heavy guns would do to the stricken men in the hospital wards. The cannonade began after we had passed by.

A few minutes later a violent blow on the head almost sent me to my knees. I thought one of the Jap guns had made a direct hit on me. My steel helmet jammed down over my eyes with a clang that made my ears ring. I pulled it clear and staggered around to see a non-commissioned Jap brandishing a club the size of a child's baseball bat. He was squealing and pointing to the dented helmet. He lifted the club again. I threw the helmet into the ditch and he motioned me to march on. Like many of my comrades, I now was without protection against the merciless sun.

Jap artillery was opening up all along the southern tip of Bataan. The area behind us re-echoed to the thud and crash of heavy gunfire. Grayish smoke puffs speckled Corregidor's sides. The Rock was blasting back at the Japs, but most of its shells were falling in the Mariveles region whence we had come.

At sundown we crossed Cabcaben airfield, from which our planes had taken off not thirty-nine hours before. Here again Jap artillery was going into action. We were marched across the field and halted inside a rice paddy beyond. We had had no food or water, and none was offered, but we were grateful of the opportunity to lie down on the earth and rest. The guards kept to the edges of the paddy, leaving us plenty of room.

I was just dropping off when there came an outburst of yelling and screeching. The Japs had charged in among us and were kicking us to our feet. They herded us back to the road and started marching us eastward again. During the brief respite leg muscles had stiffened. Walking was torture.

It was dark when we marched across Bataan field, which with Cabcaben field I had commanded two days before. It was difficult walking in the darkness. Now and again we passed the huddled forms of men who had collapsed from fatigue or had been bayoneted. I didn't kid myself that I was safe simply because I was keeping up the pace. I would not have been surprised at any time to feel a Jap blade slide between my ribs. The bloodthirsty devils now were killing us for diversion.

The march continued until about 10 p.m. When we were halted some naïve individual started a rumor that we were to be given water. Instead we were about-faced and marched back to the westward. For two more hours we stumbled over the ground we had just covered.

It was midnight when we recrossed Bataan field and kept going. We were within a short distance of Cabcaben field when the Japs diverted the line into a tiny rice paddy. There was no room to lie down. Some of us tried to rest in a half squat. Others drew up their knees and laid their heads on the legs of the men next to them. Jap guards stood around the edges of the little field, their feet almost touching the outer fringe of men.

I heard a cry, followed by thudding blows at one side of the paddy. An American soldier so tortured by the thirst that he could not sleep had asked a Jap guard for water. The Jap fell on him with his fists, then slugged him into insensibility with a rifle butt.

The thirst of all had become almost unbearable, but remembering what had happened to the colonel earlier in the day we asked for nothing. A Jap officer walked along just after the thirsty soldier had been beaten. He appeared surprised that we wanted water. However, he permitted several Americans to collect canteens from their comrades and fill them at a stagnant carabao wallow which had been additionally befouled by seeping sea water. We held our noses to shut out the nauseating reek, but we drank all the water we could get.

At dawn of the second day the impatient Japs stepped among and upon us, kicking us into wakefulness. We were hollow-eyed and as exhausted as we had been when we went to sleep. As we stumbled into the road we passed a Jap non-commissioned officer who was eating meat and rice.

"Pretty soon you eat," he told us.

The rising sun cast its blinding light into our eyes as we marched. The temperature rose by the minute. Noon came and went. The midday heat was searing. At 1 p.m. the column was halted and Jap noncoms told American and Filipino soldiers they might fill their canteens from a dirty puddle beside the road. There was no food.

During the afternoon traffic picked up again. Troop-laden trucks sped past us. A grimacing Jap leaned far out, holding his rifle by the barrel. As the truck roared by he knocked an American soldier senseless with the gun's stock. Other Japs saw this and yelled. From now on we kept out of reach if we could. Several more American and Filipino prisoners were struck down.

At 2 p.m. we were told it would be necessary to segregate the prisoners as to rank; colonels together, majors together, and so on. This separated all units from their officers and afforded opportunity for another hour of sun treatment. There was no mention of food.

The line of march was almost due north now. We reached Balanga, about twenty miles from Cabcaben field, at sundown. We were marched into the courtyard of a large prison-like structure, dating to the Spanish days, and told we would eat, then spend the night there.

At one side of the yard food was bubbling in great caldrons. Rice and soy sauce were boiling together. Jap kitchen corpsmen were opening dozens of cans and dumping vienna sausage into the savory mess. The aromatic steam that drifted over from those pots had us almost crazy. While we waited we were given a little water.

We imagined the rice and sausages were for us, though we saw hundreds of ragged and sick Filipinos behind a barbed wire barricade near-by who had only filthy, fly-covered rice to eat. After drinking we were ordered into the line for what appeared to be a routine search. When it was finished an officer shouted something and the attitude of our guards swiftly changed.

They ordered us out of the patio and lined us up in a field across the road. As we left, grinning Japs held up steaming ladles of sausage and rice. The officer followed us to the field, then began stamping up and down, spouting denunciations and abuse. When he calmed enough to be understood, we heard this:

"When you came here you were told you would eat and be let to sleep. Now that is changed. We have found pistols concealed among three American officers. In punishment for these offenses you will not be given food. You will march to Orani (five miles to the north) before you sleep."

The accusation was a lie. If a pistol had been found, the

owner would have been shot, beaten to death, or beheaded on the spot. Besides, we knew that the searchers hadn't overlooked even a toothbrush, to say nothing of a pistol. The Japs simply were adding mental torture to the physical. The Jap officer saw he wasn't believed. He did just what a Jap might be expected to do. Shortly after we resumed the march a staff car pulled up beside us.

Three American officers were dragged out of line and thrown into it. This in the words of Gilbert and Sullivan's Pooh Bah was "corroborative detail, intended to lend artistic verisimilitude to an otherwise bald and unconvincing narrative." We never saw the three officers again, though it is not hard to guess their fate. Men who had stood near two of them during the search said no guns had been found.

Our guards had been increased for the night march, and rigid discipline was imposed. We were formed into columns of fours. A new set of guards came up on bicycles and we were forced to walk practically at double quick to keep up. After two hours these guards were replaced by a group on foot who walked slowly with short mincing steps. The change of gait so cramped our leg muscles that walking was agony.

We had learned by rough experience that efforts to assist our failing comrades served usually to hasten their deaths and add to our own misery and peril. So we tried the next best thing—encouraging them with words. Talking had not been forbidden.

It was during a period of slow marching that an old friend, a captain in the medical corps, began dropping back through the ranks. Presently he was beside me. It was plain he was just about done in. I said:

"Hello, Doc. Taking a walk?"

"Ed," he said slowly, "I can't go another kilometer. A little farther and I'm finished."

"Well, Doc, I'm about in the same fix," I told him. Nothing more was said until we had covered two or three kilometers. Every now and then Doc would begin to lag a little. When this happened, the fellow on the other side of Doc would join me in slipping back some and giving him a little shove with our shoulders. He always took the hint and stepped up. At length he spoke again.

"I'm done, Ed. You fellows forget me and go on. I can't make another kilometer."

"I don't think I can either, Doc. I feel just about as you do."

That was the way we passed the night. Kilometer after kilometer crawled by, but Doc didn't fall out. If he had, his bones would be bleaching now somewhere along that road of death that led out of Bátaan.

The hours dragged by and, as we knew they must, the drop-outs began. It seemed that a great many of the prisoners reached the end of their endurance at about the same time. They went down by twos and threes. Usually, they made an effort to rise. I never can forget their groans and strangled breathing as they tried to get up. Some succeeded. Others lay lifelessly where they had fallen.

I observed that the Jap guards paid no attention to these. I wondered why. The explanation wasn't long in coming. There was a sharp crackle of pistol and rifle fire behind us.

Skulking along, a hundred yards behind our contingent, came a "clean-up squad" of murdering Jap buzzards. Their helpless victims, sprawled darkly against the white of the road, were easy targets.

As members of the murder squad stooped over each huddled form, there would be an orange flash in the darkness and a sharp report. The bodies were left where they lay, that other prisoners coming behind us might see them.

Our Japanese guards enjoyed the spectacle in silence for a time. Eventually, one of them who spoke English felt he should add a little spice to the entertainment.

"Sleepee?" he asked. "You want sleep? Just lie down on road. You get good, long sleep!"

On through the night we were followed by orange flashes and thudding shots.

At 3 a.m. of April 12, 1942—the second day after our surrender—we arrived half dead at Orani, in northeastern

Bataan, after a twenty-one-hour march from Cabcaben near the peninsula's southern tip. That thirty-mile hike over rough and congested roads had lasted almost from dawn to dawn.

Near the center of the town the Japs ordered us off the road to a barbed wire compound a block away. It had been intended for five hundred men. Our party numbered more than six hundred. Already in it, however, were more than 1,500 Americans and Filipinos.

The stench of the place reached us long before we entered it. Hundreds of the prisoners were suffering from dysentery. Human waste covered the ground. The shanty that had served as a latrine no longer was usable as such.

Maggots were in sight everywhere. There was no room to lie down. We tried to sleep sitting up, but the aches of exhaustion seemed to have penetrated even into our bones.

Jap soldiers told us there would be rice during the morning. We paid no attention. We not only didn't believe them, we were too miserable to care. The sun came up like a blazing ball in a copper sky. With the first shafts of yellow light the temperature started up and, it seemed to me, the vile stench of the compound grew in intensity. Breathing the heavy heated air was physically painful.

As the sun climbed higher, Americans and Filipinos alike grew delirious. Their wild shouts and thrashings about dissipated their ebbing energy. They began lapsing into coma. For some it was the end. Starvation, exhaustion, and abuse had been too much for their weakened bodies. Brief coma was followed by merciful death. I had a blinding headache from the heat, glare, and stench. Several times I thought my senses were slipping.

When it was observed that men were dying, Japanese noncommissioned officers entered the compound and ordered the Americans to drag out the bodies and bury them. We were told to put the delirious ones into a thatched shed a few hundred feet away. When this had been done the grave digging began.

We thought we had seen every atrocity the Japs could offer, but we were wrong. The shallow trenches had been completed. The dead were being rolled into them. Just then an American soldier and two Filipinos were carried out of the compound. They had been delirious. Now they were in a coma. A Jap noncom stopped the bearers and tipped the unconscious men into the trench.

The Japs then ordered the burial detail to fill it up. The Filipinos lay lifelessly in the hole. As the earth began falling about the American, he revived and tried to climb out. His fingers gripped the edge of the grave. He hoisted himself to a standing position.

Two Jap guards placed bayonets at the throat of a Filipino on the burial detail. They gave him an order. When he hesitated they pressed the bayonet points hard against his neck. The Filipino raised a stricken face to the sky. Then he brought his shovel down upon the head of his American comrade, who fell backward to the bottom of the grave. The burial detail filled it up.

For many of those who had been taken into the shade of the thatched shed the respite came too late. One by one their babblings ceased and their bodies twisted into the grotesque postures that mark a corpse as far as it can be seen.

During the long afternoon, stupor served as an anesthetic for most of the prisoners in the compound. There was no food. Toward evening the Japs allowed Americans to gather canteens and fill them at an artesian well. It was the first good water we'd had. Night brought relief from the heat, though there still was no room to lie down, despite the number of dead and delirious removed from the compound.

Dawn of April 13—our fourth day since leaving Mariveles—seemed to come in the middle of the night. Its magnificent colors and flaming splendor meant to us only the beginning of new sufferings. We averted our heads as the coppery light flooded our filthy prison. The temperature seemed to rise a degree a minute.

At 10 a.m., just as I was wondering how I could get through another day, there was a stir at the gates. Guards filed in and began lining us up in rows. Out of one of the dirty buildings came kitchen corpsmen, dragging cans of sticky gray rice which they ladled out—one ladleful to each man. Those of us who had mess kits loaned the lids to men who had none. There were not enough kits and lids to go around, so some of the prisoners had to receive their dole in cupped hands. The portion given each man was equivalent to a saucer or small plate of rice.

The food was unappetizing and was eaten in the worst possible surroundings, but it was eaten. Make no mistake about that. It was our first in many a day. I began feeling stronger immediately, despite the growing heat. There was not enough of the rice, however, to stay delirium and coma for the weaker prisoners. There were those for whom it came too late. Scenes of the previous afternoon were repeated. There were babblings and crazy shouts. There were additional burials in shallow graves.

The rest of us passed the afternoon in stupor. We continued to sit while the sun dropped behind the western mountains. In the twilight we were ordered to our feet. It still was light as we were marched out of the compound, toward the road. We looked at the artesian well, but the Japs warned us not to try to fill our canteens.

During the next four hours of marching we were tortured by the sound of bubbling water. Artesian wells lined the road. It seemed to me I could smell water. But we knew a bullet or a bayonet awaited the man who might try to reach the wells.

About midnight rain started falling. It was chilling, but it cleansed the filth from our stinging bodies and relieved the agony of parched dryness. Those with mess kits or canteen cups held them up toward the rain as they walked. The rain lasted about fifteen minutes and we shared the water with those who had no receptacles.

We were refreshed for a time, but as the grinding march continued men began falling down. The energy derived from the morning rice and the few swallows of rain water had been depleted. When I saw the first man go down I began counting the seconds. I wondered whether the Jap buzzard squad was following us as it had two nights before—the night of April 11.

A flash and the crack of a shot answered my question.

The executioners were on the job to kill or wound mortally every prisoner who fell out of the marching line. All through the night there were occasional shots. I didn't count them. I couldn't.

Just before daybreak the guards halted the column and ordered us to sit down. I felt like a fighter who has been saved by the bell. The ground was damp and cool. I slept. Two hours later we were prodded into wakefulness and ordered to get up. The sun had risen.

Our course was northeasterly now and we were leaving the mountains and Bataan behind. The country in which we found ourselves was flat and marshy. There were small rivers and creeks and many rice paddies. This was Pampanga province.

I was somewhat refreshed by the rest, though walking now was much more difficult. Our stay on the damp ground had caused leg muscles to set like concrete. Even my bones seemed to ache. This was the cool of the morning, yet my throat still was afire with thirst.

And just across the road bubbled an artesian well. Its splashing was plainly audible and the clear water, glistening in the morning sun, was almost too much for my self-control. I thought once if I could reach that well and gulp all the water I wanted the Japs could shoot me and welcome. The next minute I told myself I was balmy even to entertain such a thought.

The Japs were aware of the well and they must have known what was passing through our minds. I have no doubt that they were expecting the thing that happened now. A Filipino soldier darted from the ranks and ran toward the well. Two others followed him. Two more followed these, then a sixth broke from the ranks.

Jap guards all along the line raised their rifles and waited for the six to scramble into the grassy ditch and go up on the opposite side, a few feet from the well. Most of the Filipinos fell at the first volley. Two of them, desperately wounded, kept inching toward the water, their hands outstretched. The Japs fired again and again, until all six lay dead. Thus did our fifth day of the death march start with a blood bath. I needed all the control I could muster.

Men had been murdered behind me all night, but the deeds had been veiled by darkness. There had been nothing to veil the pitilessness and wantonness of the murders I had just seen. I walked a long time with my head down and my fists clenched in my pockets, fighting to think of nothing at all.

I was partly successful, enough so that from then on I practiced detaching myself from the scenes about me. I have no doubt my cultivated ability to do this saved my sanity on more than one occasion in the days to come. I remember little of the two miles we walked after the six murders at the well. We were at the outskirts of Lubao, a sprawling city of 30,000, before mutterings about me brought me back to earth to look upon a new horror.

I saw that all eyes were directed toward an object hanging on a barbed wire fence that paralleled the road. It had been a Filipino soldier. The victim had been bayoneted. His abdomen was open. The bowels had been wrenched loose and were hanging like great grayish purple ropes along the strands of wire that supported the mutilated body.

This was a Japanese object lesson, of course. But it carried terrible implications. The Japs apparently had wearied of mere shootings and simple bayonetings. These had served only to whet the barbaric appetite. What might lie ahead for all of us we could only guess.

These thoughts still were in mind as our scarecrow procession began passing through the rough streets of Lubao. We were in a residential section. Windows of homes were filled with faces turned to us that bore compassionate expressions. News of our arrival raced down the street ahead of us.

Presently from the upper windows of a large house a shower of food fell among us. It was followed quickly by other gifts, tossed surreptitiously by sympathetic Filipinos who stood on the sidewalks. There were bits of bread, rice cookies, lumps of sugar and pieces of chocolate. There were cigarettes.

The Jap guards went into a frenzy. They struck out right and left at the Good Samaritans, slugging, beating, and jabbing bayonets indiscriminately. Japs tried to stamp on all the food that hadn't been picked up. They turned their rage upon us. When the townsfolk saw their gifts were only adding to our misery they stopped throwing them.

Some Filipinos asked the Jap officers if they might not help us. The petitioners were warned to stay away. I recall a merchant who wanted to open his store to us. We could have anything we wanted free, he said. A Jap officer denounced him, warned him to keep his distance. This was at San Tomas or Santa Monica, the two small settlements between Lubao and Guagua, about three miles to the northeast.

In Guagua the Filipino civilians also tried to slip food to us. For that they were beaten and clubbed—as we were. We passed through the hot streets without a halt.

Our next stop, just outside the city of Guagua, came near being a permanent one for me. At a long, muddy ditch we were allowed to dip up drinking water. After canteens had been filled I determined to soak my aching feet in the ooze at the ditch's edge. I was doing so when the order to resume the march was sounded unexpectedly. Putting on my shoes delayed me a few seconds.

I heard a guard shout in my direction, but I continued to struggle with the footgear. When I looked up the guard was raising his rifle. I snatched my shoes and plunged through the ditch toward the column of prisoners. I dodged from side to side with a prickling feeling all over my back. But the bullet didn't come. The guard probably would have missed—the Japs are bum shots—but I didn't think so then.

As I fell in step beside Doc, he pointed toward an officer just ahead of us. This was Captain Burt, who had given the alarm on our last night at Bataan field. He was eating a long sugar lump he had managed to secrete.

"I'm glad somebody got something," Doc said.

But in a minute or two Burt had dropped back beside us and was holding out the sugar. We each took a bite and tried to give it back. Burt shook his head.

"Split it, fellows," he said. "I've already had more than that."

I've never had such a quick reaction from anything. Strength flowed into me. I told Doc I felt as if I'd had a turkey dinner. This was an exaggeration, of course, but it illustrates what just a little food would have done for all of us. The Japs were starving us deliberately.

We neared San Fernando, Pampanga province, during the afternoon of our fifth day's march. It was at San Fernando, according to rumor, that we were to be put aboard a train and carried to a concentration camp.

From among the six hundred and more American and Filipino military prisoners who had started with me from Mariveles, many familiar faces were missing. We had come almost eighty-five miles with nothing to eat except the one ladle of rice given to us more than twenty-four hours before.

We had struck the railroad at Guagua and now could see the tracks which ran alongside the highway, amid the lush vegetation of the flat, marshy countryside. We could have entrained an hour before. I doubted, therefore, that the railroad figured in the Japs' plans for us. I was becoming certain that this was to be a march to the death for all of us. And the events of the next quarter hour did nothing to banish this belief.

Just ahead of me, in the afternoon heat, were two American enlisted men, stumbling along near the point of collapse. I wasn't in much better shape. At this moment we came abreast of a calasa [covered cart] which had stopped beside the road.

An American colonel who also had been watching the two enlisted men, observed that no Jap guard was near us. He drew the two soldiers out of line and helped them into the cart, then got in also. The Filipino driver tapped his pony. The cart had moved only a few feet when the trick was discovered.

Yammering Jap guards pulled the three Americans from the cart and dragged the Filipino from the driver's seat. A stocky Jap noncommissioned officer seized the heavy horsewhip. The enlisted men were flogged first. The crackling lash slashed their faces and tore their clothing. The searing pain revived them for a moment. Then they fell to the ground. The blows thudded upon their bodies. They lost consciousness.

The colonel was next. He stood his punishment a long time. His fortitude enraged the Jap, who put all his strength behind the lash. When the American officer finally dropped to his knees his face was so crisscrossed with bloody welts it was unrecognizable.

The trembling Filipino driver fell at the first cut of the whip. He writhed on the ground. The lash tore his shirt and the flesh beneath it. His face was lacerated and one eye swollen shut. When the whipper grew weary, he ordered the driver on his way. The colonel, bleeding and staggering, was kicked back into the line of American prisoners.

I don't know what became of the enlisted men. I never saw them again. During the remaining two miles we marched to San Fernando I listened for shots, but heard none. The soldiers probably were bayoneted.

The sun still was high in the sky when we straggled into San Fernando, a city of 36,000 population, and were put in a barbed wire compound similar to the one at Orani. We were seated in rows for a continuation of the sun treatment. Conditions here were the worst yet.

The prison pen was jammed with sick, dying, and dead American and Filipino soldiers. They were sprawled amid the filth and maggots that covered the ground. Practically all had dysentery. Malaria and dengue fever appeared to be running unchecked. There were symptoms of other tropical diseases I didn't even recognize.

Jap guards had shoved the worst cases beneath the rotted flooring of some dilapidated building. Many of these prisoners already had died. The others looked as though they couldn't survive until morning.

There obviously had been no burials for many hours.

After sunset Jap soldiers entered and inspected our rows. Then the gate was opened again and kitchen corpsmen entered with cans of rice. We held our mess kits and again passed lids to those who had none. Our spirits rose. We watched as the Japs ladled out generous helpings to the men nearest the gate.

Then, without explanation, the cans were dragged away and the gate was closed. It was a repetition of the ghastly farce at Balanga. The fraud was much more cruel this time because our need was vastly greater. In our bewildered state it took some time for the truth to sink in. When it did we were too discouraged even to swear.

We put our mess kits away and tried to get some sleep. But the Japs had something more in store for us. There was an outburst of shrill whooping and yelling, then the guards poured into the compound with fixed bayonets. They feinted at the nearest prisoners with the sharp points.

Those of us who were able rose to our feet in alarm. Evidently we did not appear sufficiently frightened. The Japs outside the compound jeered the jokesters within. One Jap then made a running lunge and drove his bayonet through an American soldier's thigh.

This stampeded several other prisoners who trampled the sick and dying men on the ground. Some prisoners tripped and fell and were trampled by their comrades. The Japs left, laughing. There was little sleep that night. The stench was almost unbearable. Hundreds of prisoners were kept awake by sheer weariness. There were shouts of delirium. There was moaning. There were the sounds of men gasping their last.

At dawn of April 15, 1942, the sixth day of our ordeal, we were kicked to our feet by Jap guards and ordered to get out of the compound. The Japs did not even make a pretense of giving us food or water. Our canteens had been empty for hours. Only muddy scum inside them reminded us that we had filled them at the ditch outside Guagua the afternoon before.

Enough prisoners had been brought out of the compound to form five companies of 115 men each. In this formation we were marched to a railroad siding several blocks away where stood five ancient, ramshackle boxcars. None of these could have held more than fifty men in comfort. Now 115 men were packed into each car and the doors were pulled shut and locked from the outside.

There was no room to move. We stood jammed together because there wasn't sufficient floor space to permit sitting.

As the day wore on and the sun climbed higher the heat inside the boxcars grew to oven-like intensity. It was so hot that the air we breathed seemed to scorch our throats.

There was little ventilation, only narrow, screened slits at the ends of the cars. A large per cent of the prisoners was suffering from dysentery. The atmosphere was foul beyond description. Men began to faint. Some went down from weakness. They lay at our feet, face down in the filth that covered the floor boards.

After a seemingly interminable wait the train started with a jerk. A jolting, rocking ride began. Many of the prisoners in the boxcar in which I stood were seized by nausea, adding to the vile state of our rolling cell. The ride lasted more than three hours. Later I heard that a number of men had died in each of the five cars. I don't know. I was too far gone to notice much at the journey's end.

When the doors were opened, someone, I can't remember who, said we had reached Capas, a town in Tarlac province, and that we were headed for O'Donnell prison camp —named for the town of O'Donnell.

When the prisoners tumbled out into the glaring sunlight the wretchedness of their condition brought cries of compassion from Filipino civilians who lined the tracks. The surly Jap guards silenced these sympathetic voices with stern warnings.

We were marched several hundred yards down the tracks to a plot of bare scorching ground amid the tropical undergrowth. It was another sun treatment. There was no breeze. The ground was almost too hot to touch. The heat dried the filth into our pores.

The Jap guards formed a picket wall around us to forestall the friendly Filipinos who had come to give us food and water. Some of these, however, hurled their offerings over the heads of the Japs, hoping they would fall into our midst. Then they took to the bush, outrunning the guards who pursued them.

We sat for two hours in the little clearing before the Japs ordered us to our feet. A seven-mile hike to O'Donnell prison was ahead of us. As we filed into the narrow dirt road that wound through the green walls of the jungle, it became obvious that more than a fourth of our number never would be able to make it.

We expected mass murder of those too weak to walk. Instead, the Jap officers indicated the stronger ones might assist the weaker ones. This was something new. There were precious few stronger ones, however.

As we straggled on we had ample reason to bless the kindly Filipinos of Capas. Having seen other prisoners pass that way, they had set out cans of water among the bushes and in high grass along the road.

The Japs found many of these and kicked them over before our eyes. But some were overlooked and a few of us were able to take the edge off our thirst. One gaunt American officer said he believed he owed his life to the good and thoughtful townfolk of Capas.

My first good look at O'Donnell prison was from atop a rise about a mile off. I saw a forbidding maze of tumble-down buildings, barbed wire entanglements, and high guard towers, from which flew the Jap flag.

I had flown over this dismal spot several times, but never had given it more than passing appraisal. I wondered as I looked at it now how long I would be there; how long I could last.

As we stood, staring dazedly, there came to me a premonition that hundreds about to enter O'Donnell prison this April day never would leave it alive. If I could have known what lay in store for us all, I think I would have given up the ghost then and there.

Sharp commands by the Jap guards aroused me. We started moving.

Java Sea

On May 6, 1942, Wainwright surrendered Corregidor and the Philippines were firmly in the Japs' grasp. Guerrilla activity would increase throughout the rest of the war, with the aid of the U.S., but until the American landings in Leyte Gulf in 1944, there was no more organized fighting.

In the meantime, the Japs had attacked and overrun the islands of Wake and Guam, and had swept down the Malayan Peninsula, capturing Singapore and the thousands of British troops stationed there. And the first big naval action had been fought in the Java Sea.

In the last days of February, Japan had sent a powerful three-pronged striking force, totaling four carriers, four battleships, heavy and light cruisers, and many destroyers, to protect the troop transports for the impending invasion of Java.

Java's sea defense was in the hands of an Allied Naval Group, under the command of Dutch Adm. Doorman, and consisting of two heavy cruisers (the *U.S.S. Houston* and the British *H.M.S. Exeter*), three light cruisers (two Dutch, the *Java* and the *De Ruyter*, and the Australian *H.M.A.S. Perth)*, and eleven destroyers. On February 27th, Doorman struck at the Japanese force attacking from the northeast (a group consisting of cruisers and destroyers only). In an engagement of more than seven hours, the Allies lost half their ships including Doorman's flagship, the *Java*. The Japanese had one destroyer damaged; all their troop transports came through unscathed.

The two opposing forces were not unevenly matched, numerically speaking. The Allies took their licking because they lacked air reconnaissance, because of an astonishingly cumbersome system of communications,* and "the enemy's vast superiority in torpedo materiel and tactics." **

* S. E. Morison, in *The Rising Sun in the Pacific* (p. 342), says the Allied command under Dutch Adm. Doorman had never worked out a set of signals that were common to all; his signals

The two cruisers, *Perth* and *Houston,* escaped to fight another day, and, indeed, before the next day was over, they would be fighting for their very lives. Next morning, February 28th, they put into a Javanese port for badly needed repairs. However, orders were issued to all ships in the Java area to leave the Jap-infested waters at once. Both ships put to sea, heading for the Sunda Strait through which they hoped to escape into the Indian Ocean. They came upon Jap transports landing troops on the beaches of Banten Bay and, on the run—for their orders were to avoid action and escape—they shelled and sank four transports.

Later that night they ran head-on into a Jap force consisting of light and heavy cruisers and destroyers, which barred their entrance to the strait. The *Perth* and *Houston* fought back with everything they had, but the salvos of shells and torpedoes flung at them were simply too much to withstand.

The following selection is a description of the action from on board the *Perth.*

ACTION IN THE SUNDA STRAIT

by Ronald McKie

Saturday: 11:06 P. M.

At 10:45 p.m. Babi Island light was three miles to starboard, and a few minutes later *Perth* and *Houston* were opposite Banten Bay, near the northwest end of Java, and five miles off shore.

They were nearing Sunda Strait at last through waters where much history had been made—where Chinese battle junks had sailed, where men had fought for pepper and

---

had to be translated by a U.S. liaison officer who sent them on to other English-speaking ships; there was no recourse when the orders were conflicting, as often happens in quick actions.

** S. E. Morison, *The Rising Sun in the Pacific,* p. 358.

nutmegs and bases and personal power, where the tide of religion had ebbed and flowed. . . .

With Sunda Strait almost in sight, *Perth* increased her speed and *Houston* followed. They were steaming at 28 knots now, shuddering, straining, creaking under the vibrations of their mighty engines and thrusting screws.

In another hour, perhaps, they would be almost through Sunda Strait. In two hours or less they would be in the Indian Ocean—and out of the trap.

Then, at 11:06 p.m., when five miles from St. Nicolas Point, the extreme northwest tip of Java, with the Java Sea on its right and Sunda Strait on its left, Captain Waller sighted a ship close in to the headland.

"Challenge," he ordered. "It's probably one of our corvettes patrolling the strait."

The chief yeoman, Bert Hatwell, grabbed his Aldis lamp and winked the code letters.

The other ship replied. Her lamp was a strange pale green. Her reply was strange.

"U.B., U.B.," Waller said. "Repeat the challenge."

But as *Perth*'s Aldis winked again the other ship began to turn and make smoke, and as she showed her full silhouette Waller said: "Jap destroyer . . . sound the rattles . . . forward turrets open fire."

Then he called: "One unknown."

Perth's bow swung to bring the broadside to bear on the enemy. Then at point-blank range, her 6-inch guns spewed shells and orange flame.

In the plot below the bridge, Supply Assistant Ronald Clohesy kicked Tiger Lyons on the shin.

"It's on," he said. He might have been announcing lunch.

Lyons jerked upright and was just in time to hear the captain's order to the guns, and his words, "One unknown." That was Lyons' cue to break radio silence and report action to all shore stations. He scribbled the code signal and handed it to Clohesy who ran to the radio room behind the plot as the guns opened up.

And only Darwin, away to the southeast, ever acknowledged that signal that the Battle of Sunda Strait had begun.

Fear now was in Lyons' guts, fear cold and hard like a chunk of ice lodged between his solar plexus and his navel. Fear stayed with him for minutes, urgent and degrading, and in those minutes he felt physically dirty and hated himself. Then his panic ebbed as a shell hissed under the ship —hissed deep under the racing keel with the sound a soda siphon makes when it spits into a glass of whisky.

Now *Perth*'s guns were crashing like houses falling down, and through the speaking tube he heard someone on the bridge above say, "There are four to starboard," and another voice, "There are five on our portside"; and then a surprised "By God, they're all around us," he recognized as from Allan McDonough, the Royal Australian Air Force flying officer with the ship.

Lyons heard the captain order divided control to the guns, and soon after independent control so that each gun could pick its own target. There were plenty, too. His plot of the action already showed thirteen Japanese destroyers and two cruisers attacking them—and that was only part of the enemy force. He knew then he and his shipmates were in for a dirty night, but his early panic never returned. His plot showed that the farthest Jap was only three miles away, the closest less than a mile. The Japanese cruisers were firing over and through their own destroyers, and he thought, I hope the bastards sink one another. The Japanese and Australian and American gunners were almost looking down one another's guns.

As he plotted *Perth*'s zigzag course, Lyons, who in his steel room never saw one gun flash of that action, knew through his instruments that she was turning in a big circle with a diameter of about five miles. Waller's object, he could tell, was to circle and protect *Houston*'s blind stern and to maneuver against torpedo fire. The course changes were so frequent and violent as Waller swung his racing cruiser that Lyons jerked from one side of the plot to the other. It was like being in a car skidding badly on a slippery road. Mechanically, he recorded these course changes, watched his dials, jotted down times, speed, engine revolutions, enemy positions. He was not afraid—not even worried now. Instead, he felt a strange detachment—like being an onlooker watching the action from some independent vantage point. But his shirt stuck to him like wallpaper, and sweat dripped down his fingers and down his pencil onto his pad.

At 11:26 p.m. he noted down that *Perth* collected her first shell—in the forward funnel—with a burst of steam like a locomotive blowing off, and then another somewhere near the flag deck at 11:32. And at 11:50 she got another, near the waterline, which burst in the ordinary seamen's mess. But she was still unharmed, although the Japanese had flung thousands of shells at her. Forty-four minutes after action started she was still fighting with every gun she had, except her useless machine guns, and so was *Houston*.

Then, at 12:05 a.m., a torpedo went into the forward engine room on the starboard side, and Lyons felt *Perth* lift and hang as though she were actually floating in the air. He thought, When will she come down? Then hundreds of ship identification photographs poured on top of him from pigeonholes in a cabinet on the bulkhead above. They frightened him more than the torpedo. He cursed.

"Wouldn't it!" an assistant said. "Now it's a bloody snowstorm."

This was Fred Lasslett, one of his electrical mechanics who was waiting in the plot for damage reports. Lasslett began to pick up the photographs, and David Griffiths, the other mechanic, helped him. They gathered them in bundles, sorted them into rough order, and stuffed them back into the pigeonholes.

Then a second torpedo hit—and all the photographs poured out again. Lasslett shrugged and left them there. He took a slab of chocolate from his pocket and began to eat, gazing at the dials with their flickering needles. Shells howled over, but he didn't even look up.

"Do you reckon we'll make it?" Clohesy asked casually.

Lyons shook his head. "Doesn't look like it."

Clohesy opened a tin of biscuits scrounged from Tanjong and started munching. Lyons noticed with admiration how calm this thin-faced slender kid was. He showed no fear, no emotion except a sort of amused nonchalant detachment as though what was happening outside the plot were little concern of his. Lyons remembered then lying flat on the deck beside this youngster when the Jap bombers dropped a stick across them at Tanjong before the Java Sea fight, and watching him, amazed, as he played tittat-toe with a pencil stub on the deck as the bombs burst.

And watching him, eating biscuits now as though he were in his father's shop somewhere in Victoria, Lyons suddenly felt proud to be in action with a boy like this—and humble before such bravery.

John Woods had just reached No. 2 Lookout on the lower bridge when *Perth* opened fire. As the first gun flashes died he looked aft and saw *Houston* switch on a searchlight, and at the end of the cold blue shaft were the silhouettes of Japanese merchant ships packed close together against the Java shore like cattle sheltering against a windbreak. Then all *Perth*'s guns were firing, and the crashing against his ears from then on was continuous. It was like holding his head against a thin wall someone was trying to batter down from the other side.

All round him now the yellow lights that winked were Japanese guns, but he had no sense of fear. This surprised him. He had often wondered what point-blank action would be like, and, now he knew, he decided it was not half so exciting as a good football match.

He had nothing to do except watch. He tried to estimate the position of enemy guns by the shell splashes in the water round the ship, but soon abandoned that. There were too many guns and too many splashes. Yet in all that battle he heard only one shell—one that came in very low and skimmed the bridge like a train a few feet above his head.

When the first torpedo hit he wondered what had happened. He thought it was a shell. When the second torpedo hit, he knew, for he felt *Perth* jump out of the sea, jump ahead and fall back again. Then, quite calmly, he thought of his mother and prayed.

"Look after the family at home, God," he said, "and try to look after me if you can."

But in all that hell let loose and guns winking and metal flying, he was still not afraid.

The general alarm bells woke Len Smith. He knew what to do. He ran to his starboard torpedo tubes and took the pins off the warheads while his No. 2 and No. 3 opened the breeches and put the charges in, and his No. 4 and No. 5 swung the tubes out and trained them. Ten seconds after the alarm he reported to the bridge by phone, "All ready."

He still did not think *Perth* had run into serious trouble, but three minutes later he knew he was wrong. From the torpedo officer on the bridge came the order, "Bearing red 20. Enemy ships. All tubes ready." He waited. The next order, "Changing target," countermanded the first. The third order was, "Bearing three cruisers." Then, ten minutes after action started, came the order to fire, and the four fish leaped outward with that metallic rattling they make—like an old car jerking along a road full of potholes.

"Torpedoes running," Smith reported.

He ran to the portside and got off four more fish. As he watched them run he counted twelve Japanese destroyers under the light of star shells. Then he saw two big explosions and yelled, "You beaut!"

He grabbed the phone. "We got a couple of hits."

"We did better than that," the torpedo officer yelled back. "We killed with the first batch of fish, too."

With all his torpedoes gone, Len Smith detailed some of his crews to damage control on deck. They ran out fire hoses, while others joined the men carrying ammunition to the 4-inch guns.

But Smith still wasn't overworried. He still felt that Hec Waller would get them through, even when, just before the first torpedo hit, he counted eighteen Japanese destroyers attacking in packs of six—like gray beetles with red eyes rushing toward them. Then the second torpedo came in with a roar that even smothered the gunfire and left men dazed. Then water poured down on Smith and his men as if someone had cut the bottom out of a tank.

The water fell and slid away. Slowly he wiped his face

with his sleeve and felt the sting of salt, and thought, Now we're a goner.

Bill Davis was dreaming that a telephone was ringing beside his bed. He tried to reach for it but could not move his arm. Then he was awake and the action buzzer was going above him. He had only one feeling—surprise that of all people Bill Davis should be in two major actions within twenty-four hours.

He was supposed to get to his Red Cross action station, but, without knowing why, he joined the line of men carrying shells from the magazine to the 4-inch, and from that moment time ceased for him and noise replaced it. At first he noticed how the men about him worked as though they were at a practice, but soon they were running with the shells, talking, shouting, pushing one another out of the way, cursing. They cursed the Japs, they cursed one another, they cursed the gun crews. And the gun crews, serving the guns like maniacs, cursed everyone as they operated their mechanism.

One of the ammunition party sang in a shrill tenor that the gunfire cut to pieces, so that Davis heard only stray notes divorced from one another and high like the crying of a sick child. Another man kept yelling, "Flog the Japs, flog the Japs," in an endless chant. Another shouted, "You beaut!" as he ran cradling a shell.

Davis never doubted they would get through. He kept thinking, I wonder what time we'll get to Tjilatjap. He knew Waller would save them, even after the first torpedo hit, even after the direct hit on one of the 4-inch guns. He never forgot that. One moment he saw a gunner sliding a shell into the breech. Then a flash like a scarlet cloth seemed to wipe the man, the crew, and the gun itself into the sea. One moment there was a gun in action and men were yelling and cursing as they served it. The next moment there was only an empty space on the deck where the gun had been, and the sour stink of an exploded shell.

The guns woke Gavin Campbell, and the first thing he thought about was his tin hat. Wearily he picked it up and put it on, but forgot about his antiflash hood and gloves. He growled to Douglas Findlay, the A.B. with him on the multiple gun, "The bastards never let you sleep."

Then he heard the gong in "Y" turret just below him, and the sound reminded him of a Sydney tram bell—brassy and urgent. It told him "Y" turret was about to fire. His body tightened as he waited for the shock. Then it came and the blast, as it poured over him, was like the heat wave from a bush fire. The flash momentarily blinded him, and his sight was just back to normal when the guns fired again, and again and again. Soon, every time the 6-inch fired he pleaded with them to stop. Soon, the tension was almost pain itself, and he felt his inside would burst if the guns fired any more. But they did fire—crash, crash, crash. And then he was angry, angry because of his own helplessness above the big guns, because of the futility of standing beside his useless gun like a shag on a rock, angry because he had always wanted to fire the four black barrels and exult in their metallic argument and couldn't now because there was no time between the blinding flashes of the 6-inch for him to focus on a target. He cursed and Findlay cursed, and their faces were like quick close-ups on a screen as the guns flashed.

Once, during a sudden pause in the firing, he saw enlarging spots of light on two Japanese destroyers and knew they were opening the shutters of their searchlights. Then the 4-inch cracked and put the lights out. And as the lights went out something crashed against the gun shield close to his head and spun into the deck at his feet. A star shell flowered, high and brilliantly soft, and he looked down and saw a chunk of jagged metal, about six inches long, impaled in the deck. The jagged piece of shell looked exactly like a map of New Guinea.

He was facing astern as the first torpedo hit. He felt *Perth* rise and drop, and then everything was, for a long moment, as hushed as the bush at noon, before a great pillar of water and oil collapsed on him. When he wiped his eyes he was still facing astern and saw the dim shape of *Houston,* and from the shape was pouring stream after stream of red and blue and amber tracer as though madmen were throwing electric light bulbs across the sky.

Down in "Y" turret lobby Keith Gosden jumped up as he heard a clatter in the turret above. He knew what that meant and thought, as he always did at these moments, Is this it? Then the automatic hoist squealed and began to move, and he started feeding shells into her. And, above, the guns went off.

For an hour he worked like a machine to keep the shells up to the guns. Only twice, before he fed into the hoist a dozen practice shells, and realized, with a shock, with sudden dismay, that the magazine below was empty, did he have time to think or notice what was going on around him. Once, he shouted, "What are you doing up there?" and the turret captain, Alfie Coyne, yelled back, "You can pick your own target—there are hundreds of the bastards." Once, Jesse Garrett, one of his helpers, collapsed with the heat and lack of air, and he propped him against the bulkhead and went on feeding shells into the hungry hoist.

Then the first torpedo hit, and lifted Gosden off his feet and dropped him on his face. And as he scrambled up he saw that the lobby was leaking through the rivets. His youngest assistant, a brave boy of eighteen, saw the water, too, and began to yell. He grabbed the boy's shoulders and shook him back to control. When the second torpedo came the water poured into the lobby. At the third torpedo the three men were up to their knees in water.

They watched it rising, climbing up the sides, up the shell hoist. Then the others looked at Gosden and he thought, God, we must be sinking! We'll drown if we don't get out of this.

And then he wanted to scream.

Polo Owen woke to see two rockets falling. They were chartreuse and scarlet and soft against the night sky. They dropped lazily and he thought of Guy Fawkes Night when he was a child in Western Australia, and of how his brother once set off a Chinese basket bomb under his bottom. Then the guns opened and he jumped to his feet, but could see nothing, as he pulled on his antiflash gear, except *Perth*'s superstructure dim and high ahead and the shadowy faces of his companions.

"What the hell are we firing at?" one of the gun crew asked.

Then the cruiser suddenly increased speed, and seemed to run away from under them. The stern where they were stationed seemed to Owen to dip almost under the sea as the ship jumped forward and began to fling about like a destroyer as guns on every side flashed and went out, flashed and went out.

He noticed "Y" turret swinging on an aft bearing, and he and the others flattened behind the Carley float, which was lashed down near their gun position, as the 6-inch fired. The flash poured over them like dragon's breath and singed the hair on their arms above their antiflash gloves. The anchored Carley jumped six inches and fell back. The guns swung away, searching for the next target, and a searchlight reached out and grabbed *Perth*'s stern.

In that blinding blue glare Owen felt twenty feet high, naked and more helpless than he had ever felt in his life. It was like looking down the barrel of a gun and knowing that the gun was about to fire. The faces of his companions looked pale green and distorted—faces from another planet. In the paralytic tension of the searchlight's beam an inner voice told him that *Perth* was doomed. He heard the 4-inch snap, as though from a great distance, and the searchlight went out. Then, as "Y" turret swept round and roared again directly aft, he dived for the deck behind the Carley float.

Lying there, angrily conscious now of the futile part they were playing, he said to Ralph Lowe, "This is bloody stupid. We can't do a thing. Let's get to hell out of here."

Lowe nodded. "We'll get blown overboard if we don't."

And the others agreed.

They all ran along the quarter-deck to the torpedo space under the 4-inch-gun deck. Owen, on the starboard side, was just in time to see four torpedoes like gray cigars leap into the sea, and as he watched them he thought, Where can I go where I won't get hurt? and knew there was nowhere to go.

All along the horizon now the Japanese gun flashes were like electric lights switching on and off, and he saw the shell splashes, in the light of *Perth*'s and the Jap guns, were pale blue topped with soft white plumes which waved gently as they fell back into the sea.

Then he heard a splintering crash forward, followed by a silence, which rushed in and replaced all sound, more terrifying than the din of battle. He ran to the port torpedo space, but it was empty of men. He felt powerless, useless. He thought, This is bloody awful. If I only had something to do—something to occupy my hand or my brain. He turned to the gun at the stern, but it was now twisted metal and parts of the Carley float, draped round the barrel stumps, made the remains of the gun look like a scarecrow in a paddock. He was thinking, I missed by seconds being like that, when the second torpedo hit, and the whole ship seemed to crumple and splinter. He felt he was standing on a matchbox and it was collapsing beneath him. Three sailors ran aft bawling "Abandon ship," and with them he tried to unlash the stacked pilgrim rafts. He tore his fingernails, but the knots would not move. The blast of the 6-inch guns had made them as rigid as metal.

"Anyone got a knife?" he asked, thinking, The Carley was my abandon-ship station. Now it's the rafts or nothing.

The men shook their heads, and ran back along the quarter-deck.

Perth was already listing to port, but still moving. He went to the starboard side and looked over. The screws were slow-thumping and one was almost out of the water. It seemed so close he felt he could touch it. He went forward along the portside. The deck was deserted now, and somewhere forward steam was escaping with a thin high wail. He looked over the side and the sea seemed very near. He thought, There's nothing I can do now, as he climbed the rail.

Sam Stening swung off his bunk as the guns opened. As he pulled on his boiler suit and slid his feet into his sandals he thought, The guns shouldn't have gone off. We're done for this time. He ran across the flat to the wardroom. His men there were white-faced and silent. None of them had been in action before, except in the Java Sea.

"This is it, boys," he said, hoping desperately that the cold tightness he felt did not show in his face or voice.

"What do I do?" asked Mathieson, the chaplain.

"Just sit down," Stening said. "There's nothing to do. We just wait."

He could think of no other reply, but for some reason of association he suddenly remembered the time the chaplain, a teetotaler, had drunk cider and thought it was soft drink. Stening smiled secretly at such a stray and meaningless thought at a time like this. But he felt better, steadier. The tightness like a belt round his chest had loosened a hole or two. He said to himself, Don't panic, you bloody ape. Do your job.

But he and his men had only one job—to wait for casualties. And waiting in a closed steel room was infinitely worse than being on deck, watching, doing. Waiting was enough to break the bravest of men. He sat on a chair beside the operating table, but the ship heeled and tipped him out. He tried again, and the same thing happened. He noticed some of the men grinning and thought, They're better now—they're all better.

Perth was flying about like a crazy thing, 7,000 tons of metal changing course every few seconds it seemed. He studied his men as the racket above got worse. They were trying not to show what they felt. One man sat with his eyes closed, but could not keep his fingers still; another licked his lips with a furry tongue, like a lizard; a third . . . He thought, Thank God, they're solid.

And then, as they waited while all hell was loose above, hatred of war welled in him like sudden anger, hatred of its futility, its endless destruction of life and material, its failure to solve any of the basic problems of overcrowded, ignorant, hungry mankind.

Stening had lost all consciousness of time now, and when a man in a repair party yelled from the wardroom flat, "Casualty on the 4-inch gun deck," he did not know whether the action had lasted minutes or hours and didn't care. He detailed four of his men, and they left with a stretcher. He waited perhaps ten minutes, but they didn't return. They never returned. He noticed that boiling water was slopping from the sterilizer, and sizzling down its polished sides, and that one of the men aimlessly combed his fingers through his hair. He had another party ready to go when he heard a shout, "We've been hit forward."

"That doesn't concern us," Stening told his men.

But he thought, What a silly statement! Of course it concerns us—it concerns all of us. This is life or death for these men, for myself.

Then the first torpedo hit and *Perth* seemed to jump.

Hell, he thought, that was something pretty big!

It reminded him of the time in the Mediterranean when a bomb nearly lifted his destroyer out of the water. He had been sunk that time, by dive-bombing Stukas, in the Australian destroyer *Waterhen* along the "Spud Run" to Tobruk. He had no wish to be sunk again.

As *Perth* seemed to flop back into the sea and steady, an order came over the loud-speaker. Mixed with the crash of gunfire it sounded like "Prepare to ram," and he shouted, "Everybody lie down." The men dropped and lay there, but nothing happened, and slowly they got up and watched him—sheeplike, patient, but tense. He looked at their eyes. He could tell now they knew they would soon all have to swim. Calmly he thought, Soon I'll be in the sea.

Less than a minute after action stations, Frank Gillan had climbed into his overalls, put his torch in his pocket, and pulled on his Mae West and only partly inflated it. He was not to know until later that this last decision probably saved his life.

He left his cabin and ran forward along the alleyway, and as he ran sailors slammed the watertight doors behind him and locked the dogs. He reached the airlock above "B" boiler room, closed the steel door, and then went through and down the feet-polished ladders into the stokehold, twenty feet below the waterline. Here he was in a familiar world—so familiar that when Gillan dreams he always dreams of engine rooms—of boiler fires and steam and pumping pistons and the whine of turbines. The air stank of hot steel and oil and cordite sucked in by the turbo fans which thundered above like aero engines. The glare from the fires was terra cotta on naked chests of men in front of oil burners, and red on their cheeks as, with heads swung sideways, they watched the hand signals of Chief Stoker Reece. Above, among the tubes and ladders and wire and gauges, the white insulated steam pipes, as thick as a man's body, were like enormous copulating grubs.

"Pretty sudden, wasn't it?" Gillan yelled at Tuersley as he reached the bottom of the ladders. The warrant officer grinned.

Gillan went to the stocky chief stoker and stood beside him. Reece, his backside propped against the electric oil fuel pump, was watching the pressure gauges, and close to him were the discharge valves like rows of organ stops.

The racket now made even bellowed speech almost inaudible. The fans were pumping in the crash of gunfire, and the noise seemed to come in solid and fall on top of them. The ship was twitching like a man in an epileptic fit. The water in the long gauges above the boilers was bouncing and the water levels in the gauges reflected the light of naked bulbs like diamond facets. Every time the 6-inch fired the huge boilers, generating 20,000 horsepower, jumped up and back as though a giant fist had slugged them. They jumped, Gillan noticed, when the guns actually recoiled, not when they fired, and he could tell which way the guns were firing by the way the boilers shifted. Steam pipes, too, were vibrating and jumping as though they were alive, and from them little pieces of asbestos packing were floating down like gentle snow.

"How on earth did I get myself here?" he asked. "God knows what's going to happen."

And instantly he realized he was talking to himself—aloud.

He yelled in the chief stoker's ear, "I say, chief, it's time we had a cup of khai."

Reece just heard him because he yelled back, "I had mine before I came down, but I'll get some organized."

He signaled to a big redheaded stoker and pointed to his mouth. The stoker grinned, made the cocoa and brought Gillan a cup.

The heat, despite the gale from the fans, was getting worse. It seemed to press inward on Gillan's eyes and ears, and to press down on his cap. He was used to it—heat was part of his life—but he saw one of the stokers, a first-trip man, stagger and recover and reach for the salt tray and drop a pinch into his mouth.

Now Gillan lost all sense of time. His only concern was steam and more steam for the engines. Time became oil and burners and the thundering pulse of steam. Then the fans sucked in a terrific explosion he knew wasn't a gun or a shell. He and Tuersley and the others jerked into the air like puppets, and as they landed the plates slammed against their heels and jarred their spines and teeth. To Gillan it felt like driving a draft horse in a springless cart over a 12-inch log at a hand gallop. He knew a torpedo had got them, knew, but only later, it had hit between the forward boiler room and engine room, and in that engine room the officers he had dined with only a few hours before and all the others with them had died instantly. Three men, too, he also learned later, had been standing on a grating above the engine room when the Jap fish hit. Instantaneously the grating went red under their feet, melted in seconds, and they fell in and died in seconds. The sea followed the torpedo and boiled and thrashed among the red-hot ruin. The men there died without knowing what had hit them.

But the only damage in Gillan's boiler room was a broken water gauge. As water sprayed and sizzled down the boiler, he jumped to the turning handles and shut off the cocks sending water into the gauge. Tuersley signaled to one of the artificers, who shinned up the ladders and started fitting a new glass to the gauge.

But Gillan noticed now that the ship had lost life. One

moment she was almost human—swinging, bounding, swaying. The next she was sluggish and listing slightly to starboard. Then she straightened, but slowly, almost reluctantly. She seemed tired, listless. He looked at the sides of the boiler room and said, "If a fish comes in there it's finish." And once again he realized he was talking aloud.

Then one of the turbo fans cut out; but Tuersley, who had all the answers, knew what to do. He had been in the Mediterranean, and was no stranger to breakdowns of this kind. He climbed, hand over hand, without once using his feet, grabbing pipes and handrails until he reached the top of the boiler room where he fiddled with the fan until it came in again with a pulsating whine. Then he slid down and glanced at Gillan as much as to say, "Easy, wasn't it?"

After another big explosion, the ship listed and seemed to go down a little by the head. Then she leveled out, lost way, and rolled to port. She was still steaming, but Gillan felt the plates under him moving like a ship in a rough sea. Then came another explosion, and the boilers began to scream and blow off at their safety valves.

Gillan grabbed the phone to the engine room. It was dead. He tried to call damage control. Dead. He called the bridge. Dead. He tried to ring the telegraph to the engine room. The telegraph was jammed. As the ship listed again, Tuersley said calmly, "We'd better shut the boilers down," and Gillan nodded, and Tuersley shut off the oil supply to the burners.

Then Gillan saw that everyone, every man in that stokehold, was looking at him. The ship had a 45-degree list, he noticed, and then he thought, God, she's going! *Perth* was dead now except for the fans which were still whining and the lights which were still on, so that he knew the boiler room diesel generator was still working. The ship rolled again and seemed to slide away from him. He looked round at the men standing there, near naked, waiting, calm, and their quiet courage gave him courage. He signaled upward with both arms. But there was no rush, and he thought, What men to serve with! As they moved up the ladders, he said to Tuersley, "We ought to shut the oil fuel off completely. If we don't she'll catch fire while we're escaping." As they shut everything they could, Gillan saw that the bottom of the stokehold was now empty of stokers. Then he waved Reece and Tuersley on up the ladder.

Please God, not again! Lloyd Burgess thought as the action started. In the dark he fumbled for his shoes, found his tin hat, and stumbled on to the bridge. He was still half asleep and testy as an overtired child, and didn't care if five hundred ships were attacking them. All he wanted was sleep, but every time the guns went off he jumped and his tin hat fell down over his eyes and that woke him up and made him mad.

He could see the dim shapes of the captain standing forward on the bridge, John Harper the navigator, near the binnacle, Peter Hancox the gunnery officer, Johnson the first lieutenant, Willy Gay the officer of the watch, Guy Clarke the torpedo officer, Bert Hatwell the chief yeoman, Allen McDonough the R.A.A.F. flying officer, Frank Tranby-White the paymaster middy. And every time the guns flashed the men on the bridge were deep-etched against the violent light as though in a brilliantly clear photograph.

Between the gun bursts he heard Waller's voice, "Starboard twenty," the ship swung; "Midships," the ship steadied; "Port fifteen," the ship swung; "Midships," the ship steadied. On and on it went like a monotonous chant in a jungle of light and dark. He heard Waller call, "What about those targets on the port bow?" and the navigator's quick reply, "They're islands, sir."

The only light on the bridge was the almost hidden glow under the hooded chart table. Burgess tried to take notes of the action, writing in the dark by feel, forming his words as a child forms them, large and crude. Then the gunfire rattled the chart table to pieces. He propped the pieces up, fixed the hood, and carefully edged his head and shoulders under to check his notes. Then the table collapsed again and he backed out from under the ruin and left it there.

A searchlight got them and Waller called, "For God's sake shoot that bloody light out!"

Behind and below Burgess heard the 4-inch barking. The light blacked out.

In a silence that lasted only seconds, Burgess felt his heart hammering and all sound was within himself, so that he could almost hear the blood pumping through his body. Then the deck heaved as the first torpedo got them.

"Forward engine room out . . . speed reduced," came the report.

"Very good," Waller said.

Aft, a shell wrecked the plane and catapult with a crash like two trains meeting head on.

Then "B," "X" and "Y" turrets reported to the gunnery officer that they were out of shells and were firing practice bricks with extra cordite.

Then "A" turret reported five shells left.

Then the 4-inch reported they were firing star shells—and the last of those.

Hancox told the captain.

"Very good," he said.

The second torpedo seemed to hit right under the bridge—and among other things it jammed the hatch in "B" turret magazine, and the men there went down alive. The ship seemed to leap from the sea, straight up, and drop back. Those on the bridge went up with her and came down on their knees. When Burgess fell, he was facing aft, looking up at the director tower, and he wondered if it would fall on him. Then with a noise like escaping steam, water and oil fell on the bridge and knocked some of the men over.

"Hell," Waller said, "that's torn it! . . . Abandon ship."

"Prepare to abandon ship, sir?" Hancox queried.

"No—abandon ship."

The fateful signal went over the intercom—for those who could hear it.

"A" turret fired again—her defiant last—and Burgess' tin hat again fell over his eyes. When he pushed it back the bridge was empty, except for Waller, Gay and himself. The captain was standing far forward blowing into his Mae West.

As Burgess went down the ladder he heard Waller say, "Get off the bridge, Gay," and as Gay left Waller was standing with his arms on the front of the bridge looking down at the silent turrets.

Sunday: 12:07 A.M.

As Burgess went down the bridge ladder shells were fluff-fluffing over and Japanese searchlights were opening up like a summer carnival. He had one objective now, and only one: escape.

He yelled, "Abandon ship!" as he went across the flag deck. There were bodies among the shadows, and the darker shadows were shell gashes and blood. He crawled under the wreckage of the catapult and reached his abandon-ship station, a Carley float on the portside, and as he got there a shell hit an ammunition locker and hot metal whined and cried above him like kittens in a basket, and he dragged his tin hat down over his ears.

Three men were already at the Carley. One of them, John Harriss, an A.B., was grinning.

"Did you hear of Chips King?" he said. "He was lugging a four-inch star shell when we got abandon ship. He jumped overboard with the shell in his arms."

Burgess wasn't amused—not then. He wanted to get off, and as soon as possible. They tried to move the float, but it was too heavy. Then, as *Perth* listed, they were able to slide it down the deck and into the sea and jump after it and pull themselves aboard.

The first thing Burgess did when he was free of the ship was to go through his pockets. He threw away a sodden packet of cigarettes, tore up his notebook with the notes of the action in it, and took off his shoes and tossed them into the sea. Then he looked up, as the dying cruiser moved past them and away, and thought, Thank God, I'm clear of that!

"No—abandon ship."

The captain's voice, clear and hard, came down the

speaking tube to the plot. The men there looked at the deck-head, and then at Lyons.

"Shoot through," he said to Clohesy, who was still eating biscuits.

He shook hands with him, and with Lasslett and Griffiths, and with Tony Spriggins, the P.O. telegrapher, who was standing in the door of the plot. He followed them out, but remembered his code books and went back and heard voices on the bridge, including the captain's, but couldn't hear what was being said. He had just grabbed the code book when a shell hit the bridge, ripped the side off the plot with the clatter of a foundry at full blast as it burst upward, and flung him against his table. Then the lights went out and he thought, This is a bloody silly place for a schoolmaster to be in.

For a moment he panicked and rushed for where he knew the door must be. Then he recovered, groped back to the speaking tube and yelled, "Plot stopped." There was no answer—no voices now. He called again, "Bridge, this is the plot." Then as the ship sagged to port, he felt his way out to the flag deck where he slipped and fell to his hands and knees. He fumbled for his torch and turned it on. There were broken bodies all round him, and blood under him, and sticky on his hands, and one of the dead smiled, and another had no face. There was a pile of bodies, stacked up by blast, in an alleyway. He swung the torch. There was a body beside him, without head, legs or arms. He looked at it and wanted to be sick. He got to his feet, jumped to the ship's side, grabbed a paravane rope, swung out and dropped, and as he came to the surface through thick oil someone was calling plaintively for help and purple tracers were going over low—*zip, zip, zip*—and a sailor swam up to him and said, "Did you get any souvenirs, mate?" and before Lyons could answer lifted from the water a heavy pair of binoculars slung round his neck and added, "These bastards'll make a good hock when I get back to Sydney." Lyons was so amazed he opened his mouth and took in fuel oil, and the oil made him vomit. After that he kept his mouth shut.

He swam slowly toward voices on the water and reached *Perth*'s cutter and crawled with other men over the side. But she was jagged with shell holes and filled and sank, and a sailor panicked. He kept going up and down, up and down, screaming and gurgling until he drowned. Then a packet of Jap shells landed perhaps one hundred yards away. The concussion slammed against Lyons, and a spurt of water, as though from a pressure pump, rushed into his bowels and out again. He was sick, and someone called, "It smashed my guts," and Lyons thought, This is bloody awful. It's Saturday night—our only night free from the kids. I should be dancing with my wife.

He was on his own now, but he knew he would not die. Then he saw two men clinging to a 44-gallon drum, and as he swam up to them one said, "I'm leaving," and the other groaned, "Oh, God," and disappeared. Hanging to the drum, slippery with oil, Lyons looked about him and saw the last of *Perth*. She was over on her portside sliding down by the bows. Her screws were high in the air, naked and almost indecent above the sea, and one was still turning as though it was tired. Then she disappeared. He didn't know then, but Burgess on his float also saw the ship go and looked at his watch—the watch he had paid £5 15s. for. It was still going, and the time in the glare of searchlights was 12:25 a.m.

Lyons heard a man call, so he swam away from the drum toward him and met Yeoman of Signals Percy Stokan, who asked cheerfully, "Having any trouble?"

"Plenty," Lyons said. "The ship's sunk, I've lost thirty thousand cigarettes, my neck's stiff, and this bloody Mae is worrying me."

"Okay, okay, I'll hang onto you while you get your clothes off."

As Lyons pulled off his uniform and his shoes a sailor swam up and said, "You blokes got a knife?"

"Hell—what for?" Lyons asked.

"What for?" the sailor said. "There's a team of floggin' Japs in the water over there and I've got a few floggin' bills to pay with the floggin' little Shinto bastards."

Woods climbed down from the lower bridge and helped cut a Carley float adrift and get it into the sea on the portside. But an inner voice warned him, Don't get into it—keep away from it. He noticed that the others too seemed reluctant to leave the ship. Not a man moved, and as the float drifted away one said, "What if the old girl is afloat in the morning?" and another snapped, "Don't be a bloody fool—she's almost under now." But, still, not one of the eight men there could leave the ship, and they watched the float drift astern and disappear.

This momentary mood of indecision died as a shell hit the 4-inch-gun deck and showered sparks like an oxy-welding torch and crying lumps of metal. Woods saw a raft in the water and dived over the side, and the others followed. This was one of the pilgrim rafts—copper tanks encased in timber with trailing life lines. Soon many men were on or around it. Mechanically, Woods counted twenty-eight heads.

"Me mate here's hurt," someone called.

Those on board lifted the man from the sea and laid him across the raft. In star-shell light Woods saw that his face was green-tinged and twisted and that his eyes were closed, and he thought, What will we do? And then he got his first sickening, frightening taste of fuel oil—something every survivor will remember for the rest of his life—and for the first time he was afraid, afraid of fear, afraid of the water, afraid of dying, afraid.

Another star shell burst, and as he watched its slow sinking, brilliant yet soft way above, he remembered a book he had read before the war which described how oil fuel on the water caught fire, and how the fire swept through the lifeboats and how . . .

His guts heaved and he vomited over the man beside him in the sea.

Even when Smith knew *Perth* was sinking he was still a product of his long naval training. The average man thought instinctively of himself. But Smith thought, What needs doing before I go over the side? He went aft to the depth charges, pulled the primers out, put the keys in and made them safe. He felt glad now because he knew that if he had not done this the charges, which were set for different depths, could have exploded as *Perth* was going to the bottom and killed every man in the water. Generally, depth charges are not at the ready at night, but Captain Waller had ordered them to be kept ready. Smith had wondered why at the time.

Then he remembered the radio direction finder, near the torpedo space, which he had orders to destroy in an emergency. He found a hammer among the torpedo tools and beat the R.D.F. apparatus into scrap.

Then, for the first time, he thought of Len Smith. *Perth* was well down by the bows as he walked to the stern and sat on the rail. Will I keep my boots on? he asked himself as he listened to the propellers still churning, and the answer was, Keep them on. There's coral along this coast and you'll need them, and your knife. He never had a doubt that he would live to remember Sunda.

As *Perth*'s stern lifted higher; he said aloud, "You'd better go now, Lennie boy." He saw a Carley float and dropped almost onto it and climbed aboard where John Deegan, an A.B., and Davis, his torpedo gunner's mate, welcomed him.

They picked up twenty others as they drifted closer to the Java coast—so close that when they saw Japanese landing craft, in the light of a searchlight, going in to invade, Smith warned, "We'd better get out of this, boys, or we'll be in trouble."

They started to paddle away from the land, but the float kept turning—turning in crazy circles—like a dodgem car at a fun fair.

Davis was terrified only once during the action—right at the end when he saw his shipmates going over the side and remembered he could not swim. He was wearing his Mae West, but was afraid it would not hold him up. Frantically, he searched for a lifebuoy, but could not find one, and then, with surprised discovery, he said to himself, Don't be a fool. You can't swim more than a few yards, but you can float longer than the best swimmer can swim. You've often done it in the baths at home. He remembered the test at Garden Island, Sydney, years before when he had to swim fifty yards fully dressed, but without his boots, then float for three minutes. He had only just been able to dog-paddle the distance and then, exhausted, had turned on his back, put his arms at his sides, and floated—and gone to sleep. He had still been floating, still asleep, when the instructor discovered him a long time later and yelled, "Get to hell out of that water, you flaming seal." Remembering this he climbed the rail near the quarter-deck on the portside and tensed himself to jump.

His next memory was of lying two feet from the opposite rail on the high starboard side covered in belts of pom-pom ammunition and strips of twisted metal.

Good God, he thought, another torpedo must have got me!

In those moments he knew exactly what to do, but they were his only lucid moments for days. He pushed the belts and wreckage aside and tried to rise, but his right leg was useless. Cautiously, he felt the leg from the thigh down, and his fingers and a stab of pain told him it was smashed below the knee. The ship lurched then and he said aloud, "You'll have to leave in a hurry." He dragged himself to the side, dragged himself through the rail and fell into the sea, and saw a paddle waving above him and grabbed it and felt arms grip him.

All that night and part of the next day, as the cloud drifts in his mind lifted and closed in, he remembered pain and thought someone was twisting his leg. He didn't know that the sea was slopping against his fracture as he slumped on the side of the raft with his legs in the water.

Campbell's earphones to gunnery control clicked and went dead. He took them off and heard men on the deck below bawling, "Abandon ship!"

"Hell," Findlay said, "I've left my Mae West in my locker!"

"Then you'd better go after it," Campbell advised.

As he climbed down from his gun position he blew

into his own Mae and then, very carefully, and almost reverently, placed his beloved tin hat on the quarter-deck. He didn't drop it or throw it down. He placed it gently on the deck, and then didn't want to leave it. He had worn it in *H.M.A.S. Hobart* during a bombardment of Italian Somaliland, and again in *H.M.A.S. Canberra* off East Africa when they found the two supply ships of the Nazi pocket battleship *Admiral von Scheer*. This hat was the one thing he had always promised himself he would bring home from the war, and now he had to leave it, and he felt like saying good-by to an old friend.

From below came the grinding, tearing sounds of things shifting, sliding as the ship heeled. He went to the stern and looked over and heard the screws and said aloud, "Not for you, old son," and walked back to near "Y" turret where he straddled the rail and peered down. The swim ahead didn't worry him; he had covered two miles in the sea when at school in Melbourne and was confident he could double that distance if he had to. But he had never been able to dive or even jump from a high tower, yet now, as the same horror of height came to him, he thought, It's now or never.

Then he was falling, falling through endless space, and when he was conscious again he was floating and noticed *Houston* way ahead of him still firing, and heard shouts and saw a raft. He started to swim, but felt like a fish with a damaged fin, and knew two things had happened to him. His shoes and socks had been blown off by the torpedo blast that had knocked him overboard. And his leg was broken.

"No, no—please not that," he pleaded.

He reached under water. His left foot flopped in his hand. His throat tightened and he thought he would choke.

"I haven't a chance now," he whispered. "I'll die in the water."

Then he saw Frank Watson, a petty officer, floating near him, and called, "My leg's broken," and Watson called back. "Don't be bloody silly." But when Watson felt the break just above the ankle he said, "Sorry, but hang on. I'll blow more air into your blimp—and then we'll get you onto that raft."

But they were both only just on the raft when a Japanese destroyer passed at speed. Her bow waves were like slices of spongecake. Her wash tipped them off. In the water again, Campbell thought, calmly now, I'll be a handicap to the others. I might as well drown. And then a small voice argued, You've been unlucky so far. Hang on a bit and your luck will change. He swam, trailing his smashed leg, to another raft where Bob Collins, an A.B., asked, "What's wrong?" and Campbell told him. "Okay," Collins said, "let's see if I can help it."

He dived in, collected driftwood, split it with his knife, cut off one leg of Campbell's overalls, tore the material in strips, and splinted the broken leg. When this was done, Campbell looked at his leg and then at Collins and felt like crying. He held out his hand. The A.B. gripped it and said, "We'll get you through."

For the first time Campbell felt that luck was turning his way. But then he saw something which made him chill and weak. Two big shark fins were circling a box not ten yards away. He shivered, groping for memory of words he had once read about the sharks of Sunda Strait, and finding the words and hearing a man on a raft call, "What's that there?"

"Porpoises," Campbell said.

"They look funny to me."

"Sharks," Campbell whispered to Collins who nodded.

"We'd better tell 'em."

"Pull your legs in," Campbell said to the others, "they're sharks."

The men jerked up their legs and nearly upset the raft. Everyone watched, still suspended above a new kind of death in a sort of hideous anesthesia of frozen bodies and terrified eyes. The sharks circled—once, twice. One of the fins disappeared, there was a thrashing swirl, and the box disappeared. Then the pieces came to the surface and floated away—and slowly the other fin sank and was seen no more.

And a voice in the dark said, "If any of youse blokes see me in the Bondi surf after the war youse can kick my arse."

"Outside," Stening ordered his men, and waved his arms upward.

"Where do we go?" a youngster said.

Stening pointed. "There's a hatch right outside, and the quarter-deck hatch is on the next flat."

They ran from the wardroom and climbed the nearest ladder. As they climbed, Stening hurried to his cabin to get a block of chocolate he kept there for an emergency like this, but his cabin was a ruin of crumpled steel and splintered wood. Back in the quarter-deck lobby he saw the dogs of a hatch being turned from below. He jumped to the hatch, loosened the dogs and let three men out and followed them up the ladder, but just before he reached the deck he remembered the torch he was carrying and threw it away as now useless. On deck at last he saw men milling in the moonlight like cattle about to stampede. He climbed the ladder to the 4-inch-gun deck and tried to reach his abandon-ship station forward, but when heaps of wreckage blocked him he returned to the quarter-deck. It was now bare as a washed plate, though he had left it only a minute or two before, and all around him the silence was like sound. Then something inside the ship rolled and crashed. He ran to the stern, blew into his Mae, and was about to vault over when another torpedo struck. The rail reared and smashed his nose. He jerked into the air and fell on his back. Then water poured down and across the deck and washed him overboard. As he broke surface he saw the ship, gigantic it seemed, above him, and thought it was rolling over on him. He yelled and yelled and tried to paddle away. Chief Petty Officer Kiesey heard him, saw a blond head in the water, grabbed the hair and pulled him aboard the copper painter's punt he was on.

Stening, with a fractured skull, a broken nose, and an injured eye and knee, was shocked and silly. He stared wildly at Kiesey and yelled again because he thought the sinking ship was going to crush him. Then he jumped off the punt. Three times he jumped and three times the C.P.O. grabbed him and pulled him from the water. The third time Kiesey pulled him in he had to quieten him with a punch on the chin.

Later, Stening held out a paddle to Bill Davis in the water, and helped pull him onto the punt—but he doesn't remember that. Nor did he know at that time that the three other men on the punt with him were all badly injured. Kiesey's back had been burned by flash. Davis had a broken leg. And Leading Seaman Ben Talbot had a smashed collar-bone, cracked ribs, and other injuries.

In "Y" turret a gunner bellowed, "Abandon ship," and below in the lobby Gosden forgot about the rising water and remembered the five men in the shell room underneath him. He grabbed the phone to the shell room. It was dead. He rang the bell signals to the shell room. He got no reply. He yelled down the hoist to the shell room. There was no answer.

I must let them know, he thought, I must, I must. I can't let them die there like rats.

He waded across the flooding lobby and tried to open the door which led to a passage and the shell-room hatch. The door was jammed. There was nothing more he could do—except look at the water and want to be sick.

His two assistants had already gone up the ladder through the motor room and up again into the turret itself and out to the deck. Now he followed them.

On deck at last a searchlight blinded him. Then it swung away and he remembered his watch and £100 in notes in his locker, but decided they could stay there. He saw Alfie Coyne and with him tossed pilgrim rafts overboard, as though they were empty fruit cases, and recalled that at Tanjong four men had been needed to carry each of these heavy rafts aboard.

And then a torpedo hit. He went up, up, up—so high that he was above the top of "Y" turret. He felt extraordinarily light, and almost gay, in that mad moment. He wanted to sing and dance on the air. Then, as he fell, the torpedo wave swept across the deck and tumbled him over and over into the sea.

He went down, down. He opened his eyes against pressing blackness, like a hood over his head, but through the blackness he could see his mother crying as she opened a telegram reporting his death in action. He could see the typed words on the telegram. He felt he could touch his mother's face. Then he shot to the surface and shook the water from his eyes and saw *Perth*'s stern, clear and high, against the moon.

Near him a man called, "Help, I can't swim," but Gosden lay back in the water and laughed as the sailor swam toward him and passed him doing the finest crawl stroke he had ever seen.

If he can't swim, Gosden thought, then I'm done for.

He felt carefree now. He began to swim, but he was heavy and sluggish and realized he still had his boots on. He trod water and argued with himself. Would he get rid of them? Then he thought of the walking he would have to do when he got ashore, and decided to keep them. He began swimming again and found a Carley and got on board with Lieutenant-Commander Clarke and the R.A.A.F. corporal, Bradshaw. Later they picked up a man whose right leg was gone at the thigh. He was unconscious as they laid him across the float, and he died in twenty minutes. Then, as the float became more and more crowded, and as space was needed for the living, they slipped the body back into the warm sea.

In perhaps an hour a Japanese destroyer came alongside and tossed them ropes.

"Come aboard," a Jap shouted in English.

But Gosden and the others pushed the float away from the destroyer, and one of the boys yelled, "You know where to stick it, mug—we'd rather drown."

"So," the Jap yelled back. "You say Nippon no bloody good. You wait till tomorrow."

The destroyer went away. Later Gosden felt someone grabbing at his legs and trying to get onto the float. He looked down and saw a Japanese soldier. He was so surprised he nearly fell off the float. The soldier, as far as he could see, was wearing full equipment. He even had his rifle slung around him. Then Gosden saw other Jap soldiers in the water, their rifle barrels like periscopes. Some of the soldiers were swimming, some were floating, already drowned.

The Jap beside the float looked up and spoke. Gosden

didn't understand—and didn't care. Japs and pity did not go together. He put his boots on the flat face and pushed. The Jap clutched his boots, but Gosden jerked free and kicked at the face again and again. Around him now others on the float kicked out and splashed every time a Jap soldier tried to approach. At every kick a soldier snarled, "You killed my mate, you bastards, you killed my mate." Soon the Japs kept away or the current took them away. Soon the sea around the drifting float was empty except for the untidy bundles that were the drowned.

As Owen dived overboard he realized he had forgotten to inflate his Mae. He trod water and bent his head and tried to blow into the valve, but every time he tried he went under. In disgust, he pulled off his blimp, and then his shirt and shorts, and let them float away. Then he emptied his bowels—an act which pleased him—and for the first time was conscious of the water, warm and silky and soothing against his body, and black as the inside of a cupboard.

He began to move away from the slow-moving *Perth*, and ahead could see a long low line of fire that he knew was *Houston* burning, and from the fire leaped sparks that were guns still in action. He wanted to call for help, but could not make a sound. The small inner voice of pride prevented him. It said, Stand on your own feet, and then he smiled and thought, What a ridiculous idea with fifty fathoms of water under me! But later—much later—he heard movement near him and asked, almost apologetically, "Is anyone there?" and someone called, "Swim over here, mate." He joined three men holding to small pieces of driftwood, and hung on with them while he got his wind. Then a wavelet slapped against his face and he took in a mouthful. It was hot and salty and thick and he knew immediately it was blood. He spat. "Who's wounded?"

The man beside him spoke slowly and thickly. "Is that you, Polo?"

He knew it was Lieutenant McWilliam, and said, "Are you hurt, David?"

McWilliam didn't speak for some minutes. Then he said, "I don't think I'll live much longer, Polo."

"You'll be all right, David," Owen said, but he knew the words were meaningless. "Hang on, old boy."

Later, as they drifted among some Carleys, Owen got a mouthful of oil and began to vomit, and when the sickness eased he called to one of the floats and asked if they would take McWilliam aboard.

"Go to hell," a sailor said. "We're full."

But someone on another float called, "Sure, bring him over here. We'll make room for him."

They lifted McWilliam aboard, and Owen, before he pushed off, called, "Cheerio, David, you'll be all right now."

Soon he and Tyrell, a P.O., found a wood and metal recreation seat, which had been on *Perth*'s deck, and they hung to it. It floated with the metal back down, but held them up.

"What do you reckon our chances are?" Tyrell asked.

"We'll be all right—once we hit the beach."

Men on a raft were singing now, and farther off one man was singing "Matilda," and Owen could see the profile of Java against the sky. He felt happy—strangely happy and confident. He locked his arms across the recreation seat and felt the warm sea caressing his naked body, and a gentle peace, as soft as a woman's body, enfolding him.

He slept.

"God, you know what's going to happen, I don't." Gillan prayed as he followed Reece and Tuersley up the stokehold ladders. The ladders were almost horizontal now, and he realized, with surprise mixed with a still sort of horror, that the ship was nearly on her side.

A stoker lost his grip and fell past Reece and Tuersley, but Gillan managed to grab the man's overalls and steady him till he could start climbing again. Then the fans stopped and the only sound Gillan heard was a silent singing sound deep in his ears, and the only thing he felt was the ship sliding away beneath his feet.

When the four men reached the air lock at the entrance to the stokehold, Gillan saw that they were standing on one wall of this pressure room, and that the steel door had now become the roof. The stoker was trying to open it.

"It won't move," he yelled.

"Let's all push," Gillan said.

They heaved at the thick steel door and it began to move —up, up, until it fell aside with a crash and they pulled themselves up and through into the alleyway. Gillan now saw that the true floor of the alley had become a wall, and that they were standing on the opposite wall which had become the floor, so that the overhead lights were now burning beside them instead of above them. They all knew there was a manhole farther aft, which led into the enclosed torpedo space below the 4-inch-gun deck. They hurried along the alley, and ahead saw the other stokers climbing through. And then they stopped and looked blankly at one another.

"Hell!" Reece said in alarm.

With the ship on her side, an across-ship alleyway had now become a deep well five feet wide between them and the escape manhole.

"We'll have to jump across," Gillan said.

The lights flickered, but stayed on.

The stoker he had saved in the stokehold was first. The man jumped, but his boots slipped as he was taking off and he fell screaming into the well. The other three looked down into the awful blackness and yelled. There was no answer.

"Oh, God," Reece said.

Reece and Tuersley jumped and ran forward. As Gillan followed he saw water start coming through the manhole, and saw Reece and Tuersley get through, and then water came through the manhole in a spout like a thick green tube.

The lights went out.

For a split second Gillan could not move. Terror anchored him. Then, with the picture of the spouting manhole still before his eyes in a blackness, he dashed those last few yards, took a deep breath, and forced himself against the water and through the manhole.

Most other men would have panicked and drowned inside that ship which was at that moment nearly under water. But Gillan kept his head. In those few seconds after he had pushed through the manhole he reasoned this way: He knew that *Perth* had now turned almost turtle, and that he was not only inside her and under water, but virtually underneath her; he knew also that she must have been badly battered, that there would be wreckage about everywhere, and that if he struggled or tried to force himself anywhere he would get caught in ropes and twisted steel and drown; he knew the ship was sliding to the bottom bow first, that this forward movement would be displacing water, and that the displaced water would be flowing backward. He decided in those seconds, or split seconds, of trapped under-water reasoning, that he had one chance, and only one, of living—to float free and unresisting and to let the water itself wash him out of the ship.

He tucked himself into a ball, his knees and chin almost meeting, and let the backward-moving water roll him over and over inside that sinking ship; and as he rolled he thought, Thank God my Mae isn't fully inflated! I'd be up against the roof if it was and would never get out. He brushed against ropes, bumped into wreckage, but rolled on.

At last he hit the ship's rail and knew he was out of the enclosed torpedo space and on the submerged deck. And then he nearly drowned. The cord of the miner's lamp he was wearing on his cap became tangled in the rail wires and floating ropes. But instead of panicking, he pulled off his cap, which the water had not dislodged, broke the cord which led to a battery in his hip pocket, pulled out the battery and dropped it, and wriggled through the rails.

There the current grabbed him, as though it had hands, turned him over and over, pushed him upward, and then pushed him downward. As he went down he thought, This is like being on the big dipper at Luna Park. Then he was in a whirlpool, because he spun like a propeller, sometimes head down, sometimes feet down, and his heart was hammering and his ears were hammering and he saw scarlet, green and purple lights flicking on and off.

Suddenly the hammering ceased and everything was still. He was still within himself, and around him was stillness, and everything was stillness, and he felt peaceful and happy and never wanted to move again. And yet at that moment he thought, If I don't struggle now I'll drown.

He began to fight his way upward, to claw his way upward, like trying to climb a ladder made of treacle. He dog-paddled upward, clutching and snatching and pulling down at the water, fighting to get away from this under-water world of incredible peace and quiet he had got into where the stillness was like a charm, soft, beautiful and insidious, and where he wanted to lie back and rest and rest and rest forever.

And then, with a rush like falling upward, he catapulted up and broke surface through two inches of oil and saw a biscuit tin and grabbed it with both arms And as he hung there on the surface of the water, gulping air, he saw, thirty yards away, the tip of one of *Perth*'s propeller blades sinking into the sea.

A long 18-inch plank bumped into him, and he crawled onto it and sat on it, and past him floated a white solar topee, bobbing up and down, up and down, as though someone was walking jauntily underneath it. He thought, The sun's going to be hot tomorrow—I'll need you. So he grabbed the topee and put it on his oil-covered head, and it fitted.

Then he looked up at the stars, the brilliant clusters of stars, and spoke to them aloud.

"I'm the last man out of that ship alive," he said. "God, I thank you."

Shangri-La and Coral Sea

The *Perth* was sunk just after midnight. The heavy cruiser *Houston* continued to fight, but there was too much fire power concentrated on her. She went down, less than an hour after the *Perth,* carrying almost 700 Americans with her; 368 survivors were destined to spend the rest of the war in Jap prison camps.

The Japs struck next at Ceylon via a carrier raid, sinking two British heavy cruisers, the aircraft carrier *Hermes,* and a number of merchant ships.

On January 23, 1942, the Japanese had occupied Rabaul on New Britain, using its fine harbor as a jumping-off point for the invasion of New Guinea; on March 8th, they occupied the strategic villages of Lae and Salamaua, on New Guinea's northern coast. They were getting uncomfortably close to Australia.

So far, their conquests had been gained at a remarkably cheap price. From December 7th to May 1st, the main Jap carrier force alone, ranging from Pearl Harbor to Ceylon, had sunk five battleships, one aircraft carrier, two cruisers, and seven destroyers, damaging many other ships; the Japanese themselves lost no ship larger than a destroyer.*

The Japanese took no time out to consolidate their gains. Their strategy now called for an invasion force to sail around the eastern end of New Guinea, and take Port Moresby on the southern coast. If they succeeded, the western approach to the Coral Sea would be secured. Simultaneously, Tulagi Island in the Solomons was to be occupied, protecting the flank of the Port Moresby invasion. The ultimate aim of Japanese strategy was to bring the U.S. Pacific Fleet to decisive battle and annihilate it.

Before the Coral Sea action could take place, however, Doolittle's sixteen B-25 bombers struck Tokyo and three other cities on the Japanese mainland. The plan for the raid, conceived in January 1942 by Adm. King's staff as a much-needed shot in the arm for American mor-

* S. E. Morison, *The Rising Sun in the Pacific,* pp. 385, 386.

ale, was completely daring; close calculations were needed for the launching of the army's land-based B-25's from carriers (planes of this size had never taken off from a carrier); there was need for secrecy, too. The two carriers, *Enterprise* and *Hornet*, and their escort were to penetrate Japanese-controlled waters to within 500 miles of Tokyo, where they would be extremely vulnerable to bombers. On April 18th, the raiding force was spotted by Jap patrol boats while still more than 600 miles from Tokyo; their discovery meant the carriers must turn and run. The B-25's were launched; from this distance there was great risk they wouldn't make the China coast, their destination after dropping their bombs.

Ironically, Tokyo had just completed a trial air raid at noon on April 18th, when the first B-25's arrived overhead. While little important damage was done, the raid revived the spirit of the Allied peoples. Not a plane was lost over Japan; one landed at Vladivostok, U.S.S.R., and the rest made it to China; four crash-landed there, eleven had to be abandoned by crews forced to bail out.

This raid was the first offensive punch thrown by the U.S. The first defensive success was to come in the Battle of the Coral Sea, which was the first naval action in history fought almost entirely between aircraft carriers.

The Allied Command had prior notice from intelligence sources of the Coral Sea invasion, and guessed correctly that the main strike would be aimed at Port Moresby. On May 3rd the Japanese staged successful landings on Tulagi, but were bombed and strafed the next day by planes from the carrier *U.S.S. Yorktown*. The *Yorktown* then rendezvoused with the carrier *Lexington*, and a course was fixed for a surprise attack on the Jap invasion forces now rounding the end of New Guinea. On May 7th, a destroyer and an oiler, separated from the main U.S. forces, were destroyed by Jap carrier planes; the same day planes from the *Lexington* and *Yorktown* caught the Jap light carrier *Shoho*, and sank her.

The next day, May 8th, planes from the two big Jap carriers, *Shokaku* and *Zuikaku*, traded air attacks with the two U.S. carriers. *Shokaku* was severely damaged and *Zuikaku* lost a number of first-line fighting planes and pilots.

The *Lexington* sustained several bomb and torpedo hits. Damage seemed to have been brought under control, and it was not until some time later that fires and explosions broke out; a motor generator had been left running, igniting gasoline vapors released by an earlier torpedo hit. The condition of the ship worsened until, in the evening, the *Lexington* had to be abandoned; she was then torpedoed by one of her own escorting destroyers.

No clear-cut victory could be claimed by either side. But the U.S. had forced the Japanese to turn back their invasion forces from Port Moresby; and two of the big Jap carriers were damaged so badly they wouldn't be on hand for the battle of Midway—where they just might have turned the tide. Morison, the naval historian, says: "The Coral Sea battle was an indispensable preliminary to the great victory of Midway."

The enemy's naval commanders stuck to their grand strategy—to occupy Midway and build up an outer perimeter for the new Japanese Empire, stretching from the Aleutians to the Solomons. They intended to land on the Aleutians just before their attack on Midway to draw part of the U.S. Navy north. If they could then take Midway itself, they would hold in their hands the jumping-off point for an attack on Hawaii.

THE BATTLE OF MIDWAY

by J. Bryan, III

The Battle of Midway was one of the most furious in all history. Even before the last salute to its dead was fired, we and our Allies hailed it as a great American victory. So it was—but how great is only now becoming plain. Documents recently made available show that it was the turning point of the war in the Pacific. They also show how narrowly it missed being a defeat. If a certain Japanese scout had taken a longer look; if a young American cryptanalyst had been less acute; if a dive-bomber pilot from the *Enterprise* had guessed wrong; if the signal for an emergency turn had reached Captain Soji promptly—if any one of such seemingly trivial components had been different, years later the United States might have been struggling to dislodge the Japanese from Hawaii.

Beyond that, Midway is unique. It is the only battle in

which nine tenths of the men engaged never saw the prize for which they fought; the only battle ever waged across the one meridian where a warrior could rest tonight from tomorrow's strife.

These facts are clearly recorded, but others, far more important, are already becoming lost. Confusion is the first weed to grow on a field of combat. Historians have never ceased sifting Agincourt and Malplaquet, Brandywine and Jena, for moldy "whens" and "wheres" and "whys." Hundreds of years from now they will be sifting Midway. Today, most of Midway's veterans are vigorously alive, with memories not yet misty and papers not yet tattered. Many of these men have told me their stories. What I have learned from them I am setting down here, in the hope that it will leave fewer gaps in the chronicle of this prodigious battle, and that it will help preserve some precious fragments of American heroism that otherwise might have slipped into irretrievable oblivion.

Although Midway was fought on June 3-6, 1942, it had been precipitated six weeks before, on April eighteenth. At eight o'clock that morning, Vice Adm. William F. Halsey blinked a signal from his flagship, the carrier *Enterprise,* then 650 miles off Tokyo, to Capt. Marc A. Mitscher, of the carrier *Hornet,* near by. The signal read: LAUNCH PLANES X TO COL DOOLITTLE AND HIS GALLANT COMMAND GOOD LUCK AND GOD BLESS YOU.

As Doolittle had hoped, his raid deceived the Japanese into assuming that he had jumped off from a land base—"Shangri-La," President Roosevelt announced jocosely. Officers of the Imperial General Staff measured their charts. Excepting the sterile and unlikely Aleutians, the American outpost nearest Tokyo was Midway Island, 2,250 miles eastward. Not only must this be Shangri-La, the Japanese concluded, but it was additionally dangerous as "a sentry for Hawaii," 1,140 miles farther. They had long contemplated seizure of "AF," their code name for Midway. The commander in chief of their navy, Adm. Isoruku Yamamoto—a stocky, black-browed man with two fingers missing from his right hand—had only to designate the forces and set the date. This he now did. By the end of April the ships chosen for Plan MI—Midway Island—were being mustered from the fringes of the empire.

Right then, a full month before the first gun was fired, Yamamoto lost the battle—for the same reason that, precisely a year after the Doolittle raid, he would lose his life. Certain ingenious men in the United States Navy had broken Japan's most secret codes, and when Yamamoto flashed Plan MI to his subordinate commanders, these phantoms were eavesdropping at his shoulder.

Their hearing was not quite 20/20. They weren't entirely sure whether D Day would be at the end of May or early in June—nor whether AF was Midway or Oahu. COMINCH, Adm. Ernest J. King, thought Oahu at first, but CINCPAC, Adm. Chester W. Nimitz, thought Midway. He flew out there from Pearl on May second, along the curve of those small, sparse wave breaks with the oddly polyglot names: Nihoa, French Frigate Shoal, Gardner Pinnacles, Lisianski Island, Hermes Reef, and finally Midway.

The lagoon is about six miles across, and the islets, Sand and Eastern, lie just inside the southern reef. Sand Island is about 850 acres; its highest point is thirty-nine feet. Eastern, less than half the size, also has less freeboard. Both are arid, featureless and uninhabited, yet they are far more important than many larger, lusher islands. The name of the atoll tells why—midway across the Pacific, it is strategically invaluable.

Accompanied by Lt. Col. Harold D. Shannon, commanding the 6th Marine Defense Battalion, and Comdr. Cyril T. Simard, commanding the naval air station, Adm. Nimitz inspected both islands. Each had its own galleys, mess hall, laundry, post exchange, power house and dispensary. The chief difference was that all the aviation facilities, except the seaplane hangars, were on Eastern. For a whole hot day Nimitz strode and climbed and crawled through the establishment, peering at firing lanes, kettles, ammunition dumps, repair shops, barbed wire, underground command posts. He said nothing about his secret information, but he asked Shannon what additional equipment was needed to withstand "a large-scale attack." When Shannon told him, Nimitz emphasized the point again: "If I get you all these things you say you need, then can you hold Midway against a major amphibious assault?"

"Yes, sir."

Soon after Nimitz returned to Pearl, he wrote Simard and Shannon a personal letter, addressed to them jointly. He was so pleased with what they had accomplished that he was recommending them for promotion. The Japanese, he continued, were mounting a full-scale offensive against Midway, scheduled for May twenty-eighth. Their forces would be divided thus, and their strategy would be so. He was rushing out every man, gun and plane he could spare. He hoped it would be enough.

By now Nimitz knew for certain that Midway was the objective. A smart young officer, Comdr. Joseph J. Rochefort, in Combat Intelligence's ultrasecret Black Chamber at Pearl, had suggested instructing Midway to send a radio message, uncoded, announcing the breakdown of its distillation plant. Midway complied, and two days later Pearl's cryptanalysts intercepted a Japanese dispatch informing certain high commands that AF was short of fresh water.

Nimitz's letter had a violent impact, but Midway was not dislocated. Although its war had been "cold" so far—begging those few dozen shells—the garrison had stayed taut. Every dawn, patrol planes fanned out westward over a million and a half square miles of ocean. The galleys served only two meals a day. The Marines carried their rifles and helmets everywhere, even to the swimming beaches. At night, everyone went underground, except lookouts. So Simard and Shannon had to make no radical adjustments; they had only to assign priorities to their final efforts, and to absorb their reinforcements as smoothly as possible.

On May twenty-fifth Nimitz wrote them again: D Day had been postponed until June third. The reprieve let them put the last touches on their defenses. Shannon's garrison now numbered, 2,138 Marines. Simard's fliers and service troops numbered 1,494, of whom 1,000 were Navy personnel, 374 were Marines and 120 Army. Midway was a thicket of guns and a brier patch of barbed wire. Surf and shore were sown with mines—antiboat, antitank, antipersonnel. Every position was armed with even Molotov cocktails.

Eleven torpedo boats would circle the reefs and patrol the lagoon, to add their AA to that of the ground forces and to pick up ditched fliers.

A yacht and four converted tuna boats were assigned to the sandspit islands near by, also for rescues. Nineteen submarines guarded the approaches from southwest to north, some at 100 miles, some at 150, the rest at 200.

Defensively, Midway was as tough as a hickory nut. Before a landing force could pick its meat, a bombardment would have to crack it open. That is what worried Simard and Shannon. If enough Japanese ships stood offshore, under a fighter umbrella and out of range of Midway's coast defenses, and began throwing in a mixture of fragmentation and semi-armor-piercing shells, it would take a lot of planes to beat them off. On June third, the first day of enemy contact, Midway had 121—thirty of them patrol planes, slow and vulnerable; almost useless in combat; and thirty-seven others, fighters and dive bombers, dangerously obsolete. Worse, some of their crews were Army, some were Navy and some Marine, and interservice liaison was little more than a wishful phrase.

Midway's fliers would write one of the most heroic chapters in the history of forlorn hopes. Their glory is the glory of the Light Brigade and of Pickett's charge. But if Midway's security had depended on its air arm alone, its ground arm might have had to throw the Molotovs. Nimitz, however, in addition to fortifying the shores of his orphan island, also fortified its seas. Only a few ships were available, but he sent them all—the aircraft carriers *Enterprise* and *Hornet*, with six cruisers and nine destroyers, comprising Task Force 16; and the carrier *Yorktown*, with two cruisers and five destroyers, comprising Task Force 17. Rear Adm. Raymond A. Spruance, commanding TF 16, flew his flag on the *Enterprise*. Rear Adm. Frank Jack Fletcher, the over-all commander, flew his on the *Yorktown*.

The two task forces sortied from Pearl Harbor and rendezvoused on June second at "Point Luck," 350 miles northeast of Midway. A signal searchlight on the *Yorktown* began to blink, and Spruance's flag secretary made an entry in the war diary: "Task Force SIXTEEN [is] directed to maintain an approximate position ten miles to the southward of Task Force SEVENTEEN . . . within visual signaling distance" [so as not to break radio silence]. Next day he added, "Plan is for forces to move northward from Midway during darkness, to avoid probable enemy attack course." Then, "Received report that Dutch Harbor was attacked this morning."

Yamamoto had chosen Dutch Harbor for the opening scene of his Plan AL—Aleutians—which was parallel to Plan MI and had the dual purpose of seizing Aleutian territory and weakening Nimitz's strength by luring part of it north. Word of the attack was still flashing from command to command when another flash outshone it. Spruance's flag secretary logged it thus: "Midway search reports sighting two cargo vessels bearing 247 [degrees from Midway], distance 470 miles. Fired upon by antiaircraft."

The report was made by Ens. Jewell Reid, who had lifted his Catalina from the Midway lagoon at 4:15, forty minutes before sunrise. Chance did not lead him to the enemy in that waste of water. Nimitz had written Simard, "Balsa's air force [Balsa was the Navy's code name for Midway] must be employed to inflict prompt and early damage to Jap carrier flight decks." Rear Adm. Patrick N. L. Bellinger put it otherwise: "The problem is one of hitting before we are hit." As Commander Patrol Wings Hawaiian Area, Bellinger's job was not merely to state the problem but to find the solution. This is it:

"To deny the enemy surprise, our search must insure discovery of his carriers before they launch their first attack. Assuming that he will not use more than 27 knots for his run-in [to the launching point], nor launch from farther out than 200 miles, Catalinas taking off at dawn and flying 700 miles at 100 knots will guarantee effective coverage. With normal visibility of twenty-five miles, each Catalina can scan an eight-degree sector. It is desirable to scan 180 degrees [the western semicircle], so twenty-three planes will be needed."

Nimitz gave them to him. Not all twenty-three were Catalinas. To share the patrol, the Army sent some Flying Fortresses, Lt. Col. Walter C. Sweeney, Jr., commanding, from the 431st Bombardment Squadron; eight arrived on May thirtieth and more later. Simard assigned them to the southwest sector—the least likely source of attack—because their crews were comparatively unskilled in recognition of ships, and much depended on clear, accurate reports of the enemy's power. Besides, the heavily armed and armored Fortresses had little to fear from a brush with an overlapping Japanese patrol from Wake.

Meanwhile, one Catalina had met a direr threat than any enemy plane—a weather front, deep and wide, which developed 300 miles to the northwest and hung there, mocking Bellinger's calculations. Such a front would let the enemy creep up to its edge unseen and launch a night attack impossible to intercept. Midway's only comfort was the probability that the weather screening the enemy from observation would also screen the skies from the enemy, preventing accurate navigation and forcing postponement of his attack until dawn allowed him a position-fix.

But even though—if this guess was good—bombs would not fall until 6:00 a.m. or perhaps 6:30, Simard could not risk an earlier attack's catching him with sitting ducks. Accordingly, as soon as the search planes were air-borne, the remaining Catalinas and Fortresses also took off, to cruise at economical speed until the search had vouchsafed the first 400 miles, by which time these heavy planes—including such of the Catalinas as were amphibious—would have consumed enough gas to permit their landing on the cramped, 5,000-foot strip without jettisoning their bombs or burning out their brakes. The smaller planes—fighters, dive bombers and torpedo planes—did not take off, but they were manned and warmed up, ready to go.

The patrol crews' schedule was brutal. Midway had enough food, water and sleeping space for essential personnel only. Since maintenance crews were luxuries, the patrol crews were topping their fifteen-hour searches with hours more of repairing and refueling. Worse, a few days before, a blundering sailor had tripped the demolition charges under the aviation fuel tanks—"They were foolproof," a Marine officer said, "but not sailorproof"—and from then on, all planes had to be refueled by hand from unwieldy fifty-five-gallon drums.

The hard grind was forgotten, however, when Ensign Reid reported, "Two cargo vessels—" and twenty-one minutes later, "Main body bearing 261, distance 700 miles. Six large ships in column." Reid was wrong. This was not Yamamoto's main body; it was only a small part of one task group in his occupation force. His main body had not been sighted yet, nor had his striking force.

The occupation force, approaching from the southwest, consisted of two battleships, one seaplane carrier, six heavy cruisers, two light cruisers, twenty-nine destroyers and four assorted ships, escorting sixteen transports. The invasion troops aboard them were 1,500 marines for Sand Island; 1,000 soldiers for Eastern; fifty marines for little Kure, sixty miles west of Midway; two construction battalions and various small special units. Vice Adm. Nobutake Kondo commanded, from the battleship *Kongo*.

The striking force, hidden by the weather front in the northwest, consisted of two battleships, four carriers, two heavy cruisers, one light cruiser, sixteen destroyers and eight supply ships. Vice Adm. Chuichi Nagumo, who had commanded the striking force at Pearl, commanded again, from the same flagship, the carrier *Akagi*.

The main body, far to the west, consisted of seven battleships, one light carrier, three light cruisers, thirteen destroyers and four supply ships. Yamamoto commanded from the new battleship *Yamato*. She and her sister ship, the *Musashi*, were the most formidable in the world—63,700 tons (our *Iowa*-class battleships are 45,000) and mounting nine 18.11-inch rifles (the *Iowas* mount nine 16-inchers).

Plan MI was an exact plagiarism of Simard's and Shannon's fears. It called for the striking force to crush Midway's defenses with a three-day air attack, the main body to follow up with a big-gun bombardment, and the occupation force to put its troops ashore on beaches where only maggots moved. The Japanese unanimously admit this much, but they disagree on the plan's next provision. Some say there was none, beyond holding on. Others say that Midway and Kure were to have been steppingstones to Pearl Harbor.

All morning, radio reports crackled through Midway's earphones, as search pilots spotted the converging elements of the occupation force. Simard wanted to hit them with the Fortresses, but Nimitz had ordered "early damage to Jap carrier flight decks," and no carriers had been sighted. Then, at eleven o'clock, Ensign Reid sent a correction: there were eleven ships, not six. By now the Fortresses were back and refueled. Simard decided to attack.

Nine Fortresses, Sweeney leading, took off at 12:30, and four hours later sighted a force of "five battleships or heavy cruisers and about forty others." Sweeney broke his flight into three V's and stepped them down at 12,000, 10,000 and 8,000 feet. Extra fuel tanks in their bomb-bays left room for only half a bomb load, four 600-pounders apiece, but the bombardiers thought they hit a heavy cruiser and a transport. The Fortresses had not yet landed when four Catalinas with volunteer crews took off to make—it is still almost inconceivable—a night torpedo attack. Catalinas are not built to lug torpedoes, and their crews are not trained to drop them. Still, three pilots managed to find the enemy force—the one the Fortresses had annoyed that afternoon. They approached from down-moon, to silhouette the ships, and Lt. William L. Richards' torpedo blew a hole in the tanker *Akebono Maru*. The attack would have been no more bizarre if the tanker had torpedoed the Catalina.

The weary crews turned their planes back toward the dawn. They were almost home when Midway radioed them that it was under air attack. . . .

Reveille had sounded at three o'clock as usual, and at 4:15 as usual the dawn search took off—eleven Catalinas, scouting for Nagumo's carriers. As soon as they were clear, the Fortresses—there were now fifteen—flew out to re-establish contact with the occupation force. The planes left behind were motley. Four were Army—Marauders, normally a medium bomber, but here jury-rigged to carry torpedoes. Six more were Navy—Avengers, torpedo planes of a brand-new type. The rest were Marine, belonging to the two squadrons of Marine Air Group 22, Lt. Col. Ira L. Kimes commanding. The fighter squadron, VMF 221, had some stubby little Buffaloes, so slow and vulnerable that they were known as "Flying Coffins," and a few Wildcats, new and tough and fairly fast. The scout bombing squadron, VMSB 241, also was mongrel, with new Dauntlesses and old Vindicators—so old that the Marines called them "Vibrators" and "Wind Indicators."

All had been manned since 3:15. Their crews watched the sun rise, grumbling that battle would be better than this everlasting waiting around. Even then battle was approaching, at 200 miles an hour. For more than half the men it would be the last battle they would ever see.

The Japanese striking force had run from under its sheltering weather front shortly after midnight. Dawn gave Nagumo his position, 200 miles northwest of his target and just astride the International Date Line. At 4:30 he turned his four carriers into the southeasterly breeze and began to launch "Organization No. 5"—thirty-six fighters, Zeros, and seventy-two bombers, Vals.

Midway received its first warning at 5:25, when a Catalina reported "in clear," uncoded, "Unidentified planes sighted on bearing 320, distance 100 miles." The same Catalina reported again at 5:34: "Enemy aircraft carriers sighted 150 miles, 330 degrees." At 5:52, another Catalina corrected and elaborated this sighting: "Two carriers and battleships bearing 320, distance 180, course 135 [toward Midway], speed 25." The fourth report was from the radar station on Sand: "Many planes, 89 miles, 320 degrees."

Midway sounded the alarm, and even as its planes were taking the air, Simard radioed his flight leaders: "Fighters to intercept, dive bombers and torpedo planes to hit the carriers, Fortresses to forget the occupation force and head north—"your primary target is the carriers!" By a few minutes past six every plane was air-borne that could leave the ground, except one noncombat utility plane. Visibility was excellent, the sea calm.

Fighting 221's twenty-five operational planes were organized into five irregular divisions. The squadron's skipper, Maj. Floyd B. Parks, led a group of three divisions, consisting of eight Buffaloes and four Wildcats. The executive officer, Capt. Kirk Armistead, led the other two, of twelve

Buffaloes and one Wildcat. Parks' group made the first contact. They had climbed to 14,000 feet and had left Midway thirty miles astern when one of his pilots called, "Tallyho! Hawks at angels 12 [bombers at 12,000 feet], supported by fighters!" Parks pushed over. The time was 6:16.

The Vals were flying in two V's of V's, one far behind the other with the Zeros below both. Parks' group, then Armistead's, fell on the Vals like sheep-killing dogs, but the Zeros fell on the Marines like wolves, slashing and springing back for another slash. Outnumbered as the Marines were and—they immediately realized—hopelessly outclassed, their only chance of escape was to dive at full throttle for the cover of ground fire. Few reached it. Zeros set ablaze one plane after another, then whirled and machine-gunned two of the pilots in their chutes.

The Vals closed their ragged ranks and pressed on. Midway was waiting. All guns were manned, and radar had tracked the flight steadily since 5:55, when it had been picked up. At 6:22, D Battery reported, "On target, 50,000 yards, 320." And at 6:30, Colonel Shannon ordered, "Open fire when targets are within range." One minute later, every AA battery was firing. The first wave had arrived exactly on the schedule that Shannon and Simard had hypothesized.

These were horizontal bombers, at 10,000 feet. Of the original thirty-six, ground observers now counted only twenty-two. The opening bursts of AA were short, but the next scored direct hits on the leading plane and one other. The rest dropped their 533-pound bombs on Eastern and the northeast shore of Sand and were gone before the two broken planes had crashed to earth. Simard and his operations officer, Comdr. Logan C. Ramsey, were watching the plunge, from the entrance to their underground command post on Sand. When the Vals struck near by, Simard shouted to the gunners, "Damn good shooting, boys!"

A Negro steward's mate ran to the wreck of the leader's plane and heaved his body from the cockpit. Ramsey was searching the pockets when the guns opened up again. He and Simard ducked below.

The second wave was dive bombers, the eighteen—half of them—that Fighting 221 had left. The flight leader dropped his huge 1,770-pounder, followed it down, rolled onto his back, and flew across Eastern at fifty feet, thumbing his nose. The AA crews were too astonished to draw beads, until a storm of bombs woke them to his purpose—to distract their attention. Even so, they shot him down almost regretfully. The other Vals pulled out over the lagoon, into the torpedo boats' fire. When they crashed, they threw up white plumes instead of black. Zeros circled and strafed both islands, then followed the bombers home. Midway's only air attack of the war had lasted seventeen minutes.

The AA gunners had shot down ten Japanese planes and they swore that if their visibility hadn't been cut by smoke from a burning oil tank, they'd have shot down ten more. The Japanese admit only three losses to ground fire, but Admiral Nagumo's report mentions the "vicious" AA.

Lieutenant Tomonaga, commanding the strike, radioed Nagumo at 7:00: "There is need for a second attack," but at 7:07 another report assured him, "Sand Island bombed and great results obtained."

Simard and Shannon had assayed them by then. Casualties were few—ten dead, eighteen wounded; and ground-defense equipment had suffered only slightly—one height finder had been damaged; but many of the less important installations were either flat or sieved or in flames. On Sand, in addition to the oil tank, which burned for two days, the seaplane hangars were afire. The dispensary was a shambles—a section of its roof had been hurled high into the air, and the sight of its red cross spinning would not be forgotten.

The laundry was also gone. When Commander Ramsey reported back to Pearl on June twelfth, still in his uniform of that morning, Nimitz told him, "I understand you're crawling with—er—'eagles,' so maybe you'd like these silver ones," and showed him a dispatch recommending his promotion to captain.

Eastern lost its powerhouse, mess hall, galley and post exchange, but the airstrips, a dump of gasoline drums and all radio and radar facilities were untouched—the Japs presumably intended using them. One freakish bomb had opened the door of the brig. Another—a direct hit on the post exchange—had scattered cigarettes and beer cans like shrapnel. One can plugged a machine gunner in the solar plexus. When his wind came back, he gasped, "I never could take beer on an empty stomach!"

As soon as "all clear" sounded, Colonel Kimes broadcast the order: "Fighters land, refuel by divisions, fifth division first." No one landed. He broadcast again. Still no one landed. He changed the order to "All fighters land and re-service." Ten of the original twenty-five touched down, several blowing their tires on the jagged bomb fragments that littered the runway. Of the pilots, six were wounded. Of the planes, only two were fit for further combat.

Fighting 221 had taken fearful punishment, but how much it had inflicted was uncertain. Since there was no way to reckon the missing pilots' scores, Intelligence accepted only the claims of the ten survivors, as verified by ground observers: forty-three enemy "sures," for thirteen Buffaloes and two Wildcats. The enemy's own preposterous figures are forty-one Marine sures for four Vals and two Zeros.

Even if the Marines had known of this disparity at the time, it is doubtful if they would have roused themselves to argue it. They were too dumfounded by the performance of the Zero. Its speed, climb and maneuverability surpassed anything they had ever seen. One pilot said bitterly, "I saw two Buffaloes trying to fight the Zeros. They looked like they were tied to a string while the Zeros made passes at them."

Fighting 221 would not fight the Zeros again for nine months—its ordeal was suspended until Guadalcanal; but the other squadrons' ordeals were just beginning—the ordeals by fire that too often ended in ordeals by water.

When Simard radioed his flight leaders the bearing and distance of the enemy fleet, his intention was a simultaneous strike by all squadrons—by such a swarm of planes attacking from so many directions and elevations that, although they would neither be co-ordinated nor have fighter cover, the enemy could not protect all his carriers against them. The plan was excellent in theory, disastrous in practice.

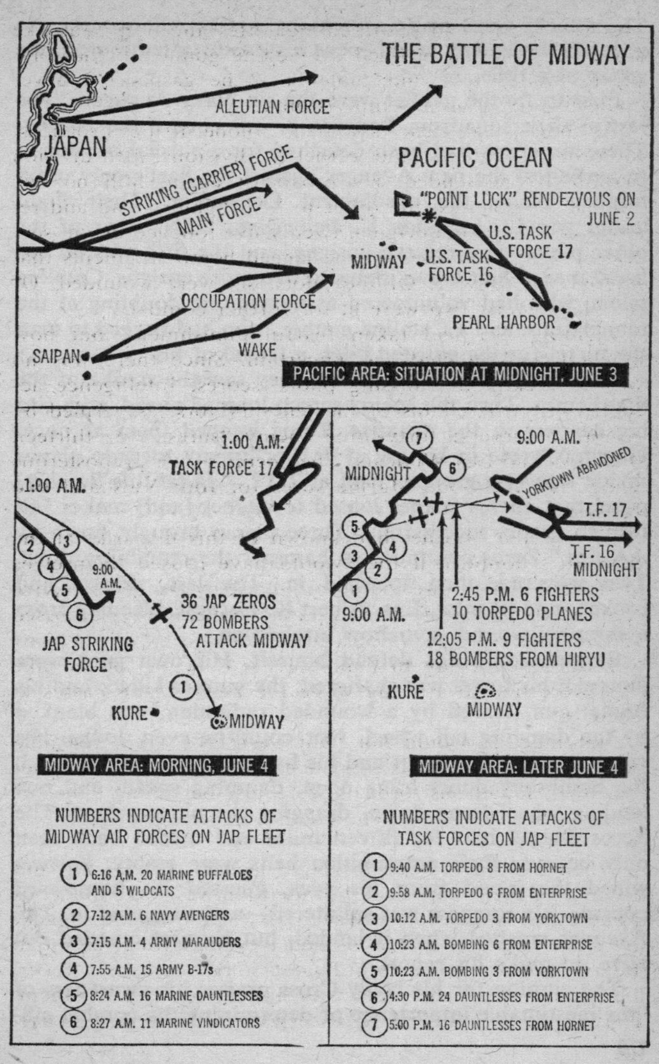
THE BATTLE OF MIDWAY
ALEUTIAN FORCE
JAPAN
PACIFIC OCEAN
STRIKING (CARRIER) FORCE
MAIN FORCE
"POINT LUCK" RENDEZVOUS ON JUNE 2
U.S. TASK FORCE 17
MIDWAY
U.S. TASK FORCE 16
OCCUPATION FORCE
PEARL HARBOR
SAIPAN
WAKE
PACIFIC AREA: SITUATION AT MIDNIGHT, JUNE 3
1:00 A.M.
TASK FORCE 17
1:00 A.M.
9:00 A.M.
36 JAP ZEROS
72 BOMBERS
ATTACK MIDWAY
JAP STRIKING FORCE
KURE
MIDWAY
MIDWAY AREA: MORNING, JUNE 4
NUMBERS INDICATE ATTACKS OF MIDWAY AIR FORCES ON JAP FLEET
1 6:16 A.M. 20 MARINE BUFFALOES AND 5 WILDCATS
2 7:12 A.M. 6 NAVY AVENGERS
3 7:15 A.M. 4 ARMY MARAUDERS
4 7:55 A.M. 15 ARMY B-17s
5 8:24 A.M. 16 MARINE DAUNTLESSES
6 8:27 A.M. 11 MARINE VINDICATORS
9:00 A.M.
MIDNIGHT
YORKTOWN ABANDONED
T.F. 17
T.F. 16
MIDNIGHT
9:00 A.M.
2:45 P.M. 6 FIGHTERS
10 TORPEDO PLANES
12:05 P.M. 9 FIGHTERS
18 BOMBERS FROM HIRYU
KURE
MIDWAY
MIDWAY AREA: LATER JUNE 4
NUMBERS INDICATE ATTACKS OF TASK FORCES ON JAP FLEET
1 9:40 A.M. TORPEDO 8 FROM HORNET
2 9:58 A.M. TORPEDO 6 FROM ENTERPRISE
3 10:12 A.M. TORPEDO 3 FROM YORKTOWN
4 10:23 A.M. BOMBING 6 FROM ENTERPRISE
5 10:23 A.M. BOMBING 3 FROM YORKTOWN
6 4:30 P.M. 24 DAUNTLESSES FROM ENTERPRISE
7 5:00 P.M. 16 DAUNTLESSES FROM HORNET

The attacks were made separately, not simultaneously. As a result, the enemy could focus his deadly attention on one group at a time.

First to fly the gantlet were the six Navy Avengers. The rest of their squadron, Torpedo 8, was aboard the *Hornet*. These six crews had been detached for a special mission—to battle-test the new Avenger against the fleet's only other torpedo plane, the obsolescent Devastator. Their flight leader was Lt. Langdon K. Feiberling, USN. Four of the other pilots were reserve ensigns, and the fifth was an enlisted man. Their crews included two more ensigns, Catalina pilots, who had volunteered as navigators, doubling at the tunnel guns, and a Catalina gunner, who had begged to man the turret for the enlisted pilot, a friend of his.

Before Midway faded astern, they saw the smoke of the first bombs. Then the enemy screen loomed ahead, with two big carriers in the distance. Zeros jumped them at once. Nagumo wrote in his log at 7:10, "Enemy torpedo planes divide into two groups," and at 7:12, "*Akagi* [his flagship] notes that enemy planes loosed torpedoes [and] makes full turn to evade, successfully. Three planes brought down by AA fire." Zeros continued to hammer the remaining three. Two wavered, then splashed in. The last, riddled and broken, and its pilot, Ens. Albert K. Earnest, bleeding from a shrapnel wound, somehow lurched on.

Earnest could not defend himself. His own guns were jammed; his turret was shattered, the gunner killed; and his tunnel gun, served by a wounded radioman, was blanked by the dangling tail wheel. Nor could he even dodge. His elevator control was cut and his hydraulic system smashed; the bomb-bay doors hung open, damping speed, and one landing wheel hung down, dragging the plane askew. The Zeros chased him for fifteen miles and turned back then only because their ammunition belts were empty. Earnest wiped the blood from his eyes, guessed his homeward course—his compass was splintered—and staggered in. The Avenger crashed when it landed, but Earnest crawled out alive, to make his report.

The citation for his Navy Cross praises his awareness of "the inestimable importance of determining the combat efficiency of a heretofore unproven plane." Admiral Spruance distilled the triumph—and sixteen men's epitaphs—into one crisp statement to Admiral Nimitz: "The new Avenger should be substituted for the Devastator as soon as possible."

Nagumo's respite was brief. He had hardly shaken off the Avengers when he was under torpedo attack again, by the four Marauders of the Army's 69th Medium Bombardment Squadron, Capt. James F. Collins, Jr., commanding. They had been the last to leave Midway, beating the bombs by mere minutes, but their speed had overtaken the Dauntlesses and Vindicators, now trudging astern. Even as Collins sighted the enemy force, a line of Zeros swung toward him. He led his flight straight at them, then ducked toward the water. One pilot yelled, "Boy, if mother could see me now!" A black wall of AA solidified ahead. Two Marauders crashed into it and fell, but Collins and Lt. James P. Muri broke through. Again the *Akagi* was the target. Collins dropped his torpedo at 800 yards; Muri closed to 450 and barely cleared her flight deck on his pull-up. Each thought he had scored, but Nagumo recorded at 7:15, "No hit sustained."

Zeros chased them out to the screen, wrecking Muri's turret and killing his tail gunner. Collins' turret could fire only in jerks, and his tail gun was jammed. Yet their two crews shot down three Zeros, maybe four, and the crippled Marauders—one's landing gear had been shot away, and the other, burning, had more than 500 holes—held together just long enough. When they touched down at Eastern, they were junk.

Meanwhile, Sweeney's fifteen Fortresses, heading westward since before dawn in search of the occupation force, had turned north as soon as they picked up Simard's six-o'clock relay of the position report on the striking force. They sighted it at 7:32, but Sweeney held his bombs. His primary target was the two carriers, and both were hidden by clouds. He began to orbit at 20,000 feet, hoping that they would venture out.

Actually, four of them were down there, all veterans of the attack on Pearl: the *Kaga* ("Increased Joy") and *Akagi*

("Red Castle"), slightly smaller than our big Essexes; and the sisters *Soryu* ("Blue Dragon") and *Hiryu* ("Flying Dragon"), slightly smaller than our light *Independence* class. The *Akagi* and *Hiryu* were unique among the type; their superstructures—"islands"—rose from their port sides.

In twenty minutes Sweeney had his hope. The *Soryu* reported, "Fourteen [sic] enemy twin-engine [sic] planes over us at 30,000 meters [sic]."

Nagumo logged at 7:55: "Enemy bombs *Soryu* (nine or ten bombs). No hits." And a minute later: "Noted that the *Akagi* and *Hiryu* were being subjected to bombings."

The carriers fired a few bursts of AA, then ran back under the clouds, leaving further defense to their CAP—combat air patrol. The Zeros had no stomach for the stalwart Fortresses; their passes were cautiously wide.

Sweeney was surprised: "Hell, I thought this was their varsity!"

As he resumed his watchful orbit, the Marines poured in—Scout Bombing 241's first attack group, sixteen Dauntlesses, Maj. Lofton R. Henderson commanding. Ten of the pilots had not joined the squadron until the week before, and thirteen were totally inexperienced in Dauntlesses, so Henderson decided not to dive-bomb, but to glide-bomb, a shallower, easier maneuver. He was spiraling down from 9,000 feet to his attack point at 4,000 when the Jap fighters caught them. The Marines rearseatmen splashed four, but the Jap pilots and their ships' AA splashed six Dauntlesses, two in flames. One was Henderson's. Seeing him burn, Capt. Elmer C. Glidden, Jr., second in command, moved into the lead. Below him was a cloud bank. He dived for it to lose his pursuit and broke through dead above the *Akagi*. Three fighters had just left her deck. She had gone to battle speed when she first spotted the Dauntlesses, and now she was writhing in her course.

Glidden pushed over and dropped his bomb from 500 feet, with the nine other pilots strung out astern. All managed to get clear of the Japanese force, but on their way home, damage dragged two more planes into the sea, and of those that landed, another two would never fly again. The pilot of one, 1st Lt. Daniel Iverson, Jr., mentioned that his throat microphone had been shot away, and added that his plane had been hit "several times." His rearseatman later counted 259 holes.

Henderson's group reported that their 500-pounders scored two hits and a near miss, and Captain Aoki of the *Akagi* has testified that this is the exact tally of her injuries, which proved fatal. However, there is also evidence that she suffered them in a subsequent attack. The *Akagi* would be a proud memorial, but the men of Scout Bombing 241 do not need her. They have another in the name of Henderson Field on Guadalcanal.

Parks, Feiberling, Henderson: three flight leaders had been killed, and the battle was not yet two hours old.

Meanwhile, the carriers' evasive tactics were intermittently taking them under open sky, so the Fortresses, still at 20,000 feet, began to potshoot. They reported three hits on two carriers, then turned homeward, their bombs exhausted.

That was at 8:24. Three minutes later, Nagumo wrote: "Enemy planes dive on the [battleship] *Haruna*." The Marines were striking again. These were VMSB 241's second attack group, eleven lumbering Vindicators, led by Maj. Benjamin W. Norris. The pilots were as green as Henderson's—nine of them had never flown a "Vibrator" before May twenty-eighth. They approached the enemy force at 13,000 feet and had just sighted it, twenty miles off, when three Zeros, doing graceful vertical rolls, ripped through their formation. One amazed Marine said, "Those Japs put on a good show—very good for us, since more attention to business might easily have wiped out eleven of the slowest and most obsolete planes ever to be used in the war."

The concentrated .30-caliber fire of four rearseatmen knocked one Zero down. More Zeros joined in, and another went down. Norris headed for the clouds at top speed. When he burst out, at 2,000 feet, he expected to find the carriers below. Instead, he was short, and directly above the *Haruna*, zigzagging in the van of the formation near her sister, the *Kirishima*.

Norris now faced a split-second decision. The carriers were his target, but his low altitude would make it suicidal to attempt taking these vulnerable planes—their skin was partly fabric—through the intense AA of the whole force. On the other hand, the *Haruna* not only was close below but might not be alert against attack, as the carriers certainly were. He chose the *Haruna.* The air was so rough with shell blasts that the Marines could hardly hold their planes in a true dive. Geysers rose near the *Haruna,* and one splashed on the *Kirishima*'s fantail, but Nagumo wrote: "No hits."

The Zeros were waiting at the screen. They shot down two Vindicators and shot away another's instruments and elevator control; the pilot limped as far as possible, then ditched in the sea near Kure. The scattered rest made it back as best they could. Even in his harried dive, Norris had radioed them: "Your course is one-four-zero," but there were only four plotting boards among the group, and most of the pilots navigated by thumb until they could home on the black pillar from the burning oil. The last of them touched down at ten o'clock.

They had left Midway neat and taut. Now it was debris. The spring morning stank of ruin. Buildings were a jackstraw pile of charred timbers. The upheaved sand, littered with thousands of dead birds, was still cold under foot. Silence lay on the once-buzzing airstrips. Two thirds of the combat planes were smashed or lost; half the aircrewmen were killed or missing. And the enemy's four deadly carriers were still intact.

Ashore, the situation seemed grave. But afloat, our own carriers had joined the battle.

Dawn on June fourth found the American forces about 220 miles northeast of Midway. A four-knot breeze blew from the southeast. Clouds were low and broken, with visibility twelve miles. Admiral Fletcher's Task Force 17, built around the [carrier] *Yorktown,* was steaming ten miles to the north of Admiral Spruance's Task Force 16, built around the [carriers] *Hornet* and *Enterprise.* Fletcher, the Senior Officer Present Afloat and Officer in Tactical Command, knew that the enemy's occupation force had been sighted west of Midway, but he did not close its position. His target was the striking force, which was expected to approach from the northwest. The *Yorktown*'s scouts had searched that sector on the third; half an hour before sunrise next morning, Fletcher sent them out again. An hour later, at 5:34, he intercepted the first of the reports that the Catalinas were flashing back to Midway, but not until 6:03 did they give him what he wanted: "Two carriers and battleships," with their bearing, distance, course and speed.

His staff laid out the data on a plotting board. The carriers were too far to be reached with an immediate strike. However, if the Japanese commander held his course—and likely he would, to take advantage of the head wind in landing his first attack wave and launching a second—an intercepting course would soon bring him within range. At 6:07 Fletcher ordered Spruance: "Proceed southwesterly and attack enemy carriers when definitely located. I will follow as soon as my planes are recovered."

Spruance headed out at twenty-five knots. The range had closed sufficiently by seven o'clock. His task force swung into the wind, and the first plane roared down the *Enterprise*'s deck. Her Air Group 6 launched fifty-seven in all: ten fighters (Wildcats), thirty-three dive bombers (Dauntlesses), and fourteen torpedo planes (Devastators). Near by the *Hornet*'s AG 8 was launching almost identically: ten Wildcats, thirty-five Dauntlesses and fifteen Devastators. Each group was ordered to attack one of the carriers, now an estimated 155 miles southwest. The launch was completed by 8:06. The task force swung out of the wind and the six squadrons sped away.

But if Fletcher blessed the scout who found Nagumo, Nagumo had one of his own to bless. At 7:28, halfway through Spruance's launch, Nagumo's scout sent back this message: "Sight what appears to be 10 enemy surface ships in position bearing 10 degrees, 240 miles from Midway. Course 150, speed over 20 knots."

Nagumo at once ordered his force, "Prepare to carry out attacks on enemy fleet units!"; then told the scout, "Ascertain ship types and maintain contact."

"Enemy is composed of 5 cruisers and 5 destroyers," the scout replied. Presently he added, "Enemy is accompanied by what appears to be a carrier."

By now the *Enterprise* had picked him up on her radar and had sent her combat air patrol to make the kill. He was still there, still transmitting—"Sight two additional enemy cruisers in position bearing 8 degrees, distance 250 miles from Midway. Course 150 degrees, speed 20 knots"—but the CAP pilots could not find him. It made little difference; the damage was already done. A few minutes later he signed off: "I am now homeward bound." The time was 8:34, he had been in the air since five o'clock, and the needles of his fuel gauges were drifting toward "empty."

Major Norris' old Vindicators were swarming over the *Haruna* and *Kirishima* just then, and Nagumo had no leisure until 8:55, when he curtly ordered the scout: "Postpone your homing. Maintain contact with the enemy until arrival of four relief planes. Go on the air with your long-wave transmitter" [to give them a radio bearing].

Nagumo then told his captains, "After completing homing operations [recovering the planes that had struck Midway], proceed northward. We plan to contact and destroy the enemy task force." They had built up speed to thirty knots when, at 9:18, a lookout sighted fifteen American planes, close to the water. They were the *Hornet*'s Torpedo 8, Lt. Comdr. John C. Waldron commanding—the rest of the squadron whose six Avengers had already flown from Midway to enduring glory.

It will never be known how, of the six squadrons launched, Waldron's plodding, 120-knot Devastators were the first by half an hour to find the enemy. It is known only that they did not rendezvous with the rest of the *Hornet*'s strike, as they should have; said a fighter pilot who saw them, "They just lit a shuck for the horizon, all alone."

Although the Japanese carrier force was now far from its predicted position—it had maneuvered radically to dodge Midway's planes, then had turned northeast to attack Spruance—Waldron flew a confident course, straight into its guns. He had lost his own fighters, and Zeros were ahead, astern and around him. The AA was almost thick enough to screen the twisting ships; it gored huge holes in wings and fuselages, cut cable, smashed instruments, killed pilots and gunners. Plane after torn plane—fourteen of them—

plunged into the sea, burned briefly and sank. A rearseatman in another squadron, miles away, overheard Waldron's last words: "Watch those fighters! . . . How'm I doing? . . . Splash! . . . I'd give a million to know who did that! . . . My two wingmen are going in the water. . . ."

The rest of Torpedo 8 is silence, except for the voice of its sole survivor, Ens. George H. Gay. He heard Waldron and he heard his own gunner cry, "They got me!" Then he was hit himself, twice, in the left hand and arm. He squeezed the bullet from his arm and popped it into his mouth. His target was the *Kaga*. He dropped his torpedo and flew down her flank, close to the bridge—"I could see the little Jap captain jumping up and down and raising hell."

A 20-mm. shell exploded on his left rudder pedal, ripping his foot and cutting his controls, and his plane crashed between the *Kaga* and the *Akagi*. He swam back to get his gunner, but strafing Zeros made him dive and dive again; the gunner sank with the plane. A black cushion and a rubber raft floated to the surface. Gay was afraid to inflate the raft; it might draw the Zeros. He put the cushion over his head and hid under it until twilight, peeking out to watch the battle. Tossed by the wash of Japanese warships, wounded, alone, the only man alive of thirty who had been vigorous a few moments before, Gay remembered their training at Norfolk, and how a farmer had complained that their practice runs were souring his cows' milk.

When Winston Churchill was told about Torpedo 8, he wept.

Gay was shot down at about 9:40. At 9:58, Nagumo wrote: "Fourteen enemy planes are heading for us." They were the *Enterprise*'s Torpedo 6, Lt. Comdr. Eugene E. Lindsey commanding. Not only had they, too, lost their fighter cover, but they were attacking an enemy alerted by the previous attack. Before a torpedo pilot can drop with any hope of a hit, he must maintain a steady course and altitude for at least two minutes. A full squadron of Zeros pounced on Torpedo 6 at this vulnerable time. Ten of the Devastators, including Lindsey's, were shot down at once, most with their torpedoes still in the slings. The other four escaped only because the Zeros were called away to meet a new threat, the *Yorktown*'s Torpedo 3.

The principal contact report had mentioned only two enemy carriers, but Intelligence had warned Fletcher that two more would be present. Rather than risk their planes' catching the *Yorktown* with hers on deck, he decided to send about half of them to reinforce the *Hornet*'s and *Enterprises*'s and to hold the rest until the two missing carriers were reported.

The *Yorktown* group—twelve Devastators, seventeen Dauntlesses and six Wildcats—was in the air by 9:30. This once the torpedo planes had the cover they needed so desperately; their fighters clung to them the whole way. Better yet, the *Enterprise*'s fighters, which had become separated from their own torpedo squadron, joined up in support. They sighted the enemy at ten o'clock, but they still had fourteen miles to go when Zeros caught them. The sixteen Wildcats were outnumbered two to one. The fast Zeros splashed three, then sped after the Devastators. By now their commander, Lt. Comdr. Lance E. Massey, had worked his way within a mile of the *Akagi*. As he turned to make his run, a Zero shot him down in flames. Six more of his squadron fell. The remaining five made their drops, then the Zeros shot down another three. The last two escaped.

Of the forty-one torpedo planes which the American carriers had sent into battle, thirty-five had now been lost. Of the eighty-two men who flew them, sixty-nine had been killed, including the three squadron commanders. And of the torpedoes they dropped, not one had scored a hit. Yet these men did not die in vain. The valor that drew the world's admiration also drew the enemy's attention. His dodging carriers could not launch a new strike. And while every gun in his force trained on the torpedo planes, and every Zero in the sky fell on them, our dive bombers—unopposed, almost unnoticed—struck the *Kaga*, the *Akagi* and the *Soryu* their death blows.

The thirty-three Dauntlesses of Scout Bombing 6, led by Lt. Comdr. Clarence Wade McClusky, Jr., commanding the *Enterprise*'s air group, had climbed up the estimated bearing of the enemy force until they should have been on top of it. McClusky cocked his wing and looked down. Visibility was perfect, except for a few small clouds. From his altitude of 20,000 feet, he could see more than 95,000 square miles of ocean. A hundred miles southeast of him was a tiny blur—Midway. But Midway was all he saw; the rest of the ocean was empty. He held on for another seventy-five miles. Still nothing, and time was running out. Merely finding the enemy carriers would not be enough. McClusky had to find them before they could launch a strike against our own carriers. Where were they? He had to guess fast and guess right.

When the *Hornet*'s group reached the estimated position and faced the same guess, their leader sent twenty-two of his bombers home and pressed forward with the rest—thirteen Dauntlesses and ten Wildcats. Like McClusky, he held southwest for half an hour, but then—with emptiness still ahead—he turned southeast, toward Midway, and then northeast. His determination to attack ignored the insistencies of his fuel tanks, and when he finally abandoned the search, it was too late for most of his planes to make even Midway. The Wildcats gasped and ditched, one after another, all out of fuel; only eight of the pilots were rescued. Two of the Dauntlesses died over the Midway lagoon; their crews waded mere yards to the beach. The other eleven landed with their last pints, at 11:20. Their welcome was something less than effusive. Not expecting the Dauntlesses, and seeing them jettison their bombs offshore, the Marine lookouts mistook them for enemy planes, blew the air-raid siren and even scrambled one of Fighting 221's riddled fighters to intercept them.

But McClusky decided that the enemy had reversed his southeast course—Capt. George D. Murray, of the *Enterprise,* called it "the most important decision of the entire action"—so he headed his bombers northwest. They had already burned up nearly half their fuel; if he didn't find his target soon, our task forces would lose his planes as well as their ships. Fifteen minutes passed, twenty, twenty-five, before his eye caught a faint white streak below—the wake of a lone Japanese destroyer; and presently, far to the north, three carriers, veering and twisting among their escorts, slid out from the broken overcast—the *Soryu* in the lead, with the *Kaga* to the west and the *Akagi* to the east. The *Hiryu,* bringing up the rear, stayed under the clouds and was never seen.

McClusky split his attack: half for the *Kaga,* half for the *Soryu.* He took a last look around—still no Zeros—and pushed over. The enormous red "meat balls" on the yellow flight decks became as sharply defined as bull's-eyes. . . .

Nagumo's strike against the American carriers was just about to take off. The *Kaga* had thirty planes on her flight deck and thirty more on her hangar deck, all armed and fueled. They were awaiting the signal when four bombs struck her, shattering her bridge and killing every man on it, including Captain Okada. Explosions leaped from plane to plane, from deck to deck. A solid pillar of fire shot 1,600 feet into the air. Smoke shrouded her, a black pall slashed with scarlet, and the blinded helmsman let her run wild.

The *Soryu* also had sixty planes aboard. Three bombs spattered blazing gasoline fore and aft on her hangar deck. A magazine exploded; both engines stopped; she lost steerageway. Captain Yanagimoto shouted from the bridge, "Abandon ship! Every man to safety! Let no man approach me! *Banzai! Banzai!*" He was still shouting *banzais* when flames rose around him. Most of the company struggled to the forward end of the flight deck, out of the fire and smoke, and huddled there until a violent explosion blew them into the sea.

The *Enterprise*'s Bombing 6 struck the *Kaga* and the *Soryu* at 10:23. At the same minute, unknown to them, the *Yorktown*'s Bombing 3 was plunging on the *Akagi,* Nagumo's flagship. Some of her Midway group had not yet returned, so she had only forty planes aboard. Her fighters tried to get clear. As the first of them gathered speed, the first bomb smashed among them, near the midships elevator, and another hit the portside aft. Damage did not seem severe, but when Captain Aoki ordered the magazines flooded, the after pumps would not function. The bridge took fire from a burning fighter below and the fire spread. Nagumo summoned a destroyer to transfer himself and his staff to the light cruiser *Nagara.* Within an hour, the *Akagi*'s flight deck flamed from end to end. When her engines stopped, an officer investigated. Her whole engine-room staff was dead.

The torpedo attacks had drawn the Zeros to water level, so they needed only a short sprint to catch Bombing 6 after the pull-out. Eighteen of McClusky's thirty-three Dauntlesses splashed in—he himself was wounded in the shoulder—but fuel exhaustion was to blame for some of them. Bombing 3 returned intact to the *Yorktown*'s landing circle, only to have her warn them away. Before the *Enterprise* could take them aboard, two of the seventeen ran dry and ditched. Worse, a *Yorktown* fighter pilot, shot in the foot, crash-landed on the *Hornet* without cutting his gun switches. His six .50's jarred off, and the burst killed five men and wounded twenty.

The *Yorktown* warned away her planes because her radar had picked up an incoming strike. Two hours before, at ten o'clock, Nagumo had reported Task Force 17's position to Yamamoto: "After destroying this, we plan to resume our AF attack." At 10:50 he admitted, "Fires are raging aboard the *Kaga, Soryu* and *Akagi,*" but added firmly, "We plan to have the *Hiryu* engage the enemy carriers." And at 10:54 the *Hiryu*'s blinker boasted: "All my planes are taking off now for the purpose of destroying the enemy carriers."

"All" was an exaggeration; the strike consisted of only nine fighters and eighteen bombers. As soon as they appeared on the *Yorktown*'s radar screen, at 11:50, her combat air patrol dashed to intercept them. Ten bombers went down at once and AA knocked down five more, but three bombs struck the ship, and one of them hurt her. It tore through to her third deck and exploded in the uptakes, blasting out the fires in two boilers and flooding the boiler rooms with fumes. It also set the paint on her stack ablaze and ruptured the main radio and radar cables. Steam pressure fell; she lost way and went dead in the water.

Fletcher took a quick turn around the flight and hangar decks. When he climbed back to the flag bridge, he found it wreathed in smoke so dense that his blinkers and flag hoists were blanketed. With all communications gone, he and the key men of his staff slid down a line and transferred to the heavy cruiser *Astoria*. Meanwhile, the *Yorktown*'s repair gangs patched her decks, and the engineering force coaxed her up to twenty knots. By two o'clock she was shipshape again—she even hoisted a bright new ensign to replace one stained by battle smoke. It had scarcely shaken out its folds when another ship's radar picked up a second attack group, thirty miles to the west—six fighters and ten torpedo planes, from the *Hiryu* as before. Fletcher's task force was now alone. Spruance was thirty miles eastward, farther from the enemy, since launching and landing had kept the *Hornet* and *Enterprise* on an easterly course. However, Spruance had sent Fletcher two heavy cruisers, and two destroyers as AA reinforcements. The *Yorktown*'s CAP and the combined AA splashed six of the torpedo planes, but four broke through and made their drops at her. The heavy cruiser *Portland* tried in vain to interpose herself. Two torpedoes struck the *Yorktown*'s port flank, almost in the same midships spot. A witness said, "She seemed to leap out of the water, then sank back, all life gone." The time was 2:45.

Dead, dark, gushing steam, she drifted in a slowing circle to port. Her list increased to twenty-six degrees; her port scuppers were awash, and she seemed about to capsize. Stretcher bearers threaded her steep passageways, collecting the wounded. At 2:55, Capt. Elliott Buckmaster ordered, "Abandon ship!" Destroyers stood in. Swimmers climbed aboard and clotted their decks in a whispering death-watch, but the *Yorktown* floated on. The late afternoon was beautiful, with a calm sea and a flamboyant sunset. A CAP pilot above Spruance's force, still steaming eastward, looked back at the stricken ship, deserted except by a destroyer. He thought of her as a dying queen, and his eyes were hot with sudden tears.

So far, no American had seen more than three Japanese carriers at one time, and three were known to have been crippled at 10:23. However, this torpedo-plane attack, nearly four and a half hours later, strongly supported the prediction of a fourth carrier. Fletcher had not long to wait for positive corroboration. Even as the *Yorktown* still reeled, one of her scouts reported, "1 CV [carrier], 2BB [battleships], 3 CA [heavy cruisers], 4 DD [destroyers], lat

31-15 N, long 179-05 W [about 160 miles west of Spruance's task force], course 000 [due north], speed 15."

Fletcher ordered the *Enterprise* and *Hornet* to strike immediately. The *Enterprise* completed her launch first. By 3:41, she had twenty-four Dauntlesses in the air, including fourteen refugees from the *Yorktown*. They had flown about an hour when they saw three large columns of smoke from the burning *Kaga, Akagi* and *Soryu*. A few destroyers were standing by them; the rest of the force was some miles to the north, fleeing with the surviving carrier, the *Hiryu*. The bombers swung westward in order to dive out of the blinding afternoon sun, and pushed over from 19,000 feet. They lost three planes to Zeros, but they laid four heavy bombs on the *Hiryu*'s deck and three more just astern, starting such enormous fires that the last pilots in line saw that she was already doomed and kicked over to bomb a battleship near by. When the second half of the strike—sixteen more Dauntlesses, from the *Hornet*—arrived a half hour later, they ignored the *Hiryu* completely and dropped on a battleship and cruiser. All the *Hornet*'s planes returned.

The *Hiryu*'s forward elevator was blasted out of its well and hurled against the bridge, screening it and preventing navigation. She had only twenty planes aboard, but they were enough to feed the fires, which quickly spread to the engine room. Her list reached fifteen degrees. She began to ship water.

Of the four carriers, the *Soryu* was the first to sink. A picket submarine, the *U.S.S. Nautilus*, spied her smoke, crept within range, and shot three torpedoes into her at 1:59. Her fires blazed up, but died by twilight, and boarding parties were attempting to salvage her when she plunged, at 7:13. Fifty miles away, Ensign Gay, under his black cushion, had been watching the burning *Kaga*. Several hundred of her crew were still huddled on her flight deck when a heavy cruiser—Japanese—began firing point-blank into her water line. Two explosions tore her apart. She sank twelve minutes after the *Soryu*.

The *Akagi* and the *Hiryu* also sank within minutes of each other, but not until next morning, June fifth. The

Akagi was stout. Her dead engines, staffed by dead men, suddenly came to life and turned her in a circle for nearly two hours, until they stopped forever. Still she would not sink. One of her destroyers torpedoed her at dawn.

The *Hiryu* was the flagship of Commander Carrier Division 2, Rear Adm. Tamon Yamaguchi, an officer so brilliant that he was expected to succeed Yamamoto as commander in chief. Burly, with a face like a copper disk, he was an alumnus of the Princeton Graduate College and had been the chief of Japanese Naval Intelligence in the United States. When he and Captain Kaki, of the *Hiryu,* saw that she could not be saved, they delivered a farewell address to the crew, which was followed "by expressions of reverence and respect to the Emperor, the shouting of *banzais,* the lowering of the battle flag and command flag. At 0315 [3:15 a.m.], all hands were ordered to abandon ship, His Imperial Highness' portrait removed, and the transfer of personnel to destroyers put underway. . . . The Division Commander and Captain remained aboard. They waved their caps to their men and with complete composure joined their fate with that of their ship." The destroyer *Makigumo* scuttled her with a torpedo at 5:10.

All four carriers were gone. With them went more than 2,000 men. Spruance reported that we now had "incontestable mastery of the air."

To the top commanders at Midway, meanwhile, June fourth had been a day of deep anxiety. The meager reports that reached them during the morning—only one enemy carrier damaged—made the ruins around them prophetic of worse. Incredibly—but for the confusion of battle—Lieutenant Colonel Sweeney, commanding the Fortresses, had not yet been told of the two United States Navy task forces offshore. Believing that Midway was fighting alone and hopelessly, he sent seven of his planes—all that were ready for instant flight—back to Oahu, both to save them from destruction and to help defend the Hawaiian Islands against the invasion which he assumed would follow Midway's imminent fall. Although Commander Ramsey, the Air Operations Officer, was better informed, even he thought it "quite possible that we would be under heavy bombardment from surface vessels before sunset."

Midway's air strength was now reduced to two fighters, eleven dive bombers, eighteen patrol planes and four Fortresses, plus aircraft under repair. Sweeney led the four Fortresses in the first strike of the afternoon, against the scattered carrier force. Two more, patched up, took off an hour later for the same target. At 6:30, as the pilots made their bombing runs, they sighted another six Fortresses a mile below—a squadron which had flown from Molokai, southeast of Oahu, straight into the battle. All three formations reported bomb hits, but Nagumo's log acknowledges none.

The Marines tried next. Their eleven dive bombers, Major Norris commanding, went out at dusk, but squalls thickened the moonless sky, and they had to abandon their search. Only the blue glare from their exhausts kept them together until Midway's oil fires guided them home. Ten returned safely; Major Norris did not return. Midway mounted one more strike that evening. Eleven torpedo boats dashed out at 7:30, hoping to cut down a straggling ship, but they, too, found nothing.

As the torpedo boats left, the Molokai Fortresses landed, with alarming news: Zeros had jumped them during their attack. Midway had learned by now that the enemy's fourth —and presumably last—carrier had been crippled at 4:30, so Zeros aloft two hours later implied that a fifth carrier was present. Actually the Zeros were orphans from the burning *Hiryu*, but Midway could not know this. Nor did it know that a patrol craft's report, at nine o'clock, of a landing on Kure, sixty miles west, derived from simple hysteria. On the contrary, each report strengthened the other. The possibility of invasion became a probability.

Midway radioed its picket submarines to tighten the line against the approaching enemy, and launched two Catalinas with torpedoes to support the interception. The Catalinas took off at midnight. At 1:20, an enemy submarine suddenly fired eight rounds into the lagoon, then submerged. Midway's belief that this was a diversion to cover a landing party seemed confirmed within an hour, when one of its own submarines, the *U.S.S. Tambor*, reported "many unidentified ships" only ninety miles westward.

The garrison already had done its utmost. There was nothing left now but the ceaseless service of the planes—eighty-five 500-pound bombs to be hung by hand, 45,000 gallons of fuel to be pumped by hand—and waiting out the direly pregnant night.

Far northeast of Midway, the American warships were also waiting. Fletcher's task force, maimed by the loss of the *Yorktown*, now merely sheltered battleships behind Spruance's. The *Hornet* and *Enterprise* were unimpaired, but Spruance was wary of the fast Japanese battleships and "did not feel justified in risking a night encounter. . . . On the other hand, I did not wish to be too far from Midway next morning. I wished to have a position from which either to follow up retreating enemy forces or to break up a landing attack on Midway. At this time the possibility of the enemy having a fifth CV [carrier] somewhere in the area . . . still existed."

Spruance had cruised slowly east, then a few miles north, east again and a few miles south, when the *Tambor*'s sighting ended his aimlessness. He headed toward Midway at twenty-five knots.

There, as the morning of the fifth dawned, the Catalinas were off at 4:15, followed by the Fortresses, and at 6:30 the first report came in: "Two battleships streaming oil," with the bearing, distance, course and speed. They were not battleships but heavy cruisers, the *Mogami* and *Mikuma*. The Catalina pilot's mistake in identification was excusable. These sister ships and their other two, the *Kumano* and *Suzuya*, were Japan's notorious "gyp cruisers"—professedly built to the conditions of the London Naval Conference, but really far larger and more powerful. They were longer, indeed, than any battleship at Pearl Harbor.

The four, a vanguard for the occupation force, had been given a screen of destroyers and sent ahead to bombard Midway in preparation for the landing. They were steaming at full speed when a lookout spotted the *Tambor* even as she spotted them. An emergency turn was ordered, but the *Mogami* missed the signal. She knifed into the *Mikuma*'s port quarter, ripping it open and wrenching her own bow askew, so that neither ship could make more than fifteen knots. The collision occurred soon after 2:00 a.m. At 2:55, Yamamoto's subordinate commanders received an astonishing dispatch: "Occupation of AF is canceled. . . . Retire. . . ."

Thus far, the enemy's motives and maneuvers at Midway have been reconstructed from official documents; but on this critical point—why Yamamoto decided to break off the battle—the files are silent. He himself is dead, so only conjectures are left. The most obvious, suggested by chronology, is that he was influenced by the collision of the cruisers, but this was, after all, only a minor mishap to his powerful fleet. Likelier, the true factors were older than the collision, but new to Yamamoto, owing to faulty fleet communications. At 6:30 the evening before, a scout pilot from one of Nagumo's ships had reported sighting "4 enemy carriers, 6 cruisers and 15 destroyers . . . 30 miles east of the burning and listing carrier. . . . This enemy force was westward bound." The pilot was myopic. The American force had only two operational carriers by then, and was bound eastward. Still, Nagumo had no reason to doubt the sighting, and although his log does not say so, presumably he informed Yamamoto at once. Yamamoto seems not to have received the message, for at 7:15 he was broadcasting:

> *1. The enemy task force has retired to the east. Its carrier strength has practically been destroyed.*
>
> *2. The Combined Fleet units in that area plan to overtake and destroy this enemy, and, at the same time, occupy AF. . . .*
>
> *4. The Mobile Force* [*Nagumo*], *Occupation Force . . . and Advance Force* [*submarines*] *will contact and destroy the enemy as soon as possible.*

Nagumo has written: "It was evident that the above message was sent as a result of an erroneous estimate of the enemy, for he still had 4 carriers in operational condition and his shore-based air on Midway was active." Accordingly, at 9:30 p.m. he repeated the pilot's sighting, and again at 10:50. One of these messages must have reached Yamamoto. When it did, the shock of learning that the

American force, which he believed crippled and quailing, was both on the offensive—which it wasn't—and stronger by two unsuspected carriers—which it wasn't—may have jolted him into ordering the retirement.

All this, it should be emphasized, is conjecture. But it is a fact that the Battle of Midway was over, except for skirmishes.

The first of them was touched off by the Catalina's 6:30 report of "two streaming oil." The Marine dive bombers jumped to the attack. Two Vindicators had been repaired overnight, so there were six now, led by Captain Richard E. Fleming, and six Dauntlesses, led by Capt. Marshall A. Tyler. As the *Mogami* and *Mikuma*, accompanied by two destroyers and trailing the *Kumano* and *Suzuya*, limped westward, their torn tanks left an unmistakable spoor, and the Marines followed it to their quarry. Through a storm of AA, the Dauntlesses dived on the *Mogami* at 8:05 and bracketed her with near misses that riddled her topsides. Then the Vindicators glided down at the *Mikuma*. Smoke gushed from a hit on Fleming's engine, but he held his course. The men behind him saw his bomb drop, saw his whole plane burst into flames, and saw him crash it into the *Mikuma*'s after turret. Captain Akira Soji, of the *Mogami*, said, "He was very brave." The Marine Corps agreed; Fleming was the first Marine aviator of the war to receive the Medal of Honor.

This was Midway's last successful action. The Fortresses made three more strikes that day, against the two cruisers and other units, but none was effective and one was tragic. Two planes, out of fuel, had to ditch, with the loss of ten men—the Fortresses' only casualties in the air battle.

The 6:30 report of "two battleships" reached Spruance too, but the weather was foul in his area, so he kept his planes on deck, hoping for better flying and a fatter target. Presently he had both. At eight o'clock, with the skies clearing, another Catalina reported: "2 battleships, 1 carrier afire [imaginary: the last enemy carrier had sunk three hours before] and 3 heavy cruisers, speed 12." Their position, far to the northwest, was beyond Spruance's range, but he headed out and waited for his superior speed to narrow the gap. No further reports came in, however, and as the day wore on, Spruance felt that the morning position was growing "rather cold." It was the best target offered, though; and at 3:00 p.m., when he had closed to an estimated 230 miles, he began to launch.

A group of *Enterprise* dive bombers searched for 265 miles while a *Hornet* group searched 315 miles on a slightly different bearing. By now the weather had worsened. Each group found one small ship—the same one, a straggling destroyer; each attacked it unsuccessfully; and each lost a plane—the *Enterprise* to AA, the *Hornet* to fuel exhaustion. The weary rest landed in darkness. Disheartened, Spruance set a westward course, although the empty ocean ahead promised little for next day, especially since he had to slack off his full-speed pursuit—his destroyers were low on fuel—and there was always the possibility of a night ambush by fast battleships. Still, luck might bring him across those two lame cruisers. . . . He ordered the *Enterprise* to send a dawn search over the whole western semicircle.

The *Kumano* and *Suzuya* had taken no part in defending their sister against the Marines; they merely stood by a few miles away, and when Fleming's crash further reduced the *Mikuma*'s speed, they increased their own and fled. Through the fifth and the early hours of the sixth, the cripples limped on with their two loyal destroyers. Their plight was desperate; they knew it, and Spruance soon learned it. The *Enterprise*'s scouts spotted them at 7:30 and shouted their position. The *Hornet* began to launch her dive bombers and fighters at 7:57. They struck at 9:50, and as they returned, the *Enterprise* launched. They, too, struck and returned, and the *Hornet* launched again.

In all, the Dauntlesses dropped eighty-one bombs. Five hit the *Mogami*, killing more than 100 men. Ten gutted the *Mikuma*. Her survivors climbed aboard the destroyer *Arashio*, where a direct hit killed nearly all of them. Another bomb burst open the second destroyer's stern. Between bombings, the Wildcats spattered the burning hulks with .50-caliber bullets. The last planes, racks empty, headed home at 3 p.m. The *Mikuma* sank about two hours later. The *Mogami* and the two destroyers, all afire, their broken decks littered with dead men, made their painful way back to Japan.

Spruance's fuel was almost gone; enemy submarines were prowling the area, and further pursuit would take him within range of Wake, which was packed with Japanese planes once expected to base at Midway. He reversed course and withdrew toward his tankers. As his pilots stripped off their flight gear and relaxed, the Fortresses made their final attack—and Midway's. Flying at 10,000 feet, they dropped their bombs on a vessel which they reported as "a cruiser that sank in fifteen seconds." The "cruiser" proved to be the *U.S.S. Grayling*, a submarine. Happily, her sinking was only a crash dive.

Midway's fighting was done, but its work was not—the work that had begun early on June fourth, when the first American pilot parachuted from his flaming plane. All that day, the next, and for weeks afterward, Catalinas searched the ocean for rafts and life jackets. They found Ensign Gay on the afternoon of the fifth. A medical officer asked what treatment he had given his wounds.

Gay said, "Soaked 'em in salt water for ten hours."

On the sixth, they picked up another pilot, a lieutenant (j.g.) who had been clutching the bullet holes in his belly for two days. The Japanese had strafed him in his raft—to prove it, he brought in his splintered paddle. The Catalinas rescued more than fifty men. Thirty-five were Japanese, from the *Hiryu's* engine room. They had drifted thirteen days and some 110 miles.

The biggest aftermath job was salvaging the *Yorktown*. It started auspiciously. The destroyer *Hughes*, standing by her on the night of the fourth, rescued two wounded men, who had been overlooked when she was abandoned, and one of her fighter pilots, who paddled up in his raft. Early next morning, Captain Buckmaster and a working party of 180 returned with three other destroyers, and that afternoon a mine sweeper took her in tow for Pearl Harbor. Repairs crept as slowly as the *Yorktown* herself, but by noon of the sixth, jettisoning and counterflooding had begun to reduce her list, and with the help of the destroyer *Hammann,* lashed to her starboard side and supplying power and water, her fires were being brought under control. Then, at 1:35, a lookout sighted four torpedo wakes to starboard. The *Hammann*'s gunners opened fire, hoping to detonate the warheads, and her captain tried to jerk her clear with his engines, but nothing availed. One torpedo passed astern. One hit the *Hammann*. The other two hit the *Yorktown*. They were death blows for both ships.

Geysers of oil, water and debris spouted high and crashed down. The convulsive heave of the decks snapped ankles and legs. Stunned men were hurled overboard, then sucked into flooding compartments. The *Hammann*'s back was broken; she settled fast and sank by the head. Almost at once, her grave exploded. The concussion killed some of the swimmers outright; others slowly bled to death from the eyes and mouth and nostrils.

The *Yorktown*'s huge bulk absorbed part of the two shocks, but her tall tripod foremast whipped like a sapling, and sheared rivets sang through the air. The rush of water into her starboard firerooms helped counter her port list at first, but Buckmaster knew that she was doomed. Too many safety doors had been sprung, too many bulkheads weakened. He mustered the working party to abandon ship. A few did not appear—the torpedoes had imprisoned them in compartments now inaccessibly submerged. An officer phoned one compartment after another. When a voice answered from the inaccessible fourth deck he asked, "Do you know what kind of a fix you're in?"

"Sure," said the voice, "but we've got a hell of a good acey-deucey game down here. One thing, though—"

"Yes?"

"When you scuttle her, aim the torpedoes right where we are. We want it to be quick."

They did not need to scuttle her. Early the next morning, "she turned over on her port side"—in Buckmaster's words—"and sank in three thousand fathoms of water, with all her battle flags flying." As her bow slid under, men on the destroyers saluted.

So ended the Battle of Midway. The United States had lost a carrier, a destroyer, 150 planes and 307 men. Japan had lost four carriers, a heavy cruiser, 253 planes and 3,500 men. It was a decisive American victory. Exactly six months after Pearl Harbor, naval balance in the Pacific was restored. It was also Japan's only naval defeat since 1592, when the Koreans under Yi Sunsin, in history's first ironclad ships, drove Hideyoshi's fleet from Chinhai Bay.

Tactically, Japan's sunken carriers and dead combat pilots—some 100 of her finest, plus another 120 wounded—caused drastic changes in her whole naval establishment. To replace the carriers, she had not only to convert seaplane tenders, thereby curtailing long-range reconnaissance, but to rig flight decks on two battleships. The pilots could never be replaced. Said Capt. Hiroaki Tsuda, "The loss affected us throughout the war."

Strategically, Midway canceled Japan's threat to Hawaii and the West Coast, arrested her eastward advance and forced her to confine her major efforts to New Guinea and the Solomons. Moreover, her efforts were no longer directed toward expansion, but toward mere holding.

The initiative that Japan dropped, the United States picked up. We moved forward from the "defensive-offensive," in Adm. Ernest J. King's phrases, "to the offensive-defensive," and thence to Tokyo Bay. What ended there had begun at Midway. Said Rear Adm. Toshitane Takata, "Failure of the Midway campaign was the beginning of total failure."

Our commanders may have recognized it at the time, but they restrained their optimism. Immediately after the battle, Admiral Nimitz announced only that "Pearl Harbor has now been partially avenged. Vengeance will not be complete until Japanese sea power is reduced to impotence. We have made substantial progress in that direction." Then his jubilation broke out in a pun: "Perhaps we will be forgiven if we claim that we are about midway to that objective."

Guarding Australia

The enemy had failed to turn the corner of New Guinea by sea; now they were to try it by land. In the late months of spring and early summer, 1942, the Australians kept the Jap troops pinned down along the northern coast; except for minor land actions, the main battles had been fought in the air, with the Australians and Americans slowly but surely wresting control of the air from the Japs. However, in late July, the Japs landed 5,000 troops at Gona Mission. From there they drove the Australian forces back through the jungle to the Kokoda Trail, sixty miles south; this was the route over the Owen Stanley Range and down through the jungle to Port Moresby. The Australian defenders were outnumbered five to one, but they fought a stubborn withdrawing action as they retreated southward up the Owen Stanley Mountains.

Gen. MacArthur, then in Australia, was determined to hold Port Moresby; it was the base from which he would fight his way back to the Philippines. Gen. Kenney, his air commander, flew pursuit fighters in; he used bombers to bring up fresh troops and badly needed supplies to the Australians in the mountains, and, as the Aussies withdrew toward Port Moresby, the flying time shortened enough to let the air force hit the Japs in their front lines.

"The Japs covered the sixty miles of their advance from Buna in five days. To push ahead another thirty miles took fifty days, and the speed of their advance slackened every day." * The Japs got all the way to the village of Ioribaiwa, thirty-two miles from Port Moresby, but here the Australians held, and a counteroffensive was soon launched.

* George H. Johnston, *The Toughest Fighting in the World*, p. 138.

FIGHTING BACK IN NEW GUINEA

by George H. Johnston

The limit of the Japanese advance toward Port Moresby—the mountain ridge and village of Ioribaiwa—was captured today, Sept. 28, 1942, and our troops are pushing ahead through a heavy rainstorm toward the scattered villages that line the "Kokoda Trail."

The Japs offered little resistance, although they had built up a high timber palisade across the top of the ridge in front of an involved system of weapon pits and trenches. 25-pounders blew great holes in the palisade and the Australians went in with the bayonets and grenades. The Japs didn't wait for any more. They scuttled northward through the jungle, abandoning a stack of unburied dead, a great dump of equipment and ammunition, and leaving to us the steep ridge down which we retreated only a couple of weeks ago with the Japs rolling stones and grenades down on us and plastering our rearguard with fierce mortar and machine-gun fire.

The Japs have left a lot of graves on Ioribaiwa Ridge, and trampled in the mud between the bodies of the dead is an elaborate shirt of scarlet silk with a black dragon embroidered on it. Most of the corpses are emaciated. General Blamey, the Australian Field Commander, was right about letting the jungle beat the Japs. The evidence scattered everywhere along the track and through the jungle is that this Japanese army was at the point of starvation and riddled with scrub typhus and dysentery. The stench of the dead and the rotting vegetation and the foetid mud

Condensed from the author's *The Toughest Fighting in the World.*

is almost overpowering. One of our doctors carried out a couple of autopsies. Many of the Japs, he said, had died because hunger had forced them to eat the poisonous fruits and roots of the jungle. It's clear now that the enemy stopped at Ioribaiwa Ridge because he was humanly incapable of thrusting ahead any farther.

The Australians are pushing ahead very cautiously, profiting by these grim reminders of an advance that went too fast, building up store dumps and medical posts as they go, taking meticulous care about sanitation and hygiene, advancing in three prongs that are exploring every side track and cleansing every yard of jungle as they go.

In this dense terrain of matted vegetation and half-hidden native pad-pads and steep gorges there are the ever present threats of ambush, counter-infiltration and outflanking. But the Australians are climbing slowly and grimly up the southern flanks of the Owen Stanley's with the knowledge that the only Japanese behind their thrusting spearheads are dead ones.

VALLEY OF SILENCE

From the crest of Imita Ridge the vast valley of Ua-ule Creek lay like a bowl of tumbled green jungle held between the jagged purple peaks of the lower Owen Stanley's. The three-toothed ridge of Ioribaiwa guarded the other side of the valley with an almost unbroken wall of jungle, clear in the tropical light. Beyond the afternoon thunderheads were massing above and between the rising peaks of the range. The rolling clouds had beheaded the great bulk of Mount Urawa and scattered tufts and wisps of cotton-wool across the flanks of distant Maguli.

The valley below was silent. The only sound was the soft hiss and drip of rain among the great jungle trees of Imita Ridge. But no sound came from Ua-ule Valley for no man lived there—not even a native—and the only movement was the play of shadows across the matted trees.

Down the north wall of this valley came the Japanese one day last month. For three bitter weeks they had driven everything before them. They had fought courageously, fanatically, mercilessly. Ragged, exhausted, hungry Australians straggled through the silent valley on their retreat to Imita Ridge, while the rearguard fought to stem the yellow tide on the crest of Ioribaiwa. Just as the enemy was hidden by that silent blanket of jungle so were the countless deeds of heroism.

In one tiny clearing a young Australian lay wounded by a sniper's bullet. His patrol was coming up behind him unaware of the hidden ambush. He could have feigned death and escaped when darkness came. Instead he shouted warnings and directions to his comrades. The enraged Japanese pumped more bullets into him but the Australian continued to direct his patrol. He was dead when his comrades returned after having wiped out the Japanese.

On this same terrible slope six Victorians had squirmed to within six yards of the Japanese positions to silence a troublesome enemy gunpit and had killed every man in it. Across this mysterious valley had shrieked the 25-pounder shells from the Australian guns that held the Japanese and blasted them out of Ioribaiwa. For the Japanese never reached the foot of that valley of silence, never climbed the southern wall of Imita. Across this valley last week went the grim-faced green-uniformed Australians on the terrible march back to the crest of the path through the Owen Stanley's—and beyond.

The silence of centuries returned to the valley of Ua-ule. It was just as it had always been as we looked across to jagged Ioribaiwa, its edges softened by the veil of falling rain. That rain would be falling gently on those few crude crosses. Some would bear the crudely penciled names of Australians . . . one or two the simple words: "Unknown Australian Soldier."

No man can give more than life itself. These men had given that to the valley of silence that somehow seemed part of Australia itself. Their sacrifice was a heritage to their country's history.

By some freak of the valley and the lowering shroud of rain clouds a thin sound tinkled up from the silent green depths—the sound of biscuit tins clanking together. . . .

Five days ago the Japanese began their resistance again—on the wide shallow plateau of the Gap, the pass through the forbidding spurs of the main range. The weather is bad, the terrain unbelievably terrible, and the enemy is resisting with a stubborn fury that is costing us many men and much time. Against the machine gun nests and mortar pits established on the ragged spurs and steep limestone ridges our advance each day now is measured in yards. Our troops are fighting in the cold mists of an altitude of 6,700 feet, fighting viciously because they have only a mile or two to go before they reach the peak of the pass and will be able to attack downhill—down the north flank of the Owen Stanley's. That means a lot to troops who have climbed every inch of that agonizing track, who have buried so many of their cobbers and who have seen so many more going back, weak with sickness or mauled by the mortar bombs and bullets and grenades of the enemy, men gone from their ranks simply to win back a few more hundred yards of this wild, unfriendly, and utterly untamed mountain. Tiny villages which were under Japanese domination a few weeks ago are back in our hands—Ioribaiwa, Nauro Creek, Menari, Efogi, Kagi, Myola—and we are fighting now for Templeton's Crossing.

Already a new language is springing up on this green and slimy trail. Whenever Australians are in an area for long enough they soon invent a new slang to describe it. They adapt themselves to discomforts, give them ironical names and laugh them off. A few weeks ago these troops were still talking the language of the Middle East, which has been their home for more than two years. They talk now like the men who have been in New Guinea for months. The curses of New Guinea are varied enough to provide troops with their main subjects of conversation but, in rough order, the worst are mosquitoes, mud, mountains, malaria and monotony. The "mozzies" and malaria are worst down near the coast, but they are speedily replaced by the mud and mountains as you go inland. The monotony, of course, is everywhere, except where the fighting provides something special to think about.

They love mosquito stories, and the more fantastic they are the better they like them.

There was one about a Jap airman who was found lying on a hill. The official explanation was that he had been shot down by our fighters, but the boys in the know say that he was picked up at Lae by a mozzy, who carried him over the Owen Stanley's, looking for a nice quiet place to eat him. He saw a flight of Fortresses heading north, and, mistaking them for his wife and kids, he dropped the Jap and fell into formation.

I heard another one on the same lines about an ack-ack gunner who caught a mosquito in his sights, and, mistaking it for a Zero, opened fire with a Bofors gun. The third shell chipped one wing, and the fourth exploded right under his tail. The boys raised a cheer as they saw him come down smoking, but instead of crashing he picked up a rock and threw it at them. They can show you the rock, too.

They all grew out of the old tale about the two mosquitoes who found a good, juicy-looking staff sergeant asleep under his net one night. One of them politely lifted the net for the other to fly in, and his friend returned the compliment by turning over his identity disc to see if he belonged to the right blood group.

"Well, he's okay," one of them said. "Shall we eat him here or take him down to the beach?"

"Don't be silly. If we take him down to the beach the big chaps will grab him."

I can't vouch for that one. I never met the staff sergeant.

Moresby's best mosquito joke, I think, is a perfectly authentic signboard that stands alongside a shallow pool on the main road in the garrison. It was erected by an anti-malaria squad which forgot to paint in the hyphen. The pool was filled with gamboesia, the little imported minnow that eats mosquito larvae, and the sign reads:

And everybody who passes always makes the customary remark of awe that tradition dictates: " 'Struth, are they that big?"

On the Kokoda track, however, after you've been walking a few hours, you soon get above the mosquito country. As the troops toiled and grunted up they would often stop and gasp with amazement at the enormous butterflies that drifted to and fro, or alighted on their arms to drink the sweat. The insect life, from scorpions to butterflies, is impressive.

Only for a time though. You eventually reach a stage when flora and fauna, and even the Japs, gradually lose interest. Your mental processes allow you to be conscious of only one thing—"The Track," or, more usually, "The Bloody Track." You listen to your legs creaking and stare at the ground and think of the next stretch of mud, and you wonder if the hills will ever end. Up one almost perpendicular mountain face more than 2,000 steps have been cut out of the mud and built up with felled saplings inside which the packed earth has long since become black glue. Each step is two feet high. You slip on one in three. There are no resting places. Climbing it is the supreme agony of mind and spirit. The troops, with fine irony, have christened it "The Golden Staircase"!

Life changes as you push up the track. Standards of living deteriorate, sometimes below normally accepted standards even of primitive existence. Thoughts become somber, humor takes on a grim, almost macabre quality. When men reach the nadir of mental and physical agony there are times when sickness or injury and even death seem like things to be welcomed. Near Efogi, on a slimy section of the track that reeks with the stench of death, the remains of an enemy soldier lie on a crude stretcher, abandoned by the Japanese retreat. The flesh has gone from his bones, and a white, bony claw sticks out of a ragged uniform sleeve, stretching across the track. Every Australian who passes, plodding up the muddy rise that leads to the pass, grasps the skeleton's grisly hand, shakes it fervently and says "Good on you, sport!" before moving wearily on.

In this territory the Japanese are fighting, with a stubborn tenacity that is almost unbelievable, from an elaborate system of prepared positions along every ridge and spur. Churned up by the troops of both armies, the track itself is now knee deep in thick, black mud. For the last ten days no man's clothing has been dry and they have slept—when sleep was possible—in pouring rain under sodden blankets. Each man carries all his personal equipment, firearms, ammunition supply and five days' rations. Every hour is a nightmare.

"BUT KOKODA WAS EMPTY"

The Australians have re-conquered the Owen Stanley Range. Today, on November 2, they marched into Kokoda unopposed, through lines of excited natives who brought them great baskets of fruit and decked them with flowers. They marched back to the little plateau where Colonel Owen had died so many weary weeks before. They marched downhill through Isurava and Deniki, where many of them had fought the bloody rearguard action of August. The Japs had fled. Patrols cautiously went ahead to scout, squirmed their way through the rubber trees to test out Kokoda's defenses. But Kokoda was empty. There was no sound but the droning of insects and the noise of the rain pattering through the trees. Kokoda, "key to the Owen Stanley's," had been abandoned by the Japanese without a fight. Their defense of Kokoda had been the pass through the range, and they had failed to hold that defense line.

Today Australian troops in ragged, mud-stained green uniforms, in charred steel helmets that had been used for cooking many a meal of bully beef on the Kokoda trail, stood in ranks round the flagpole in front of the administrative building while an Australian flag (dropped with typical courtesy, friendship and thoughtfulness by an American fighter pilot) was slowly hoisted in the still air. There was no cheering. There was no band playing. There was merely the packed lines of these hundreds of weary Australians, haggard, half-starved, dishevelled, many wearing grimy, stained bandages, standing silently at attention in the rain. For weeks their muttered "Kokoda or bust!" had been the most quoted saying of the track. Well, here was Kokoda, and lost in the rain clouds behind was the great blue rampart of the Owen Stanley's, with the shaggy 13,600-foot crest of Mount Victoria hidden by the afternoon thunderheads.

The shadow of the Australian flag, hanging limply in the still, moist air, fell across the lines of Japanese graves sheltering beneath the shattered debris of what once had been the Government station buildings. Within 12 feet of the flagstaff was the tall, simple memorial erected by the Japanese "in memory of the many soldiers of Nippon who fell in the great battle for Kokoda." And near by was the grave of Colonel Owen.

Littered all over the area were discarded Japanese anti-aircraft shells, smashed boxes which had contained stores, wicker baskets in which food had been dropped by parachute. In a valley beyond was the Japanese cemetery, with its hundreds of neat graves.

Within an hour the Australian spearhead was snaking down the narrow track leading from the little plateau on to the flat, jungle-choked plain below. They were marching on to try to catch the fleeing enemy.

TWO MEN ARE SITTING

On an upturned packing case alongside an air-strip in the Kunai 20 miles behind Gona sat a blindfolded Japanese prisoner, awaiting the transport plane that would carry him back to Port Moresby. He had bitten off the end of his tongue to ensure that he wouldn't talk. He could hear the roar of powerful aircraft engines as our transports swept in with guns and ammunition and food. He could hear the fainter throbbing of our bombers and fighters streaking over toward Buna. His share of the war was over, but in the tangled swamps and kunai patches of the Buna plain thousands of his fellow countrymen were facing up for the final battle of a tough campaign.

The allies were closing in from seven directions. The Americans had gone into action twenty-four hours before, and three columns of green-uniformed doughboys were even now assaulting the tough defense perimeter around Cape Endaiadere, Buna and Giropa Point. The Australians were pushing up the track to Sananande Point and another force, advancing with staggering speed, had reached to within a mile of the north coast at Gona. The village of Soputa, south of Sananada, had just fallen to Australians and Americans after tough fighting.

But the surly little Jap with the bristly hair and with the dried blood caked at the corner of his mouth didn't know anything about these things.

It's been a tense week for the senior officers. General Harding, of the American 32nd Division, had to swim two miles to the shore when the lugger in which he was moving along the north coast was strafed and sunk by Zeros. Australia's General Vasey and America's General MacNider have been strafed and sniped at.

Back at headquarters are the senior generals—MacArthur, Blamey and Kenney, all now established in New Guinea to direct operations on the spot. Blamey, who lives in a camouflaged tent lined with maps on which colored pins illustrate the inexorable advance of the troops under his command, is cautious, and wisely planning to meet the worst contingency that can happen.

The senior soldier of them all, General Douglas MacArthur, miraculously retains complete privacy in a garrison area where there has never been privacy before, where even American and Australian nurses have had to avert their eyes from the roadside spectacles of nude soldiers showering under roadside hydrants, and naked men wandering carelessly everywhere.

MacArthur is just as remote, just as mysterious as he has been ever since he reached Australia eight months ago. He lives with Kenney in a white-painted bungalow surrounded by a riotous tropical garden of frangipani and hibiscus and flametrees. He is rarely seen. I remember how one American soldier came up to me in a state of great excitement because he had seen the great man. "I got a glimpse of him before breakfast," he said. "He was walking beneath the trees in a pink silk dressing gown with a black dragon on the back." Another man told me he had seen MacArthur in the afternoon with signal forms in one hand and a bunch of green lettuce which had been flown up from the mainland in the other. Between munches he doubtless analyzed the progress of the carefully prepared plan to take Papua back from the Japs.

That plan probably had its beginning at a special press conference in July which I had flown down to Melbourne to attend. That conference was—and unfortunately still is—off the record, but one remark of the general's can be told. "We suffer because our forces are split over many fronts," he said, "but so long as we can keep fighting on every one of those fronts we keep the enemy fighting there, too, and his forces are similarly split. We must attack, attack, attack!"

Well, that is what is happening in Papua today. The Japs, for the moment, are on the defensive everywhere. There are many problems that the three generals must overcome. The Australians call this a "Q War"—a quartermaster's war, in which supply and movement are everything that matters, except fighting courage. Those problems have been largely solved by the dynamic General Kenney who has built up his air transport organization to an enormous scale. Almost every foot of our advance from Ioribaiwa across the Owen Stanley's and across the northern plain to Buna has been made possible only by the endless job of innumerable young pilots—many of them American kids from flying schools who flew the great Douglases and Lockheeds across the Pacific and straight to New Guinea—who have dropped or landed thousands of tons of food, equipment, munitions and guns.

If this is a Q War we have just seen a perfect example of efficiency in fighting that sort of war. The Japs have been beaten in the air, beaten on supply, beaten in straight-out fighting ability. Today we can see the end of the picture in sight. The Japs have lost almost all that they have struggled so hard for during the last one hundred and twenty-one days.

And today two men are sitting. They are many miles apart. One is a blindfolded Japanese prisoner. I wonder what he is thinking? The other is the mysterious, aloof American general from the Philippines sitting beneath the frangipani and munching Australian lettuce as he reads the reports coming in from the front, where allied troops are battering down the enemy's final Papuan resistance. Perhaps he sees in this little jungle campaign the first complete justification of his months old theory of "Attack, attack, attack!" But I'm not sure. Because, you see, I don't know what he is thinking either. . . .

TWENTY-FOUR MARCHED OUT

Along the narrow, winding Sananada track, flanked by swamps and thick jungle, both sides had dug in in small pockets. Little isolated battles were raging to the noise of thudding mortars, chattering machine-gun fire, and the zip and whine of bullets.

Sometimes our men advanced with blood-curdling yells to rout out Japanese nests at the bayonet point or with grenades. But the progress generally was pitifully slow.

Soon after we had smashed through the Japanese defenses at Soputa village, the enemy had brought up a 75-millimeter mountain gun, and for two days its shelling of the allied forward positions had held up any appreciable advance.

An order was issued that the gun was to be silenced at all costs. The job was allotted to 90 men of an A.I.F. battalion which had been fighting with magnificent courage and determination in the slimy Papuan jungles for two and a half months.

Under the command of Captain Basil Catterns, of Sydney, the 90 mud-stained, heavily armed men crept into the flanking underbush at dawn one morning.

The enemy gun position was only two miles away, but

the Australians had to make a wide detour to get round the deep, evil smelling swamps.

For more than eight hours the men hacked and smashed their way through the entangling vines and rotten trees, their direction plotted and corrected by the noise of the enemy gun in action.

Just before dusk, Catterns saw ahead of him a Japanese camp with strong defenses all round, and the mountain gun firing from a pit in front of the camp and sending shells over the trees into the Australian positions two miles away.

After a few moments' consideration the Australians decided to launch their first assault on the camp to clean out the Japanese troops.

The Australians were drawn up in a wide, sweeping curve. Zero hour was fixed at sunset, and they crouched in the jungle until the order to charge was given.

The sun dropped swiftly behind the darkening trees. Catterns gave the order. Within a few seconds one of the most spectacular and bloody battles of the New Guinea war was raging in the tiny clearing.

The Australians tore their way through two barricades of plaited vines that the Japanese had erected, and swept across three lines of trenches with Bren guns and tommy guns blazing. Others lobbed showers of grenades into the Japanese posts.

The Japanese were taken completely by surprise as thousands of bullets whacked into native huts. Screaming, they came pouring from the huts, but within a few seconds every exit had been blocked by a pile of Japanese dead. More were blown to pieces by Australian grenades, and others were mown down like ripe corn as the Australians continued their terrorizing rush through the camp.

Grenades burst among the fires on which the Japanese evening meal was cooking, and in the great flash of flame some of the huts caught fire.

Some Australians had been killed and many wounded. The enemy had recovered from his surprise, and was hitting back hard. The Australians circled round their wounded with blazing guns, and slowly retreated into the jungle, carrying their wounded with them, behind the screen of gunfire. In the darkness the Australians dug defense positions as best they could while the wounded were attended to, and half the men fought a defensive action against more than a hundred Japanese, who maintained a constant night-long fire from machine guns, mortars, and grenades. Other Japanese were pouring from a second camp nearby.

By dawn the Australians were completely surrounded and there was no way of getting a message through to inform their unit of their plight.

"We were holding a sausage-shaped perimeter sixty yards long and thirty yards wide," said Captain Catterns. "We had stacked our wounded around a large tree in the center of our position, but as the Japanese counter-attacked throughout the day the wounded were systematically picked off one by one by snipers. The Japanese sniped at the slightest movement.

"Under the protection of heavy machine-gun fire, their grenade throwers would advance and concentrate on one of our weapon pits or trenches, and plaster it until they were satisfied it was wiped out.

"Then they would turn to another Australian position. It was evidently their intention to whittle our defenses away one by one until we were exterminated."

Lieutenant Stewart Blakiston, of Geelong, one of the few officers to survive, said: "When we first occupied our little defense position we were hemmed in by jungle. When we left it looked like a sports field. Every blade of grass had been levelled and all the scrub and trees had been cut down by machine-gun fire. Even six-inch trees had been levelled to the ground by Japanese heavy machine guns. The parapets of trenches had been blown in and flattened by the constant hail of bullets, and the sides of weapon pits were shot away. Sometimes the Japanese would circle our defenses with their gunfire like Red Indians attacking a wagon train in the old wild western films. How any of us survived throughout that day I still don't know.

"Some of us almost cried with relief when, just before sunset, we heard the rattle of musketry as an Australian battalion advanced up the track towards us. Some of the Japanese who were around us sped through the jungle to meet the new threat. There were enough of them left to keep us busy until after dark, when we were able to retire a few hundred yards to better defenses behind."

When the tide of battle had rolled on, by dawn next day, only four officers and 20 other ranks of the gallant 90 lived to march out from that terrible jungle clearing. But near the bodies of the 66 brave Australians who had not died in vain were the bodies of more than 150 Japanese.

And the Australians had done their job. They had silenced a dangerous enemy pocket; they had paved the way for an almost bloodless advance of two miles by the troops behind them.

And buried in the mud beside the tangled jungle track was the 75-millimeter gun—abandoned by the Japanese—which the Australians had been ordered to put out of action.

"THE WILDEST, MADDEST, BLOODIEST FIGHTING"

The Japanese are trying desperately to reinforce their last garrison in Papua. Under cover of darkness and bad weather several destroyers have succeeded in running the allied air blockade and have landed reinforcements at Buna. Other formations of fresh enemy troops have been brought down the coast from Salamaua in small boats, landing barges and even native craft. Today they continued their plan of reinforcement with submarines, at least nineteen (including one big fellow of 3,000 tons) of which were sighted heading for Buna on the surface in convoy formation. They crash-dived within sixty seconds when our planes came over.

Nevertheless our forces are closing in everywhere. At Gona the Australians have cut their way through to the beach and are now trying to silence the immensely strong pillboxes and gunpits that the Japanese have established near Gona Mission. At Buna the Americans have driven a wedge to within 800 yards of Buna government buildings, where the Japanese apparently have their focal positions. But it's a tough job. Deep swamps of black mud in which a man would drown limit the terrain over which we can attack. Every logical and practical line of approach is covered by a network of fortifications which the Japs have been working on for months.

Every weapon pit is a fortress in miniature. Some are strengthened by great sheets of armor and by concrete, but the majority are merely huge dug-outs—several are 150 feet long—protected from our fire and bombs by sawn logs and felled trees which form a barrier six, ten, and sometimes 15 feet thick. The logs are held in place by great metal stakes, and filled in with earth in which the natural growth of the jungle has continued, providing perfect camouflage. Many of the pits are connected by subterranean tunnels or well protected communication trenches. The pits are heavily manned and each is filled with sufficient food, water and ammunition to enable the Japs to withstand a long siege. From every trench or pit or pillbox all approaches are covered by wide fields of sweeping fire along fixed lines.

At the moment the most desperate fighting is taking place on the Gona beach sector, where the A.I.F. is gradually whittling away the enemy's grip in a series of ferocious, but costly, bayonet charges. One private described a typical attack to me today:

"We'd been advancing for hours through stinking swamps up to our knees when we reached better country in the coconut groves, but when we pushed through the plantation to the beach we met heavy machine-gun fire from a strong Jap post on the beach. We attacked in a broad, sweeping line, charging across the sand with fixed bayonets and grenades, and stormed our way right into the position.

"It was the wildest, maddest, bloodiest fighting I have ever seen. Grenades were bursting among the Japs as we stabbed down at them with our bayonets from the parapets above. Some of our fellows were actually rolling on the sand with Japs locked against them in wrestling grips. It was all over within a few minutes. A few of the Japs had escaped, but the bodies of 30 were tangled among their captured guns.

"A bayonet charge like that is a pretty terrible business when you see your cobbers falling, when you can only see ahead of you a tree. You can't even see the Japs hidden among the roots until you're right on top of them, and they are still firing and yelling as you plunge the bayonet down. But it's the only way to clean them out. Those bastards fight to the last. They keep fighting until your bayonet sinks into them."

Another incident yesterday provided a typical illustration of Japanese desperation. A brawny American tommy gunner, 6 feet 3 inches tall, was patrolling alone down a track near Gona when a completely unarmed Japanese, slightly built and not much more than five feet tall, leaped out of the undergrowth, seized the big American by the throat and brought him crashing to the ground. They wrestled wildly for a few minutes, but the American broke the grip of the Jap, scrambled to his feet and brought the butt of his gun crashing down on the head of his assailant. The Jap fell to the ground, but when the American stooped over, he was grabbed by the ankle and again brought down. In the end the American was forced to strangle the Jap to death with his bare hands.

BOTTCHER'S SALIENT

Today the greatest individual act of heroism among the American forces in New Guinea came to an end when a grimy party of twelve men under the leadership of a tough sergeant who can scarcely speak English were relieved in the salient on Buna beach that they held against an overwhelming force of Japanese for seven days and nights. The establishment of that tiny salient and the holding of it might well prove one of the vital factors in breaking the Japanese grip on the entire Buna sector. Sergeant Herman Bottcher, of "Bottcher's Salient," richly deserves the D.S.C. he's going to be awarded, and also the promotion to commissioned rank which is being rushed through the "usual channels."

Bottcher is 37 and he comes from San Francisco. He is German-born, from Landsberg, near Berlin, worked in Australia for some years in the late twenties, and then went to the United States to try his luck. He knows modern war, because soon after he received United States citizenship he lost it when he enlisted with the International Brigade to fight against the Axis in Spain. He was a good soldier and a brave fighter for the Republicans, in whose army he rose from the rank of private to that of captain. He enlisted later with the United States Army and found himself in Papua, fighting his second war against the Axis.

Bottcher is of medium size, wears a magnificent black beard, looks at you with fierce eyes, and speaks almost unrecognizable English with a thick German accent.

On December 5 the Americans were hammering in vain at the strongly defended Japanese posts outside Buna. The enemy held the village on one side and the Government station on the other. There had been a disheartening series of failures by the Americans to breach the defenses. Bottcher was in the thick of it. He came back to get a pail of water for some of his wounded and saw two or three American officers sitting on the ground trying to work out ways and means of assaulting the enemy line. Bottcher glared at them as he filled the bucket. "If you guys would get up off your goddam tails and start fightin' maybe we'd get something done!" he snarled and strode back to the forward positions.

Bottcher decided to do something himself. He called for volunteers to drive a wedge right into the Japanese positions and through to the beach. It was a tough job. Many men volunteered and Bottcher picked twelve of them.

They squirmed through the swamps and coconut palms toward their objectives through a hail of heavy fire, but the tommy guns and grenades of Bottcher and his men cleaned up enemy machine-gun posts, and brought snipers toppling from trees. After several hours of heavy fighting the little force reached its objective, where Bottcher ordered his men to dig in on the beach and stay there.

Trenches and weapon pits were dug. At dawn the Japanese attacked from both flanks, one force rushing from the village and one from the Government station. Both attacks were repulsed by fierce machine-gun fire, and the Japanese retired, dragging some wounded with them, and leaving forty dead on the beach. A few hours later a Japanese machine-gun post brought harassing fire to bear on the American post, so Bottcher crawled out with a pocketful of grenades, squirmed across the bullet-torn sand, and blew the post to pieces with grenades. He crawled back to his little garrison.

That night the watchful doughboys saw enemy barges moving offshore, and opened up on them with heavy machine-gun fire. One barge was set on fire, and Japanese could be seen scrambling from it on to the other, which escaped at full speed to the northward.

Next day a party of Japanese was seen sneaking across a bridge over Buna Creek, and Bottcher's guns brought down six of them before the others fled.

All this time the little beachhead was constantly under fire from strong enemy positions on both sides, but the thought of retiring never occurred to the German-born sergeant who had been wounded several times. The American post was causing great concern to the Japanese, and on the night of December 9 another double attack was made from both sides. Again the Japanese were driven back in confusion.

Next morning Bottcher and a few of his men crawled out of their trenches into no-man's-land. They counted seven more Japanese dead added to the pile of corpses in front of their weapon pits, and found two abandoned Japanese machine guns with ammunition. These were dragged back to the post to increase its armament.

Once or twice Bottcher had visitors. On one occasion the American commanding officer—General Eichelberger, a brave man and a fine soldier—crawled along to Bottcher's Salient, and did a bit of useful sniping while he was there! But most of the time the thirteen men were alone, with hundreds of Japanese all round them.

Today a stronger party of fresh troops went in to relieve them. But before he came out Bottcher was able to get a final crack at the Japs. For some hours they had watched the Japanese building a heavy timber barricade leading from Buna Village toward the American post. It was obviously their intention to launch an attack from behind the barricade. Bottcher got his mortars ranged and waited until the palisade was almost completed. Then he sent over a string of bombs and blew the timber wall and all the Japanese working on it to pieces. Since then the Japanese haven't attempted to begin the job again.

By a conservative count it is believed that Bottcher and his twelve men have killed more than 120 Japs from this little salient.

MASSACRE AT MAMBARE

The Japanese lost one north coast beachhead today, with the fall of Buna Village, and gained another at tremendous cost well up the coast near the Mambare Delta, 53 miles away. Attacking in force from Bottcher's Salient, the Americans smashed right through Buna Village to the coast, completely cleaned up the area, which is littered with the bodies of hundreds of Japanese, and effectively isolated the enemy's Sananda force from the main garrison which holds a strong line from Giropa Point to Cape Endaiadere. General Eichelberger practically led his troops into the attack. This is every man's war up here. Senior officers will be found in the trenches with the troops, and right in the front line you will see commanding generals directing machine-gun and mortar fire and blazing away with tommy guns at Japanese snipers in the tree-tops!

I was just behind the front line at Gona, crouched down in the kunai grass with a party of 21 A.I.F. infantrymen from South Australia. They had been in action almost constantly for two months. They were thin, haggard, undernourished, insect-bitten, grimy, and physically near the end of their tether. They were fighting on fighting spirit alone.

And because that spirit was good they were still superlative troops.

They were talking among themselves about a Japanese weapon pit which was concealed in the butt of a huge jungle tree at the end of a clearing which lay beyond the kunai patch. The pit had held them up for two hours. Two of their number had been killed and five wounded when they first pushed through the kunai and ran into a scythelike sweep of fire from the Japanese positions. A twenty-three-year-old subaltern from Glen Osmond was talking quietly to the men.

"No use sitting round, I guess. We might as well get stuck into it!"

The men grinned. The lieutenant—who wore no badges of rank and was clad in the same green jungle uniform as the troops—turned to a lanky sergeant. "How much of that grass do you reckon they've cleared away between the post and the edge of the kunai?"

"Seventy or 80 yards, I'd say," replied the sergeant. A couple of privates nodded and a lance-corporal estimated it as "nearer a hundred."

"Well, there are 21 of us now," said a stocky little private from Renmark. "Once we get up to the bloody pit it would only take about six of us to dig the little blighters out."

He tossed a hand grenade a few inches into the air and caught it nonchalantly.

"You ought to be one of the six, sport," interjected another private, lolling on his back with his net-covered steel helmet over his eyes, and a piece of yellow grass moving up and down rhythmically to the slow champing of his jaws. "You're so bloody short, Tojo'll never be able to get a sight on yer!" A soft ripple of laughter ran round the little group.

But even that little burst of laughter was heard. From the Japanese post came the *pap-pap-pap* of a short machine-gun burst. The bullets zipped harmlessly high overhead. The man who was chewing grass tipped his helmet back and looked in the direction of the enemy post, invisible behind the screen of kunai. "Use 'em up, Tojo," he muttered. "You ain't got much longer to go."

The lieutenant buckled his belt and looked round at his men. They grinned and reached for their rifles and Brens and tommy guns. "According to Shorty here, this job's going to mean 15 of us won't get through," he said, as if it were a grand joke.

"Wouldn't count on that," said the lanky man, spitting out the well-chewed piece of grass. "He always was an optimist!"

Another ripple of laughter. "Well, some come back, they say," grinned the lieutenant. He motioned to the men. They took a final look at their weapons, saw the grenades were ready, and began to squirm slowly toward the edge of the long grass. As he moved past the lanky man winked at me. "Give us a good write-up," he said.

The movement of the 21 men made little movement in the grass and the occasional shaking of the thick blades might have been only the wind blowing in from the beach. They reached the edge of the kunai. A few yards out in the cleared area were the twisted bodies of their comrades killed a couple of hours before. There was a sudden flash of steel as the Australians sprang to their feet and started running. They were yelling like madmen. For a split second there was no sound from the enemy position. Then it started. The wild *brrrrpppppp-brrrrrop* of machine guns firing with fingers tight on the triggers, the crack of grenades, once the scream of a man.

The Australians were running in a straight line. It's no use swerving or dodging when you're charging into machine-gun fire. Their bayonets were at the high port. Men were falling. One threw up his hands, stopped dead, and stumbled to one side. Another fell as he was running, rolling over and over like a rabbit hit on the run. Another was spun around like a top before he crumpled up and slid to the ground. The little man who had predicted that six would get through had almost reached the Japanese pit when he fell. He went over backwards as if somebody had delivered a terrific uppercut.

He didn't live to find out, but his estimate was wrong.

Nine of the Australians got through. They wiped out the post, killing every one of the 19 Japs inside.

That is the meaning of morale. I saw that happen. I saw many other incidents just as expressive of the fighting spirit that makes these young Australians and Americans the world's best assault troops. These men, after the endless weeks of short rations, the gruelling fight across the Owen Stanley's, the sight of their comrades killed or wounded or evacuated with the mysterious malady known generally as "jungle fever," would not have been condemned had their spirit wilted, their morale weakened in the final bitter struggle that preceded the fall of Gona and Buna. But that morale had been tempered in the flame of hardship, adversity, and peril. It did not wilt.

"OF HUMAN THINGS"

The show is over. It is January 23, 1943. The last Japanese soldier in Papua has been killed or captured. Buna station, Giropa Point and Cape Endaiadere, where the Japanese resisted stubbornly from their foxholes for two bitter months, were crushed by Australian and American infantry charging behind Australian-manned and American-built light tanks. On the Sananda track the last pockets, which had held out longer than any others, were crushed. Some of the Japanese gave themselves up. Others stayed in their foxholes to be killed or to die of starvation and disease. Yesterday fighting ceased.

It was on this date twelve months ago that the war in New Guinea began, when Rabaul succumbed to the furious onslaught of the men of Nippon. Much has happened since then. The 16,000 men that General Horii threw into the attempt to conquer Papua have been killed or wounded or captured. Mostly they have been killed. And General Horii himself is dead. So are many other uncounted Japanese, destroyed in their planes and destroyed in the scores of ships that have become twisted junk on the sea floor for the sake of Japanese aggression in the South Seas.

The Solomons

While the Australians and the Americans were fighting in New Guinea, American Marines had invaded Guadalcanal in the Solomon Islands. Once Tulagi was occupied (the only successful part of the enemy's original Coral Sea scheme), the Japanese had begun work on

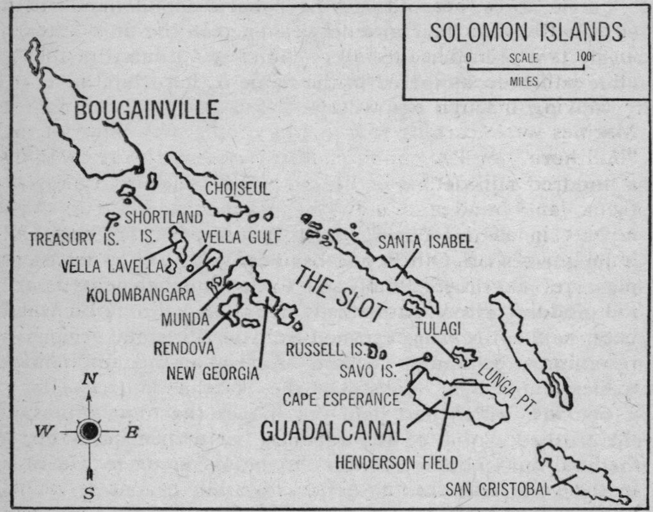

an airfield on nearby Guadalcanal. When the American naval commanders heard this news, they rushed the 1st Marine Division, then in New Zealand, to attack Guadalcanal. Japanese air forces, once firmly established on Guadalcanal, could raise havoc with the supply lines stretching from New Zealand and Australia back across the Pacific to Hawaii and the U.S.

The account which follows is a chapter from Maj. Frank Hough's remarkably fine book * about the Marines in action in the Pacific.

* *The Island War.*

GUADALCANAL: THE TURNING POINT

by Maj. Frank Hough

"Now hear this! *Now hear this!* All hands man your battle stations. . . . *Darken Ship! Darken Ship!* Secure all ports and bulkhead doors. The smoking lamp is out on all weather decks. . . . *Now hear this!* . . ."

Moving through empty, placid seas, some thousands of Marines were learning to obey the omnipotent voice of the "bull horn," or PA (public address system); were learning a hundred dull details of life aboard a transport. Many of them, landbound until now, had found a certain thrilling novelty in all this during the first few days, but that had quickly worn off. Others had been denied even this transient pleasure: old-timers, who had traveled a dozen seas aboard the plodding Navy transport *U.S.S. Henderson,* which had been hauling Marines around for thirty years; organized reservists, who had spent months on extended amphibious maneuvers in the Caribbean and off the Atlantic coast.

For the First Marine Division was going to war, though the truth was that none of them, from the Commanding General down, expected that they would actually meet war in the very near future. Although much of the personnel had been in training for more than a year, the units had been brought up to war strength only recently by incorporation of many men fresh from boot camp, and the full combat teams had had comparatively little opportunity to work together as units. The plan was to set up training bases in New Zealand where this deficiency could be remedied. The word was that they would not be called upon for combat action until January, 1943. And this was only late spring of 1942. . . .

Condensed from the author's *The Island War.*

So they settled down resignedly to the dullest life the mind of modern man has been able to devise: to a routine of boat drills, calisthenics, mess formations; to monotony-whiling poker and blackjack (craps showed a notable decline in popularity), cribbage, checkers and a surprising amount of chess. At night they sweltered four and six deep in fetid holds served by overworked blower systems which too often broke down, or groped about the darkened decks, watching the bright tropic stars close above the gently swaying mastheads, speculating vaguely on the strange land toward which they were headed.

The forward echelon, including Division Headquarters, had left Norfolk, Virginia, on 20 May aboard the *U.S.S. Wakefield* (former *S.S. Manhattan*) and two smaller ships, and had reached Wellington, via the Panama Canal, on 14 June. The men liked the people and the country. For two weeks they worked hard and cheerfully at establishing their training base, anticipating a long period of abundant liberty among a hospitable, congenial populace.

But that dream was to be short lived. On 25 June the High Command arrived at a momentous decision, and the Division was ordered to prepare to move into combat at the earliest possible moment. The second echelon, which had traveled by train from New River to San Francisco, reached Wellington on 11 July, only to be put immediately at unloading their ships and reloading, combat style.

Combat-loading, at this stage of the war, was mainly a theory, and not a fully developed theory, at that. Its object was to stow the gear aboard in such fashion that those items most urgently needed on a beachhead could be got at easily and unloaded quickly, the less urgently needed items to follow according to a complicated system of priorities. Space economy was no object; at least, not the primary object. Thus, trucks, jeeps and other rolling stock which had been disassembled on the trip out to conserve space, now had to be reassembled for immediate use and loaded with ammunition, food, etc. This was highly wasteful according to commercial standards, and much valuable cargo was necessarily crowded out.

Furthermore, there was considerable lack of unanimity

of opinion regarding priorities, which led to what turned out to be some regrettable errors. From the outset it had been the fate of the First Division to do things the hard way. As the pioneer unit in the field, it had served as the proving ground in which trial and error developed the methods and techniques of the entire Marine Corps. And it was destined to continue so until, as some cynics put it later, the Division kept on doing things the hard way throughout its career from sheer force of habit.

Other things went wrong, too, unavoidably. The Quartermaster Department, not having expected to go into combat for some months, was lacking in certain essentials which were all but impossible to obtain on short notice. New Zealand labor unions placed some difficulties in the way of loading at first, and with the exception of a few civilian crane operators the Marines handled all the cargo themselves, working continuously in shifts. Then the rains came: torrential downpours which ruined supplies, equipment and dispositions. It was a disgruntled and exhausted Division which shoved off from Wellington on 22 July for a destination still unknown to most.

It was not unknown, of course, to the Division command. Our smashing naval victory at the Battle of Midway had set the stage for a quick followup offensive on our part, and the activities of the Japanese themselves provided the cue to where it could be launched with the best prospects of decisive success.

The archipelago known as the Solomon Islands runs from a point about five degrees below the Equator, adjacent to New Britain, for several hundred miles in a southeasterly direction. The several large islands and innumerable smaller ones lie in two parallel chains, separated by a wide channel which came to be known as the "Slot." Geologically they were described as old coral deposits on an underwater mountain range which had been thrust above the surface by volcanic action at some time in the remote past. This made for rugged, mountainous country, slashed by precipitous ravines and gullies, abounding in natural caves. Centuries of tropical climate had blanketed this with lush jungle.

All through the spring, Coastwatchers lurking in the hills had reported steady Japanese penetration southeastward along both of the twin chains. By mid-May, the Japanese had seized the provincial capital of Tulagi, located on a small island in a splendid harbor formed by the larger adjacent island of Florida. Captain W. F. M. Clemens, a British officer who had been a member of the civil Government, had escaped across the channel to Guadalcanal where he had taken up the duties of Coastwatcher, together with two Australians and supported by a small group of loyal natives. From this point of vantage, he was able to verify, early in July, what up until then had been mere rumors: that the Japanese had sent troops and laborers into Guadalcanal where they were building a sizable airfield near the mouth of the Lunga River with such despatch that it might be expected to be operational by mid-August.

Guadalcanal was the next to the last island in the southern end of the two chains which bounded the Slot. It was about ninety miles long, with width up to twenty-five miles over much of its length, its longitudinal axis roughly paralleling that of the chain itself. In common with the other larger Solomons, it possessed a backbone of high, rugged mountains—but with a notable difference. Whereas on the southern shore the mountains dropped sharply to the sea, to the north, save for the northwestern area, they gave way to foothills which in turn flattened out to a comparatively level coastal plain which reached a depth of eight miles in some places.

This was practical terrain for the construction of airfields. Furthermore, it was more open than is usually the case with tropic islands. The jungle was dominant, being thickest and most continuous along the courses of the numerous rivers which drained the region. Elsewhere it was frequently broken by glades and prairies. Much of the shore line was taken up with the evenly spaced palms of extensive coconut plantations. Inland, the plain was checkered with open patches grown to coarse kunai grass, often six to seven feet tall.

These general features were known, but that was about

all. No reliable maps could be located. Aerial surveys showed the outline of the coast and location of possible landing beaches, but little else in the inland tangle of jungle and kunai grass. And time was desperately short, because it was imperative that we strike before the enemy aircraft could begin using the new field.

A few New Zealanders were found who had visited one part or another of the Solomons, or had worked in the coconut plantations or missions there. Colonel Goettge, Division Intelligence Officer (D-2), flew to Australia to solicit the services of others with similar knowledge. Little information of value was obtained, but several men with some firsthand knowledge of the area volunteered to accompany the expedition. This would be all we would have to go on until contact could be made ashore with Captain Clemens and his friendly natives.[1]

The Division was far from complete as a unit. Earlier in the year one of the infantry regiments, the 7th Marines,[2]

[1] Captain Clemens entered the Marine lines a week after the landing, as soon as convinced that this was not a hit-and-run raid. Like the proverbial Englishman-in-the-tropics, he emerged from the jungle immaculately clad and accompanied by his retinue. Among his followers was a remarkable native, Sergeant Major Vouza, recently retired from the local constabulary, whose subsequent yeoman service was to win him high decorations from both Britain and the United States.

[2] In the Marine Corps, regiments are designated by the term "Marines" following the regimental number, as above. Infantry regiments are numbered 1 through 9 and 21 through 29; artillery regiments 10 through 15; engineer regiments 16 through 20. Army regiments are numbered and designated by branch of service, i.e., 9th Infantry, 25th Field Artillery, 5th Engineers, etc. A common mistake even among well-informed newspapermen was to refer to the Fifth Marine Division, for example, as the 5th Marines. This led to some unfortunate misunderstandings, as at Iwo Jima where a dispatch about the heavy casualties being suffered by the "Fifth Marines" scared the daylights out of relatives of men in the 5th Marines (regiment) which happened to be some two thousand miles from Iwo at the time.

with reinforcing elements, had been detached to strengthen the defense of Samoa, where they were still in garrison. To make up the deficiency, the 2nd Marines, of the Second Division, were temporarily attached, together with the 1st Raider Battalion, 1st Parachute Battalion (minus parachutes), and 3rd Defense Battalion, the composite being designated First Marine Division, Reinforced.

The two convoys carrying the several elements rendezvoused near the Fijis. Off the island of Koro it was planned to hold a dummy run (rehearsal for the coming operation). Again the business was fouled up. The new elements had not been fully integrated into the Division as a whole. Control facilities proved inadequate for an operation of such magnitude. Landing boats milled around aimlessly trying to find the line of departure or figure out what they were supposed to do. When the first wave was finally formed and rushed shoreward, many landing boats piled up on the fringing reef hundreds of yards from dry land, while others barely managed to swerve away. None of them ever did get to shore.

Again, the First Division had done things the hard way. And, again, events were to prove that their efforts had not been wasted.

From there on in, the Division's luck seemed to change. The sea was calm, the weather hazy for the most part. The last two days were overcast, with a low ceiling which hid the convoy from aerial observation. Unmolested, apparently unobserved, the transports and their naval covering force rounded the northwestern end of Guadalcanal during the night of 6/7 August at 0310. Here the convoy separated into two parts for the two primary missions of the operation. The northern force passed to the north of Savo Island and headed for Tulagi Harbor. The main force slipped silently, darkly, between Savo and Guadalcanal, moving to the southeast. Not a sound broke the night stillness, and dawn commenced breaking with tropical placidity.

Then, at 0614, there came a thundering unfamiliar to these parts, and great tongues of crimson and orange flame lit the graying sea. . . .

The beaches selected for the Guadalcanal landing were situated about three miles east of the nearly completed airfield, primary objective of the operation. They were fine wide beaches, backed by the evenly spaced trees of a big coconut plantation. The day was clear and calm, the surf running low. Not a shot sounded from the island as the assault waves swept shoreward. Here began the legend of "First Division landing-luck," which was to endure to a bloody termination on the beaches of Peleliu, more than two years later.

The naval covering force and carrier-based aircraft had given the beaches a quick going over and had thoroughly plastered the airfield area, where aerial reconnaissance and such meager intelligence as had been obtained indicated the Japanese were concentrated. In contrast to the fiasco off the Fijis—and mainly because of it—the assault waves formed with quiet efficiency, crossed the line of departure on schedule and moved in to hit the beach at 0910. While units assembled and moved inland to predetermined phase lines, the Higgins boats returned to the transport area for more troops and for supplies which had been so painfully combat-loaded for the occasion. All was quiet, and it was a fine war, that clear morning of 7 August. Later waves, rushing ashore with high consciousness of history in the making, found members of the waves which had preceded them eagerly trying to hack open coconuts with machetes and bayonets.

The initial assault troops consisted of two battalions of the 5th Marines which landed abreast, the 1st Battalion (1/5) [3] on the right, the 3rd Battalion (3/5) on the left. Their mission was to set up a perimeter defense some distance inland which would secure the beach against counterattack, thus covering further troop landings and obtain-

[3] This form of designating battalions of regiments is standard in reports from the field and is used here for economy and convenience. Thus, 1/5 without further designation was 1st Battalion, 5th Marines. There were three battalions to a regiment, each consisting of four companies, lettered "A" through "M." This number was later reduced to three.

ing dispersal areas for the supplies to be brought ashore. The 1st Marines began landing in column of battalions at 1100 and advanced immediately inland through the perimeter in a generally westerly direction. 1/5 thereupon moved up on their right, following the shore in the direction of Lunga Point, leaving beachhead security to 3/5.

Once through the coconut grove, they met the jungle. The time would come when these Marines would be as much at home in the jungle as any fighters in the world; when, upon rare occasions, they would find it a friend. But that time was in the future. On this, their first meeting, it was an enemy, enigmatic and implacable, which impeded their progress, caused units to lose contact and direction, and filled them with a hundred unnamed fears as night closed in.

The jungle of the Solomons is the type known as "rain forest," indigenous to the larger islands of that general area of the Pacific, notably New Guinea and the Bismarck Archipelago. It is characterized by giant hardwoods, which tower well over a hundred feet into the sky, with boles six and eight feet in diameter, flared out at the base by great buttress roots. Among and beneath the trees thrives a fantastic tangle of vines, creepers, ferns and brush, impenetrable even to the eye for more than a few feet. Exotic birds inhabit its upper regions; the insect world permeates the whole in extraordinary sizes and varieties: ants whose bite feels like a live cigarette against the flesh, improbable spiders, wasps three inches long, scorpions and centipedes. The animal kingdom is less numerous, represented by species of rats, some distant relatives of the possum, lizards ranging in length from three inches to three feet, a few snakes mostly of the constrictor type, and some voracious leeches peculiar in that they live in trees and drop upon the unwary passer-by from above.

No air stirs here, and the hot humidity is beyond the imagining of anyone who has not lived in it. Rot lies everywhere just under the exotic lushness. The ground is porous with decaying vegetation, emitting a sour, unpleasant odor. Substantial-looking trees, rotten to the core, are likely to topple over when leaned against, and great forest giants crash down unpredictably in every windstorm. Freshly killed flesh begins to decompose in a matter of a few hours. Dampness, thick and heavy, is everywhere, result of the rains which give the forest its name; unbelievably torrential in season, never ceasing altogether for more than a few days at a time. Mosquitoes, bearers of malaria, dengue and a dozen lesser-known fevers, inhabit the broad, deep swamps which are drained inadequately by sluggish rivers where dwell giant crocodiles, the most deadly creature of this particular region.

Through this steaming wonderland, Marines of the First Division moved toward the airfield, hacking their way through the undergrowth, bogging down in swamps, fording sluggish streams, struggling through occasional "open" patches of tough kunai grass higher than a man's head. Units lost contact and alignment, wandered about aimlessly, wondering where they were. Men shouted and cursed and fired at shadows and generally created sufficient din to reveal their positions to anyone within hundreds of yards. Later, jungle-hardened officers and men alike looked back with horror at this amateurish advance. A wily and determined enemy, familiar with the ground, might have wiped out great segments of the force in detail.

But there was no determined opposition; only a few scattered snipers. Progress was euphemistically described as "satisfactory," and advanced units set up perimeter defenses for the night.

The 1st Marines reached the airfield late on the second day (D+1), the 5th continuing along the shore to Kukum, a native village beyond the mouth of the Lunga. The Japanese bivouac areas showed every sign of having been precipitately abandoned. Many of the enemy had been cooking their breakfasts when the bombardment had struck, and their pots still hung over dead fires. Damage was surprisingly light. Later intelligence disclosed that the defenders had orders to take to the hills in case of attack, but this would not account for their failure to destroy the large stocks of food and building materials which were shortly to prove a boon to the captors, or the fine refrigerating and generating plants which were captured intact. All in all, the Guadalcanal attack can be rated as one of the greatest strategic and tactical surprises achieved in this or any other war.

Meanwhile, matters on the beach were anything but "satisfactory." The dummy run off Koro which had ironed out the worst difficulties in landing procedure had never reached the beach; hence, there had been no rehearsal for the shore party. Both planning and personnel proved wholly inadequate to cope with the flood of supplies which poured ashore in the wake of the troops. As big tank lighters and ramp boats brought in the artillery, rolling stock and other heavy equipment, the scene on the beach passed through confusion to chaos.

As anticipated, the enemy's reaction was prompt and violent. The first air alert sounded about 1300 on D-Day, practically par for the Japanese getting a flight down from Rabaul after receipt of the alarm. Fighter-escorted bombers swept in fearlessly through a sky blossoming with flak air bursts—and proceeded to ignore their main chance with a shortsightedness which seemed incredible at the time, and still does. Perhaps they were acting under orders; perhaps the temptation was simply too great to resist. Whichever the case, this flight and those that followed concentrated entirely on the convoy, ignoring the supplies piled all over the beach in plain sight. Had those supplies been destroyed or even seriously damaged, the expedition would have been doomed at a single stroke, as events were to prove. As it was, all the Japanese accomplished was to inflict minor damage on the shipping, including one destroyer. A heavier raid[4] the following day caused a few casualties and set fire to the transport *George F. Elliott* which burned brightly all night before sinking with a large quantity of much needed supplies.

But that we could still outblunder the Japanese at this stage of the war was soon to be demonstrated. Early the following morning (0200, 9 August) disaster struck.

[4] Coastwatchers on Bougainville radioed the word as soon as this flight passed over, thus furnishing the first concrete example U.S. troops were to have of the value of these gentry.

Throughout the day air reconnaissance had reported enemy naval units lurking to the west and northwest within striking distance of Guadalcanal. About dusk a delayed report came from a Coastwatcher of a heavy cruiser task force on the move. In order to screen the vulnerable transports, two cruiser-destroyer groups, including both Australian and U. S. ships, were posted on either side of small Savo Island, in the channel between the northwestern tip of Guadalcanal and Florida, to intercept any Japanese coming down the Slot from the direction of their bases.

How the enemy were able to elude the alertness of a force posted specially in expectation of their arrival has never been entirely explained. But approach they did, undetected. The first intimation of their presence to the men aboard the loafing ships came when they were suddenly blasted at point-blank range by the big guns of what were apparently a number of heavy cruisers. Wholly unprepared, silhouetted by flares and the light from the burning transport *Elliott*, our ships were so many sitting ducks. In approximately thirteen minutes from the opening salvo, the heavy cruisers *U.S.S. Astoria, Quincy* and *Vincennes* and *H.M.A.S. Canberra* were either sunk or sinking, and *U.S.S. Chicago* severely damaged.

Whereupon the Japanese, with that curious knack for losing opportunities which they were to display so often, hurried back the way they had come without entering the transport area where their attentions might well have been catastrophic.[5]

As events proved, this would be the most brilliant and effective naval victory the enemy would achieve in the whole course of the war. But there was no way of knowing that at the time. The Savo Island action had to be taken as a routine demonstration of the efficiency of Japanese

[5] Long after the event, it was learned that a lucky shell from one of our dying cruisers struck the Japanese admiral's control room, destroying his charts and evidently giving him the jitters. This, together with fear of being caught in daylight by our aircraft, caused him to turn back without attacking the transports, as he had orders to do.

sea power, and viewed in that light the U.S. Navy faced a grim prospect indeed.

When dawn came the transports began weighing anchor. With what remained of their convoying warships in attendance, they silently stole away to the south, and by evening the Marines were on their way. Very, very much on their own.

The reasons behind this unexpected move were not clear at the time. It was only natural to associate it with the Savo debacle and conclude that the Navy had simply taken to its heels in panic, an impression which caused much bitter criticism and hard feeling. Actually, Admiral Turner had notified General Vandegrift of the proposed move more than three hours before anyone had any inkling that the Japanese were going to strike. The more rational explanation is that the planes of the carrier task force had suffered considerable casualties and were running out of fuel, and it was deemed inadvisable to leave the helpless transports in so dangerous a region without air cover.

Anyway, go they did, taking with them more than half of the cargoes—inadequate to begin with—which they had not had time to unload. All that the Marines ashore had to sustain them during the month to elapse before another convoy arrived was that piled-up litter on the beach which the enemy aviators had not bothered to destroy: that and the supply of rice and fish heads which the hurriedly departing Japanese had considerately left in their bivouac area.

The Marines, of course, could not foresee all this at the time. Most of them did not even know what had happened off Savo Island; they had heard the guns and some had seen the flashes, but so sanguine had their own experience made them it never occurred to most of them that we could have suffered a serious setback. Nor did they realize the full significance of the convoy's departure.

With the men and supplies available, it was obviously impossible to attempt any extensive mopping up of enemy remnants in this unfamiliar territory and still insure the safety of the important ground already taken. Indeed, there were not enough men to form a continuous perimeter cordon at a safe distance around Henderson Field, as the Marines had named the captured airdrome.[6] A defense system was set up with flanks resting on the sluggish Tenaru River to the east and a grassy ridge two miles short of the Matanikau to the west.

Patrols exploring the near-by territory encountered enough opposition to show definitely that there were Japanese fighting men on the island and that they were organizing, mainly to the northwest, farther along the coast. But the men in the ranks were not greatly concerned. Even as the rate of enemy air attack stepped up and increasing patrol activity was encountered along the perimeter, they were more uncomfortable than worried.

Hadn't they accomplished their primary mission as Marines? They had seized and secured an excellent beachhead and a strategic airfield; from here on, the job was the Army's. It was just a case of holding until the Army relieved them, then all hands would go back to New Zealand, about which fabulous stories had already grown up. How long would that be? Scuttlebutt said three weeks, maybe four. . . .

Actually there were no really heavy air attacks during the first two weeks on Guadalcanal; not heavy, that is, judged by the standard of what was to come. But there were repeated small raids: six or seven bombers cruising the field at leisure and unloading just about as they pleased. That was the aggravating part of it: the lack of opposition. The air strip had been completed within the first few days, and a PBY had landed as early as 12 August; yet no fighter protection arrived during those two weeks. AA guns of the 3rd Defense Battalion brought down an occasional raider,

[6] Named after Major Loften R. Henderson, Marine flier killed at Battle of Midway. As planned by the Japanese, the original landing strip was 3,778 feet long by 160 feet wide. At the time of its capture, it had been completely graded and all but 197 feet surfaced with coral, clay, gravel and dry cement.

but were inadequate for complete protection and altogether lacking in camouflage netting, one of the many items which turned out not to have been unloaded from the hurriedly departing transports.

And there were various minor nuisances. A carrier-based Japanese fighter plane known as "Louie the Louse" came by occasionally to drop light bombs or flares over the airfield. The latter usually signalized naval action coming up, whereupon Louie would hang around and call the shots for his friends. More persistent was "Washing Machine Charlie," a big twin-engine flying boat, so nicknamed because of the irregular sound of its unsynchronized motors. Charlie had great staying power and would cruise up and down over the Marine positions most of the night, dropping bombs at intervals just to make sleep difficult and wear down the nerves. A submarine (or submarines) called "Oscar" loafed around offshore, surfacing now and again to observe the situation and throw a few rounds into the area or at the slow Higgins boats which were all the water transportation our people had at this stage. Japanese destroyers moved about as they pleased, shelling our installations when the spirit moved them and, it was rumored, landing troops beyond our perimeter. So long as they stayed out of range of our half-track 75's, they were as safe as though in their home waters; coast defense guns were another of the many items which had failed to come ashore. The implications of this complete air and sea superiority did nothing to raise the Marines' morale.

The enemy on shore also proved more of a nuisance than a menace during this period. After the first few days, increasing numbers of sad-looking characters began slinking out of the bush and giving themselves up in hopes of getting something to eat for a change. But as we soon found out, these were not soldiers, but laborers; most of them not even Japanese, but Koreans. The men christened them "termites." They showed no compunctions against telling all they knew of the enemy's strength and dispositions; but they didn't know much, having been kept in a condition of virtual slavery by the military, who had abandoned them to their own devices once the shooting had started.

From what our Intelligence could piece together, there had been about two thousand of these people on the island when we had landed, guarded and supervised by some six hundred troops: naval personnel and members of the Special Landing Forces, the Japanese equivalent of our own Marines. This force had evidently regained some semblance of cohesion following their inglorious flight on D-Day, and indications were that their point of assembly was Matanikau village, just beyond the mouth of the river of that name, some three miles west of our perimeter.

One of this group was finally wounded and captured. From him it was learned that his companions were running short of supplies and that some of them might be inclined to surrender. At least, this was what some of his interrogators believed they learned. On the whole, the prisoner was sullen and unco-operative, not one to inspire any great degree of confidence. At this time there was much we did not know about Japanese psychology, and our technique of prisoner interrogation was still rudimentary.

On the basis of this dubious information, Colonel Frank B. Goettge, Division Intelligence Officer (D-2), determined to lead a patrol into the Matanikau region. The project did not arouse much enthusiasm in other quarters, but Colonel Goettge was insistent. "The way to get intelligence about the enemy is to go where the enemy is," he declared.

And go he did, taking a patrol of twenty-one enlisted men and four officers, including a surgeon and an interpreter. The now terrified prisoner was also brought along.

The party set out in a Higgins boat late on the evening of 12 August and proceeded down the coast beyond Point Cruz. Some time was wasted as they cruised about offshore while the prisoner tried to pick a likely spot to land. Whether he deliberately led them into ambush is problematical; the din of the boat's motor was quite sufficient to alert all the Japanese in the neighborhood. In any event, they had scarcely moved inland from the beach when they were greeted by a withering fire. Colonel Goettge and the prisoner, in the lead, were killed, apparently instantly, and the rest of the patrol pinned down on the beach.

A desperate fire fight lasted through the rest of the night. The Marines, fighting in strange territory in total darkness, did not have a chance. The captain who succeeded to the command dispatched a sergeant in an effort to get through to the perimeter and bring help. The sergeant drew fire some distance down the beach, and, fearing he had been killed, the captain sent a corporal on a similar mission. Actually both men got through safely but not in time to save the doomed patrol. Only one other survived: just before dawn a sergeant, the only one remaining who was not too badly wounded to swim, plunged into the sea, by-passed the Jap-held territory and finally reached the small naval operating base at Kukum. With the coming of daylight, the Japanese closed on the helpless survivors on the beach and massacred them all.

The fate of the Goettge patrol resulted in the first really earnest efforts to wipe out the troublesome pocket of the enemy. Three company-strength patrols of the 5th Marines moved into the region immediately west of the Matanikau. Two native villages were cleared out and a number of Japanese killed in a series of skirmishes, but final results were inconclusive. Veteran jungle fighters, with the great advantage of knowing the terrain intimately, the enemy's major parties were able to slip away from any enveloping movement we tried to throw about them.

Our greatest difficulty was the lack of men to do the job as it needed doing. The object of the campaign had been to seize and hold the airfield. The area included was sufficiently large to stretch the perimeter defense dangerously thin. To draw men in any number from this line might well be fatal to the safety of the field, and the mobile reserve was absurdly small for a mission of these proportions.

The entire Marine force on the island at this time included only two infantry regiments with their reinforcing elements. The Raider Battalion, Parachute Battalion and most of the 2nd Marines were still in the Tulagi area. The 7th Marines, one of the Division's original components, was still on garrison duty in Samoa. General Vandegrift had requested urgently that it be brought to the scene as soon as possible. Until it arrived, however, his scope of offensive action was strictly limited. He and his staff had to strike a delicate balance of safety factors against the urgency of the situation practically every time a combat patrol was organized.

With these inadequate means, he was still trying to eliminate the enemy to the west, when, to the east, the enemy struck what was to prove his first major blow.

This fell on the night of 20/21 August. Only the previous afternoon, the first squadron of Marine fighter planes had, at long last, established themselves on Henderson Field. They were to prove their usefulness sooner, perhaps, than even the most optimistic had expected.

There were many features connected with the so-called Battle of the Tenaru[7] which were puzzling to people as slightly acquainted with Japanese military psychology as were our officers at that early stage. They learned much during that night and the day that followed, but much that they learned remains inexplicable to the American mind to this day.

What, for instance, could the enemy reasonably hope to accomplish by attacking two reinforced regiments with a mere twelve hundred men? True, they could throw an overwhelming weight of numbers against any point of the thinly held perimeter line they might select; yet that force amounted to a small fraction of the strength we could muster against them once the breakthrough was made (if it were made) and we were able to concentrate. They could hardly have expected to drive us into the sea, or even to hold the airfield permanently—provided they ever got to the field. They could not have been planning destruction of our planes because, when their plans were made, we had no planes on the island; the first ones arrived by pure chance only after the Japanese were moving into position for the attack.

[7] Really the Ilu. A former resident, accompanying our troops, mistakenly transposed the names of these two rivers, and they were carried thus on our makeshift maps for some months. They are used here as they were during the campaign.

Perhaps they grossly underestimated our numbers; there were plenty of instances later to demonstrate the faulty functioning of enemy combat intelligence. Perhaps they took their own propaganda too literally and honestly believed themselves supermen, each worth easily ten of us decadent democrats. Whatever went on in their oriental minds, the net result was that twelve hundred first-class Japanese fighting men became unavailable for more important operations to come where their strength might conceivably have proved an important factor.

They not only failed to get to the airfield; they failed even to break through the thin perimeter. In fact, they didn't even come close.

This force had been landed within the past few days, apparently from destroyers, some distance to the east of our positions. We had had some intimations of such an event, but the lack of air observation had prevented us from verifying it or estimating the numbers involved. The enemy was commanded by one Colonel Ichiki.

On the nineteenth a Marine patrol in the Koli Point region had surprised and annihilated an enemy patrol which was obviously the advance party of a much larger force. The dead were found to be clean, well dressed and splendidly equipped, obviously new to the island.[8] Very evidently, something was cooking. A few strands of barbed wire were strung in front of our most exposed positions; wire salvaged from an old plantation fence, since our own wire was another of the necessities which had failed to come ashore in sufficient quantity before the flight of the transports. All hands were exhorted to remain especially alert.

These precautions paid off richly. The Japanese did not bother to bring up artillery. They did not call for a preliminary fire mission from their ships, which had been able to shell us with complete impunity for the past two weeks.

[8] Later one of the few prisoners taken declared, perhaps with tongue in cheek, that not only had he never heard of Guadalcanal but thought they were attacking Catalina Island off the California coast.

Relying entirely on surprise, they moved as silently as possible from their assembly area to the east bank of the Tenaru, then suddenly hurled an overwhelming force of infantry across the sand spit that completely blocks the mouth of that sluggish river at this season.

The alert Marines opened up with everything they had. The carnage on that narrow spit was ghastly. But the impetus of their rush carried the Japanese forward over their own dead and dying. Until they hit the newly installed wire. This seemed to take them completely by surprise, though a few actually got into Marine foxholes; the rest milled around in bewilderment. High-pitched screams of pain, fury, frustration rose above the raving of the automatic weapons which were piling up their dead.

It was hot work for many minutes for the handful of Marines at the point of contact. Japanese grenades reached the nearer foxholes, and men were killed and wounded there. Then the crazy tide receded, leaving its broken debris strewn across the sand spit.

The enemy attacked again and again, both across the spit and at other points just inland from the river's mouth. A hardy handful succeeded in reaching the western bank a couple of hundred yards farther inland, only to be pinned down there and eliminated at leisure when daylight came. A few managed to get around the wire and, creeping along the reverse slope of the beach, attempted unsuccessfully to infiltrate our shore positions. That was all.

The sector where the assault struck was manned by elements of the 2nd Battalion, 1st Marines, plus two platoons of the Special Weapons Battalion, operationally attached to that regiment. It was commanded by Lieutenant Colonel E. A. Pollock, battalion CO. He proceeded as quickly as possible to where things were hottest and took the situation in hand personally. By skillful employment of his few reserves, he had the position greatly strengthened by the time dawn came.

With the new day, Colonel Ichiki contributed another Japanese tactical gem to the general confusion. Instead of drawing off his battered force while he still had time, he chose to dig in among the widely spaced trees of the coconut plantation on a narrow point at the mouth of the river, and opened a fire fight with the Marines on the opposite bank. The Japanese used mortar and small-arms fire; the Marines replied in kind, with the addition of artillery and strafing attacks by the newly arrived planes. It was an absurdly unequal contest from the outset.

Having failed to break through a thinly held line in the darkness, did Ichiki really believe he had a chance of doing so in broad daylight, with the entire Division alerted? It was all quite incomprehensible to the occidental mind. Some officers clung to the belief that he was acting as spearhead for a more powerful force, or at least staging a feint to cover a major attack on some other sector. But when scouting planes failed to detect troop movements elsewhere, all hands decided that theirs was not to reason why. If this strange character wanted to encompass his own destruction, far be it from us to disoblige him.

The 1st Battalion, 1st Marines, currently in Division reserve, was brought up from its bivouac in the Lunga area. The men forded the Tenaru more than a mile above its mouth, deployed to cut off retreat inland or toward the east, and moved slowly through the jungle toward the coconut grove on the point. Downriver the unequal fire fight continued. Some Japanese, frantic with shell shock or terror, plunged into the ocean and tried to swim away. Marine veterans of a dozen rifle ranges happily lined the sights of their 03's upon the futilely bobbing heads.

On the east bank an increasing volume of small-arms fire could be heard as 1/1 closed in inexorably. About three o'clock five light tanks ambled across the corpse-strewn sand spit and into the grove, maneuvering easily among the well-spaced trees. Then 1/1 debouched from the jungle, and the final trap was sprung. Colonel Ichiki wrote "finis" to his peculiar campaign by burning the regimental colors and shooting himself through the head.

Nothing remained now but to bury the dead. With rare consideration, many of the Japanese supplied their own shovels, another of the many implements of which the Marines stood in sore need.

The first flight of Marine planes which moved in to base on Henderson Field on 20 August consisted of one fighter squadron and one dive bomber squadron: Captain John L. Smith's VMF-223 (19 Gruman Wildcats) and Major Richard C. Mangrum's VMSB-232 (12 Douglas Dauntlesses). None of the personnel had ever been in combat, but this was a deficiency which was remedied in short order. It so happened that their very timely arrival coincided with a marked stepping-up of Japanese activity in all departments. From the outset, the air force—these units and others which were to reinforce and relieve them from time to time—was employed as a tactical arm of the utmost importance. Never have two arms of any service worked in closer co-ordination than did the Marine Air and Ground Arms at Guadalcanal, and seldom have such efforts been so successful.

The Japanese had begun landing troops on the island in comparatively small contingents within the first few days of our occupation. Aside from the Ichiki detachment, their first—or first-known—attempt to bring in reinforcements on a large scale precipitated the Battle of the Eastern Solomons, 23-25 August. This occurred when a U.S. carrier task force intercepted an enemy convoy some distance short of Guadalcanal. The surface forces did not make contact; it was a case of planes vs. ships on both sides, with the dive bombers from Henderson Field flying missions in support of the Navy carrier-borne planes.

The result was not especially conclusive, and the enemy losses were never fully verified. They are believed to have been considerable. At any rate, for some time after this flight the Japanese showed a marked disinclination to risk their vulnerable heavy transports within range of our land-based bombers and resorted to other methods of piecemeal reinforcement of their garrison: bringing the troops down in smaller craft, traveling only by night along a chain of staging points on other islands; and carrying them as deck loads on destroyers and fast cruisers which could slip in under cover of darkness, unload, and be well out of the area before our planes could spot them in the morning.

Perhaps this was not the fastest way to build up a formidable attacking force, but obviously it was working after a fashion. There were increasing indications that another major assault to recapture the field was impending. If the Japanese had learned anything at all from the fate of the unlamented Colonel Ichiki, this one might really be serious. Marine combat patrols resumed their activities in the Matanikau-Kokumbona region in an effort to nip the threat in the bud, but with the resources at hand they were still unable to bring the enemy to decisive action.

The Japanese could land to the east of us or to the west, and all that made it impractical for them to land directly behind us, to the south, was the width of the island and the height and ruggedness of the mountains which formed its backbone. The same factors—jungle and lack of roads—which deterred the enemy from moving about freely, operated against us whenever we tried to get at them.

The air force was very useful in detecting these landings and helping to frustrate them, but the planes were helpless to a great extent in coping with the night sneaks. To handicap them still further, the Japanese began staging more frequent and heavier air attacks on Henderson Field. Life on Guadalcanal was becoming distinctly unpleasant.

Except for Colonel Ichiki's detachment the persistent landings of the Japanese had been concentrated to the northwest, where a force of formidable dimensions was being built up in the Tassafaronga-Kokumbona region. At 0200 on 2 September, however, a convoy was spotted unloading troops near Taivu Point, some miles to the east. When such activities were observed on several nights following, and ground patrols had verified them, it was decided to strike there by land.

This assignment was given to the Raider Battalion, newly arrived from Tulagi, with the Parachute Battalion in reserve. They embarked at Kukum on APD's[9] and landed under covering fire of the ships' guns early on the morning of 8 September. From here they moved against the rear of the main Japanese position, which had been located at Tasimboko village, not far to the west.

[9] Old destroyers converted into light transports.

There had been reports, subsequently verified, that the enemy force numbered up to five thousand. Yet all that the Raiders encountered was disorganized and unusually ineffectual resistance from what turned out to be a small rear echelon. In what had been the enemy bivouac area, supplies and equipment in considerable quantities were captured, together with six field guns. The main enemy forces had moved inland a day or two earlier, cutting a trail as they went, in a generally southwesterly direction.

The Raiders were to meet them a few nights later, however, when the whole howling mob boiled bloodily up out of the jungle to hurl themselves against the south-central sector of the airfield perimeter.

The enemy attack was planned with all the elaborate detail of which Japanese staffs are occasionally capable. It called for a co-ordinated three-pronged drive against the east, center and west sectors of the inland perimeter, supported by heavy air bombing by day and naval gunfire by night. In fact, it took practically everything into consideration—except the terrain in which it would have to be executed.

As a result of this omission, plus some hard fighting by us, the effort ended in as complete frustration as Colonel Ichiki's, and on a considerably larger scale. So difficult were communications in that country that the three assaults were poorly co-ordinated. The eastern force, after days of cutting trail and lugging gear through the dense jungle, arrived in position late and too exhausted to attack with determination. The western force did not attack at all until the main effort, in the center, had been completely defeated, and they were beaten off with comparative ease.

There was nothing easy about the fight in the center, however. This action, known as the Battle of the Ridge—sometimes called Bloody Ridge, Raiders' Ridge or Edson's Ridge—turned out to be one of the hottest things of its kind the campaign was to produce. It began in the evening of 12 September, accompanied by heavy naval shelling, and lasted with varying intensity all that night and the following day, not to be definitely decided until shortly before dawn on the morning of the fourteenth. The defense line was breached at several points, some units were temporarily cut off, and there was wholesale infiltration, one small group of Japanese even penetrating to the Division command post which had been placed dangerously far forward. At one stage, Colonel Edson found himself holding a particularly vital position with some three hundred men against an attacking force estimated at two battalions.

The Ridge extended about a thousand yards due south from a point about a mile beyond the airstrip, which it commanded. Its crest and upper slopes were open and grassy, but the lower slopes and the valleys which flanked them were densely jungled. The defense line ran across the ridge itself and down into the jungle on either side. The left was held by two attenuated companies of the Parachute Battalion, the right by "C" Company of the Raiders whose flank lay near the Lunga River.

The right bore the brunt of the first night's fighting and was forced back, necessitating a withdrawal all along the line in order to maintain contact. When daylight efforts on the thirteenth failed to drive the enemy from their newly won positions, Colonel Edson decided on a further strategic withdrawal. This shortened his lines to about 1,800 yards, but they were still dangerously thin and not so well integrated as would have been desirable, owing to the rugged terrain.

The second night's attack was concentrated mainly on the Ridge itself, where the Paramarines and Company "B" of the Raiders were now in position. The Japanese reached deeply into the bag of tricks with which we were to become increasingly familiar as the war progressed. They talked in loud voices when approaching in order to draw fire that would reveal our position prematurely. They spread a smoke screen and shouted, "Gas attack!" They shouted other things in English of varying quality: insults, threats, faked commands. They cut in on the wave length of the portable radios to issue confusing reports. They charged down the length of the Ridge and swarmed up out of the jungles that flanked it. They obliged Colonel Edson to rectify his lines again. At one crucial point he had only sixty men holding the Ridge proper. But they held it.

Action was intense from six in the evening until past midnight, with enemy cruisers and destroyers firing occasional missions on our positions as they had done the previous night. Our own artillery was in action on a large scale all night, firing with amazing speed and accuracy. Often the infantry of both sides were too intermingled in the viciousness of close combat for the fire of the 75's and 105's to be effective, but its end result was devastating. A lull in the fighting occurred during the early hours of the morning, broken by a large infiltration to the left rear. This, too, failed of accomplishment, and by 0500 there were unmistakable signs that the pressure was relaxing.

The reinforced defenders, attacking in their turn, succeeded in pushing the enemy back along the Ridge. Our planes, coming over to strafe at dawn, found a general retreat in progress toward the south and west. More than six hundred Japanese dead [10] were counted on the field of battle; how many were killed elsewhere or died during the retreat is problematical, though the number is known to be considerable.

The Japanese secondary attack to the east was delivered against elements of 3/1 holding a sector southeast of the airfield and a short distance west of the bank of the Tenaru. It began shortly after nine on the evening of the thirteenth with a fire fight, developed several assaults in considerable strength, and flickered intermittently all night. Our troops here were well dug in, behind wire, and the enemy was unable to penetrate anywhere. Throughout this engagement, their troops displayed a lack of spirit and determination remarkable for the Japanese at that time and place. It was not until later that we discovered that they were close to exhaustion before the assault even started. This futile gesture cost them about two hundred dead. Our losses were four dead, three wounded.

[10] Freshly killed Japanese turn a curious shade of lemon-yellow, the characteristic death pallor of their race. This does not last long, however; in the tropics decay sets in in a few hours.

The attack to the west did not even commence until late afternoon on the fourteenth, by which time the main enemy force was in full retreat. It struck a sector about midway between Kukum and the Matanikau, held by the 3rd Battalion of the 5th Marines. The Japanese charged in with the bayonet in broad daylight, one of the very few instances of daylight attacks in the entire campaign, and they were beaten back easily. Other sporadic attacks occurred during the day, uniformly futile.

What made the Guadalcanal campaign such a terrible experience for the personnel participating was the unending pressure to which all hands were subjected. There were no rest areas on the island, no recreation facilities; nowhere a man could go and nothing he could do to recuperate nerves rubbed raw by the strain of what amounted to perpetual combat. There was scarcely a day or night during the four months the First Marine Division was on Guadalcanal when they were not attacking or being attacked, by land, sea or air, and in many instances all three. Few troops in all the world's history have been subjected without relief to a pounding so intense and so sustained.

They had to do everything the hard way. Guadalcanal was a laboratory in which the techniques of future victories were developed by painful experimentation. We knew nothing of the Japanese except that up until now they had swept everything before them in this war. They were an oriental people; their tactics, psychology and battle ethics were utterly foreign to us. Our knowledge of the jungle and jungle fighting proved to be rudimentary. We lacked much in knowledge and in the means to cope with tropical diseases: malaria, dengue, scrub typhus, dysentery, the ever-present fungus infection familiarly known as "the crud."

Furthermore, the Marines who landed on Guadalcanal were essentially assault troops; their mission was to seize and secure a limited objective, then turn it over to troops better prepared to hold and exploit it. They were neither trained nor equipped for a protracted defensive action, and much of the equipment they had intended to bring ashore had been hauled away upon the premature departure of the first transport convoy. But the first Army troops did not arrive until mid-October: one regiment, that came as reinforcements, not relief.

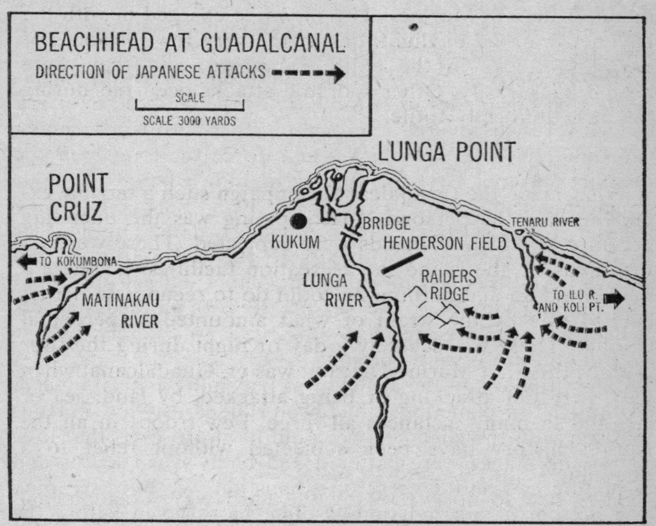

The complete domination of air and sea which the Japanese had enjoyed at the outset had been considerably diminished by the arrival of our planes at Henderson Field. The enemy could harass and retard, but not seriously check, the arrival of our supplies and reinforcements, and we could do just about the same to him. During the two weeks' lull that followed the Battle of the Ridge, nightly parades of warships and landing craft poured Japanese into the Tassafaronga area, to the northwest, while we in turn received an important reinforcement by the arrival, on 18 September, of the last remaining regular element of the First Division: the 7th Marines.

Inside the Marine perimeter tension was mounting, and no clairvoyant was needed to figure out the shape of things to come. The Japanese had begun stepping up the intensity of their air attack late in September, and the tempo continued to mount as October progressed. They were obviously trying to knock out Henderson Field and its planes in preparation for a major landing. They paid a staggering price in men and planes, but they came perilously close to succeeding. In a sense, they did succeed.

On 11 October so heavy and continuous were the air attacks that our planes were too busy or too battered to attack a task force discovered approaching early in the afternoon. Fortunately, our Navy had a task force of its own in the vicinity and took over the job that night in a fierce half-hour engagement off Cape Esperance. They sank one heavy cruiser, four destroyers and a transport, damaging another cruiser and destroyer, with loss to themselves of one destroyer. And the next morning our planes did get up, found the limping survivors and set fire to two more destroyers which were believed to have sunk.

But still more were coming.

The situation on the airfield was becoming critical indeed. Although our plane losses had been ridiculously low in comparison with the enemy's, we could ill afford even that loss. Surviving planes were battered and badly worn, pilots and ground crews on the verge of exhaustion. We were scraping the bottom of our aviation-gasoline barrel even before the thirteenth when two flights of enemy bombers caught our planes on the ground, set fire to one of our few remaining fuel dumps and made a shambles of the landing strip. Clearly a crisis was near. It came that night.

The Japanese heavy artillery had opened on the field early in the evening, and there had been repeated air alerts. Beyond the Matanikau, enemy ground troops were throwing up signal rockets. All hands were expecting a land attack. This never materialized, but it was about the only thing that didn't.

Later in the evening Condition Red sounded again. This time it was Louie the Louse. He dropped a flare over the airfield, and all hands dove for their dugouts. They knew the invariable signal for a naval bombardment. They had lived through many. But they had never lived through anything like that night and, praise God, would never have to again.

This time the Japanese had battleships. For an hour and twenty minutes they lay off Savo Island, pouring in a steady stream of twelve- and fourteen-inch shells. Cruisers added their sixes and eights. Destroyers swung in close with their fives, while bombing planes came over in relays and the heavy artillery ashore contributed its bit to the general chaos.

Of thirty-nine Marine dive bombers which had been operational the day before, only four were in condition to leave the ground in the morning—after the strip had been repaired sufficiently for them to take off.

Late that afternoon one of these hardy survivors, scouting between more air raids, discovered the enemy's main troop convoy coming down the Slot: seven large transports, escorted by destroyers. Meanwhile, ground crews had repaired nine more of the Dauntless dive bombers. These attacked as evening was drawing on, sinking one transport and damaging another. The five survivors plodded on and were soon lost in the closing night. Another naval shelling, lasting from 0105 to 0220, provided them further cover, and at dawn we needed no scouting planes to locate them: they were calmly discharging troops and cargo about fifteen miles up the coast to the west.

The night's bombing and shelling had left us only three bombers in operating condition, and so badly pitted was the runway that two of these were wrecked attempting to take off. The Wildcat fighters, which had been less hard hit, went at the transports with machine guns. More dive bombers were hurriedly put in shape. The Japanese responded with flights of Zeros, float planes, and a storm of AA from the screening warships. Before the day was over, we had thrown in everything we could glue together, including General Geiger's PBY (big, clumsy Catalina flying boat), which attacked successfully in the guise of a torpedo bomber. The Army sent over a flight of B-17 Flying Fortresses from their base at Espiritu Santo in the New Hebrides. 1100 that morning found one of the transports sunk, two beached and burning, the other two damaged and in flight.

But no doubt the Japanese considered them expendable. A large part, at least, of their mission had been accomplished.

It was during this hectic period that the first U.S. Army troops reached the island. If ever soldiers were pitchforked abruptly into battle, it was the men of the 164th Infantry. They landed under air attack on the thirteenth and reached their bivouac area just in time for the naval shelling that the Japanese dished out that night. They were to prove themselves one of the finest fighting units it has ever been the privilege of Marines to serve with. This was fortunate, for their mettle was to be tested in short order.

The Japanese attack which was now in the making was under the direction of Lieutenant General Hyakutake, Commanding General of the XVII Army, recently arrived from Rabaul to take personal charge. Essentially the attack was similar to the one which had failed at Bloody Ridge more than a month before. Hyakutake had fresher men and more of them, that was the main difference: a full division, heavily reinforced. It never seemed to occur to him that the basic tactics might be faulty. Or were these the only offensive tactics the Japanese knew? As the war progressed, we were to see them repeat previous mistakes time and time again.

Once more they moved deep into the jungle to the south, cutting trail and lugging gear. This time, at the cost of prodigious labor, they achieved a degree of tactical surprise: the trail went through so far below the perimeter that our patrols failed to discover it. We were expecting an attack from somewhere in the general direction of the Matanikau for obvious reasons, and we got it, though it proved only a single phase of the whole complicated operation. What prevented the troops to the south from effecting serious surprise was that all hands in our perimeter had been alerted for so long that they were prepared for practically anything, anywhere. That—plus the steadiness and determination of the Marines and soldiers who bore the brunt of the assault; plus, again, the same lack of co-ordination which had doomed the enemy's previous all-out effort.

Japanese patrol activity increased along the lower Matanikau on 20 October. During the following night, tanks could be heard moving up toward the west bank. Artillery chased them back, how far we did not know, and we took the hint to bring half-tracks and 37's into the area. To make their intentions even more evident, enemy planes came over at dusk and strafed our forward positions along the river. But nothing further developed that night or the next. The lone battalion which constituted our sole mobile reserve was not lured into that sector.

The Matanikau attack finally developed shortly after dark on the night of the twenty-third, with Hyakutake trying to throw two full infantry regiments against the narrow front held by 3/1. It was preceded by the closest equivalent of a barrage that the Japanese, with their odd ideas of using artillery, had yet put on. Then their tanks, which we had been hearing for some time, dashed out of the jungle and started for our positions. There were ten of them, in two waves: little 18-tonners, exceedingly vulnerable. The only practicable crossing was the sand spit at the river's mouth, narrow and without cover. Only one made it, overrunning a machine gun emplacement and several foxholes. A Marine, crouching in one of the latter, calmly slipped a hand grenade under one tread, crippling its steering mechanism. It reeled around into the surf where a half-track 75 destroyed it.

Meanwhile, the 11th Marines had opened up with the heaviest massed fire the campaign had produced to date, saturating the area. They had been registered on this particular target for weeks. The carnage was terrible. The Japanese infantry, which had been grouped to follow the tanks, never left the cover of the jungle, where they could be heard yelling and screaming. One column did attempt to force a crossing farther up but was easily repulsed. When our patrols explored the region a few days later, they counted some six hundred dead. Japanese reports captured subsequently indicated that two battalions of the 4th Imperial Infantry had been annihilated.

This abortive attack failed entirely of effect. Again that lack of co-ordination: the troops who were to stage the enemy drive from the south, which presumably was to be simultaneous, did not get into position until the following night, while a secondary blow evidently designed to distract us still further did not come off until the night following that.

The main attack from the south developed about midnight of 24/25 October, hitting a sector below and to the east of Bloody Ridge where the previous drive had been turned back. This was held by the 3rd Battalion, 164th Infantry, with the 1st Battalion, 7th Marines, tying in with their right. After ten days of being bombed, shelled and strafed, the soldiers were spoiling for a chance to fight back. They got it that night and handled it like veterans.

The Japanese attack followed the familiar pattern: a power thrust against a narrow front. Our artillery quickly zeroed-in on the ground it would have to cross, and pounded the enemy assembly area in depth. A torrential downfall of rain hampered both attackers and defenders. Men of the 2nd Battalion, 164th, posted in reserve, groped forward through the pitch darkness to reinforce their comrades. The position, well wired-in, stood firm as a rock. With the approach of dawn, the surviving Japanese fell back sullenly to regroup.

That day (25 October) became known to the battered defenders of Guadalcanal as "Dugout Sunday." Intense enemy air activity gave ample evidence that they considered the battle far from over despite the two bloody repulses they had already suffered. This air activity was unopposed at first, the rains of the night before having reduced the airfield to such a state that it was impossible for our fighters to take off. Japanese warships moved in with impunity to sink or chase away the few auxiliary vessels we had available, before turning their guns on the shore positions, the first occasion when they had approached so close during the daytime since arrival of our planes.

Prodigious work by Engineers and Seabees, however, finally got the field operational again despite hell and high water, bombs, shells and mud. And once our planes did get aloft, the toll was enormous. Fighters went after the enemy's Zeros and bombers, and presently the sky was full of falling aircraft—not ours. Dive bombers chased off the surface ships, sinking a cruiser and seriously damaging at least one other craft.

All these signs and portents were not lost on the men at the front, who spent the day repairing wire and generally improving their positions. Sure enough, with darkness the enemy to the south began to move again. This time their immediate objective was a little to the west of the previous night's attack: the sector held by 1/7, under Lieutenant Colonel Lewis B. Puller.[11]

The first assault hit the defenders' wire about 2200, and from then until after dawn the firing was almost incessant. It would rise to a furious crescendo as each successive onslaught reached its full height, then gradually taper off as the Japanese fell back to reorganize and work themselves up to the proper pitch for another try. The battle developed a rhythm of its own as the same thing happened time after time; a tempo you could almost set your watch by.

And the full force of the attack always struck in the same place, which made it very convenient for the strung-out defenders. Later Colonel Puller asked a captured Japanese sergeant why, after repeated repulses, they had not probed other parts of the line for weak spots, something they had proved quite adept at doing in some other instances. The Japanese shrugged. This particular attack, he explained, had been very thoroughly planned, and no unit would think of deviating from the letter of its orders. Here was another instance of that curious inflexibility of the Japanese military mind which we were to encounter so often.

By 0530 the following morning, Colonel Puller's command had withstood six separate assaults of undiminishing fury. Now a seventh, launched with final desperation,

[11] Much-decorated "Chesty" Puller has never been noted as one of the Marine Corps' least colorful characters. With seven assorted shell fragments in his anatomy, he submitted reluctantly to medical attention. The corpsman on the scene took one look and began writing out an evacuation tag. "Take that damned label and paste it on a bottle!" yelled the colonel furiously. "I remain in command here!"

achieved a small breakthrough; but even this was to be short lived. Before they could exploit their gain or even dig in to hold it, daylight came. Caught in a savage cross fire, the pocket became a deathtrap. Few, if any, of the enemy got back through that gap in our wire.

Once more the Japanese wave subsided into the jungle, beyond artillery and mortar range. After the toll exacted by these two nights of savage fighting, they were through as a major offensive force. And they had not come within a mile of the airfield they had set out to capture.

While the fighting just described had been in progress, during the early morning hours of 26 October, another enemy force launched a furious assault against the inland flank of the Matanikau sector, about four miles to the west. As a diversion, this came at least two days too late to have any effect. It was not organized in sufficient strength to constitute a major threat in itself, but it did provide plenty of trouble during the time it lasted.

Dawn showed 227 Japanese dead in, and immediately in front of, the position, with many more in the ravine below. By conservative estimate, the enemy had lost 3,400 killed during the entire three-way, three-day action.

The Matanikau ridge sector was not attacked again, but the next two days saw some further fighting south of the airfield. It was directed mainly against Colonel Puller's sector and the point where his flank joined that of the 164th. It never achieved the proportions of the first two nights and gradually diminished until it petered out into random sniping.

It was the Japanese who chose to make Guadalcanal a major issue. This was all to the good, as things turned out, but at the time we would have preferred to pay a minimum purchase price, had the choice been ours.

Perhaps they were motivated by that strange oriental fear of losing face. Perhaps, clinging to their singular conceptions of decadent democracies, they fully believed that a serious setback at this remote spot would convince our nation once and for all of the futility of attempting to compete with supermen. Whatever the reason, they threw at us everything that they had within reach, and that was a good deal. As someone expressed it, Guadalcanal became a sink-hole: a bottomless pit into which they poured ships and planes and men: ships and planes and men which would never be used against us elsewhere. Nowhere in the Pacific did they pay so high a price to lose a piece of real estate of comparable size and strategic importance.

Before the end of the campaign fifty thousand Japanese, by conservative estimate, had died either on Guadalcanal or on ships attempting to reach it. Dark rumors of the "Island of Death" seeped back to more remote posts of the Imperial Army, and more than a year later Radio Tokyo was still referring to the First Marine Division as "the Guadalcanal butchers."

The part played by the Navy air and surface forces in the campaign cannot be minimized. Without their daring and skillful efforts not even survival would have been possible, let alone victory. Already we have seen how, after the initial setback off Savo Island, they had turned the enemy back in the Battle of the Eastern Solomons on 23-25 August and off Cape Esperance 11 October. On 26 October, while the Marines ashore were still beating back the major Japanese threat, opposing carrier task forces were fighting the plane vs. ship Battle of Santa Cruz, seven hundred miles to the northeast, again inflicting losses that hurt. And our greatest and most decisive victory was yet to come.

But the troops ashore could not know this as that bloody October drew to a close. All they knew was they had smashed the enemy, that they were deathly tired from heavy fighting and months of bombing and shelling—and that, instead of getting the rest they had so well earned, they were moving out to attack once more.

The Japanese were coming again; coming in the greatest strength they had yet displayed. Several separate naval task forces were on the prowl. A transport convoy of twelve large ships lurked somewhere to the northwest, prepared to make the final dash. If their previous defeats had taught them anything, it was that they needed more of everything: more ships, more planes, more troops. This time they planned to land two reinforced divisions to join the battered, scattered survivors of earlier catastrophes.

But we had received some additional troops ourselves. The 8th Marines, Reinforced, a Second Division unit, had landed on 4 November, and much needed replacements arrived on the eleventh. By the twelfth, with the landing of two battalions of the 182nd Infantry, together with reinforcing elements, a large part of the Army's Americal Division was ashore. These included more artillery: 105's and big 155's. Air reinforcements had brought our strength on Henderson Field to five Marine squadrons, four Navy squadrons and one Army squadron. The ground forces shortened and strengthened their lines and waited confidently.

The Japanese employed the same tactics which had so nearly succeeded in mid-October: to neutralize Henderson Field by intensive air and naval attack in order to permit the vulnerable transports to come in unmolested by our air force. The intensity of their bombing attacks was stepped up sharply on 11 November and during the succeeding day. But now we had much greater strength with which to oppose them. Few of their bombers were able to get through to the field; those which were not shot down in the attempt wasted their ammunition in ineffectual attacks on the shipping which had brought in the reinforcements, still unloading offshore.

During the night of 12/13, a powerful Japanese task force closed in for the kill. About 0100 Louie the Louse flew over the field and dropped flares, the conventional signal that the shelling was about to begin. But at this juncture something occurred which seems to have been quite outside the enemy's expectations.

The transports which had brought in our reinforcements had been escorted by a small task force of cruisers and destroyers in two groups, under command of Rear Admiral Daniel J. Callaghan and Rear Admiral Norman Scott, respectively. As night drew on, Admiral Turner, in over-all command, had herded his transports out to sea and dispersed them in order to avoid the enemy force which was bearing down, turning his combat vessels over to Admiral

Callaghan. About the time Louie's flares were lighting up Henderson Field, this able officer hurled his force with stunning suddenness squarely into the enemy fleet northwest of Savo Island.

He was ridiculously outnumbered and outweighed. The enemy were moving in three parallel columns, and Callaghan led the American force straight down between them, blazing away to port and starboard with fine impartiality. Within fifteen minutes practically every U.S. ship had been damaged. In approximately half an hour the survivors had passed through the entire enemy fleet, whereupon they broke off the action and slipped away into the darkness, leaving the enemy milling about in too great confusion to shell anybody ashore, what remained of the several columns firing into each other long after their attackers had disappeared.

This was an exploit of which any Navy could be proud. But it was not achieved without cost. A shell struck the bridge of the flagship, *U.S.S. San Francisco,* instantly killing Admiral Callaghan and the ship's commander, Captain Cassin Young. Admiral Scott went down with his flagship, the light cruiser, *U.S.S. Atlanta,* another light cruiser and four destroyers were also lost, two cruisers and three destroyers badly damaged.

Japanese losses were one heavy cruiser, one light cruiser and one destroyer definitely sunk, and one battleship crippled. Two additional cruisers and at least three destroyers were left burning furiously and presumed sunk.

As usual when their preconceived plans were upset, the Japanese seemed incapable of adapting themselves to the altered situation. The bewildered task force limped off to the west to reorganize, their mission completely frustrated. Not a shell fell on Henderson Field that night. Our search planes, going up without hindrance the next morning, discovered the crippled battleship previously mentioned and summoned torpedo planes and dive bombers. These left her at dusk dead in the water and being abandoned by her crew; though they did not actually see her sink, next day only an oil slick remained where she had been.

The following night, however, a task force did get

through and shelled the field. Perhaps this was what remained of the same force, or perhaps another like it; so many enemy task forces were prowling the Solomons those days that it was hard to tell which was which. Again there was at least one battleship, plus cruisers and destroyers. Again the Japanese displayed that singular ineptness which characterized their operations throughout the Guadalcanal campaign. In October an intensive bombardment lasting an hour and twenty minutes had failed to knock out Henderson Field; now they shelled for only forty-five minutes and departed precipitately before the dire threat of a handful of PT boats which was all we could muster to throw against them.

One dive bomber and two fighters had been destroyed on the field. A few others had been damaged, none beyond prompt repair. There was no damage to the runway which could not be remedied in short order. The search planes were off with the dawn—and when they reported back, all hands knew that This Was It.

The Japanese transports were making their run for the island: twelve of them, crammed with troops and equipment, convoyed by five cruisers and six destroyers. Our air arm hit them with everything we had. Marine, Navy, Army: dive bombers, torpedo bombers, scout bombers, even B-17's; they attacked in swarms, in relays, shuttling from the scene of action back to Henderson Field to refuel and rearm, then back to the slaughter. They blasted everything that floated, concentrating on the transports. One after another sank or caught fire. Late afternoon found the survivors, abandoned by their protecting escort, still staggering forward.

Under cover of darkness, four of them actually made the run and beached near Tassafaronga. It was a brave but futile gesture. With the coming of daylight on 15 November, planes and long-range artillery destroyed them before they could unload. The number of bomb-happy soldiers who may have come ashore could not constitute more than a minor nuisance. The bulk of these two Japanese divisions had made their beachhead on the bottom of the Pacific.

But even as darkness was closing mercifully over the helpless transports, the Japanese Navy was rushing, hellbent, toward another major disaster. A strong task force was hastening down from the north, evidently intending to shell the airfield into helplessness in order to save the surviving troop ships. This included two battleships in addition to the usual heavy and light cruisers and destroyers. But coming up from the opposite direction were the two much more powerful U.S. battleships *South Dakota* and *Washington* escorted by four destroyers, under Rear Admiral Willis A. Lee.

The ensuing action did not last long. The Japanese lighter craft attempted to break through the thin destroyer screen in an effort to get at the big ships. They succeeded in sinking three of the destroyers, but that was all the good it did them. While the remaining destroyer was picking up the survivors from her sisters, the battlewagons opened up with radar-directed fire from their 16-inch guns. In the roaring half-hour before the enemy scattered and fled ignominiously the Japanese lost one battleship, three heavy cruisers and a destroyer sunk; another battleship, cruiser and destroyer, heavily damaged.

These three days of diverse but almost continuous action became known as the Naval Battle of Guadalcanal. Its effect on the Japanese was crippling; temporarily, at any rate: it left them without the ships to send more troops in to Guadalcanal, even if they had the troops to send after the terrible losses they had sustained in these attempts.[12]

And without these troops, Japanese offensive operations

[12] There were anxious days in the United States before this denouement became known. Certain of those self-appointed oracles, the news commentators, began writing off the whole Guadalcanal operation, to the great dismay of relatives of the men fighting there. The Navy, they declared, was unable either to reinforce or to evacuate the Marines ashore and had decided to abandon them to their fate rather than lose more lives and ships trying. A short-wave broadcast to this effect was picked up on the island where it caused much surprise and indignation. Apparently about the only people who refused to believe that the First Marine Division was licked were the men of the First Marine Division.

on the island itself came necessarily to a standstill. The decisive phase of the Guadalcanal campaign had closed.

As far as Guadalcanal was concerned, the First Marine Division was through to all intents and purposes as November drew to a close. For four months they had fought in one of the foulest climates on earth; had been bombed, shelled and shot at between periods of actual fighting. Now, as American troops continued to pour in, and Japanese troops were unable to reach the island, it was possible to start relieving these units on the lines. Soon they would be able to leave the island altogether. It seemed an age ago that they had arrived, expecting a stay of three to four weeks. . . .

Among the newly arrived troops was one especially spectacular unit, commanded by a spectacular man: the 2nd Marine Raider Battalion, under Lieutenant Colonel Evans F. Carlson. These were the people who had made the hit-and-run attack on Makin in mid-August, landing from submarines. At Guadalcanal they wrote another brilliant entry in their, and their leader's, record.

All of the Raider battalions were specially picked, specially trained. By nature, they were light, swift-moving, hard-hitting troops, mentally alert and physically hardy. Much was expected of them in training and in combat, and in recompense they were accorded certain special privileges in camp. This occasionally irked the line troops beside whom they did most of their fighting, since occasions for the employment of their specialty were comparatively rare. But when such occasions did arise, the Raiders were magnificent.

Carlson's battalion had landed at Aola early in November. Immediately they set out in pursuit of those Japanese who had fled into the interior.

What followed was a month of strenuous campaigning, covering some of the most difficult terrain on the island. Relentlessly the Raiders tracked down the Japanese they were pursuing. Their course carried them farther inland than Marines had ever been. Here they encountered groups of stragglers, flotsam and jetsam of the many columns which had beaten their brains out against the Marine defense.

Swinging far south of the perimeter, they came upon the trail cut by the Japanese for their ill-fated October assault. Here they found well-organized detachments of the enemy occupying well-stocked bivouac areas. Moving with incredible speed for that type of country, striking with stunning surprise and annihilating power, the Raiders cleared out all the territory below the airfield position for a depth of many miles in every direction.

When they entered the perimeter on 4 December, they had destroyed more than four hundred Japanese troops in twelve separate engagements, with a total loss to themselves of seventeen killed.

Following the enemy's crushing naval defeat, the nature of ground operations underwent a marked change. This did not become apparent immediately. For nearly a month our activities were confined mainly to patrolling, punctuated by infrequent clashes with an enemy who, unable to attack, appeared to have withdrawn a considerable distance from our lines.

Within the perimeter, there was a wholesale realignment of units. The First Marine Division completed evacuation on 9 December.

On this date Major General Vandegrift turned over command to Major General Alexander Patch, USA, Commanding General of the Americal Division. This unit was at full strength now, following the arrival of the 132nd Infantry, and more troops of the XIV Corps were pouring in. With the Japanese clearly incapable of attacking, General Patch judged the time ripe to inaugurate the offensive which was destined to drive them forever from the island.

It proved painfully slow going. As became evident, the Japanese, abandoning hope of resuming the attack with the resources at hand, had utilized the breathing spell to dig in defensively. They attempted to establish no continuous lines of resistance, no organized defense in depth; instead, they prepared isolated strong points to take full advantage of the rugged, jungled ground: in ravines, on reverse slopes, in other areas in defilade from our artillery fire where often a single machine gun nest could pin down an entire battalion. The consummate skill of the Japanese in the utilization of terrain and camouflage, which was to feature all Pacific campaigns, now came conspicuously to the fore.

And with it went that dogged persistence which caused men, without hope of escape or of gaining anything more than a little time, to fight grimly to the death. With equal grimness the Marines and soldiers learned to contain the pockets of resistance and push on, leaving them for the reserve troops to clean out at leisure.

The Army's Twenty-fifth Infantry Division arrived in mid-January. Expecting that the enemy was planning a last desperate stand in prepared positions in the high, rugged ground of Cape Esperance, General Patch moved this fresh unit far inland to converge on the cape from the southeast in conjunction with the drive along the northern coast. New as they were to the jungle, the Twenty-fifth pushed on relentlessly through some of the worst campaigning terrain in the world, and reached Cape Esperance, to find—nothing much. A few miserable stragglers showed a semblance of fight or slunk off into the jungle. Of the high officers who were known to have been on the island, of the formidable force which it had been thought was assembling here for a last stand, there was no trace. Organized resistance on Guadalcanal had ceased.

What had happened? Radio Tokyo promptly announced that the Japanese High Command, deeming Guadalcanal of little value, anyway, had withdrawn their troops intact without interference from the badly beat-up Americans. The Americans, inured by now to the reliability of Japanese broadcasts, paid no more attention to this claim than to a dozen previous fatuous boasts.

It was not until the end of the war gave us access to official enemy reports that we found out exactly what had happened. For one of the very few times during the entire war, Tokyo had told the literal truth. The Japanese Navy had actually accomplished what hardly an American on Guadalcanal would have believed possible. Using submarines, destroyers, any swift craft available; taking full advantage of the moonless nights, which grounded our aircraft, to shuttle back and forth to the nearest islands still in their possession, they had successfully evacuated not only their high officers, but some sixteen thousand troops: rather more than our Intelligence believed still existed on the island. Here was a truly brilliant achievement to crown as bungling and inept a campaign as was ever waged by a major power.

These reports unearthed after the war disclosed another interesting and somewhat sinister fact not known at the time. By late January, 1943, the Japanese had managed to concentrate at Rabaul some fifty thousand mobile troops, together with the ships to transport them and the war vessels to convoy them. They had been definitely earmarked for another all-out effort to recapture Guadalcanal when the unexpected successes of the Australian-American drive in northern New Guinea caught the enemy command on the horns of a dilemma. This Japanese expeditionary force might well prove decisive in either theater, but it could hardly be divided between the two with any prospect of success. After much soul searching, the High Command decided to evacuate the Guadalcanal garrison to reinforce the central Solomons in hopes of making a stand there and assigned the troops at Rabaul to New Guinea—where the great bulk of them were to meet a watery grave in the Battle of the Bismarck Sea in early March.

The Guadalcanal campaign was the longest in the entire Pacific war. Ground fighting lasted for six months. And even after this had ceased, the Japanese were still able to reach the island with occasional air strikes which inflicted damage and casualties.

It was far from being the bloodiest in point of actual battle casualties. Marine units listed 1,242 as killed in action, died of wounds and missing; wounded numbered 2,655. But if the number of men knocked out by sickness were counted, casualties would have been close to total. Very, very few of the Marines who fought there—and not many of the later-arriving soldiers—failed to contract at least malaria. And malaria incapacitated men as effectively as wounds, not once but recurrently, sometimes over a period of years.

The importance of the operation has a number of facets.

It marked our assumption of the offensive, which we were never to relinquish; and by the same token, the end of the Japanese offensive. The strategic and tactical gains were obvious: guaranteed safety for our supply line to Australia; an air base and advanced staging area from which to strike toward the heart of the enemy's gains. It taught us much; and as the first head-on meeting with the Japanese, it set the pattern in many respects for things to come.

It demonstrated clearly to the world at large that the Japanese soldier was something less than the superman he had been pictured on the strength of his early, easy conquests.

What was he, then?

A Marine sergeant, interviewed by an Army intelligence officer at the height of the fighting, stated the point of view of the men in the ranks with admirable succinctness. "Hell," he said, "they ain't supermen; they're just a bunch of tricky little bastards."

A more scholarly analysis, written by a staff officer long after the heat of battle had subsided, put it somewhat differently:

"He (the Japanese soldier) fought, as an individual, as well and as bravely as any warrior the world has ever seen; he bore privation and hardship that would have put out of action most of the troops of the Allied forces, and in spite of those hardships and that privation, he attacked with determined ferocity whenever he came in contact with the American troops. In attack he was single minded and reckless of his life; in defense he was bitterly tenacious. He was in all ways except intelligence a worthy enemy and one to be respected." [13]

The word "respected" is correct in the sense it is used here, but it is open to connotations which would not win widespread approval. The men who fought him respected the danger that the Japanese soldier represented; they did not, with very rare individual exceptions, respect him as a man.

[13] Captain J. L. Zimmerman, USMCR, in "The Guadalcanal Campaign," monograph published by Historical Division, U.S. Marine Corps.

It was often too difficult to differentiate his bravery from sheer stupidity. Too often his tenacity was without point, and his Banzai charges, which never in the course of the entire war achieved any results of importance, seemed plain silly.

In his willingness to die, he frequently let death become an end in itself, losing sight of the fact that by dying he was supposed to accomplish something for his country, not merely earn himself a one-way ticket to that odd oriental Valhalla reserved for men killed in battle. Indeed, so engrossed did he sometimes become with the death fixation that he did not wait to be killed. In the course of the war many thousands, high officers as well as men in the ranks, were to follow the illustrious example of Colonel Ichiki and take their own lives rather than die fighting. Whether the Japanese war gods allow full credit for this type of exit has never been clearly established.

The Japanese soldier possessed great endurance, patience and the ability to subsist on a minimum of nourishment, but man for man he was smaller and less powerful physically than the American. Though his publicists made a great to-do about the manly virtues of fighting hand to hand with cold steel, he seldom resorted to this in actual practice, and nearly always came out second best when he did. Contrary to early belief, he was no better adapted by nature to the jungle than were our people; he had simply been there longer and received more special training, an advantage which was soon overcome. Nor was he any less vulnerable to tropical diseases. His people had cornered the natural sources of quinine, then the only specific against that ubiquitous scourge, malaria, yet, before the war had progressed far, American medical science had developed repressives equal or superior.

He did possess at the outset one great advantage: complete lack of inhibiting battle ethics, as defined by modern civilization and the precepts of the Geneva Convention. He would as soon kill a chaplain administering the last rites to the dying as he would an active enemy. Nothing delighted him more than killing our wounded lying helpless between the lines, unless it was killing the doctors and hospital corpsmen who went out to attend them. For one thing, chaplains, doctors and corpsmen, under the terms of the Geneva Convention, were not armed—not at the beginning, anyway.[14]

What we did not realize at the outset was that we were fighting what was essentially a medieval nation, with the medieval conception of total war, total destruction. And it was this conception which carried Japan down to the most abject defeat ever suffered by a supposedly first-class power since the Middle Ages. For once they had showed us the way, there was nothing for it but to play the game the way they wanted it played.

The Japanese High Command was full of surprises and paradoxes. The officer class was thoroughly professional and had been for generations, yet they proved grossly negligent, or ignorant, in several matters which the armies of other nations considered military fundamentals.

One of these was combat intelligence. Although their prewar espionage system was a model of far-reaching thoroughness, their officers in the field were nearly always without accurate knowledge of their enemy's strength and intentions, and seemed quite incapable of devising means for gaining such knowledge. Some of the egregious errors into which this led them have already been seen. There were to be many more.

Security, both internal and external, was another glaring weakness. Troops went into combat carrying diaries, letters, maps showing their dispositions, and even orders outlining in detail the action in which they were participating. Literally tons of documents were captured in enemy command posts; it never seemed to occur to anyone that they should have been destroyed. Japanese prisoners of war talked freely about everything they knew, even guiding our troops upon occasion. They had never been taught differently; their officers, having ordered them to die rather than be captured, could not consistently instruct them on how they should behave as prisoners.

Troop security in the field was treated with equal negligence. Patrols were constantly being taken by surprise.

[14] Japan never signed the Geneva Convention.

Columns marched through unknown country, shouting and jabbering at the top of their lungs, without benefit of a point or flankers. Time after time, patrols of ours simply walked undetected into the midst of their bivouac areas.

Their staff work was spotty: there was nearly always either too little of it or too much. That is, their operations were either impromptu affairs without adequate preparation, or planned in such intricate and elaborate detail as to be unworkable under combat conditions. And they were completely without ability to improvise when things failed to work out as expected.

Their only tactical innovation was the development of infiltration on a wide scale. In this they appear to have had a childlike faith. To anyone fighting a war by the book, the presence of active enemy elements on his flanks or in his rear is a serious matter, and this tactic had caused the British some trouble in Malaya and Burma, and the Dutch in the Indies. But in the Pacific we threw the book overboard and came to recognize infiltration for what it was: a minor nuisance to be dealt with by troops in reserve.

Aside from this, their idea of winning battles was to achieve surprise if possible, otherwise to overwhelm by sheer weight of numbers and indifference to losses. These means failing, they became what the sergeant previously quoted had called them: they abandoned tactics for trickery.

This assumed an almost infinite variety of forms. Individuals would feign a desire to surrender in order to get close enough to blow their captors—and themselves—to kingdom come with concealed grenades. They booby-trapped our dead and even their own. English-speaking Japanese cut in on our radio frequencies and tapped field telephone lines in order to issue false orders or misleading reports, or they shouted such orders in the midst of battle. Whole companies memorized catch phrases of English which they would yell for one reason or another. Snipers in ambush simulated wounded Marines by calling "Corpsman! Corpsman!" in order to lure to their deaths men engaged in errands of mercy.

Officers up through the rank of colonel were generally

brave and conscientious, if unimaginative and unresourceful. Above that, the qualities varied amazingly. We were to encounter the case of one general who carried through an exceedingly clever operation for the sole purpose of assuring his own safety, then abandoned to its destruction the army which had made his escape possible. Another, after ordering his men to their death in an effulgent proclamation, proceeded to kill himself rather than lead them. Not until Iwo Jima were we to meet a Japanese commander to whom high Marine officers could accord genuine professional respect.

Officers and men alike were essentially attack minded. All of their manuals and field regulations heavily emphasized the offensive aspects of warfare. And despite its general nature, the Guadalcanal campaign, save for its opening and closing phases, had been basically a Japanese offensive, or at the very least, a counteroffensive. There was a widespread belief at this time that they were physically and temperamentally incapable of sustaining protracted action of a purely defensive character; that that curious phenomenon, the Banzai charge, was in reality a form of combat fatigue: the crack-up of men whose nerves could no longer stand being on the receiving end of battle.

How infinitely wide this was of the truth, we were soon to learn. For following Guadalcanal, we would be the ones on the offensive. It would be our men's flesh and blood that were pitted against the emplaced weapons of the enemy. It might be said, without too great risk of contradiction, that Japan's greatest military achievement of the war was the conversion of a fighting force imbued for generations with the philosophy of attack into what were quite likely the most stubborn defensive fighters in all military history.

For that, unfortunately for us, is precisely what the Japanese became as the war moved westward.

Strategy for Attack

American forces now had the initiative, and meant to keep it. The question no longer was how to hit the enemy, but where.

Early in the war, the Joint Chiefs of Staff in Washington had given Gen. MacArthur command of all operations in the southwest Pacific; Adm. Nimitz had been given command in the south, north and central Pacific. As the Japs were pushed back in both theaters, it was natural for both commanders to argue for priorities; each wanted the main attack route on Japan to be staged in his area. MacArthur argued for the New Guinea-Mindanao route, liberating the Philippines and then hitting the Japanese mainland. Nimitz, and his superior on the JCS, Adm. King, favored the island-hopping route through the central Pacific to Formosa and perhaps the China coast, invading Japan from there. A compromise was finally reached, with each commander given his head in his own theater, once his strategy was approved by the Joint Chiefs of Staff.

For example, Nimitz had agreed with MacArthur that Adm. Halsey's offensive in the Solomons would cover only Guadalcanal and Tulagi; but after the Japs had been driven off Guadalcanal, more airfields were needed to mount attacks farther north, and Halsey was given the task of pushing the Japs out of New Georgia, Bougainville and eventually New Britain. MacArthur was still involved in New Guinea; by the terms of the compromise, Halsey's operations were subject to MacArthur's approval. Rabaul, on New Britain, was to be neutralized or destroyed, whichever suited the strategic purpose when the time arrived.

New Georgia was invaded on June 30, 1943, by the 37th and 45th U.S. Infantry Divisions, together with several Marine battalions. Five new airfields had been captured by August 9th, from which U.S. planes could now stage operations against the Japs farther up the Slot.

In the New Georgia campaign, four PT squadrons, totaling about fifty boats, sank and harassed Jap troop barges sent down the Slot. One such action involving Jap destroyers occurred in the beginning of

August, in which Lt. John Kennedy, USNR (now U.S. Senator from Massachusetts), commanded one of the PT's.

The account of that action is written by John Hersey, then a war correspondent.

PT BOATS IN THE SLOT

by John Hersey

Our men in the South Pacific fight nature, when they are pitted against her, with a greater fierceness than they could ever expend on a human enemy. Lieutenant John F. Kennedy, the ex-Ambassador's son and lately a PT skipper in the Solomons, came through town the other day and told me the story of his survival in the South Pacific. I asked Kennedy if I might write the story down. He asked me if I wouldn't talk first with some of his crew, so I went up to the Motor Torpedo Boat Training Centre at Melville, Rhode Island, and there, under the curving iron of a Quonset hut, three enlisted men named Johnston, McMahon, and McGuire filled in the gaps.

It seems that Kennedy's PT, the 109, was out one night with a squadron patrolling Blackett Strait, in mid-Solomons. Blackett Strait is a patch of water bounded on the northeast by the volcano called Kolombangara, on the west by the island of Vella Lavella, on the south by the island of Gizo and a string of coral-fringed islets, and on the east by the bulk of New Georgia. The boats were working about forty miles away from their base on the island of Rendova, on the south side of New Georgia. They had entered Blackett Strait, as was their habit, through Ferguson Passage, between the coral islets and New Georgia.

The night was a starless black and Japanese destroyers were around. It was about two-thirty. The 109, with three officers and ten enlisted men aboard, was leading three boats on a sweep for a target. An officer named George Ross was up on the bow, magnifying the void with binoculars. Kennedy was at the wheel and he saw Ross turn and point into the darkness. The man in the forward machine-gun turret shouted, "Ship at two o'clock!" Kennedy saw a shape and spun the wheel to turn for an attack, but the 109 answered sluggishly. She was running slowly on only one of her three engines, so as to make a minimum wake and avoid detection from the air. The shape became a Japanese destroyer, cutting through the night at forty knots and heading straight for the 109. The thirteen men on the PT hardly had time to brace themselves. Those who saw the Japanese ship coming were paralyzed by fear in a curious way: they could move their hands but not their feet. Kennedy whirled the wheel to the left, but again the 109 did not respond. Ross went through the gallant but futile motions of slamming a shell into the breach of the 37-millimetre anti-tank gun which had been temporarily mounted that very day, wheels and all, on the foredeck. The urge to bolt and dive over the side was terribly strong, but still no one was able to move; all hands froze to their battle stations. Then the Japanese crashed into the 109 and cut her right in two. The sharp enemy forefoot struck the PT on the starboard side about fifteen feet from the bow and crunched diagonally across with a racking noise. The PT's wooden hull hardly even delayed the destroyer. Kennedy was thrown hard to the left in the cockpit, and he thought, "This is how it feels to be killed." In a moment he found himself on his back on the deck, looking up at the destroyer as it passed through his boat. There was another loud noise and a huge flash of yellow-red light, and the destroyer glowed. Its peculiar, raked, inverted-Y stack stood out in the brilliant light and, later, in Kennedy's memory.

There was only one man below decks at the moment of collision. That was McMahon, engineer. He had no idea what was up. He was just reaching forward to slam the starboard engine into gear when a ship came into his engine room. He was lifted from the narrow passage between two of the engines and thrown painfully against the starboard bulkhead aft of the boat's auxiliary generator. He landed in a sitting position. A tremendous burst of flame came back at him from the day room, where some of the gas tanks were. He put his hands over his face, drew his legs up tight, and waited to die. But he felt water hit him after the fire, and he was sucked far downward as his half of the PT sank. He began to struggle upward through the water. He had held his breath since the impact, so his lungs were tight and they hurt. He looked up through the water. Over his head he saw a yellow glow—gasoline burning on the water. He broke the surface and was in fire again. He splashed hard to keep a little island of water around him.

Johnston, another engineer, had been asleep on deck when the collision came. It lifted him and dropped him overboard. He saw the flame and the destroyer for a moment. Then a huge propeller pounded by near him and the awful turbulence of the destroyer's wake took him down, turned him over and over, held him down, shook him, and drubbed on his ribs. He hung on and came up in water that was like a river rapids. The next day his body turned black and blue from the beating.

Kennedy's half of the PT stayed afloat. The bulkheads were sealed, so the undamaged watertight compartments up forward kept the half hull floating. The destroyer rushed off into the dark. There was an awful quiet: only the sound of gasoline burning.

Kennedy shouted, "Who's aboard?"

Feeble answers came from three of the enlisted men, McGuire, Mauer, and Albert; and from one of the officers, Thom.

Kennedy saw the fire only ten feet from the boat. He thought it might reach her and explode the remaining gas tanks, so he shouted, "Over the side!"

The five men slid into the water. But the wake of the destroyer swept the fire away from the PT, so after a few minutes, Kennedy and the others crawled back aboard. Kennedy shouted for survivors in the water. One by one they answered: Ross, the third officer; Harris, McMahon, Johnston, Zinsser, Starkey, enlisted men. Two did not answer: Kirksey and Marney, enlisted men. Since the last bombing at base, Kirksey had been sure he would die. He had huddled at his battle station by the fantail gun, with his kapok life jacket tied tight up to his cheeks. No one knows what happened to him or to Marney.

Harris shouted from the darkness, "Mr. Kennedy! Mr. Kennedy! McMahon is badly hurt." Kennedy took his shoes, his shirt, and his sidearms off, told Mauer to blink a light so that the men in the water would know where the half hull was, then dived in and swam toward the voice. The survivors were widely scattered. McMahon and Harris were a hundred yards away.

When Kennedy reached McMahon, he asked, "How are you, Mac?"

McMahon said, "I'm all right. I'm kind of burnt."

Kennedy shouted out, "How are the others?"

Harris said softly, "I hurt my leg."

Kennedy, who had been on the Harvard swimming team five years before, took McMahon in tow and headed for the PT. A gentle breeze kept blowing the boat away from the swimmers. It took forty-five minutes to make what had been an easy hundred yards. On the way in, Harris said, "I can't go any farther." Kennedy, of the Boston Kennedys, said to Harris, of the same home town, "For a guy from Boston, you're certainly putting up a great exhibition out here, Harris." Harris made it all right and didn't complain any more. Then Kennedy swam from man to man, to see how they were doing. All who had survived the crash were able to stay afloat, since they were wearing life preservers—kapok jackets shaped like overstuffed vests, aviators' yellow Mae Wests, or air-filled belts like small inner tubes. But those who couldn't swim had to be towed back to the wreckage by those who could. One of the men screamed for help. When Ross reached him, he found that the screaming man had two life jackets on. Johnston was treading water in a film of gasoline which did not catch fire. The fumes filled his lungs and he fainted. Thom towed him in. The others got in under their own power. It was now after 5 a.m., but still dark. It had taken nearly three hours to get everyone aboard.

The men stretched out on the tilted deck of the PT. Johnston, McMahon, and Ross collapsed into sleep. The men talked about how wonderful it was to be alive and speculated on when the other PT's would come back to rescue them. Mauer kept blinking the light to point their way. But the other boats had no idea of coming back. They had seen a collision, a sheet of flame, and a slow burning on the water. When the skipper of one of the boats saw the sight, he put his hands over his face and sobbed, "My God! My God!" He and the others turned away. Back at the base, after a couple of days, the squadron held services for the souls of the thirteen men, and one of the officers wrote his mother, "George Ross lost his life for a cause that he believed in stronger than any one of us, because he was an idealist in the purest sense. Jack Kennedy, the Ambassador's son, was on the same boat and also lost his life. The man that said the cream of a nation is lost in war can never be accused of making an overstatement of a very cruel fact. . . ."

When day broke, the men on the remains of the 109 stirred and looked around. To the northeast, three miles off, they saw the monumental cone of Kolombangara; there, the men knew, ten thousand Japanese swarmed. To the west, five miles away, they saw Vella Lavella; more Japs. To the south, only a mile or so away, they actually could see a Japanese camp on Gizo. Kennedy ordered his men to keep as low as possible, so that no moving silhouettes would show against the sky. The listing hulk was gurgling and gradually settling. Kennedy said, "What do you want to do if the Japs come out? Fight or surrender?" One said, "Fight with what?" So they took an inventory of their armament. The 37-millimetre gun had flopped over the side and was hanging there by a chain. They had one tommy gun, six 45-calibre automatics, and one .38. Not much.

"Well," Kennedy said, "what do you want to do?"

One said, "Anything you say, Mr. Kennedy. You're the boss."

Kennedy said, "There's nothing in the book about a situation like this. Seems to me we're not a military organization any more. Let's just talk this over."

They talked it over, and pretty soon they argued, and

Kennedy could see that they would never survive in anarchy. So he took command again.

It was vital that McMahon and Johnston should have room to lie down. McMahon's face, neck, hands, wrists, and feet were horribly burned. Johnston was pale and he coughed continually. There was scarcely space for everyone, so Kennedy ordered the other men into the water to make room, and went in himself. All morning they clung to the hulk and talked about how incredible it was that no one had come to rescue them. All morning they watched for the plane which they thought would be looking for them. They cursed war in general and PT's in particular. At about ten o'clock the hulk heaved a moist sigh and turned turtle. McMahon and Johnston had to hang on as best they could. It was clear that the remains of the 109 would soon sink. When the sun had passed the meridian, Kennedy said, "We will swim to that small island," pointing to one of a group three miles to the southeast. "We have less chance of making it than some of these other islands here, but there'll be less chance of Japs, too." Those who could not swim well grouped themselves around a long two-by-six timber with which carpenters had braced the 37-millimetre cannon on deck and which had been knocked overboard by the force of the collision. They tied several pairs of shoes to the timber, as well as the ship's lantern, wrapped in a life jacket to keep it afloat. Thom took charge of this unwieldy group. Kennedy took McMahon in tow again. He cut loose one end of a long strap on McMahon's Mae West and took the end in his teeth. He swam breast stroke, pulling the helpless McMahon along on his back. It took over five hours to reach the island. Water lapped into Kennedy's mouth through his clenched teeth, and he swallowed a lot. The salt water cut into McMahon's awful burns, but he did not complain. Every few minutes, when Kennedy stopped to rest, taking the strap out of his mouth and holding it in his hand, McMahon would simply say, "How far do we have to go?"

Kennedy would reply, "We're going good." Then he would ask, "How do you feel, Mac?"

McMahon always answered, "I'm O.K., Mr. Kennedy. How about you?"

In spite of his burden, Kennedy beat the other men to the reef that surrounded the island. He left McMahon on the reef and told him to keep low, so as not to be spotted by Japs. Kennedy went ahead and explored the island. It was only a hundred yards in diameter; coconuts on the trees but none on the ground; no visible Japs. Just as the others reached the island, one of them spotted a Japanese barge chugging along close to shore. They all lay low. The barge went on. Johnston, who was very pale and weak and who was still coughing a lot, said, "They wouldn't come here. What'd they be walking around here for? It's too small." Kennedy lay in some bushes, exhausted by his effort, his stomach heavy with the water he had swallowed. He had been in the sea, except for short intervals on the hulk, for fifteen and a half hours. Now he started thinking. Every night for several nights the PT's had cut through Ferguson Passage on their way to action. Ferguson Passage was just beyond the next little island. Maybe . . .

He stood up. He took one of the pairs of shoes. He put one of the rubber life belts around his waist. He hung the .38 around his neck on a lanyard. He took his pants off. He picked up the ship's lantern, a heavy battery affair ten inches by ten inches, still wrapped in the kapok jacket. He said, "If I find a boat, I'll flash the lantern twice. The password will be 'Roger,' the answer will be 'Willco.' " He walked toward the water. After fifteen paces he was dizzy, but in the water he felt all right.

It was early evening. It took half an hour to swim to the reef around the next island. Just as he planted his feet on the reef, which lay about four feet under the surface, he saw the shape of a very big fish in the clear water. He flashed the light at it and splashed hard. The fish went away. Kennedy remembered what one of his men had said a few days before, "These barracuda will come up under a swimming man and eat his testicles." He had many occasions to think of that remark in the next few hours.

Now it was dark. Kennedy blundered along the uneven reef in water up to his waist. Sometimes he would reach forward with his leg and cut one of his shins or ankles on sharp coral. Other times he would step forward onto emptiness. He made his way like a slow-motion drunk, hugging the lantern. At about nine o'clock he came to the end of the reef, alongside Ferguson Passage. He took his shoes off and tied them to the life jacket, then struck out into open water. He swam about an hour, until he felt he was far enough out to intercept the PT's. Treading water, he listened for the muffled roar of motors, getting chilled, waiting, holding the lamp. Once he looked west and saw flares and the false gaiety of an action. The lights were far beyond the little islands, even beyond Gizo, ten miles away. Kennedy realized that the PT boats had chosen, for the first night in many, to go around Gizo instead of through Ferguson Passage. There was no hope. He started back. He made the same painful promenade of the reef and struck out for the tiny island where his friends were. But this swim was different. He was very tired and now the current was running fast, carrying him to the right. He saw that he could not make the island, so he flashed the light once and shouted "Roger! Roger!" to identify himself.

On the beach the men were hopefully vigilant. They saw the light and heard the shouts. They were very happy, because they thought that Kennedy had found a PT. They walked out onto the reef, sometimes up to their waists in water, and waited. It was very painful for those who had no shoes. The men shouted, but not much, because they were afraid of Japanese.

One said, "There's another flash."

A few minutes later a second said, "There's a light over there."

A third said, "We're seeing things in this dark."

They waited a long time, but they saw nothing except phosphorescence and heard nothing but the sound of waves. They went back, very discouraged.

One said despairingly, "We're going to die."

Johnston said, "Aw, shut up. You can't die. Only the good die young."

Kennedy had drifted right by the little island. He thought he had never known such deep trouble, but something he did shows that unconsciously he had not given up hope. He dropped his shoes, but he held onto the heavy lantern, his symbol of contact with his fellows. He stopped trying to swim. He seemed to stop caring. His body drifted through the wet hours, and he was very cold. His mind was a jumble. A few hours before he had wanted desperately to get to the base at Rendova. Now he only wanted to get back to the little island he had left that night, but he didn't try to get there; he just wanted to. His mind seemed to float away from his body. Darkness and time took the place of a mind in his skull. For a long time he slept, or was crazy, or floated in a chill trance.

The currents of the Solomon Islands are queer. The tide shoves and sucks through the islands and makes the currents curl in odd patterns. It was a fateful pattern into which Jack Kennedy drifted. He drifted in it all night. His mind was blank, but his fist was tightly clenched on the kapok around the lantern. The current moved in a huge circle—west past Gizo, then north and east past Kolombangara, then south into Ferguson Passage. Early in the morning the sky turned from black to gray, and so did Kennedy's mind. Light came to both at about six. Kennedy looked around and saw that he was exactly where he had been the night before when he saw the flares beyond Gizo. For a second time, he started home. He thought for a while that he had lost his mind and that he only imagined that he was repeating his attempt to reach the island. But the chill of the water was real enough, the lantern was real, his progress was measurable. He made the reef, crossed the lagoon, and got to the first island. He lay on the beach awhile. He found that his lantern did not work any more, so he left it and started back to the next island, where his men were. This time the trip along the reef was awful. He had discarded his shoes, and every step on the coral was painful. This time the swim across the gap where the current had caught him the night before seemed endless. But the current had changed; he made the island. He crawled up on the beach. He was vomiting when his men came up to him. He said, "Ross, you try it tonight." Then he passed out.

Ross, seeing Kennedy so sick, did not look forward to the execution of the order. He distracted himself by complaining about his hunger. There were a few coconuts on the trees, but the men were too weak to climb up for them. One of the men thought of sea food, stirred his tired body, and found a snail on the beach. He said, "If we were desperate, we could eat these." Ross said, "Desperate, hell. Give me that. I'll eat that." He took it in his hand and looked at it. The snail put its head out and looked at him. Ross was startled, but he shelled the snail and ate it, making faces because it was bitter.

In the afternoon, Ross swam across to the next island. He took a pistol to signal with, and he spent the night watching Ferguson Passage from the reef around the island. Nothing came through. Kennedy slept badly that night; he was cold and sick.

The next morning everyone felt wretched. Planes which the men were unable to identify flew overhead and there were dogfights. That meant Japs as well as friends, so the men dragged themselves into the bushes and lay low. Some prayed. Johnston said, "You guys make me sore. You didn't spend ten cents in church in ten years, then all of a sudden you're in trouble and you see the light." Kennedy felt a little better now. When Ross came back, Kennedy decided that the group should move to another, larger island to the southeast, where there seemed to be more coconut trees and where the party would be nearer Ferguson Passage. Again Kennedy took McMahon in tow with the strap in his teeth, and the nine others grouped themselves around the timber.

This swim took three hours. The nine around the timber were caught by the current and barely made the far tip of the island. Kennedy found walking the quarter mile across to them much harder than the three-hour swim. The cuts on his bare feet were festered and looked like small balloons. The men were suffering most from thirst, and they broke open some coconuts lying on the ground and avidly drank the milk. Kennedy and McMahon, the first to drink, were sickened, and Thom told the others to drink sparingly. In the middle of the night it rained, and someone suggested moving into the underbrush and licking water off the leaves. Ross and McMahon kept contact at first by touching feet as they licked. Somehow they got separated, and, being uncertain whether there were any Japs on the island, they became frightened. McMahon, trying to make his way back to the beach, bumped into someone and froze. It turned out to be Johnston, licking leaves on his own. In the morning the group saw that all the leaves were covered with droppings. Bitterly, they named the place Bird Island.

On this fourth day, the men were low. Even Johnston was low. He had changed his mind about praying. McGuire had a rosary around his neck, and Johnston said, "McGuire, give that necklace a working over." McGuire said quietly, "Yes, I'll take care of all you fellows." Kennedy was still unwilling to admit that things were hopeless. He asked Ross if he would swim with him to an island called Nauru, to the southeast and even nearer Ferguson Passage. They were very weak indeed by now, but after an hour's swim they made it.

They walked painfully across Nauru to the Ferguson Passage side, where they saw a Japanese barge aground on the reef. There were two men by the barge—possibly Japs. They apparently spotted Kennedy and Ross, for they got into a dugout canoe and hurriedly paddled to the other side of the island. Kennedy and Ross moved up the beach. They came upon an unopened rope-bound box and, back in the trees, a little shelter containing a keg of water, a Japanese gas mask, and a crude wooden fetish shaped like a fish. There were Japanese hardtack and candy in the box and the two had a wary feast. Down by the water they found a one-man canoe. They hid from imagined Japs all day. When night fell, Kennedy left Ross and took the canoe, with some hardtack and a can of water from the keg, out into Ferguson Passage. But no PT's came, so he paddled to Bird Island. The men there told him that the two men he had spotted by the barge that morning were natives, who had paddled to Bird Island. The natives had said that there were Japs on Nauru and the men had given

Kennedy and Ross up for lost. Then the natives had gone away. Kennedy gave out small rations of crackers and water, and the men went to sleep. During the night, one man, who kept himself awake until the rest were asleep, drank all the water in the can Kennedy had brought back. In the morning the others figured out that he was the guilty one. They swore at him and found it hard to forgive him.

Before dawn, Kennedy started out in the canoe to rejoin Ross on Nauru, but when day broke a wind arose and the canoe was swamped. Some natives appeared from nowhere in a canoe, rescued Kennedy, and took him to Nauru. There they showed him where a two-man canoe was cached. Kennedy picked up a coconut with a smooth shell and scratched a message on it with a jackknife: "ELEVEN ALIVE NATIVE KNOWS POSIT AND REEFS NAURU ISLAND KENNEDY." Then he said to the natives, "Rendova, Rendova."

One of the natives seemed to understand. They took the coconut and paddled off.

Ross and Kennedy lay in a sickly daze all day. Toward evening it rained and they crawled under a bush. When it got dark, conscience took hold of Kennedy and he persuaded Ross to go out into Ferguson Passage with him in the two-man canoe. Ross argued against it. Kennedy insisted. The two started out in the canoe. They had shaped paddles from the boards of the Japanese box, and they took a coconut shell to bail with. As they got out into the Passage, the wind rose again and the water became choppy. The canoe began to fill. Ross bailed and Kennedy kept the bow into the wind. The waves grew until they were five or six feet high. Kennedy shouted, "Better turn around and go back!" As soon as the canoe was broadside to the waves, the water poured in and the dugout was swamped. The two clung to it, Kennedy at the bow, Ross at the stern. The tide carried them southward toward the open sea, so they kicked and tugged the canoe, aiming northwest. They struggled that way for two hours, not knowing whether they would hit the small island or drift into the endless open.

The weather got worse; rain poured down and they

couldn't see more than ten feet. Kennedy shouted, "Sorry I got you out here, Barney!" Ross shouted back, "This would be a great time to say I told you so, but I won't!"

Soon the two could see a white line ahead and could hear a frightening roar—waves crashing on a reef. They had got out of the tidal current and were approaching the island all right, but now they realized that the wind and the waves were carrying them toward the reef. But it was too late to do anything, now that their canoe was swamped, except hang on and wait.

When they were near the reef, a wave broke Kennedy's hold, ripped him away from the canoe, turned him head over heels, and spun him in a violent rush. His ears roared and his eyes pinwheeled, and for the third time since the collision he thought he was dying. Somehow he was not thrown against the coral but floated into a kind of eddy. Suddenly he felt the reef under his feet. Steadying himself so that he would not be swept off it, he shouted, "Barney!" There was no reply. Kennedy thought of how he had insisted on going out in the canoe, and he screamed, "Barney!" This time Ross answered. He, too, had been thrown on the reef. He had not been as lucky as Kennedy; his right arm and shoulder had been cruelly lacerated by the coral, and his feet, which were already infected from earlier wounds, were cut some more.

The procession of Kennedy and Ross from reef to beach was a crazy one. Ross's feet hurt so much that Kennedy would hold one paddle on the bottom while Ross put a foot on it, then the other paddle forward for another step, then the first paddle forward again, until they reached sand. They fell on the beach and slept.

Kennedy and Ross were wakened early in the morning by a noise. They looked up and saw four husky natives. One walked up to them and said in an excellent English accent, "I have a letter for you, sir." Kennedy tore the note open. It said, "On His Majesty's Service. To the Senior Officer, Nauru Island. I have just learned of your presence on Nauru Is. I am in command of a New Zealand infantry patrol operating in conjunction with U.S. Army troops on New Georgia. I strongly advise that you come with these natives to me. Meanwhile I shall be in radio communication with your authorities at Rendova, and we can finalize plans to collect balance of your party. Lt. Wincote. P. S. Will warn aviation of your crossing Ferguson Passage."

Everyone shook hands and the four natives took Ross and Kennedy in their war canoe across to Bird Island to tell the others the good news. There the natives broke out a spirit stove and cooked a feast of yams and C ration. Then they built a leanto for McMahon, whose burns had begun to rot and stink, and for Ross, whose arm had swelled to the size of a thigh because of the coral cuts. The natives put Kennedy in the bottom of their canoe and covered him with sacking and palm fronds, in case Japanese planes should buzz them. The long trip was fun for the natives. They stopped once to try to grab a turtle, and laughed at the sport they were having. Thirty Japanese planes went over low toward Rendova, and the natives waved and shouted gaily. They rowed with a strange rhythm, pounding paddles on the gunwales between strokes. At last they reached a censored place. Lieutenant Wincote came to the water's edge and said formally, "How do you do. Leftenant Wincote."

Kennedy said, "Hello. I'm Kennedy."

Wincote said, "Come up to my tent and have a cup of tea."

In the middle of the night, after several radio conversations between Wincote's outfit and the PT base, Kennedy sat in the war canoe waiting at an arranged rendezvous for a PT. The moon went down at eleven-twenty. Shortly afterward Kennedy heard the signal he was waiting for—four shots. Kennedy fired four answering shots.

A voice shouted to him, "Hey, Jack!"

Kennedy said, "Where the hell you been?"

The voice said, "We got some food for you."

Kennedy said bitterly, "No, thanks, I just had a coconut."

A moment later a PT came alongside. Kennedy jumped onto it and hugged the men aboard—his friends. In the

American tradition, Kennedy held under his arm a couple of souvenirs: one of the improvised paddles and the Japanese gas mask.

With the help of the natives, the PT made its way to Bird Island. A skiff went in and picked up the men. In the deep of the night, the PT and its happy cargo roared back toward base. The squadron medic had sent some brandy along to revive the weakened men. Johnston felt the need of a little revival. In fact, he felt he needed quite a bit of revival. After taking care of that, he retired topside and sat with his arms around a couple of roly-poly, mission-trained natives. And in the fresh breeze on the way home they sang together a hymn all three happened to know:

Jesus loves me, this I know,
For the Bible tells me so;
Little ones to him belong,
They are weak, but He is strong.
Yes, Jesus loves me; yes, Jesus loves me . . .

Atoll War

Bougainville was the next objective; it was on the way to New Britain, where the Jap stronghold of Rabaul supplied the enemy in both New Guinea and the Solomons. Assault forces, made up of the 3rd Marine Division, the 37th Infantry Division, a Marine raider regiment, several Marine battalions, and the 8th New Zealand Brigade Group, landed November 1, 1943, in swampy terrain at the center of the island, where the Japs least expected them. The assault forces secured their landings against little opposition, but they had long, hard fighting ahead of them, with the miserable terrain giving them as much trouble as the Japs. Bougainville was not officially secured until the end of March.

Quite another kind of battle was fought that same November, by the 2nd Marine Division on Tarawa. It had fought at Guadalcanal and Tulagi, where "they had learned much about Jap fighting methods. Practice had made them one of the finest jungle outfits in the world. But when it came to atoll fighting they had nearly as much to learn as the totally green 27th Division.* At Tarawa they learned." **

Tarawa was an atoll in the Gilbert Islands which had been a British possession before the war began. The Japs had occupied it and Makin, a near-by atoll, and fortified them. Betio Island, in the Tarawa atoll, had a three-strip airfield; its capture would be the first step toward the powerful Jap naval base of Truk in the Carolines.

On the 21st of November, after three days of shelling and bombing by both navy ships and carrier-based bombers, the first landing waves were waiting for the final shelling, which was supposed to give the *coup de grâce* to the Japs on shore. To the astonishment of the Marines,

* Simultaneously, the 27th Infantry Division was to assault Makin Island close by. Compared to Tarawa, Makin was lightly held, but the 27th had had no combat experience at all.

** Maj. Frank Hough, *The Island War*, p. 126.

the enemy answered this last concentration of fire, and H-Hour was postponed several times before the first wave was sent in.

"Naval gunfire ceased,* and the dive bombers returned to give the island a final pasting. As the amphibious tractors carrying the first assault waves entering the lagoon left the line of departure and waddled forward . . . they soon came under mortar, machine-gun and anti-boat fire. This was scattered and poorly controlled at first, showing the enemy were still dazed by the heavy bombing and shelling they'd received. The first three waves, all in amphtracks, got ashore without serious losses. But the Japanese were recovering rapidly. As the boats carrying the fourth wave (these were not amphtracks, but cargo carriers) piled up on the reef hundreds of yards from shore, there began a terrible carnage which will always be associated with the name Tarawa.

"The position (of the first three waves) was precarious in the extreme. The beach averaged only about twenty feet in width, bounded on the landward side by a four-foot revetment of logs forming a sea wall. This provided fair cover for men crouching close to it, but it was a major obstacle for any advance inland. And until they could establish a beachhead in depth and wipe out some of the weapons which were raking the reef and the top of the sea wall, they could not hope for substantial reinforcements or supplies.

"Wading 700 yards of coral reef is a slow laborious process under the best of circumstances. You trip over jagged boulders, climb hummocks, sprawl into sudden deep depressions where a heavily armed man can drown unless rescued. Now a storm of assorted shells threw geysers from the shallow water, and machine-gun bursts marched their precise ranks across it. Some of the men landed on the pier [this ran out 500 yards from shore to the end of the fringing reef, built partly on pilings, partly on coral] and made their way along that open, narrow, fire-swept roadway. Others crept through the water close along the pier's side. But to most, even this scant cover was denied. They came in straight across the reef, through the tortured water that was turning red around them. Tiny black dots of men, holding their weapons high above their heads, moving at snail's pace, never faltering. Some of them, miraculously, made it. Many others did not.

"At last, to stop the hopeless slaughter, the order was passed that

* Maj. Frank Hough, *The Island War,* pp. 133-139.

no more waves were to go in unless some of those guns could be silenced, or arrival of darkness would cover the landings.

"There was no jungle on this portion of Betio; only scattered coconut palms badly shattered by shell fire, and the open airstrips, most of their visible installations in ruins. Yet nothing moved about the ground. Few live Japanese were seen during all of the three days of intensive fighting. For, in a sense, the enemy had created their own 'jungle.' Their emplacements had become virtually integral parts of the island.

"Mostly they were below ground, dug deeply and sometimes reinforced with concrete. They were roofed with thick logs and steel beams or rails, on top of which coral rock was piled in considerable depth, sometimes sand.

"The small size of the firing apertures enhanced this concealment feature. It is characteristic of Japanese defense tactics to emphasize concealment, relying upon interlocking and overlapping lanes of fire rather than wide traverse of individual weapons. That is, the narrow firing opening limited the sweep of the gun to a lane directly to its front. Within that lane it was deadly; to either side it was helpless and dependent for protection upon the next gun whose fire lane was laid to tie in with that of the first gun, upon which, in turn, it was dependent for flank protection. And so on, until the defense sector became actually a series of separate mutually protective pillboxes, further defended by strategically placed riflemen in trenches, trees and camouflaged rifle pits.

"Such a position was deadly from the front and extremely difficult to flank. The individual components were all but impervious to small-arms fire and must be destroyed by close-up work with grenades, demolition charges and flame throwers. To get close enough, the attackers had to neutralize at least temporarily not only their immediate objective but the pillboxes and riflemen which covered its flanks.

"Such a system had the disadvantage of inflexibility: once one pillbox was taken, the problem of taking the rest was greatly simplified. But it remained to the end a case of destroying individual installations and individual Japanese who fought in concealment to the death.

"The situation was grim as evening drew on. . . . The men were ordered to dig in and hold what they had regardless.

"They did not have very much. The entire extent of shore line held amounted only to some 300 yards. Fractions of four battered battalions held a perimeter line which ran inland about fifty yards to the edge of the airfield on the east, circled the base of the pier, and reached a maximum depth of 150 yards on a narrow front behind Red 2.*

"No artillery had been brought ashore. There was no room to set it up. All the Marines ashore had to depend on for fire support was naval gunfire and carrier-borne aircraft, neither of which could be very effective in the darkness against the sort of counterattack which was almost inevitable should the Japanese react according to precedent.

"But now events proved that the shelling and bombing, so disappointing on the whole, had been extraordinarily effective in an unexpected way. However slight the vital damage to the enemy's major installations, their communications had been completely destroyed, and harassing fire throughout the night kept them inoperative. Japanese in pillboxes, blockhouses and dugouts remained isolated from their command post and from each other, quite incapable of massing for any concerted action. There was no important counterattack and only a few ineffectual efforts at infiltration.

"The troops of the later waves still crouched in their landing boats beyond range outside the reef. During the night a number of these tried to make it ashore under cover of the darkness. But the darkness supplied little cover that night. Gasoline and supply dumps were burning all over Betio, adding their lurid glare to that of a small but tropically bright quarter moon. The white coral of the pier stood out starkly against the dark water. Black figures moved along it, antlike, to and fro: members of the shore party carrying in vital supplies of ammunition, water, food. The Japanese shelled them mercilessly. The Navy shelled the Japanese. Combat engineers repaired the pier as fast as the enemy blasted it. The shore party took their losses and carried on.

"All in all, it was quite a night. But when daylight found that thin perimeter still intact, a new feeling began to imbue the weary, hungry, thirsty men who held it: a conviction, tacit but implicit, that the crisis had passed. Although ninety percent of Betio smoked and smoldered in front of them, although enemy fire rose in frenzy and volume from every side, and there was no sign of weakening resistance anywhere,

* Designation of an assault beach. (Ed.)

all hands knew now that the issue was no longer in doubt—if it ever had been really."

The story of the second day on Tarawa is taken from Robert Sherrod's memorable *Tarawa*.

TARAWA: THE SECOND DAY

by Robert Sherrod

This is how things stood at dawn of the second day: the three assault battalions held their precarious footholds—Major Crowe's was about midway of the island's north beach, just east of the pier; Lieutenant Colonel Jordan's held a portion of the beach a couple of hundred yards west of Crowe, on the other side of the pier; and the third assault battalion, I learned, had landed on the strongly fortified western tip of the island. This last-named battalion, although separated from its staff and part of its troops, actually had been more successful than the first two. Under the leadership of one of its company commanders, Major Mike Ryan, who took over when the battalion c.o. landed in another pocket, it had fought its way inland until it held a seventy-yard beachhead before dark of the first day. The naval gunfire had been particularly effective on this western end of the island, knocking out all the big guns which had been the chief defense, and Major Ryan's men, had, in the words of Colonel Shoup, proved themselves "a bunch of fighting fools." The battalion, of course, was isolated from the rest of the Marines on the island.

During the first night the Japs, apparently because their communications had been disrupted and many of their men undoubtedly had been stunned, had not counterattacked. Probably as many as three hundred Japs, we learned later, had committed suicide under the fierce pounding of our naval guns and bombs.

Meanwhile, the Marines had landed Colonel Shoup's combat team reserve battalion, the first battalion of the Second Regiment. During the night considerable quantities of ammunition, some artillery, some tanks (light and medium), and other supplies had also been brought in.

General Julian Smith had sent a message from his battleship headquarters: "Attack at dawn; division reserve will start landing at 0600." The division reserve was the first and third battalions of the Eighth Marines.

Our casualties had been heavy on the first day, but well over half the dead, and practically all of the wounded, had been shot, not in the water, but after they had reached land and climbed the seawall. Those wounded more than lightly in the water had little chance of reaching shore. The amphibious operation up to that point, therefore, could have been called better than successful. The hell lay in the unexpectedly strong fortifications we had found after we landed.

It was not possible—and never will be possible—to know just how many casualties the three assault battalions had suffered D Day. Most officers agreed afterward that thirty-five to forty percent was as good a guess as any. Organization was ripped to pieces. The percentage of casualties among officers had been heavier than among the men, and key men such as platoon sergeants, virtually irreplaceable, had been killed or wounded. Therefore, we had to have more men quickly, and General Smith had said they were on the way.

Because the second day was even more critical than the first, and because it was the day the tide finally turned in our favor, I have written a play-by-play chronology (as I saw it) from my notes:

0530: The coral flats in front of us present a sad sight at low tide. A half dozen Marines lie exposed, now that the water has receded. They are hunched over, rifles in hand, just as they fell. They are already one-quarter covered by sand that the high tide left. Further out on the flats and to the left I can see at least fifty other bodies. I had thought yesterday, however, that low tide would reveal many more than that. The smell of death, that sweetly sick odor of decaying human flesh, is already oppressive.

Now that it is light, the wounded go walking by, on the beach. Some are supported by corpsmen; others, like this one coming now, walk alone, limping badly, their faces contorted with pain. Some have bloodless faces, some bloody faces, others only pieces of faces. Two corpsmen pass, carrying a Marine on a stretcher who is lying face down. He has a great hole in his side, another smaller hole in his shoulder. This scene, set against the background of the dead on the coral flats, is horrible. It is war. I wish it could be seen by the silken-voiced, radio-announcing pollyannas back home, who, by their very inflections, nightly lull the people into a false sense of all-is-well.

0600: One of the fresh battalions is coming in. Its Higgins boats are being hit before they pass the old hulk of a freighter seven hundred yards from shore. One boat blows up, then another. The survivors start swimming for shore, but machine-gun bullets dot the water all around them. Back of us the Marines have started an offensive to clean out the Jap machine guns which are now firing at our men in the water. They evidently do not have much success, because there is no diminution of the fire that rips into the two dozen or more Higgins boats. The *ratatatatat* of the machine guns increases, and the high *pi-i-ing* of the Jap sniper bullet sings overhead incessantly. The Japs still have some mortars, too, and at least one 40- or 77-mm. gun. Our destroyers begin booming their five-inch shells on the Jap positions near the end of the airfield back of us.

Some of the fresh troops get within two hundred yards of shore, while others from later waves are unloading further out. One man falls, writhing in the water. He is the first man I have seen actually hit, though many thousands of bullets cut into the water. Now some reach the shore, maybe only a dozen at first. They are calm, even disdainful of death. Having come this far, slowly, through the water, they show no disposition to hurry. They collect in pairs and walk up the beach, with snipers still shooting at them.

Now one of our mortars discovers one of the machine

guns that has been shooting at the Marines. It is not back of us, but is a couple of hundred yards west, out in one of the wooden privies the dysentery-fearing Japs built out over the water. The mortar gets the range, smashes the privy, and there is no more firing from there.

But the machine guns continue to tear into the on-coming Marines. Within five minutes I see six men killed. But the others keep coming. One rifleman walks slowly ashore, his left arm a bloody mess from the shoulder down. The casualties become heavier. Within a few minutes more I can count at least a hundred Marines lying on the flats.

0730: The Marines continue unloading from the Higgins boats, but fewer of them are making the shore now. Many lie down behind the pyramidal concrete barriers the Japs had erected to stop tanks. Others make it as far as the disabled tanks and amphtracks, then lie behind them to size up the chances of making the last hundred yards to shore. There are at least two hundred bodies which do not move at all on the dry flats, or in the shallow water partially covering them. This is worse, far worse than it was yesterday.

Now four of our carrier-based fighters appear over the water. The first makes a glide and strafes the rusty freighter hulk, then the second, third, and fourth. Thousands of their fifty-caliber bullets tear into the old ship, each plane leaving a dotted, blue-gray line behind each wing. "The god-damn Japs must have swum out there last night and mounted a machine gun in that freighter," says an officer beside me. "I thought I saw some bullets coming this way."

Three more Hellcats appear. These carry small bombs under their bellies. The first dives for the freighter and misses by at least fifty yards. The second does likewise. But the third gets a direct hit and the old freighter gushes a flame fifty feet into the air. But the flame apparently is from the bomb explosion alone, because it dies out immediately. "May kill some of our own men out there with that bombing and strafing," observes the officer, "but we've got to do it. That Jap machine gun is killing our men in the water." A dozen more bomber-fighters appear in the sky. One after another they glide gracefully to within a few hundred feet of the freighter, drop their bombs, and sail away. But only one of the twelve gets a hit on the freighter. I am surprised at their inaccuracy—one bomb is two hundred yards beyond the target. These fighter-bombers are less accurate than the more experienced dive bombers.

0800: Back at Colonel Jordan's command post nobody is happy. Things are still going badly. Colonel Jordan is talking to Major Crowe: "Are there many snipers behind your front lines? Uh, huh, we have a hell of a lot, too."

"Where is my little runner? Where is Paredes?" asks Colonel Jordan.

"He is dead, Colonel. He was killed right over there," a Marine answers. Corporal Osbaldo R. Paredes of Los Angeles was a brave Marine. All during the first day he had carried messages through intense fire, never hesitating to accept the most dangerous mission. "Oh, hell!" says the misty-eyed colonel. What a fine boy! I'll certainly see that his family gets the Navy Cross." He stops suddenly. The Navy Cross seems quite inadequate now, only a few minutes after Paredes has been killed.

By now all the coconut trees from which snipers had been shot yesterday are filled again with more snipers. The sniper fire seems more frequent than ever and nobody can stick his head out of the battalion shellhole without getting shot at. The hell of it is that they are in trees only a few yards away, and they are hard to spot. They are not dangerous at any respectable range, but from their nearby positions they can kill a lot of Marines. A Marine comes by headquarters grinning. "I just got one," he says. "He dropped his rifle on the third shot, and it fell at my feet. But I swear I haven't seen him yet. I guess they tie themselves to trees just like they did at Guadalcanal."

0830: By now most of the Marines have arrived who will ever get ashore from those waves that were hit so badly early this morning. Those lying behind the tank blocks and the disabled boats get up once in a while and dash for shore. But I'm afraid we lost two hundred of them this morning, mavbe more.

A captain comes by and reports that one of his men has

single-handedly knocked out eight machine-gun nests—five yesterday and three this morning. Another unattached officer, whose normal duty is a desk job, not combat, drops in and reports that he finally killed a sniper. He had been out looking all morning—"How can you kill the bastards if you can't see them?"—and he finally had fired a burst into a coconut palm. Out dropped a Jap, wearing a coconut-husk cap. We feel that we are eliminating a lot of Jap machine gunners and snipers now. As the last men come ashore, there is only one machine gun firing at them, and it hits nobody.

0940: Now the high explosives are really being poured on the Jap positions toward the tail end of the island. Our 75-mm. pack howitzers are firing several rounds a minute. The strafing planes are coming over by the dozens, and the dive bombers by the half-dozens. Now we have many 81-mm. mortars joining the deathly orchestra. Betio trembles like a leaf, but I ask myself, "Are we knocking out many of those pillboxes?"

We know the Japs are still killing and wounding a lot of men. The stretchers are passing along the beach again, carrying their jungle-cloth-covered burdens. One Marine on a stretcher is bandaged around the head, both arms, and both legs. One of the walking wounded, his left arm in a white sling, walks slowly along the beach in utter contempt of the sniper who fires at him.

1100: Finally at Colonel Shoup's headquarters. And what a headquarters! Fifteen yards inland from the beach, it is a hole dug in the sand back of a huge pillbox that probably was some kind of Japanese headquarters. The pillbox is forty feet long, eight feet wide, and ten feet high. It is constructed of heavy coconut logs, six and eight inches in diameter. The walls of the pillbox are two tiers of coconut logs, about three feet apart. The logs are joined together by eight-inch steel spikes, shaped like a block letter C. In between the two tiers of logs are three feet of sand, and covering the whole pillbox several more feet of sand are heaped. No wonder our bombs and shells hadn't destroyed these pillboxes! Two-thousand-pound bombs hitting directly on them might have partially destroyed them, but bombing is not that accurate—not even dive bombing—on as many pillboxes as the Japs have on Betio. And when bombs hit beside such structures they only throw up more sand on top of them.

Colonel Shoup is nervous. The telephone shakes in his hand. "We are in a mighty tight spot," he is saying. Then he lays down the phone and turns to me, "Division has just asked me whether we've got enough troops to do the job. I told them no. They are sending the Sixth Marines, who will start landing right away." Says a nearby officer: "That damned Sixth is cocky enough already. Now they'll come in and claim they won the battle."[1]

From his battalion commanders Colonel Shoup receives regular telephone reports. One of them is now asking for air bombardment on a Jap strongpoint on the other side of the airfield, which we can see a few hundred feet from regimental headquarters. "All right," says the colonel, putting down the telephone. "Air liaison officer!" he calls, "tell them to drop some bombs on the southwest edge of 229 and the southeast edge of 231. There's some Japs in there giving us hell." The numbers refer to the keyed blocks on the map of the island. It seems less than ten minutes before four dive bombers appear overhead, then scream toward the earth with their bombs, which explode gruffly: *ka-whump, ka-whump, ka-whump, ka-whump.* Even nearer than the bombs, destroyer shells in salvos of four are bursting within ten minutes after a naval liaison officer has sent directions by radio.

Next to regimental quarters rises a big, uncompleted barracks building, which withstood our bombing and shell-

[1] The Sixth is one of the two Marine regiments which fought so bravely and brilliantly in France in World War I. But other regiments are jealous of the Sixth's honors. Examples: (1) in Shanghai it used to be said that the "pogey-bait" Sixth ordered $40,000 worth of post-exchange supplies—one dollar's worth of soap, the rest in candy ("pogey-bait"); (2) in New Zealand other Marines spread the rumor that the *fourragère* which the Sixth's men wore on their shoulders indicated that the wearer had a venereal disease.

ing very well. There are only a few small holes in the roof and wooden sides of the building. Five-foot tiers of coconut logs surround the building, to protect it against shrapnel. I run the thirty feet from Colonel Shoup's command post eastward to the tier and leap over it. Some Marines are in the unfloored building, lying on the ground, returning a Jap sniper's fire which comes from we know not where. Says a Marine: "That god-damn smokeless powder they've got beats anything we ever had." Then I cross the interior of the building, go through a hole in the wall and sit down beside some Marines who are in the alleyway between the wooden building and the tier of coconut logs.

"This gets monotonous," says a Marine as a bullet whistles through the alley. We are comparatively safe, sitting here, because we are leaning against the inside of the log tier, and the vertical logs that act as braces are big enough for us to squeeze behind. The problem is to flatten one's legs against the ground so that they are not exposed to the sniper's fire.

1130: These Marines are from H Company, the heavy-weapons company of the battalion I came with. "We've already had fifteen men killed, more in twenty-four hours than we had on Guadalcanal in six months," said the Marine sitting next to me, "and I don't know how many wounded.

"We started in in one amphib, and it got so hot the driver drove off before he had unloaded all of us. Then the amphib sank—it had been hit—and another one picked us up and brought us ashore."

Where had they landed? "Right over there by that pillbox with the four Japs in it," he replies. "You know who killed those Japs? Lieutenant Doyle of G Company did it—that's P. J. Doyle from Neola, Iowa—he just tossed a grenade in, then he jumped in with the Japs and shot them all with his carbine before they could shoot him."

By now it is fairly raining sniper bullets through our alley, as if the sniper is desperate because he isn't hitting anybody. The sniper is evidently a couple of hundred yards away, because there is a clear space that is far back from the open end of the alley. Japs can hide behind a coconut log without being seen all day, but nobody ever heard of one hiding behind a grain of sand.

A bullet ricochets off the side of the barracks building and hits the leg of the private who is second down the line. "I'm glad that one was spent," he says, picking up the .303-caliber copper bullet, which is bent near the end of the nose. I reach out for the bullet and he hands it to me. I drop it quickly because it is almost as hot as a live coal. The Marines all laugh.

These Marines calmly accept being shot at. They've grown used to it by now, and I suddenly realize that it is to me no longer the novelty it was. It seems quite comfortable here, just bulling. But I am careful to stay behind the upright coconut log which is my protection against the sniper.

Into the alleyway walks a Marine who doesn't bother to seek the protection of the coconut logs. He is the dirtiest man I have seen on the island—men get dirty very quickly in battle, but this one has a good quarter inch of gray-black dust on his beardless face and his dungarees are caked. A lock of blond hair sticks out from under his helmet.

"Somebody gimme some cigarettes," he says. "That machine-gun crew is out there in a shellhole across the airfield and there's not a cigarette in the crowd." One of the Marines throws him a pack of Camels.

The new arrival grins. "I just got me another sniper. That's six today, and me a cripple." I ask if he has been shot. "Hell, no," he says, "I busted my ankle stepping into a shellhole yesterday." His name? "Pfc. Adrian Strange." His home? "Knox City, Texas." Age? "Twenty."

Pfc. Adrian Strange stands for a few minutes, fully exposed to the sniper who has been pecking at us. Then the sniper opens up again, the bullets rattling against the coconut logs.

Pfc. Strang sings out, "Shoot me down, you son-of-a-bitch." Then he leisurely turns around and walks back across the airfield, carrying his carbine and the pack of cigarettes.

"That boy Strange," says the Marine next to me, "he just don't give a damn."

1200: Colonel Shoup has good news. Major Ryan's shorthanded battalion has crossed the western end of the island and the entire eight-hundred-yard beach up there is now ours. There are plenty of Japs just inside the beach, and the fortifications on the third of the island between Shoup's command post and Ryan's beach are very strong. And the entire south shore of the island, where there are even stronger pillboxes than there were on the north, remains to be cleaned out. That is the job of the Sixth Regiment, which will land this afternoon.

A young major comes up to the colonel in tears. "Colonel, my men can't advance. They are being held up by a machine gun." Shoup spits, "Goddlemighty, one machine gun."

1215: Here the Marines have been sitting in back of this pillbox (Shoup's headquarters) for twenty-four hours. And a Jap just reached out from an air vent near the top and shot Corporal Oliver in the leg. In other words, there have been Japs within three feet—the thickness of the wall—of the Marines' island commander all that time. Three Japs had been killed in the pillbox yesterday, and we thought that was all there were.

There is very bad news about Lieutenant Hawkins. He may die from his three wounds. He didn't pay much attention to the shrapnel wound he got yesterday, but he has been shot twice this morning. He wouldn't be evacuated when he got a bullet through one shoulder. "I came here to kill Japs; I didn't come here to be evacuated," he said. But a while ago he got a bullet through the other shoulder, and lower down. He lost a lot of blood from both wounds.

Said the corporal who told me this, "I think the Scout and Sniper platoon has got more guts than anybody else on the island. We were out front and Morgan (Sergeant Francis P. Morgan of Salem, Oregon) was shot in the throat. He was bleeding like hell, and saying in a low voice, 'Help me, help me.' I had to turn my head."

Lieutenant Paine, who had been nicked in the rear as he stood talking to us—"I'll be damned. I stay out front four hours, then I come back to the command post and get shot"—has more news about Hawkins. "He is a madman," says Paine. "He cleaned out six machine-gun nests, with two to six Japs in each nest. I'll never forget the picture of him standing on that amphtrack, riding around with a million bullets a minute whistling by his ears, just shooting Japs. I never saw such a man in my life."

The young major whose men were held up by a single machine gun was back again. "Colonel, there are a thousand goddamn Marines out there on that beach, and not one will follow me across to the air strip," he cries, desperately. Colonel Jordan, who by this time was back at his old job as observer, our battalion having been merged with Major Wood Kyle's reinforcing first battalion, speaks up, "I had the same trouble. Most of them are brave men, but some are yellow." I recall something a very wise general once told me, "In any battle you'll find the fighting men up front. Then you'll find others who will linger behind, or find some excuse to come back. It has always been that way, and it always will. The hell of it is that in any battle you lose a high percentage of your best men."

Says Colonel Shoup, "You've got to say, 'Who'll follow me?' And if only ten follow you, that's the best you can do, but it's better than nothing."

1300: Now they are bringing up the dead for burial near the command post. There are seven laid out about ten yards from where I sit. They are covered with green and brown ponchos, only their feet sticking out. I think: what big feet most American soldiers and Marines have! None of those looks smaller than a size eleven. The stench of the dead, as the burial detail brings them past and lines them up on the ground, is very heavy now.

Somebody brings in the story of a Jap sniper whose palm-tree roost was sprayed repeatedly. But he kept on firing, somehow. Finally, in disgust, a sergeant took a machine gun and fired it until he had cut the tree in two, near the top. The fall is supposed to have killed the Jap.

1430: Things look better now. The amphtracks—those that are left—are bringing stuff ashore and carrying the wounded regularly, and they get shot at only occasionally when they head back into the water. Major Ryan and his crowd are doing very well at the western end of the island,

and the Sixth Marines are about to land there and start down the south shore. We've got another company of light tanks ashore, and they are going up as close as possible to the Jap pillboxes and firing high explosives into the slits. The improved situation is reflected in everyone's face around headquarters.

1600: Bill Hipple and I head east along the beach to Major Crowe's headquarters. By this time we are so confident that the battle is running in our favor that we do not even crouch down, as we walk four feet apart, one ahead of another. After we cross the base of the pier the inevitable sniper's bullet sings by. "Jesus," says Hipple, "do you know that damned bullet went between us?" We crouch down under the protection of the seawall during the rest of the journey.

That tough, old-time Marine, Jim Crowe, is having a tough time yet, but he is still as cool as icebox lettuce. "We kill 'em and more come filtering up from the tail of the island," he says. I ask him about his casualties. "Already had about three hundred in my battalion," he says.

A young tank officer, Lieutenant L. E. Larbey, reports to the major as we are talking to him. "I just killed a Marine, Major Crowe," he says bitterly. "Fragments from my 75 splintered against a tree and ricocheted off. God damn, I hated for that to happen."

"Too bad," mutters Crowe, "but it sometimes happens. Fortunes of war."

The heavy tanks are being used against the pillboxes. They have tried crushing them, but even a thirty-two-ton tank is not very effective against these fortifications. "We got a prisoner last night," said Crowe, "and we have four more, temporarily, sealed up in a pillbox. I suppose they'll kill themselves before we get 'em out."

The strafing planes are coming overhead in waves now and the grease-popping sound of their guns is long and steady. "Don't know how much good they do," says Crowe, "but we know their bullets will kill men if they hit anything. One fifty-caliber slug hit one of my men—went through his shoulder, on down through his lung and liver. He lived about four minutes. Well, anyway, if a Jap ever sticks his head out of his pillbox the planes may kill him."

1630: Crowe is talking on the phone, apparently to Colonel Shoup: "I suggest we hold a line across from the pier tonight." That means his men have advanced about two hundred yards to the east of the island, and he believes they can hold a line all the way across the island, which is about six hundred yards wide at that point. Meantime, my old battalion, plus the reinforcements, are cleaning out the center of the island, Major Ryan's battalion is holding the western end, and a battalion of the Sixth Marines is landing to start down the southern shore.

1700: Hipple and I are surprised to see two more correspondents—we had long since decided that none of the others was alive. But Dick Johnston, a young, pencil-thin U.P. man, and Frank ("Fearless") Filan, A.P. photographer, had also managed to land with the assault waves. "Filan, here," says Johnston, "is a hero. The Marine next to him was shot as they waded in. Filan started helping him back to the boat. But then a sniper opened up on the boat from the side. The Marine beat Filan to the shore. And Filan ruined all his cameras and equipment helping the Marine." The two correspondents report that at least one more correspondent arrived this morning. Don Senick, the newsreelman. "His boat was turned back yesterday," says Johnston, "but they got ashore this morning. Senick ought to get the Purple Heart. He was sitting under a coconut tree. A bullet hit above his head and dropped on his leg. It bruised him."

Lieutenant Larbey sits down beside us. "Were you ever inside a tank when it got hit?" he asks. "The spot inside the tank where the shell hits turns a bright yellow, like a sunrise. My tank got two hits a while ago." Larbey walks back to his iron horse. Says Johnston, "That guy is a genius at keeping his tanks running. He repairs the guns, refuels them somehow, and reloads them with ammunition."

A tall, grinning Marine is here at headquarters getting ammunition. He has a bandage on his arm, and a casualty tag around his neck like those the corpsmen put on every man they treat—in case he collapses later from his wound.

"Get shot in the arm?" asks Jim Crowe.

"Yes, sir," says Morgan.

"What'd you do, stick your arm out of a foxhole, eh?"

"No, sir, I was walking alongside a tank." And Morgan goes on about his business, gathering ammunition. Crowe looks up at the sky, which is full of planes. "Look at them goddamn strafing planes. They haven't killed fifty Japs in two days," he growls.

A grimy Marine seated alongside us muses: "I wonder what our transport did with those sixteen hundred half pints of ice cream that was to be sent ashore yesterday after the battle was over."

An officer comes in and reports to Major Crowe that a sniper is raising hell with the people working on supplies at the end of the pier. By this time we are stacking great piles of supplies on the end of the pier. The officer thinks the fire is coming, not from the beach, but from a light tank that is half sunk in the water. It is the same tank that I saw the naked figure dive into as I came ashore. These devilish Japs!

A destroyer standing so close to shore that it must be scraping bottom has been ordered to fire at a big concrete blockhouse a couple of hundred yards away from us. First, it fires single rounds—five or six of them. Then, when the range is found, it opens up with four guns at a time and to us it seems that all bedlam has broken loose. After about eighty rounds it stops. "They never hit it squarely," says Major Crowe, "but almost."

1803: Now, at three minutes past six, the first two American jeeps roll down the pier, towing 37-mm. guns. "If a sign of certain victory were needed," I note, "this is it. The jeeps have arrived."

1900: Back at regimental headquarters, Colonel Shoup wipes his red forehead with his grimy sleeve and says, "Well, I think we are winning, but the bastards have got a lot of bullets left." I ask him how much longer it would last. "I believe we'll clean up the entire western end of the island tomorrow, maybe more. It will take a day or two more to root them all out of the tail end of the island."

A surgeon grunts and rises from where he has been working feverishly over a dozen wounded Marines who lie on the beach. His blood-plasma containers hang from a line strung between a pole and a bayoneted rifle stuck upright into the ground. Four deathly pale Marines are receiving the plasma through tubes in their arms. "These four will be all right," the doctor thinks, "but there are a lot more up the beach that we probably can't save." He continues, "This battle has been hell on the medical profession. I've got only three doctors out of the whole regiment. The rest are casualties, or they have been lost or isolated. By now nearly all the corpsmen have been shot, it seems to me."

Lieutenant Colonel Presley M. Rixey, a blue-eyed, mustachioed Virginian who commands the artillery attached to Colonel Shoup's regimental combat team, is the first man I have heard pick the turning point of the battle, "I thought up until one o'clock today it was touch and go. Then I knew we would win. It's not over yet, but we've got 'em." Supplies are beginning to flow over the pier in quantity now. The last of Colonel Rixey's 37's and 75's are being landed, "At long last," he says.

"You know what," says Colonel Rixey, "I'll bet these are the heaviest casualties in Marine Corps history. I believe we've already lost more than ten percent of the division and we haven't landed all of it." Until now I haven't considered Tarawa in the light of history. It has only seemed like a brawl—which it is—that we might easily have lost, but for the superb courage of the Marines. But, I conclude, Colonel Rixey may have something there. Maybe this is history.[2]

-1930: Hipple and I begin digging our foxhole for the night—this time a hundred yards further up the beach, next to Amphtrack No. 10. "This one came in on the first wave," says a nearby Marine, "there were twenty men in it, and all but three of them were killed."

As we dig deeper, the smell from our foxhole becomes oppressive. "Not all the Japs used those privies over the

[2] At Soissons July 19, 1918, the Marines suffered 1,303 casualties. They probably took more the first day on Tarawa, and the ratio of dead to wounded was 1 to 2 instead of 1 to 10.

water," I commented. Hipple has finished digging with the shovel, and now he begins smoothing the foxhole with his hands—all foxholes should be finished by hand. The smell is so oppressive we throw a few shovelfuls of sand back into the hole to cover at least some of the odor.

Then we lie down to sleep. It has been more than sixty hours since we closed our eyes and the danger of a night attack has been all but eliminated, so we sleep soundly.

2400: We are rudely awakened after three hours' sleep. The tide has come up and flooded our foxhole. This is unusual, because the tide has not been this high since we reached the island. We sit on a bank of sand, wide-awake and knowing that there will be no more sleep tonight. Besides, Washing Machine Charley will be due soon and nobody can sleep while being bombed.

0500: Washing Machine Charley was over at four o'clock. He dropped eight bombs in his two runs over the island. Said Keith Wheeler, later, "He was absolutely impartial; he dropped half his bombs on us and half on the Japs." Water or no water, we lay face down in our foxhole as he came over. As the bombs hit, there was a blinding flash a couple of hundred yards up the beach, to the west. A few minutes later a Marine came running up the beach, shouting, "There are a lot of men hurt bad up here. Where are the corpsmen and the stretchers?" He was directed to a pile of stretchers nearby. Soon the stretcher bearers returned, silhouetted by the bright half-moon as they walked along the beach. Washing Machine Charley had killed one man, had wounded seven or eight.

0530: At first sight, Bill Hipple looks at what had been our foxhole. Then he learns that the odor was caused, not by Jap excrement, but by the body of a dead man who had been buried beside the foxhole. Bill had been clawing the face of a dead man as he put the finishing touches on the foxhole.

Jungle War

On November 23, 1943, Tarawa was secured. The 2nd Marine Division had lost approximately 3,000 casualties, with less than 1,000 dead; but the enemy had lost almost every man on the island. Out of 4,000 Japanese, hardly more than 100 were taken alive as prisoners.

On December 26, 1943, the 1st Marine Division landed on Cape Gloucester, at the northwestern end of New Britain. While the landings here were comparatively unopposed, there would be at least three months of hard jungle fighting. With the western third of New Britain in U.S. hands, Rabaul would be effectively neutralized for the duration.

The fighting at Cape Gloucester was "a jungle slugging match,* where flame throwers were useless, it was often impossible to throw a grenade more than ten feet ahead, and the bazooka usually failed to detonate upon striking the soft earth of the Jap field works.

"The terrain was as rugged and treacherous as the Japanese. The direction of the advance necessitated what is known technically as cross compartment fighting; i.e., moving at right angles to the natural watershed. This meant that instead of following valleys and ridges, an interminable succession of these had to be crossed. Men would scale one ridge, wiping out the prepared positions, which cluttered both the forward and reverse slopes, then plunge down into another valley where they might or might not find a river which showed on none of their crude maps, with the enemy entrenched on the far bank. One such stream had to be crossed nine times before a bridgehead could be secured. Or perhaps there would be a swamp, neck-deep or worse. Then another fortified ridge, another unknown valley. . . .

"And always the rain and the mud, torrid heat and teeming insect life, the stink of rotten jungle and rotting dead; malaria burning the body and fungus infection eating away the feet, and no hot chow

* Maj. Frank Hough, *The Island War*, p. 168.

for weeks. And fury by day and terror by night and utter weariness all the time. "And death."

In the following narrative, T/Sgt. Asa Bordages describes a small but bitterly fought action at one of the creeks—aptly called Suicide Creek—which held up the advance on Cape Gloucester for a time.

SUICIDE CREEK AT NEW BRITAIN

by T/Sgt. Asa Bordages

They came to "Suicide Creek." It had no name and it was not on the map, but that is what the Marines called it after they had fought two days in vain to win a crossing. The creek is swift, two or three feet deep, perhaps twenty feet across at the widest, twisting between steep banks. It flows over rocks that make footing difficult, and here and there a tree had fallen into the stream. The banks rise steeply from ten to twenty feet, up to little ridges in the jungle of Cape Gloucester.

The Marines didn't know the creek was a moat before an enemy strong point. They couldn't see that the heavy growth across the creek was salted with pillboxes—machine-gun emplacements armored with dirt and logs, some of them dug several stories deep, all carefully spotted so they could sweep the slope and both banks of the stream with interlacing fire.

Only snipers shot at the Marine scouts who crossed the creek, feeling their way through the thickets. More Marines followed, down into the creek, up the steep bank, on into the jungle. Then they got it. The jungle exploded in their faces. They hit the deck, trying to deploy in the bullet-lashed brush and strike back. Marines died there, firing blindly. Snipers picked off some of them as they lay there. It's perfect for snipers when machine guns are firing; you can't hear the single pop above the heavier fire. You don't know you're a target until you're hit.

From the American side of Suicide Creek, Marines gave the trapped platoon overhead fire. The idea is to fling such a volume of fire at the enemy's position that he must hug cover and slacken his fire. The overhead fire spread an umbrella of bullets above the pinned-down platoon, enabling them to crawl out and crawl back across the creek, pulling out their wounded.

That's how it went all day as Marine detachments felt for a gap or a soft spot in the enemy's positions along the creek. They would be hit and pull back, and then detachments would push across the creek at other points. They'd be blasted by invisible machine guns, and leave a few more Marines dead in the brush as they fell back across the creek. Then they'd do it all over again.

There was nothing else they could do. There is no other way to fight a jungle battle—not in such terrain, when the enemy is dug in and your orders are to advance. You don't know where the enemy is. His pillboxes are so camouflaged that you can usually find them only when they fire on you. So you push out scouts and small patrols, until they're fired on. Then you push out patrols from different directions until they too draw fire. Thus you locate the enemy. Then you have to take the emplacements, the pillboxes, one by one in desperate little battles.

Private First Class Calvin B. King, of Pen Mar, Pennsylvania, remembers his platoon crossed the creek four times in a single day and four times had to stumble back under enemy fire. And not until the last time did they see a Jap.

"That time we got maybe a hundred and fifty feet into the brush and then we saw them coming at us," he said. "They had slipped around and were coming in from our flank to wipe us out. There were a lot of 'em. I don't know how many. It looked like they was everywhere.

"They didn't make a sound. They were just coming at us through the trees. We were firing, but they kept coming at us. There were too many of them to stop. We had to pull out. Machine guns were shooting at us from everywhere. And all them Japs coming. We'd pull back a little way and stop and fire, and then we'd fall back a little more.

"Somebody was saying, 'Steady . . . Steady there . . .' But I don't know who it was. I just kept firing. You don't think about nothing. You just shoot. Guys were getting hit. We had to pull them along with us. You can't leave a guy for the Japs. The things they do to 'em . . ."

There was a private first class from Oakland, California. He was blinded by powder burns. He couldn't know it was only temporary. All he knew was that he was blind in the middle of a battle. He was saying, "I can't see." He was fumbling around, trying to feel his way in the brush. The bullets were cutting all around, but he didn't ask anybody to stop fighting to help him. He just hung onto his rifle, like they tell you to, and tried to crawl out, though he couldn't see where to crawl. Corporal Lawrence E. Oliveria, of Fall River, Massachusetts, grabbed the blind boy by the arm, pulling him along as they withdrew. He'd pause to fire, and the blind Marine would wait beside him, and then Corporal Oliveria would lead him back a little farther. "The boy didn't moan or pray or nothing. He just kept saying, every now and then, 'I can't see.' "

By the time they got back to the creek, the Japanese were close on them, charging now. But the Marines had machine guns at the creek. They piled the Jap dead in the brush and broke the charge.

Another platoon tried crossing the creek at another point. Near the head of the line was "the Swede," a private first class from some place out west. He was a big guy, built like a truck, the last man in the world you'd ever suspect of being sentimental. His big ambition was to send his kid sister through college. It took some doing, but he was doing it on his service pay. The Swede was just stepping into the creek when he got it.

"You could hear the bullet hit him in the stomach," said Platoon Sergeant John M. White. "He just stood there a minute. He said, 'Them dirty bastards!' Then he fell down. He was dead.

"When we got across the creek, the fire was so hot we couldn't do a thing. You couldn't see a single Jap. All you could see was where the bullets were hitting around us. And men getting hit. But no matter how bad it got, I never saw one of the boys pass up a wounded man."

Private First Class Charles Conger, of Ventura, California, was one of those hit. A machine gun cut his legs from under him. Nobody saw him. Nobody could have heard him if he'd yelled—the firing was too heavy. He was as alone as a man can be. It was slow, painful, dragging through the brush, crawling head first down the bank, dragging limp legs. He had to pull himself on by inches, then belly down the bank sprayed with bullets as thick as rice thrown at a bride. He tumbled into the creek. The rocks were sharp. He was gasping in the swift water, struggling across against the force of the stream. It was only blind luck that White saw him. White was too far away to help, but he stopped and waved his arms to attract attention, ignoring cover until two Marines who were nearer saw the wounded man in the creek. Those Marines were almost across. Safety lay just ahead. They didn't have to stop. But they went sloshing through the water to the wounded man. They half carried, half dragged him with them.

The battalion tried all day to win a crossing at the creek. In the end, they could only withdraw to the ridge on the American side and dig in for the night. It was getting dusk as one machine-gun platoon finished its gun emplacements. Then the men began digging their foxholes. Most of them were stripped to the waist and they laid aside their weapons as they dug.

That was the moment the enemy chose to charge. They must have slipped across the stream and up the slope and watched the digging. They must have seen that if they could reach those emplacements and get those machine guns, they could swing them and smash the infantry company holding the next section of the line. That is why the Japanese, perhaps fifty of them, did not yell and did not fire a shot. They rushed with bayonets.

Down among his infantrymen, Captain Andrew A. Haldane, of Methuen, Massachusetts, was talking with First Lieutenant Andrew Chisick, of Newark, New Jersey. They heard a Marine yell. They looked up and saw the Japs racing toward the emplacements, and weaponless Marines scattering out of the way. Some had no chance of getting to their weapons. The Japs were hardly thirty yards from the nearest gun and closing fast.

Then more Marines were firing, but it wasn't enough to stop the charge. The nearest Japs were hardly ten feet from the guns. Captain Haldane ran toward the guns, firing as he ran. Lieutenant Chisick ran with him. Others joined the charge, some with bare hands, some with clubs or entrenching tools snatched up from the ground. The Japs reached one gun and swung it to enfilade the line. A Jap was in the gunner's seat. The Marines' charge hit the gun before he could fire a shot. He got a bayonet through the chest. The enemy broke, and the Marines cut them down. More than twenty dead Japs were scattered in the brush by the time it was quiet again.

The Marines were bombed that night. Dive bombers. The enemy set up a heavy fire of tracer bullets to show the bombers where their own lines were and where they should drop their bombs in the dark. Nobody will ever be able to describe a bombing. You can't describe hell. You can only go through it.

The Marines had to take the bombing after a day of battle, without any way of hitting back. The next morning, January 3, they attacked again. The enemy threw mortar shells. Sergeant White saw a shell explode, and ducked down the line to see if anyone was hit. "A kid was sitting there in his foxhole. He didn't have any head. He just had a neck with dog tags on it."

All through that second day, the Marines pushed small units across the creek at different points, still trying to find a soft spot in the Japanese defenses. Each time they were hit. They knocked out some of the machine guns, but each time, in the end, they had to fall back across the creek.

There was a boy firing from behind a log. His face was gray. He stopped firing and looked around. His eyes were dull, without hope.

"It don't do any good," he said. His voice was flat. He

wasn't speaking to anybody. He was just saying it. "I got three of 'em, but it don't do any good."

Platoon Sergeant Casimir Polakowski—known as Ski—said, "What the hell are you beefing about? You get paid for it, don't you?"

The kid managed a grin. As Ski crawled on down the line, the boy was fighting again, squeezing them off.

A platoon was pinned down in the jungle on their flank. They could neither go forward nor withdraw. They could only lie in the brush, held there by a crisscross net of machine-gun fire, while snipers took pot shots at them. Ski's platoon was ordered to lend a hand. They were bone-tired, but Ski said, "Let's get going," and they got.

Three of them were Denham, Melville, and O'Grady. Private Harry Denham, of Nashville, Tennessee, was called "Pee Wee" because he was so small. They say he went to "some fancy military school." But he didn't ask favors of anybody and he wouldn't back down before the biggest man in the regiment. Just a bantam rooster of a kid who'd take on anything that walked. Private First Class John O'Grady, of Ogdensburg, New York, left the talking for the trio to Denham and Melville. He was a quiet guy who never had much to say to anybody, but he seemed to talk plenty when the three of them were off by themselves. Maybe he told them what he wanted to be after the war. The kids all think about that. It's something to look forward to—and a guy needs something to look forward to. Private First Class John William Melville was called "Pete," but nobody seemed to know why. His home was Lynn, Massachusetts. He was twenty-six, almost an old man. He quit a white-collar job with the General Electric Company in Boston to join the Marine Corps.

Denham, Melville, and O'Grady—and Levy, Jones, and Brown—flung themselves at the enemy's flank so he'd have to break the fire that had the other platoon caught. Men dropped, but they kept going forward, fighting from tree to tree. They pushed the enemy back and held him long enough for the trapped platoon to pull out. That was long enough for the Marines to form a line so they couldn't be rolled up by counterattack.

Another lull then. The jungle was still. First Sergeant Selvitelle asked Ski how it was going. Ski was smoking a cigarette. His voice sounded tired.

"They got Denham, Melville, and O'Grady," he said. They were lying out there in the brush somewhere and he was smoking a cigarette.

The word came to move up. There was firing ahead. Maybe an hour later Ski was behind a tree when he saw a wounded Marine lying in the open. A sniper was shooting at the boy. Ski could see the dirt flung up when the bullets hit. The boy was trying to crawl away, but he couldn't.

Ski ran from cover and pulled him to a tree. The sniper saw him. All the sniper had to do was wait until Ski started to return to his post. Then he shot Ski in the back.

That was about the time Tommy Harvard's platoon crossed Suicide Creek, lugging their heavy machine guns. "Tommy Harvard" was the code name for First Lieutenant Elisha Atkins, who played football at Harvard, belonged to the Dekes and the Owls, and got his B.A. in 1942. "Very quiet and polite as hell" is the way a sergeant described him.

The enemy let First Lieutenant Atkins and about half his men cross the creek before they opened up. Six automatic weapons blasted them at point-blank range. There were at least three machine guns with perfect fields of fire. It happened too quickly for anybody to duck.

Sergeant Wills says, "I saw a man ahead of us and just as I saw he wasn't a Marine they all let fly."

Marines were hit. Somebody was screaming. Corporal John R. Hyland of Greenwich, Connecticut, was frowning as he tried to knock out the nearest machine-gun nest with rifle fire. The screaming man stopped.

Corporal Hyland said, "We ought to get the hell out of here." But he didn't move to go. He kept his place, still shooting at the spot of jungle where he guessed the gunport was, until the order was passed to withdraw.

The machine guns swept the brush just higher than a man lying flat. The trapped Marines rolled down the bank or pushed backward on their bellies until they could tumble into the creek. The screening bush was their only protection against the snipers perched in trees. As they rolled into the stream, they hunkered down as low as they could in the water. Some got down so only their faces showed above the water. All of them pressed against the Japanese bank as bullets slashed through the undergrowth above them, splattering the creek and the American bank beyond.

Two of the Marines had fallen on a big log lying in the creek. One of them was hit in the leg and couldn't move, but he was near enough for Sergeant Wills to pull him into the creek. Other Marines dragged him up against the brush-choked bank; but they couldn't reach the other boy on the log. He lay too far out in the field of fire. He'd caught a full machine-gun burst. He must have had twenty holes in him, but he was still alive. He was hung over the log, partly in the water. He was calling weakly, "Here I am, Wills . . . over here . . ."

They couldn't help him. They could only listen to him.

"Wills . . . I'm here . . . Wills . . ."

There were other wounded in the creek above them. They couldn't help them either. Most of those crouching in the bushes against the bank were wounded, too. The kid on the log was getting weaker. Just listening was harder than anything Sergeant Wills ever had to take.

"He was calling me, and I couldn't help him. All of them were guys we knew, but we couldn't do a thing. We had to lay in the water and listen to them. It was the coldest damn water I ever saw. Their blood kept flowing into our faces."

Their only chance was to creep downstream close against the bank and then make a dash, one by one, for the American shore. A little way down the twisting stream there was a spot where a man would have a chance to make it. Most places, he would have to stop to climb the bank. Only a man who wanted to commit suicide would try that.

It was slow work for the men in the creek, crawling downstream in the racing water, hampered by the thick tangles of vines and brush. Men caught in the vines struggled helplessly.

"Everybody had to cut everybody else loose as we went

along," says Private First Class Luther J. Raschke, of Harvard, Illinois.

He found young Tommy Harvard tangled in the vines and cut him loose. "I tried to help him along, but he wouldn't come. He'd been hit three times. A slug had smashed his shoulder. He was losing blood pretty fast. But he wouldn't leave. He was trying to see that everybody got out first. He told me, 'Go on, go on!' He wouldn't let anybody stop for him. He said, 'Keep the line moving!' He made us leave him there."

They made their dash; got safely out and reached the line of foxholes to which the battalion had fallen back again after that second day.

But Raschke couldn't forget the wounded officer they'd left in the creek. He said, "I guess everybody else is out."

"Yeah," said Corporal Alexander Caldwell, of Nashville, Tennessee.

"Well . . ."

"Yeah," said Corporal Caldwell.

So they got permission to go back into no man's land to hunt for their platoon leader. Corporal Caldwell took along two more volunteers, for they might have to carry Lieutenant Atkins, if they found him, and they might have to fight their way out. They were Louis J. Sievers, of Johnstown, Pennsylvania, and Joseph V. Brown, of Middletown, New York, both privates first class.

It was getting hard to see when they crawled down to the creek. Raschke stopped. They lay listening, but they could hear nothing except the rushing stream and, now and then, the sound of the Japanese talking. They had to make their choice then. They could go back without the lieutenant. Or they could risk calling. Nobody would blame them if they went back. Nobody would know they hadn't done everything they could do to find him.

Raschke lay on the edge of the stream and he remembers clearer than anything else how close the water was under his nose. The others were in the bush, rifles ready to fire if the enemy discovered him. Not that it would do any good. He'd be dead. For that matter, if the machine guns opened up, they'd all be dead.

"I was scared stiff," Raschke says. "I called as softly as I could, 'Tommy Harvard . . . Tommy Harvard . . .'

"A voice said, 'I'm down here.'

"It sounded weak, but we figured it might be a trap. So I said, 'What's your real name?'

"The voice said, 'Elisha Atkins.' So we knew it was him. We crawled down and pulled him out. He said, 'God! Am I glad to see you!' "

He was shaking from hours in the chill water, weak from loss of blood, but still calmly Harvard as they carried him to the rear.

During the two days the 3rd Battalion had been fighting vainly to win the crossing of Suicide Creek, the outfit on its left had been trying as stubbornly and as vainly to get across its segment of the stream.

During those two days, Marine Pioneers were toiling to build a corduroy road through the swamp in their rear so that tanks could be moved up to the line. The tanks finally reached the outfit on the 3rd Battalion's left, but they found the banks of the creek too steep for crossing. The gully formed a natural tank trap. So a Marine bulldozer was called to cut down the banks of the creek and make a fill in the stream so that the tanks could cross against the enemy.

The Japanese saw their danger. They concentrated fire on the bulldozer. Man after man was shot from the driver's seat—some killed, some wounded. But there was always a Marine to jump in the seat. He had no shield, no protection at all. He sat up in the open like a shooting-gallery target for all the enemy's fire. But the Marine bulldozer kept on till the fill was made and the tanks were rolling across the creek.

The advance of the tanks made the positions of the enemy opposing the 3rd Battalion untenable. If they tried to hold against the frontal attack of the 3rd Battalion, they would be hit by tanks and infantry from the flank. They'd be a nut in a nutcracker. They had to retreat or be crushed, and they retreated. The crossing of Suicide Creek had been won.

Island-Hopping

Neutralizing Rabaul relieved the Jap threat to MacArthur's flank. He could now continue his drive along the New Guinea coast toward the Philippines.

With the successful strikes at the Gilberts, and the beginning of heavy bombing and strafing attacks on the Marshalls, our strategy in the Pacific was beginning to jell. "The new technique had been perfected: neutralize and by-pass all enemy strongpoints not essential to our purposes in order to seize a strategically important airdrome or naval anchorage, which could be used to neutralize further strongpoints, and open up the next strategic objective." *

The next blow fell, early in 1944, on the Marshalls, a large cluster of coral islands (one of which—Kwajalein—was the largest coral atoll in the world). The Marshalls were to the north and east of the Carolines, which included the great enemy base at Truk. And the Marshalls were part of the prewar Japanese Empire—the first to be attacked by U.S. forces. They were thus the outer edge of the main Japanese defenses, but the enemy High Command had decided not to risk the fleet in their defense. The Japanese troops on the spot were ordered to hold fast—to the bitter end, if necessary.

The assault forces which hit Kwajalein, under the command of Maj. Gen. Holland M. Smith, were made up of the 4th Marine Division, not yet bloodied in battle, and the 7th Infantry Division, which had seen service in the Aleutians.

Although the Kwajalein assault came close on the heels of Tarawa, the naval commanders quickly put to use the lessons learned at Tarawa: i.e., longer periods of bombing and shelling to lighten the load for the assault troops; many more amphtracks to get the troops across the reefs usually found encircling atolls; artillery and tanks put quickly on the beaches to give the troops fire support.

Resistance on Kwajalein Atoll was crushed completely by February

* Maj. Frank Hough, *The Island War,* p. 211.

7, 1944. One week later, an assault force moved out to invade Eniwetok, another atoll in the Marshalls, with two good airfields only 669 miles from Truk. The Marshall Islands conquest gave the Allies bases for new air and sea operations, fanning out over a radius of 2,000 miles to the Marianas and Palau. Airfields on the Marshalls, once in operation, effectively neutralized Truk. "Island-hopping had evolved into island-leapfrogging. In the process tens of thousands of soldiers on whom Japan had depended to retard the progress of the U.S. sat impotently on their arms without firing a shot from the beginning to the end of the war." *

END ON SAIPAN

by Maj. Frank Hough

The seizure of the Marshalls and MacArthur's drive along northern New Guinea had effectively flanked Truk; had provided us with bases from which it could be kept neutralized and from which we could mount an attack against it should we so desire. But it had not been cut off from the homeland and its intermediate bases. Troops and supplies could still be poured in. This was an expensive process now, but we had reason to believe that it was being done, and with some success. Truk, a tough nut to begin with, was getting no softer fast, despite the knocking out of its air power.

The same applied to a number of other places. Our swift conquest of Tarawa had startled the Japanese. Seriously alarmed by the success of our operations in the Marshalls, they set about a hurried modification of their basic strategy. So long as their outer defense line held, their intermediate defenses had been of secondary importance. Now, in a kind of frenzy, they began pouring troops, equipment and sup-

* Maj. Frank Hough, *The Island War*, p. 211.

plies into the Marianas and western Carolines at an unprecedented rate.

Experience had proved that there was no foretelling with any certainty where we would strike next; therefore, they were obliged to reinforce all of their garrisons in this area, giving such priorities as they could to those spots which, to their minds, appeared our most probable objectives. As usual, when they had any leeway at all for their calculations, they guessed wrong.

The strain on their resources was severe, aggravated as it was by the brilliant work of the U.S. submarines in the waters which their convoys must traverse. How many thousands of lives and tons of supplies and shipping were lost during this period probably never will be known.

To obtain the necessary troops, they were obliged to draw upon armies in the homeland, China, and Manchuria. One aspect of the long-range effect of this was brought out dramatically more than a year later. When the Russians attacked in Manchuria on the eve of the war's end, they, and the world in general, were somewhat astonished to discover that the vaunted Kwantung Army was only an ineffective hollow shell of its former self. But the men who had fought their way across the Pacific were not surprised; they knew that the cream of that army had died long since, out there in the islands.

But all this is second-guessing; utilizing knowledge obtained during and after the operation in question. At the time the Marianas campaign was determined upon, we knew only enough to convince the planners that, while this would constitute a bold stroke, the indications were that it would not be a rash one. The threefold advantage to be gained in the shortest possible time was the determining factor: (1) Truk would be absolutely and irrevocably cut off; (2) we would be established firmly in the enemy's intermediate defense line; (3) we would have air bases within heavy-bomber range of Tokyo itself.

Reliable intelligence had been exceedingly difficult to obtain. We had some fair estimates of the respective garrison strengths at the time of the Marshalls operation and we knew that these had been heavily reinforced since, but whether they had been doubled, tripled or even quadrupled we had no sure way of estimating. This was especially the case with the main Japanese base, Saipan, which also served as a staging point for the entire area, as well as for Truk, Woleai and other strong points in the central and western Carolines. Any attack here would be certain to encounter an inestimable number of transient troops standing by for shipment elsewhere, over and above the greatly augmented garrison.

Second only to Saipan in strength and importance was Guam, our former possession which had been lost in the early days of the war. Guam was the southernmost of the Marianas and the largest of the group—indeed, the largest island in the Central Pacific between the Hawaiians and the Philippines. Of lesser importance but known to contain garrisons and airfields were: Rota, thirty-two miles northeast of Guam; Tinian, two and one half miles southwest of Saipan and within easy artillery range of that island; and Pagan, 172 miles north of Saipan.

To strike this vital blow against what was, in many respects, an unknown quantity, the High Command mustered the most powerful force to operate in the Pacific up to this time; the largest force ever to operate under Marine command. This included both Amphibious Corps, embracing three Marine divisions and one Marine brigade, all reinforced, and two reinforced Army Infantry divisions, plus Corps and miscellaneous supporting troops. Here was every assault unit the Marine Corps had in the Pacific at the time, with the sole exception of the First Division, as yet unrecuperated from the protracted New Britain campaign.

The chain-of-command was unique and somewhat confusing, although it worked out excellently. The plan called for division of the whole force into two groups under single over-all command: the Northern Group[1] (V Amphibious Corps, Lieutenant General Holland M. Smith) to attack Saipan, and, when the situation warranted, to stage a shore-to-

[1] For official purposes this group was given the unwieldy title: Northern Troops and Landing Force (NTLF). Southern Group was similarly designated STLF.

shore assault on Tinian; and the Southern Group (III Amphibious Corps, Major General Roy S. Geiger) to attack Guam. The Marine Corps at this time had no echelon in the field higher than an amphibious corps; yet here was a situation where two amphibious corps must operate together under a single over-all command which, according to book, simply did not exist.

The troops assigned to the Northern operation numbered altogether about 77,413, not all of them, of course, strictly assault troops. The combat units included the Second Marine Division, veterans of Guadalcanal and Tarawa; the Fourth Marine Division, veterans of the Marshalls; and the Twenty-seventh Infantry Division (Army), one regiment of which had fought at Makin, another at Eniwetok. Supporting these were various corps troops, notably artillery, both Army and Marine, the 7th Field Depot, four Marine and four Army Amphibian Tractor battalions operating a total of 722 vehicles, and one Army DUKW (amphibious truck) battalion plus one separate company.

Also brought along was an odd orphan battalion whose somewhat enigmatic status might better be cleared up at the outset. This was made up of men, many of them combat veterans, who had been crowded out of the divisions by the revision of the Tables of Organization. Known originally as the 2nd Marine Provisional Battalion, on the eve of sailing for Saipan it was designated 1st Battalion, 29th Marines, the remainder of that regiment being currently in training at New River, North Carolina, and due overseas shortly. Throughout this operation 1/29 was attached to the 8th Marines, Second Division, forming in effect a fourth battalion of that regiment and proving a very useful addition.

Just what strength the Japanese could muster against this array was not known with any certainty. Estimates ranged from twenty thousand to twenty-five thousand combat troops, which would seem to give us fair assurance of having the minimum three-to-one numerical superiority deemed necessary to success in an amphibious assault against a strongly held position. This proved a remarkably shrewd estimate for all practical purposes. Later studies, during and after the operation, indicated that actually there were

29,662 enemy troops on Saipan on D-Day, but the discrepancy was largely compensated for by the fact that the most recently arrived were virtually unarmed as a result of U.S. submarine attacks on their convoy on the way out.

The Marine divisions assigned to this operation had had combat experience, but not in terrain even approximately resembling this. Here was no small, flat atoll island to be overrun in a matter of hours of concentrated, savage fighting: like Tarawa, where the Second Division had fought, or Roi-Namur, where the Fourth Division had received its baptism of fire. Nor was it, by any stretch of the imagination, another Guadalcanal. There the Second Division had mastered the close-in bitterness of jungle fighting; here they would be mostly in the open, against a dug-in enemy strongly supported by artillery.

Another novel feature was provided by the civilian inhabitants of the place. Hitherto, the only natives encountered on target areas in the Pacific had been scattered handfuls of Melanesians and Micronesians, semisavages who had no special stake in the outcome and were interested only in keeping out of the way until the issue was settled. But Saipan, as a result of Japanese development and immigration, had attained a reasonably high degree of civilization and boasted a civilian population reliably estimated to number in the vicinity of twenty thousand persons.

The attack on Saipan achieved tactical surprise, to a greater degree, perhaps, than the planners had dared to hope. Although repeated air strikes had neutralized the airfields, so had similar strikes neutralized all the other islands within reach. It was not until the intensive two-day prelanding naval bombardment was well under way that the Japanese High Command on Saipan became convinced that their island, not any one of a dozen others, was to be our true objective.

There was a reason for this. In spite of the urgency of strengthening their intermediate defense line, the Japanese were physically incapable of strengthening all these islands simultaneously; hence, had been obliged to work out a system of priorities. In their infinite wisdom, they reached the conclusion that MacArthur's drive along the New

Guinea coast would outrun the drive across the Central Pacific and therefore assigned to the Palaus, far to the southwest, top priority on men, armament, building materials. The Marianas' elaborately planned defenses were not scheduled for completion until November.

But this was all to the good on 15 June, 1944: beaches and reefs were unmined, heavy coast defense guns lay unmounted beside their half-finished emplacements, permanent defense positions were makeshift or negligible, and there was no organized system of defense in depth on all of Saipan.

Once they had determined our intentions, however, the Japanese command reacted with their customary vigor, and somewhat unaccustomed acumen. They picked our landing beaches accurately and refused to be fooled by any feints elsewhere, although a last-minute demonstration by the floating reserve off Tanapag Harbor did delay transfer of one regiment temporarily. Already they had considerable artillery in position to defend the threatened area, and more was rushed to the scene with all possible expediency. Unfortunately for them, the ferocity of the naval gunfire and air strikes caused such heavy casualties that they were obliged to move the guns to the reverse slopes of the low ridges in that neighborhood where their full effectiveness could not be brought to bear until the landings were well under way.

As in the Gilberts and Marshalls, the landing had to be made over coral, the fringing reef here extending seaward a distance of eight to twelve hundred yards. There was a narrow deep-water passage through to the docks at Charan Kanoa, but enemy artillery had this so well zeroed-in that it proved unusable until these guns could be put out of action. So it was over the reef that the Marines came, and so well had the technique been developed as a result of previous operations that seven hundred-odd amphtracks landed some eight thousand men in the first twenty minutes.

But such are the complications of any ship-to-shore movement that even an unopposed landing is bound to be fouled-up in one way or another. And enemy artillery, mortar and anti-boat gunfire made the Saipan landing a grim and bloody business, for all the expedition with which it was carried off. The amphibious tanks, which were supposed to support the assault waves across the reef and then spearhead the drive inland, proved so slow and clumsy that they were soon outstripped by the LVT's, thus losing much of their effectiveness.

The invasion began as a toe-to-toe slugging match and continued that way throughout the first two days. The Japanese were supremely confident. They had an unusual proportion of heavy weapons and tanks. Despite the fact that they had not really expected to be attacked until the last minute, they had managed to get plenty of troops to the scene; even though these did not have permanent prepared positions of the sort they might have liked, terrain features were all in their favor. And, as so often happened, they underestimated the strength of the attackers.

The evening of D-Day found the 10,000-yard beachhead pushed inland to a maximum depth of about 1,500 yards. Artillery was set up and firing, tanks and the Division command posts were ashore. But the situation was far from good. The Japanese still held dominating heights in front of the Marine positions, still had plenty of artillery and heavy mortars. Our lines were not integrated in places, units being out of direct contact with their neighbors. The largest and most serious gap was the one which had existed all day between the two divisions. In an effort to close this, 1/29 (the orphan battalion previously described) had been landed during the afternoon on the right of the 8th Marines, to which regiment they remained attached throughout the campaign. But the gap still remained at nightfall, and the two divisions dug in with their inner flanks deeply refused (bent backward).

There was artillery fire all night; heavier artillery fire than troops of ours had ever before received from the Japanese.

The second day saw a continuation of the dogged slugging match, and again the situation at nightfall was one to cause concern. We still lacked possession of the ridge which marked the O-1 Phase Line. The 165th Infantry, of the Twenty-seventh Infantry Division, had been thrown in on the left of the 23rd Marines in another attempt to close the gap between the divisions; another futile effort. Casualties for the two days already ran over 3,500—twenty per cent of those to be sustained during the entire campaign. Tanks had proved largely useless in the face of so much enemy artillery. With all Marine reserve troops ashore and committed, there was real danger of losing the initiative should fighting continue on such a scale, a serious business at this stage of an operation.

One puzzling feature of those first two days was the small number of enemy dead found in the overrun positions. Past experience indicated that, with such heavy shelling and intensive fighting, heavy casualties to the defending side were inevitable. Yet few indications were found that this was the case here. Not until later, when the advance began to discover concentrations of Japanese bodies well behind the former lines, was it definitely established that the enemy had been carrying off their own dead. This was a new wrinkle with them, and it fooled, or partially fooled, a number of our people. It was to recur repeatedly, however, in subsequent operations.

With the swinging of the main drive toward the north, clearing the southeastern corner of the island was assigned to the Twenty-seventh Infantry Division, two regiments of which were now ashore. The 165th Infantry secured Aslito airfield on D + 3 and drove on to the eastern shore. Here they wheeled southward, with the 105th on their right, gradually driving the enemy back to the narrowing confines of Nafutan Point. The terrain here was rugged and heavily jungled, making progress slow and difficult. After several days of strenuous work, however, the surviving Japanese were penned into a small pocket on high ground near the tip of the point, where the 2nd Battalion, 105th Infantry, was left to contain them while the 165th and 106th, which had landed on D + 5, were transferred northward to join the main drive.

The dual aftermaths of this move did not occur until some days later and will be discussed here in their chronological relation to the campaign as a whole.

D + 3 definitely marked the conclusion of the initial phase of the Saipan operation. Matters had not worked out strictly in accordance with expectations. Casualties had been higher than anticipated, for one thing: 4,856 altogether, including six battalion commanders, some of the assault units sustaining up to sixty per cent. Somewhat makeshift means had to be devised for evacuation of the wounded. These were taken offshore by such craft as happened to be available for the purpose and transshipped to such transports as had the means to care for them, often before adequate records could be made. Since these transports were departing from time to time for widely divergent ports, men carried on the casualty lists as missing in action often turned up weeks and even months later in hospitals in such unexpected places as the Admiralty Islands, Guadalcanal, even Nouméa.

Another difficulty was caused by the civilian population. Civil Affairs officers were included on both Division and Corps T/O's (Table of Organization), but this was the first time they had been called upon to cope with the problem on anything but the smallest scale. They were wholly unable to obtain adequate personnel for the job, or to get priorities on food, transportation or gear necessary for caring for their charges.

Although the island's second town lay directly in the zone of the initial assault, it was assumed for some obscure reason that few, if any, civilians would be taken during the first few days. Actually there were some four hundred in our hands on D-Day, 1,500 by the end of D + 2; wretched, homeless creatures for whom we had no food, no clothes, no guards and not even the beginnings of a stockade where they might be secured and sheltered. Fortunately they proved patient, docile people, and soon supplies of Japanese food were captured which proved sufficient for their immediate needs, although the conditions under which they were obliged to exist for some time reflected little credit upon their captors.

There were three other features of the Japanese defensive effort during those first four days which, although their effect on the outcome was negligible, deserve mention here.

Early on the morning of D + 3, the Japanese injected an element of novelty into the proceedings by attempting an amphibious operation of their own. Intelligence had been aware for some time that the enemy had organized special units whose object was to effect landings behind our lines, on the not wholly ridiculous theory that, once the assault troops were well engaged some distance inland, the beaches would be exceedingly vulnerable. These special units had, on paper, well worked-out T/O's and quite elaborate tactical instructions, which we had never had the opportunity of seeing them attempt to carry out until that morning of 18 June. Then, in the first light of dawn, thirty-five landing barges were discovered making their way out of Tanapag Harbor, heading south with bland disregard for the powerful naval force standing by some distance to seaward. Not that this force was necessary; with the aid of a lone destroyer, the LCI gunboats blew the whole flotilla out of the water in a matter of minutes.

Another feature was air attack. The first Condition Red sounded early in the night of D-Day, and because the enemy air potential in the area was known to be considerable, caused the transport convoy to put to sea. They might as well have saved themselves the trouble. Only two to six planes came over, dropped a few poorly directed bombs and departed hurriedly. Such raids became almost nightly features throughout the campaign, with never anything resembling a serious attack in force. In the course of twenty-six small raids during fourteen nights, fourteen of the raiders were shot down by AA fire, and after the captured airfield had been made operational for our own planes the danger was still further lessened.

Long-range artillery fire from neighboring Tinian, five thousand yards to the southwest, also proved an occasional nuisance, nothing more. Some of our own 155's were assigned to deal with this. Time after time they seemed to have knocked out the enemy emplacements, only to have the guns open up again a day or so later. It was merely harassing fire, however, poorly directed and in the main ineffective.

By now the Japanese failure must have been evident even to themselves. Far from driving the invaders into the sea, they themselves had been driven from their strong positions, forced back all along the line. Their communications had been so disrupted that, although this was not immediately apparent, they lacked the means to organize major counter-attacks with sufficient promptness to cope with changing situations. Yet their morale remained unimpaired, as it would for many days to come before the bitter, desperate end.

One reason for this was their extraordinary powers of self-deception. A complete log of incoming and outgoing radio messages, captured later, illustrated this graphically. Abject failure did nothing to diminish the confident boastfulness of the island command. Over the air waves, the battle they fought was terrific indeed, with every retreat a brilliant victory inflicting fantastic losses upon the rash invaders. No one reading through those dispatches, without knowledge of what was actually happening, could avoid the conviction that the Japanese were winning, and handsomely. And that, apparently, is just what the people at home believed. Not until the last suicide-bent straggler leaped into the sea from Marpi Point did the Government have any real inkling that the battle was going against them, that Saipan had been irrevocably doomed for three weeks, and the blow hit with such stunning force as to bring the Tojo Cabinet down with a crash that shook the whole Greater East Asia Co-Prosperity Sphere.

But the home Government had been practicing precisely the same sort of mumbo jumbo on its own part. For encouragement of the brave boys at the front, it cooked up a series of smashing victories all over the Pacific and sank the whole U.S. Navy two or three times more. And the fighting men seemed to accept all this as no more than the literal truth. What if a considerable portion of the "sunken" enemy fleet lay in plain sight offshore shelling the daylights out of them at leisure, and the skies were dark with the invaders' planes from carriers and the captured airfield? The mighty Navy of Nippon would soon take care of those interlopers, sink them as many times more as might be necessary.

On D + 4 (19 June) realignments for the northward drive had been completed, and the advance began. The going was slow and produced some hard though unspectacular fighting. The southern portion of the island, low and comparatively level, with canefields and much cleared land, had been mostly secured by now, and the advance lay across rising ground, increasingly brush covered, toward the dominating height of Mount Tapotchau.

Here were encountered with increasing frequency those geological phenomena common to such formations, which were to play such an important part in all operations in the western islands: coral-limestone caves, occurring naturally as a result of the upward pressure of volcanic forces which had created the island and broken its surface into sharp ridges and ravines. These caves furnished splendid defensive positions, particularly to a people with the naturally underground tendencies and endless patience of the Japanese. They occurred usually in the faces of cliffs, in defilade from artillery or naval gunfire and all but invulnerable to aerial bombing. They were susceptible to man-made improvements, but fortunately on Saipan there had been little time or materials available for such work. Here were few of the reinforced concrete bulkheads, steel doors, elaborate galleries which would be encountered in some later operations. Nor had many of the natural positions been developed to obtain scientifically interlocking fields of fire for mutual protection.

The caves on Saipan could usually be by-passed, and this was precisely what was done. The assault troops pushed on, keeping unrelenting pressure on the enemy, leaving the reduction of the caves and their immobilized occupants to special mopping-up details from the reserve, liberally equipped with flame throwers and demolition charges.

The movement pivoted on the 2nd Marines, holding the extreme left, on the island's western shore. This unit had seized its sector of the designated final beachhead line and held there, making no advance at all until D + 9, when they moved to the outskirts of Garapan. They had received special training in town fighting, hitherto unknown in the Pacific, and had as one of their principal objects the capture of the island capital.

The 6th Marines, on the right of the 2nd, did not do much advancing either during the early stages but patrolled extensively to their front. On their right the 8th (with 1/29 attached) faced exceedingly difficult terrain, rising ruggedly to Tapotchau itself.

At the beginning of the drive, the Fourth Division adjoined the Second Division on the right, with the 23rd and 24th Marines in line, the 25th in reserve, though these regimental positions were shifted from time to time. This was comparatively simple while they were traversing the narrow waist of the island where Magicienne Bay cut deeply inland. By the evening of D + 7, however, they had reached the upper end of the bay where the broad, blunt projection of the Kagman Peninsula adds another two miles, approximately, to the island's width. To cope with this suddenly expanded front, it was necessary to bring the Twenty-seventh Infantry Division forward to take over the center of the lines while the Fourth took over the new sector on the right, thereby giving rise to one of the most unfortunate incidents in the whole Pacific war.

For a fair understanding of this controversial subject, it may be well to consider the position in which the members of the Twenty-seventh Division found themselves when they were moved into the front lines on D + 8.

Although the 165th Infantry had seen action on Makin and the 106th on Eniwetok, this had been of brief duration and fought under utterly different conditions than those encountered on Saipan. Furthermore, the Army's training differed in several essentials from that of the Marines, as did certain tactical conceptions of its leaders. Yet now three infantry regiments (less 2/105) were placed between two veteran Marine divisions to advance across naturally difficult terrain contested by a determined enemy.

The result was that, not only did they fail to keep pace with the advance of the elements on either flank, but for the first two days they failed to achieve any essential advance at all.

They had been trained to conserve their strength; to rely upon artillery and air strikes to knock out major obstacles in their path before committing the infantry to assault, regardless of how long this might take. The Marine hypothesis, on the other hand, held time to be of the essence. An amphibious operation against a sizable land mass was utterly dependent upon the uninterrupted flow of supplies across the landing beaches: the offensive must be sustained and the enemy kept off balance until a final beachhead line is established beyond artillery range of these beaches and deep enough to insure against a sudden breakthrough in force to the rear areas, otherwise the beaches cannot be considered secure and the whole operation remains in jeopardy. This had been the main tactical consideration at Guadalcanal, Bougainville and Cape Gloucester.

Cut from the same cloth was a difference in tactical method which contributed further to slowing down the advance in the center. With the object of keeping unremitting pressure on the enemy, the Marine units continued advancing until dusk, when they dug in on a continuous line of double foxholes, either with no flanks or with the flanks deeply refused. The Army units, on the other hand, halted an hour or more before dark and established a series of mutually supporting strong points: ideally, two companies of a battalion forward, each dug in on a full perimeter defense, and the third some distance behind and covering the gap between them.

Each method had its characteristic advantages—and disadvantages. The Marines claimed that theirs, in addition to maintaining the utmost pressure on the enemy, provided the greatest possible protection against that Japanese tactical specialty, infiltration. It was, however, much harder on the men and might have proved a serious weakness in the event of a major breakthrough since nothing remained behind the front line except for the mortars and the command posts. They contended further that the Army method was a setup for infiltration, especially since the early hour of digging-in gave the enemy plenty of time to scout the position by daylight and form their plans accordingly.

That the Army method constituted a stronger defense in depth was undeniable, but this appeared a minor point in view of the enemy's apparent inability, since D + 2, to attack in force. And even this argument was weakened subsequently when the only two major breakthroughs achieved by the Japanese during the campaign were effected at the expense of the ill-starred 105th Infantry.

There were other minor differences, all stemming from the same root, notably methods of using artillery and the Army's refusal to by-pass enemy pockets of resistance, however ineffectual and immobilized these might be. The difference in theory was, at this stage, a fundamental one. The Army contended that Marine methods were reckless of human life; unnecessarily so. The Marines held the Army to be overcautious to the point of timidity; that securing with all possible speed was all important in an amphibious operation, and that the smaller number of initial casualties incurred by the Army method was more than counterbalanced in the end owing to the necessarily longer duration of the campaign.

What it all added up to was that, on this first attempt at a unified operation, the two theories were not readily reconciled. When the Twenty-seventh Division could not, or would not, keep pace with the two Marine divisions, the inside flanks of those units were left dangerously exposed, to the peril of the entire effort. And when, after two days, Major General Ralph Smith, Commanding General of the Twenty-seventh, could not (or, again, would not) take the steps necessary to remedy the situation, Lieutenant General Holland M. Smith, Commanding General of the V Amphibious Corps and Northern Marianas Attack Group, arbitrarily relieved him of his command.

There is nothing novel about an officer being relieved of his command in the field. It has occurred in every major war which has ever been fought. It occurred numerous times in this war; in the Army, Navy and Marine Corps. What raised the hue and cry in the case of Smith vs. Smith was the fact that the two officers involved belonged to different branches of the service; that a general in the senior and vastly larger branch had been removed by a general in the junior and much smaller service, regardless of the fact that the Marine Corps held the command and responsibility for this particular operation, and furnished the bulk of the troops.

But the Saipan affair did not involve arbitary imposition of Marine command upon an Army division, as many were led to believe from the heated and none-too-clear debate in the press, and elsewhere. The officer succeeding to the command of the Twenty-seventh Division was Major General Sanford Jarman, U.S. Army, who had been brought along to be Commanding General of Saipan garrison forces once the island was secure. Under General Jarman and his successor, the Twenty-seventh gradually pulled itself together, rectified its tactical position, and carried on successfully against the enemy until close to the end of the campaign.

The change in command of the Twenty-seventh Division took place on D + 9 (24 June). In the meanwhile, the advance had continued steadily, inexorably but slowly, against stubborn opposition, complicated by difficulties in getting supplies forward over the rugged, jungle-choked terrain.

On D + 7 the 6th Marines cleared the way for an assault by the adjoining 8th Marines upon Mount Tapotchau by capturing the hill known as Tipo Pale, dominating the strongly held valley which flanked the main elevation. For the next two days the 8th Marines and their attached elements fought their way stubbornly upward. On D + 10, supported by a heavy mortar barrage, elements of 1/29 and the Second Division Reconnaissance Company executed a brilliant encircling movement behind the Japanese troops dug in on the forward slope and occupied the summit, nearly surprising the enemy CP located in a tunnel dug all the way through the narrow crest.

A strong counterattack was beaten off during the night, but the hill was not really secured until the remaining elements of the 8th Marines had cleared the enemy entirely from the reverse and flanking slopes, a job which took the better part of the next two days. This accomplished, all units with any excuse for doing so proceeded to establish observation posts up there, affording them a remarkably clear view of the entire northern half of the island.

With the fall of Tipo Pale, which dominated Garapan, the 2nd Marines had advanced along the western shore to the lower edge of that town, where they dug in to await straightening of the whole front line. On the extreme right the Fourth Division completed mopping up of the entire Kagman Peninsula in three days and anchored their flank firmly on the shore again. Early in the morning of D + 11, the 2nd Battalion, 25th Marines, from the reserve, was moved into the gap on the left of the 8th Marines caused by the clearing of the Tapotchau slopes, tying in with the Twenty-seventh Division, in the center, which was still in the process of getting straightened out under its new commanding general. Thus, by D + 12 (27 June) a firm and well-integrated line had been established across the full width of the island, firmly securing dominant Mount Tapotchau and somewhat more than the entire southern half of Saipan.

About this time occurred a novel incident which, though it had no effect upon the outcome of the campaign, brought some passing excitement to the people in the rear areas who had begun to believe themselves pretty remote from the war.

As previously related, a Japanese detachment of undetermined size had been cut off in the south when the 25th Marines had reached the eastern shore. The Twenty-seventh Division, taking over this sector, had driven them gradually into a corner on Nafutan Point, the southeastern tip of the island, where 2/105 had been left to contain them and finish them off at leisure. During the night of D + 11 (26 June) a sizable group of these broke out of the trap and started hellbent for the airfield where our planes were now freely operating.

The effort was unusually well organized as such things go, complete with written orders, a chain-of-command and a slogan deemed fitting for the occasion: "Seven lives to repay our country"—meaning, evidently, that each man was supposed to kill seven Americans before going to join his ancestors. In addition, they were to do as much damage as possible to installations and equipment, and try to get through to their own lines to the north.

Exactly how many started out on this fantastic sortie it would be impossible to say. Some five hundred bodies were counted in the morning, and it is quite possible that some got through to their own lines, or at least to the cover of the hilly jungle.

They were singularly unsuccessful in all respects. Not only did they fail to kill "seven for one"; it is improbable that they killed much more than seven for the whole five hundred. They got as far as the edge of the airfield where they destroyed one parked plane and damaged two others before being driven off by an aroused crowd of Seabees and aviation ground personnel. The survivors then struck out toward the north where presently they came up against the CP of the 25th Marines, currently in reserve. There, to all intents and purposes, the effort ended, though irritated Marines from artillery and other infantry units were still blasting stragglers out of bushes and holes well into the morning.

On the front the next few days were spent in minor advances and consolidating positions. Then on D + 17 (2 July) the whole line surged forward. On the left the 2nd Marines, specially trained in town fighting, occupied the high ground behind Garapan and fought their way about halfway through the rubble of the town itself. Farther inland the remainder of the Second Division scored substantial advances against diminishing opposition, the rejuvenated Twenty-seventh Division in the center keeping pace. The Fourth Division also moved with alacrity, except on the extreme right, along the shore, where strong Japanese concentrations in prepared positions were encountered.

The advance continued in much the same manner for the next three days. On the left the 2nd Marines completed the occupation of Garapan on D + 18, and the 6th pushed on to Tanapag Harbor, by-passing enemy strong points on swampy Mutcho Point. On the following day they advanced another 1,500 yards, securing the important dock area, and the 8th Marines took the sea plane base. The center, too, scored steady, substantial gains, but the extreme right continued to encounter difficulties, causing that flank to bend backward rather sharply. No substantial advance was made there until D + 19; then on D + 20 (5 July) the 23rd Marines broke through crumbling resistance to straighten out the line.

The narrowing of the island meanwhile had pinched the Second Division out of the line, their sector being taken over by the Twenty-seventh. The 105th Infantry, now holding the extreme left flank, advanced to a point near the lower edge of Tanapag town and dug in there to serve as pivot for a new turning movement. It had become clear that such Japanese resistance as remained was concentrated along the western shore. The decision was, therefore, to swing the right around until the line roughly paralleled the island's axis and attack downward from the high ground.

This maneuver took most of the next two days. The 105th stood fast, as did the 165th on its right, consolidating positions on the high ground behind Tanapag. The Fourth Division, meanwhile, continued to drive northward on a front about two thousand yards wide, pivoting on the right of the Twenty-seventh Division. The 2nd Marines had been attached to the Fourth Division for this phase of the operation, so that they now had four regiments in the line; the line itself, as a result of this turning movement, running roughly northeast to southwest, facing the western shore except at the extreme north and extreme south where the flanks bent to face northward.

That, then, was the tactical situation on the critical night of D + 22 (7 July), when the initiative on Saipan passed briefly to the Japanese.

General Saito, an elderly man rendered more infirm by the rigors he had gone through, had recognized the handwriting on the wall for some time. Extravagant promises from the homeland of naval and air relief could no longer blind him to reality. General Saito was a brave man, brought up under the code of Bushido, indoctrinated with the standard of battle ethics known as "senjinkun." His thoughts on the matter are incorporated in his remarkable last message to his troops, one paragraph of which will suffice for present purposes:

> *The barbarous attack of the enemy is being continued. . . . We are dying without avail under the violent shelling and bombing. Whether we attack or whether we stay where we are, there is only death. However, in death there is life. We must utilize this opportunity to exalt true Japanese manhood. I will advance with those who remain to deliver still another blow to the American Devils, and leave my bones on Saipan as a bulwark of the Pacific.*

What Saito planned was, in short, a Banzai in the grand manner. It was to be frankly suicidal, dedicated to the "Seven lives to repay our country" slogan which had motivated the Nafutan Point breakthrough, but without even the tactical objective of those men: to rejoin their own main force. This was their main force.

To insure its being the largest mass suicide yet staged in the Pacific, Saito laid his plans sufficiently far in advance to allow for concentrating such troops as he had left. With his communications so thoroughly disrupted, he had to rely entirely upon runners. He figured on a minimum of three days, and the orders were issued accordingly: all units still functioning as such, and all other personnel still able to navigate under their own power were to rendezvous at a designated spot near the village of Makunsho by the night of 6 July.

The runners had to do most of their work at night, under constant harassing fire. It was impossible for them to reach all of the elements concerned in the time allowed, inevitable that some of their dispatches should fall into American hands. Our people were aware well in advance that something on a large scale was coming up, and all hands were alerted accordingly. What they could not predict with any certainty was exactly when it would break or what direction it would take.

General Saito issued his "Last Message" at 0800 on the morning of 6 July, even as his troops were beginning their rendezvous. He had decided by that time that he was too old and weak to be of any use in such an operation. His closing words: "I advance to seek out the enemy. Follow me!" were not intended to be taken literally. Actually he proposed to depart this world ahead of his troops, to meet them later on in the place all of them were going.

The message issued, the old general sat down to the most sumptuous meal his attendants could prepare from what was left of their food supplies: saki, canned crab meat, etc. Then, after the traditional goings on associated with such a ceremony, he repaired to the mouth of the cave which served him as a CP, bade farewell to his staff and seated himself crosslegged, facing in the general direction of the emperor's palace. A ceremonial dagger was handed to him. Perhaps his hand trembled as he went through the motions of drawing his own blood. The instant that blood flowed, his adjutant, acting upon well-rehearsed orders, shot him in the right temple. His body was subsequently recovered by the Marines and buried with military honors.

It is believed that Admiral Nagumo [2] followed a similar procedure in his own CP at about the same time. From the best evidence available, it appears that command of the actual attack devolved upon Colonel Suzuki of the 135th Infantry.

Exactly how many participated in this attack, the Japanese themselves could never be sure. From the best available evidence, bodies subsequently buried, it appears that the number ran upward of three thousand. The advance elements, at least, were well organized. They started southward from Makunsho about 0400 on the morning of 8 July, moving in formation, following in general the right-of-way of the narrow-gauge railway near the shore. They scattered the American outposts and slammed head on into the 1st and 2nd Battalions of the 105th Infantry at 0510. And broke through; there was no stopping that many men whose only thought was to kill and be killed. Our artillery pounded furiously the area from which the attack was developing, but was necessarily ineffective at the point of contact for fear of hitting our own people.

Dawn revealed a situation of chaotic confusion. 1/105 and 2/105 had been shattered. Savage fighting swirled about a dozen isolated American pockets of resistance. Some were overrun; some held out. Some battleshocked soldiers escaped into the hills. Those nearest the shore were driven into the sea. Wading, swimming, they fled across the reef, with machine-gun bullets cutting the water around them and mortar shells dropping in their midst, to be picked up by naval craft at the reef's edge.

The Japanese drove on. Marine observers in the hills, watching proceedings through glasses, now glimpsed a strange phenomenon. Behind the enemy assault formations

[2] An obscure end for a conspicuous career. It was Nagumo who commanded the task force which attacked Pearl Harbor with such disastrous results, and also that other task force which sought to attack Midway—with the disaster in reverse.

moved a weird, almost unbelievable procession: the lame, the halt and the blind, literally. The sick and wounded from the hospitals had come forth to die. Bandage-swathed men, amputees, men on crutches, walking wounded helping each other along. Some were armed, some carried only a bayonet lashed to a long pole or a few grenades, many had no weapons of any sort. If they could manage to kill a few Americans, that would be all to the good. But it was not important; theirs was not to reason why but to die in battle. Later it was discovered that some three hundred patients too weak to move had been killed in the hospital by their own people. This was IT: the end, the works, everything.

About one thousand yards behind the infantry positions, Batteries "H" and "I" of the 10th Marines (Second Division Artillery) were working their 105's furiously. As the enemy broke through and surged toward them, they lowered to point-blank range. The Japanese kept coming. The artillerymen cut their fuses to burst the shells at 150 yards, at 100 yards, and fired straight into the seething mass of their assailants. Many Japanese died here; the survivors kept coming. Hastily the Marines removed the firing blocks to make the guns useless and fell back fighting as infantry, and the enemy overran the emplacements.

But the end was at hand. Men from the other batteries of the 10th Marines hurried to their comrades' aid with rifles, carbines, machine guns, BAR's. Clerks, messmen, CP personnel, came in with whatever weapons they could lay their hands on. Roaring in over the heaped bodies of enemy dead, they recaptured the guns and put them into operation again. The greatest of all Banzais was over, as such.

The rest of the day was devoted to mopping up the remnants. The 6th and 8th Marines, which had gone into reserve a few days earlier upon being pinched out of the line, were moved forward again for this messy work. The 165th Infantry and the 23rd Marines attacked westward from the high ground. Thus died those Japanese who had survived their madness up until then. Nightfall found only two pockets of stubborn resistance pinned against the shore, and these were cleaned out the following day.

The carnage had been ghastly beyond belief. Burial parties needed days to deal with the great number of dead. One observer visiting the scene described exhausted soldiers and Marines lying down to sleep amid already rotting corpses for the simple reason that no spot in the area was free of corpses. One single space about an acre in extent was entirely covered with them. As regards its only conceivable object, suicide, General Saito's Banzai had been an unqualified success.

The campaign was soon over after that. On D + 23, while mopping up of the Banzai remnants was still going on, the Fourth Division swung its line around to face northward again, extending the width of the island. With the 2nd Marines (temporarily attached) on the left, the 24th in the center and the 25th on the right, they drove northward against trifling resistance. Here and there a handful of Japanese who had missed the Banzai for one reason or another tried to fight and died miserably in their holes. Others fled before the advance; fled to the edge of the cliffs that dropped away from the plateau to the low shelf of the rocky beaches. More died here, by their own hands or those of the Marines. Some struggled down the cliffs to the shore.

Here was enacted the crowning horror of the whole campaign. Some hundreds of fleeing civilians had taken refuge on the northern shore and in the caves in the cliffs which faced it. Now, believing themselves to have reached the last extremity, they set about a veritable orgy of self-destruction. Mothers and fathers stabbed, strangled or shot their screaming children; hurled them into the sea and leaped in after them, all in plain view of the Marines atop the cliffs or trying to get to the beach. Men hardened in one of the bloodiest campaigns of the Pacific turned away from the sight, sick at heart and physically ill.

Surrender pleas were largely in vain. These people had been told repeatedly that the Americans would kill them, preferably by torture. Now when a few of the miserable creatures showed a disposition to tempt this fate, they were shot down by Japanese soldiers in their midst or others still holed up in the caves in the cliff faces. LCI gunboats lay offshore while Japanese language interpreters exhorted surrender through loudspeakers. Japanese soldiers, using the helpless civilians for cover, fired upon them. One such character was seen to shoot, one by one, a group of about fifteen, mostly women and children, pausing systematically to reload his rifle when necessary, capping the performance by blowing himself up with a hand grenade.

Unable to accomplish their humanitarian mission, the LCI's finally turned their guns against the caves from which the sniping was coming. When the Marines were able finally to occupy the beach, their prisoners totalled a bare handful, most of these badly wounded children whose parents had failed to finish them off before taking their own lives.

Saipan was formally declared secure at 1615 on D + 24 (9 July). All this meant was that organized resistance had ceased and the entire island had been overrun. At long last the artillery was silent, having no areas left in which to fire. But actually some thousands of armed Japanese still lurked in the jungles, hills and caves. For weeks afterward they were being hunted out and killed, often at the rate of more than a hundred a day, in one of the biggest mopping-up operations in history. More than a year later, when final peace came to the Pacific, there were still Japanese soldiers at large on Saipan.

But for all practical purposes the campaign, as such, ended on 9 July. Americans, to the number of 3,143, had died there, 13,208 had been wounded and 335 were still carried as missing on the casualty report dated 12 August. Against this, were 23,811 known Japanese dead and 1,810 military prisoners, the largest number taken in any campaign to date. How many civilians died could not be estimated. There were 14,735 interned in the stockades.

The price had been high, but no one disputed that the purchase had been worth it. The Marines on Saipan had little time to think about that matter, however. They could only lick their wounds, get such rest as was possible and try to absorb in the minimum time the new blood which had come to them in the form of fresh replacements from the States.

TURKEY SHOOT

While the Marines were fighting on Saipan, Adm. Spruance had a huge naval force drawn up west of the Marianas to ward off expected Japanese sea strikes; Task Force 58 comprised fifteen carriers, seven battleships, eight heavy cruisers, thirteen light cruisers and sixty-nine destroyers, under the tactical command of Adm. Marc Mitscher.

The Japanese had hoped to entice the U.S. naval forces into battle farther southwest, in waters within range of their land-based planes, to offset U.S. numerical superiority in carrier aircraft. But once news of the Marianas invasion reached Adm. Toyoda, commander of the Japanese Combined Fleet, he ordered a rendezvous of his forces in the Philippine Sea to attack the U.S. fleet. His tactical commander, Adm. Ozawa, had forces inferior to Mitscher's in every category except heavy cruisers—nine carriers to Mitscher's fifteen, five battleships to Mitscher's seven, etc.—and the plane disparity was even more striking—in everything but float planes, the U.S. outnumbered Ozawa's forces two to one.

However, once the battle began, Ozawa expected major support from planes based in the Marianas and at Truk, where reinforcements had been ordered before the action began. And his search planes had a greater range, giving him the chance to spot the enemy's position before his own forces were detected.*

Ozawa's planes did discover Task Force 58 on June 18, 1944, the day before the battle. Mitscher's task force was drawn up in five circles, four carrier groups approximately four miles in diameter, with perimeters of battleships, cruisers and destroyers to provide fire screen; to the west of the carriers a battle line (circular) of six battleships, four cruis-

* S. E. Morison, *New Guinea and the Marianas,* p. 233: Jap planes could search in a radius of 560 miles, while the more heavily armored U.S. planes' range was only 325-350 miles; also, Jap attacks could be launched from 300 miles, U.S. attacks from about 200.

ers and a dozen destroyers to engage enemy strikes, with two picket destroyers further west to warn of their approach.

Adm. Spruance wanted the fleet to remain close to Saipan, fearing the Japs might feint to the center, then attempt an end run around the U.S. fleet to get at the Marianas invasion forces. He "ordered the fleet to advance westward during the daylight and retire eastward at night —until information of the enemy requires other action." *

This tactic would forestall the discovery of the Jap fleet until the second day of battle, too late to enable Task Force 58 to close for decisive action.

The next day, June 19th, Ozawa's carrier planes launched four separate raids. But their approaches were plotted by radar on the U.S. carriers in time for intercepting planes to meet them. What few planes got through to the fleet were destroyed by anti-aircraft fire or driven off. The Japanese lost about 315 planes that day, in such a slaughter that the June 19th action became known as "The Great Marianas Turkey Shoot." In the meantime U.S. submarines sank two big Jap carriers—the *Shokaku* and *Taiho*.

The next day Air Search gave Mitscher the correct position of the Jap forces, approximately 275 miles away; the range was risky for the U.S. carrier planes, and their return would require night landings on the flight decks, but the air groups were launched. They met resistance from the remnants of the Jap planes, but sank an enemy carrier, *Hiyo*, destroying two-thirds of Ozawa's remaining aircraft. American losses from the action were only twenty planes.

Adm. Ozawa had 35 planes left out of 430. He turned his fleet homeward, beaten in the greatest carrier battle of the war. His failure can be attributed to the inexperience of his carrier pilots (their training hadn't been completed before they were sent into battle), and his dependence on land-based aircraft, which he'd expected to operate from the Marianas and Truk; unknown to him, the reinforcements he'd asked for had been diverted at the last moment to hit MacArthur's invasion of Biak.

The Battle of the Philippine Sea stirred up much argument among the U.S. naval commanders. Adm. Spruance was charged with being too cautious, not allowing the ships of Task Force 58 to steam westward on the 19th to make contact with the Jap fleet (subs had signaled their approximate position). If they had, they would have been in position, early on

* S. E. Morison, *New Guinea and the Marianas,* p. 251.

June 20th, for day-long strikes at the Japs, and the toll of ships could have been much greater.

Two weeks after Saipan fell, Tinian was assaulted; on July 24th, the 4th Marine Division and two regiments of the 2nd Marine Division landed, the remainder of the 2nd Marine Division being brought over the next day. Tinian was declared secured on August 1st, and, together with Saipan, would soon be turned into a base for bombing attacks on Japan itself by the new long-ranging B-29's.

Guam was to have been assaulted during the middle of June, but when Saipan turned out to be a tougher nut than expected, Adm. Spruance held up the Guam attack. D-Day was set for July 21st. The 3rd Marine Division were aboard the transports seven weeks, waiting.*

Two separate landings were made on Guam; because of the long delay prior to the actual assault, the U.S. Navy conducted the longest bombardment of any of the Pacific Island campaigns. The beaches were softened up as never before, and the landings went off as close to perfection as one could hope for, with the tanks and artillery being put ashore on D-Day.

"The story of the next four days is one of dogged, bitter fighting. The 3rd Marines battled their way inch by inch up the Chonito Cliff, suffering heavily from casualties and exhaustion. The 21st Marines moved toward the higher ground across successive ridges only to find beyond each, another jungle-packed ravine filled with Japs covered by mortar and artillery concentration, on the reverse slopes of higher ridges beyond." **

The battle for Guam was reported by Sgt. Alvin M. Josephy, then a Marine Corps Combat Correspondent.

* Hough says, *The Island War,* "No one who has never traveled to combat aboard an overcrowded assault transport in the tropics, can comprehend what those men went through during the 48 to 52 days the various elements were at sea" (p. 264).

** Maj. Frank Hough, *The Island War,* p. 270.

BANZAI ON GUAM

by Alvin M. Josephy, Jr.

The battle for Guam was, from the news perspective back home, just a battle for "another little island"—good for a few days' headlines.

On Guam, however, it was another story. Some of the fiercest moments of the struggle were still ahead of us. Our Division CP was in an amphitheater near the shore, in an area that lay beyond the right flank of our original beachhead. The amphitheater was formed by towering hills and coral bluffs. The open (or shore) side was bounded by a road. It was a fairly secure spot, guarded by rings of MPs and free from Jap mortar fire. Here, General Turnage and his staff set up tents from which to direct the deepening of our beachhead.

Our line was now many thousand yards long, and that it was a thin line was no secret. We were only one division, and we had no reinforcements. We had to push and keep pushing; and the more we pushed, the wider our perimeter became and the more men we needed to hold it. We looked forward to the day when we would join the Provisional Brigade on the other beachhead. They had elements of the 77th Army Division with them as reinforcements. The 77th had begun landing its men late on D-Day on that beachhead. As soon as we all joined, we could possibly count on reinforcements from the Army. Until then, however, we had to hold and deepen our perimeter alone.

During the night of July 25—D plus four—it rained. Toward morning we noticed the sound of gunfire coming closer to our Division CP. Then the guards up on the hills that formed the amphitheater began to shoot. At first there were just sporadic shots—a rifle or a carbine shot into the night. Then they came oftener. There were hand-grenade blasts, and the sudden bursts of BARs and machine guns.

Wheaton and I could hear men stirring in the holes around our foxhole. Occasionally a shot rang out very near to us. Then a hand grenade popped, so close that it might have been thrown by a man in a nearby hole. We peered cautiously over the lip of our foxhole and waited for a form to show itself.

Nothing happened, but by dawn the woods on top of the hills above us were resounding with shots. We got out of our holes carefully. Soon the word spread: the Japs had broken through. Several thousand of the enemy were behind our front lines, threatening all our rear units.

Things occurred then with terrible speed. Our artillery CP was overrun. Japs, carrying land mines and picric-acid charges around their belts, emerged from a draw and, throwing grenades, hit the artillery unit to which Wheaton and I had originally been attached. Our men fought back with rifles and hand grenades from the foxholes in which they had been sleeping. The Japs screamed in English (Staff Sergeant Jim Hague, one of our combat correspondents who was caught in the middle of the battle in his foxhole, reported that men that day heard Japs cry, "One, two, three, you can't catch me!") and charged into one of our machine-gun positions, taking the gun away from the crew. The Marines fought back with another machine gun and drove the Japs back up the draw. Lieutenant Rodgers, with whom we had sailed to Guam, collected a squad of men and boldly led it after the Japs. A flurry of shots from among some rocks stopped the group. One shot hit Rodgers, and he fell. The next moment there was an explosion; a hand grenade or a stick of dynamite—no one knew which—had hit the Lieutenant, and his body blew apart. Several other Marines were killed there, men who had been in our hold sailing to Guam.

While the artillerymen were fighting off the Japs, a second band of enemy rushed down another draw to appear suddenly at our Division hospital. The corpsmen and patients could hear firing coming nearer but thought nothing of it until a wounded man appeared, running at top speed and yelling: "The Japs are coming! The Japs are coming!"

There was no time to wonder how the Japs had broken so deeply into our rear. The corpsmen grabbed rifles and carbines and flung themselves behind cots and cartons of plasma and dressings. Some of the ambulatory patients hopped out of bed and ran for the beach. A cook, whose foot had been wounded the night before when he had been carrying ammunition, scrambled from his cot without a stitch of clothing on and hobbled as fast as he could to the shore. The Japs soon appeared at the hospital, screaming and throwing grenades. The corpsmen fired at them and tried to stop them. One corpsman killed seven Japs with a carbine. Patients inside the ward tents grabbed their weapons and joined the fight as hand-grenade fragments ripped into the canvas flaps. A doctor, in the middle of an operation, paused an instant, trying to decide what to do. The next moment two mortar bursts shredded the top of the surgery tent. The doctor ordered corpsmen to take up positions around the tent. Then he finished the operation.

It was a wild, swirling fight, but it was soon over. Reinforcements arrived from the Division CP and helped the corpsmen wipe out the Japs. Every enemy in sight was killed. But no one knew how many more were still behind our lines and out of sight. Reports from the front lines estimated that at least two thousand Japs had broken through during the night. There must still be almost that number wandering through the brush and hiding temporarily in caves behind our perimeter—a menace, since at any moment groups of them might attack other units, as they had attacked our artillery CP and the Division hospital.

Every Marine and Seabee on our beachhead was mobilized. Squads were formed to look for and attack the enemy that had broken through. All normal activity behind our front lines ceased. Cooks, drivers, clerks, telephone operators, unloaders on the reef—everyone available—went into the hills that morning to eliminate the threat to our beachhead.

Meanwhile we wondered what had happened. How had

so many Japs gotten through, and when? The story, when it came down to us from the front lines, was the story of the first banzai charge our Division had ever met: a vicious, drunken, night counterattack designed to hurl us off of Guam and back into the sea.

The Japs' preparations for it had begun two nights before. That evening two of our PFC's, Joseph Basso and Russell Elushik, had been in an advanced foxhole in front of B Company, the 21st Marines. Basso, a husky former machinist, had been trying to get to sleep when Elushik, who was on guard, fired into the night with his automatic rifle. Basso leaped to his feet, to find the ground around the foxhole swarming with Japs. The two men stood back to back and fired as fast as they could at the enemy forms. The Japs, however, quickly overwhelmed them. The two men were dragged out of the foxhole and across the ground toward the Japanese lines. They struggled and yelled, but they were too far away from other Marines to make themselves heard.

At last Elushik, who weighed about two hundred pounds, twisted himself free and broke away. The Japs dragging Basso let go and chased after Elushik. Basso scrambled breathlessly back to his foxhole and retrieved his automatic rifle. He saw the Japs overtake Elushik and knock the big man down. At the same moment, Basso emptied his rifle at the Japs, trying not to hit the form on the ground. Several of the enemy fell. There was a sudden silence. A few Japs crawled stealthily away. Basso utilized the pause to scramble back to his own lines, get a man to cover him, and go back after Elushik. When he reached Elushik, the big man was still alive, despite the fact that his left hand had been cut off by a Jap saber, both his arms and legs had been broken, and he had a bayonet wound through his neck and back. Elushik and Basso were both evacuated that night. Elushik later died, but Basso, suffering from severe shock, recovered and rejoined his unit.

Nothing more was thought of the episode until two nights later when it became evident that the Jap raiding party had tried to take our men prisoners in order to obtain information. The enemy had chosen to hit the 21st Marines' sector in a counterattack and had needed an appraisal of our strength. Although they failed to secure information from Basso and Elushik, the Japs by themselves estimated our situation correctly. They narrowed the main force of their attack down to our weakest unit— the 1st Battalion of 21st Marines. Here, in the very center of our whole beachhead line, no more than 250 men manned a position that ran for more than two thousand yards—a frontage normally requiring about 600 men. Company B, in the center of the 1st Battalion zone, was down to approximately 75 men out of an original landing strength of 217. The Marines, dug in on a ridge top a couple of miles from the shore, were organized in small knots to cover areas around them—islands of resistance, so to speak.

On the night of July 25 the Japs prepared to strike this sector.

That night, unaware of what lay ahead, our men on the ridge ate a dinner of cold K rations. The hours passed, and it began to pour and drizzle alternately. The Marines tucked ponchos around themselves and squirmed sleepily in the mud. Toward midnight one of the men on watch noticed that the Japs were throwing a lot of grenades. On both sides of him, other Marines were hurling their own grenades back into the night. Many of these burst five and ten feet above the ground, the fragments showering on the wet dirt.

At about three a.m. a rifleman named Martinez heard a swishing of grass out ahead of him, like men moving about. Then he noticed the *pang* of pieces of metal hitting each other and a busy stirring in the darkness that made him uneasy. He peered into the mist but was unable to see anything. Then, as he listened, other things happened. A barrage of hand grenades flew through the darkness and exploded behind him. They kept coming, and he noticed mortar shells beginning to crash more frequently on the ridge.

He woke the other two men in his foxhole. They had been curled in their ponchos, and they got to their feet uncertainly. At the same moment an orange signal flare shot up from the Japanese lines. A singsong voice shouted into the night, and an avalanche of screaming forms bounded suddenly into view. With their bayonets gleaming in the light of sudden flares, they charged toward the Marine foxholes, throwing grenades and howling: "*Ban-zai-ai!*" like a pack of animals.

The Marines awoke with a start. Along the ridge, wet, groggy men bolted to their feet and grabbed their weapons. Grenades exploded like a crashing curtain against the onrushing Japs. A man on a telephone yelled for uninterrupted flares, and flickering lights began to hang in the air like giant overhead fires.

All along the line the enemy attack was on. Red tracer bullets flashed through the blackness. Japanese orange signal flares and American white illumination shells lit up the night like the Fourth of July, silhouetting the running forms of the enemy. On the right and the left the attack was stopped cold. As fast as the Japs came, they were mowed down by automatic rifles and machine guns. The enemy assault gradually focused on a draw where some American tanks were parked. The tanks fired their 75s at the charging masses. At first the Japs attacked the steel monsters like swarms of ants, firing their rifles at the metal sides and clambering up and over the tanks in a vain attempt to get at the crews inside. They screamed and pounded drunkenly on the turrets and locked hatches, but in their excitement they failed to damage a single tank. Finally, as if engaged in a wild game of follow-the-leader, many of them streamed past the tanks, down the draw toward the beach.

The rest, cringing before the tank fire, moved to the left, hoping to break through our lines and get to the draw farther down the slope of the ridge, behind the tanks. The front they now charged was that of B Company. Here, against the 75 men, the full force of the Japanese attack broke.

In their three-man foxhole, the rifleman Martinez and his two companions had maintained steady fire directly ahead, diverting the first rush of Japs to other sections of the line. During a pause in the fighting, one man left the hole to go back for more hand grenades. Martinez and a Marine named Wimmer were left alone. Around them they saw some of the other Marines withdrawing, sliding down the ridge to a secondary line of foxholes about ten yards to the rear. Here and there, in the light of the flares, they could see them pulling back wounded men.

Trying to decide whether to withdraw themselves, Martinez and Wimmer were confronted suddenly by the first wave of Japs. With bayonets fixed, the enemy came more slowly, throwing grenades and then falling to the ground to wait for the bursts. The first grenades exploded around the Marines without harming them. Then one shattered Wimmer's rifle, and the two men decided it was time to withdraw.

As they crawled out of their foxhole and ran and slid down the slope of the ridge, they noticed a group of screaming figures pour over the crest farther to the right and run headlong down the hill. It was the first indication that the enemy were breaking through. Now the Japs would be in our rear, and it would no longer be easy to tell friend from foe.

Martinez and Wimmer reached their platoon command post—an old shellhole ten yards from the top of the ridge, held by Second Lieutenant Edward W. Mulcahy. When the two Marines reached him, Mulcahy was trying desperately to make his field telephone work; but the wires to the rear had already been cut by mortar shells.

Wimmer slid into the hole beside the Lieutenant, and Martinez lay on the forward lip of earth as protection with his rifle. The night was hideous with explosions, lights, screaming enemy, and the odor of *sake*. Against the skyline a handful of Japs appeared. Martinez fired at them, and they backed out of sight. A moment later a string of hand grenades rolled down toward the Marines. Though most of them bounced harmlessly by to explode behind them, one blew up in front of Wimmer's face. Fragments shattered Mulcahy's carbine and struck him on the left side of the head and body. It felt as if he had been slammed with a two-by-four plank.

When he regained his breath, he saw Wimmer holding out his pistol.

"You take it, Lieutenant," Wimmer said in a strange voice.

The Lieutenant protested. The enlisted man would need the weapon for himself.

Wimmer raised his head and smiled. "That's all right, sir," he breathed. "I can't see any more."

The shocked Lieutenant tried to bandage Wimmer's splintered face. The noise from the top of the ridge showed that Marines were still up there, fighting back. It gave the three men hope. The Lieutenant began to shout in the night, like a football coach, "Hold that line, men! You can do it!"

The Marine line on the crest, however, had by now disintegrated into a handful of desperate knots of men, fighting together with the fury of human beings trying not to be killed.

Action around two heavy machine guns was typical of what was occurring. A Jap grenade hit one gun, temporarily putting it out of action. The crew members fixed it quickly and started firing again. A second grenade hit the gun's jacket and exploded, knocking off the cover and putting it completely out of the fight. The same blast wounded one of the men. His three companions moved him to a foxhole ten yards behind the shattered gun. One man jumped in beside him, and the other two ran back to the machine-gun foxhole with their carbines. Heaving grenades like wild men, they managed to stall any Jap frontal charge for the moment.

Meanwhile, the other gun was also silenced. Riflemen in foxholes near by heard a sudden unearthly screaming from the gun position. By the wavering light of flares, they saw one of the crew members trying to pull a Japanese bayonet out of another Marine's body. The same instant a wave of Japs appeared from nowhere and swept over both men. Three of the enemy, stopping at the silent machine gun, tried to turn it around to fire at the Marines. In their hysteria, one of them pulled the trigger before the gun was turned, and the bullets sprayed a group of Japs racing across the top of the ridge. Finally the Japs tried to lift the entire gun on its mount and turn the whole thing. A Marine automatic rifleman blasted them with his BAR, and the Japs dropped the gun. Two of them fell over the bodies of the Marine crew. A third pulled out a grenade and, holding it to his head, blew himself up. A moment later another band of Japs appeared. Again, several paused at the gun and tried to swing the heavy weapon around. They had almost succeeded, when from the darkness a lone, drunken Jap raced headlong at them, tripped several feet away over a body, and flew through the air. There was a blinding flash as he literally blew apart. He had been a human bomb, carrying a land mine and a blast charge on his waist.

Other units all along the line had equally serious moments during the night. Though none had been overrun like B Company, several withdrawals occurred. On the left of B Company, however, A Company also stood firm, inspired by Captain William G. Shoemaker, one of the most popular officers in the 3d Division. As wave after wave of Japs rushed A Company's lines, only to be hurled back, Captain Shoemaker made his way calmly among his men, exhorting them to hold.

"If we go, the whole beachhead goes," he explained. "It's up to us to stay here."

Once a rumor swept along the line that the order had been given to withdraw. Men looked around wildly for confirmation. Captain Shoemaker heard the rumor. He leaped to his feet—a hulk of a man, wrapped in a captured Jap trenchcoat—and roared into the night: "By God, we hold here! The beachhead depends on us!"

His men held.

At about 0600, three hours after the enemy attack had begun, a last wave of Japs charged over the top of the hill. It was the wildest, most drunken group of all, bunched together, howling, stumbling and waving swords, bayonets, and long poles. Some were already wounded and were swathed in gory bandages. The Marines yelled back at them and chopped them down in their mad rush. In a moment it was over. The last wave of the three-hour attack died to a man.

But daylight revealed in all their seriousness how successful the earlier charges had been. It was then that the furious, pellmell Jap attacks had begun to hit our rear units.

Immediately behind the punctured 21st Marine line, engineers, artillerymen, and 21st CP personnel formed a secondary line of defense. Other groups, armed with grenades and automatic weapons, moved through the wooded draws and valleys behind our front, in a roving attempt to find the Japs.

The prompt action saved a potentially serious situation. The Jap plan had counted on driving our Marine line straight back into the sea, first piercing it so that the remnants would have to withdraw, and then fanning out in the rear, disrupting our communications and disorganizing the elements on the beach. The attacking enemy, never well organized and from the start under the influence of alcohol, disintegrated once it got through our lines until it became a hodge-podge of wandering bands and individuals without leadership, communications, or well-defined aims. Some of them managed to do damage, like the group that hit our artillery CP. Others caused temporary disruptions, like the mob that stumbled on our Division hospital. But they were only small groups without tactical coordination, and they became easy prey for our mopping-up bands. By noon we had wiped out most of them. The rest of the enemy took to caves to hide and—like bewildered, sick animals—to puzzle over their fate.

As our units re-formed their lines, it was found that Company B had almost been wiped out during the night. Only 18 men remained out of the 75 who had dug in the evening before. The survivors were put into another company, and B Company temporarily ceased to exist.

Many more of our men were killed or wounded that morning mopping up the scattered Jap bands behind our lines. What happened at the artillery CP, where Lieutenant Rodgers and some of our shipboard comrades lost their lives, occurred also around other units. One of our most tragic losses was that of Captain William O'Brien, the 3d Division's Legal Officer, who was liked by everyone who knew him. Although a staff officer, he voluntarily led a squad through the hills above the Division CP looking for Japs. Somehow the other men lost sight of him, and they came back without him. One of his closest friends was our adjutant, Major Bob Kriendler, who had been busy keeping tabs on our casualties as they piled up during the night. It had been a sad job for him, for many of the dead and wounded had been his friends. Then someone came in to say that Bill O'Brien was missing. Major Kriendler couldn't believe that anything had happened to the Legal Officer. He kept his fingers crossed and assured everyone that his friend would turn up during the day. But just after noon, a man came into Kriendler's tent on some other business. "Say, it's too bad about Bill O'Brien, isn't it?" he said to the Major.

Kriendler thought the newcomer was merely repeating the rumor. "He'll turn up," he replied.

But the newcomer leaned forward. "I don't think you understand," he went on. "I just saw Bill down at the cemetery —they brought him in. No one saw him get killed. They just found his body."

The banzai charge on Guam was never fully reported by the civilian press. Most of the civilian correspondents at the time were on the other beachhead with the 1st Brigade and the Army. In front of our lines our bulldozers and burial squads found some eight hundred Japs. Behind our lines we killed or sealed in caves about two thousand more. The newspapers in the United States put it simply: an enemy counterattack was repulsed with severe losses to the Japanese. Such reporting could not convey the terror of the night attack or the businesslike devotion to duty of our men. Because the eighteen survivors of B Company and the others who stood all along the line that night failed to give way, the beachhead was saved, as Captain Shoemaker had said it would be. By maintaining their line, our men were able to close the gaps, trap the enemy in the rear, and the following day launch a new attack of their own.

The Jap charge had wasted the cream of the enemy troops on the island. After the failure of the charge they had nothing more to oppose us with. They continued to hurl smaller attacks against us at night—some of them drunken assaults—and retreat before us by day; but their offensive power was broken.

As we pushed inland, some of our units continued to have desperate moments among the wooded hills and valleys. In many places the hills were steep coral formations that afforded the Japs numerous caves in which to hide. Many of these caves were neutralized by "Slug" Marvin's flame-throwing team. Once a company commander sent for Marvin and told him that he had seen a Jap duck into a cave. He asked Marvin to get him to surrender or seal him up. So Marvin climbed on top of the cave and hollered: "Nipponese, take off your clothes, come out with your hands up, and we'll take you prisoner and treat you well."

Instead of one voice replying from inside the cave, several called back: "Go to hell!"

Marvin then threw in three thermite grenades and listened. With the hiss of the grenades quieted, he still heard jabbering inside. He ordered a flame-thrower used. A thirty-foot stream of fire flashed into the cave and licked the walls and floor. The jabbering continued.

"TNT!" Marvin yelled.

They threw in twenty-five pound TNT charges, used the flame-throwers again, and then sprayed the inside with an automatic rifle. At last everything was still. Marvin pushed impatiently into the cave's mouth. Inside he counted thirty dead Japs. Later, when rear elements came up and made a thorough check of the cave, they found sixty-three dead enemy. The cave, which the company commander had seen *one* Jap enter, was big enough to hold five hundred men at a time!

Marvin's team eventually got worn out. Of twenty-one men who had landed with him, only six were left on their feet. Marvin sent the survivors back for a rest and volunteered to take over a rifle platoon whose commanding officer had been a casualty. Leading the platoon forward one day, "Slug," in his usual fashion, got far out ahead.

He turned and yelled back. "Come on up here, you men! I'm not a scout!"

Just then something hit his cartridge belt: a Jap hand grenade, a rifle shot—no one ever knew. "Slug's" ammunition exploded into him and around him like a fireworks display. Litter bearers carried him back to the beach, and he died a few days later on a ship. He was awarded the Navy Cross posthumously.

Close-range fighting and sudden death from small arms and occasional artillery shells characterized the remainder of the battle for Guam. By D plus 8, we seemed to be well in control of the situation, although we were still suffering casualties. Our Division line swung around, joined the Brigade and the 77th Division who had pushed inland from the other beachhead, and established a line of attack clear across the island. Then we moved abreast, heading for the northern coast of Guam.

About this time, I left Wheaton and went to the 9th Marines, whose three combat correspondents had all been casualties on D-day. The 9th Marines were pushing the attack in the center of our line and meeting little resistance. We entered Agana, the capital city of Guam, and found nothing there. The town in which our men had looked forward to having their first liberty in a year was a complete shambles and deserted. The Japs did not choose to defend it, possibly because by then their communications and command were thoroughly disrupted. It would have made an excellent site for defense, however. Our naval and aerial shelling had turned it into a jungle of ruins.

Moving quickly, we left Agana and occupied the Japanese Tiyan airfield on the other side of town. The field looked like a country airport back home, though not so good. A few scattered buildings had been smashed to ruins. About twenty-five shattered Jap planes lay in the bushes and among trees along the strip. The area was deserted, and we pushed on, entering the jungle of the northern half of Guam.

It was impossible to see more than a few feet ahead through the thick foliage. We moved in skirmish lines but knew that we were leaving enemy stragglers behind. They were cut off and leaderless and were mostly wandering around in the jungle trying to stay out of our sight. They hid in caves during the day and came out to try to find other Japs at night. We were leaving them to rear elements for mopping up. Our commanding officers wanted the rifle units to keep going and wipe out any large band of Japs they found, so that no sizeable enemy group could get its breath and reorganize.

What happened when the Japs got a chance to reorganize was made grimly evident to us soon after we passed the Tiyan airfield. We had emerged on a narrow jungle road, leading to a village called Finegayan. It was about noon, and I was helping to guide a member of an artillery forward observing team up to our front-line company. A radioman, he was relieving someone who had been with us five days. The FO team members each worked five days with the forward companies, then rested in reserve a couple of days.

Along the road Jap snipers took potshots at us. We clung to the side of the trail beneath the protection of tall grass and bushes. We passed many Jap bodies, lying on the road and in the brush. They had just been killed, their skin was loose and wrinkled, and the blood was still red on their clothes.

We noted an unusual amount of firing ahead of us. Rifle and machine-gun shots cracked through the grass. Mortar shells crashed among the trees, sending up columns of black smoke. Overhead one of our observation planes was whirring back and forth. Going on, we reached a green wooden house by the side of the road. About thirty Marines lay on stretchers in front—it was an aid station. Doctors and corpsmen were working over a line of men. Two jeep ambulances were being filled with wounded. It looked like the biggest battle since we had left the ridges above the beachhead.

We found the company CP to which the radioman had been ordered to report. The Marines were crouched in shell-holes and newly dug foxholes. The dirt—red and moist, almost like mud—covered the men's clothes and faces and hands. We were ordered to get down and stay down. The firing ahead was sharp. Bullets were striking trees around us. Men scurried back and forth through the grass, hunched over, the way they had moved along the beach on D-Day.

"This war ain't over yet," a sergeant said, chewing on a wad of tobacco. "I guess you know they got a lot of our guys here just now." He waved his arm around at the grass. "We got over a hundred Nips in the past half-hour, I reckon."

Although the sounds of battle were all around us, we couldn't see anything. After some time we could reconstruct what had happened. It had been an enemy ambush. The

Japs had had two road blocks in parallel lines across the road, about a hundred yards apart. There were mines in the roads, then antitank and heavier guns on both sides of the road, and, stretching inland, round spider pits dug into the ground to keep the tanks from going around the traps. The pits had been filled with Japs ordered to halt the tanks.

Somehow the tanks got through, but the infantry didn't. The first row of Japs let most of our men through, then opened fire on their backs. At the same moment the second row of Japs opened fire in our men's faces. The rear line of Japs were eliminated in bloody, hand-to-hand fighting. Some of the Japs jumped out of their pits to run. Our men cut them down. One Marine, PFC Francis P. Witek, killed fourteen Japs with his BAR, fearlessly standing up in the open to get a good aim at them. Then he was killed by a Jap hand grenade. (Witek received the Congressional Medal of Honor posthumously for this gallantry.)

The battle ended almost as suddenly as it had begun. A short time after the radioman and I arrived, the firing slackened and then ceased. Men lifted themselves warily and poked around in the grass. We went forward along the road about fifty yards and saw the road block that had trapped our men. A Jap 77, with big wooden wheels, stood silently against the trunk of a breadfruit tree; around it sprawled dead Japs. In from the road was a line of spider pits—round holes about two feet across and three feet deep. In each one there were two dead Japs, mashed and gory. Some had been hit with grenades, other looked as if tanks had run over them. Around the lips of their holes lay unused ammunition, black and red hand grenades, and Molotov cocktails—green *sake* bottles filled with gasoline. None of the bottles had been used. Some of our men poked for souvenirs, using their bayonets to cut the belts and buttons of the dead Japs so as to see whether they were wearing flags underneath their clothes. One Jap had a battle flag wrapped around his leg beneath a puttee. The white of the flag was covered with characters in black ink—good-luck messages from his friends and family back home. One of our interpreters, glancing at the flag, pointed to one set of characters. "That," he said, "reads: 'Death to the Anglo-American devils.' "

The man who had gotten the flag grinned. "Now ain't that sweet?" he muttered.

The road was open now, and I left the radioman and went back to the aid station. Somebody there said we had killed one hundred and nine Japs and had had almost as many casualties ourselves. Stretcher bearers were still looking around through the tall grass for our dead. A jeep came up, pulling a trailer full of new shoes and dungarees.

"Them's for my boys," the driver shouted gleefully. "I never forget them. Tonight I'm bringing up hot soup and doughnuts!"

He unhitched the trailer and took me back in the jeep. The smell along the road was growing stronger. The dead were turning ivory-colored. We passed a Marine lying on his back just off the road.

"Keep low," the driver said. "A sniper just winged that poor guy while I was coming up."

We got back without incident, and I returned to the Division CP. Some of the civilian correspondents were there. They had brought mimeographed copies of the day's news from one of the transports off shore—news that had been picked up by radio from San Francisco. One of the items said that the battle of Guam was almost over. I felt a little bitter when I went to bed that night.

The next day Captain Shoemaker of A Company, the 21st Marines—the officer who had gallantly exhorted his men to hold the line on the ridge the night of the banzai charge—was killed. Ironically, he was doing nothing at the time but resting. His men were taking a breather, lying along both sides of the same road on which we had been ambushed. Suddenly an enemy 77 shell swooshed through the air from somewhere up north and crashed with a burst of smoke. Fragments ripped into the Captain, and he died almost immediately. The men gathered around his body while they waited for a jeep ambulance, and many of them cried. One man with tears staining his dusty face turned away. "All the good ones go," he said.

On the 11th of August we reached the cliffs along the northern shore of Guam and looked down at the surf breaking on the reef six hundred feet below. We sent patrols down the cliffside and out to the breakers. Then we announced that Guam had been secured.

That night I went back to the Division CP that had been moved into the jungle about halfway up the island. We had set up a fly tent and slept on top of the ground beneath the canvas. In the middle of the night somebody in a foxhole on one side of us began shooting—past us. Someone on the other side returned the fire. Others joined in, and the bullets flew back and forth. Suddenly a grenade hissed through the night and exploded. The fragments rattled against our fly tent. We pressed ourselves as flat against the ground as we could, praying that nothing would hit us. Suddenly in the darkness one of the other men in our tent yelled: "God damn it, don't you know this rock is secured!"

It would be a nice ending to the story to say that this stopped the senseless firing around us, but it didn't. And it would also be nice to say that the island at that time was *really* secured, but it wasn't. There was still a lot of fighting on Guam ahead of us.

War Under Water

There was always speculation as to what motivated the Banzai attacks; at Guam, it was obvious that most of the Japs had revved up their courage with hard liquor. American troops came upon huge stores of Scotch and American whisky, *sake* and beer on Guam, which led to the discovery that the Japanese apparently had their main liquor supply dump there for the whole central Pacific area.*

For all the comprehensive planning that went into these island operations, there was frequently a scarcity of good maps. Oddly enough this was so at Guam; even though Guam was an American possession before the war, there wasn't a single good map the planners could depend on. Reconnaissance of the islands to be assaulted was therefore doubly important; most of it was in the capable hands of the air forces. But submarines were also used, particularly in the first island campaigns, when airfields weren't within range. Submarines surfaced offshore to look over the fortifications on the beaches, the underwater demolition problems that had to be solved before the troops could go in, etc. This was a minor part of their job, of course; the submarine was an immensely important assault weapon in the Pacific Theater. In 1943, American submarines sank Japanese merchant tonnage of 1,335,000 gross tons, plus 22 warships. In the first months of 1944, well over a million and a half gross tons were sunk.

By the end of 1944, the total tonnage of the Jap merchant marine fell to less than 2,000,000 tons, a crippling drop from 5,500,000 tons two years earlier.

The submarine service did not encourage publicity during World War II. Of the publications since the war, Samuel Morison's histories of naval operations are excellent sources for the accomplishments of the submarine. And *Battle Submerged*, by Adm. Harley Cope and Capt. Walter Karig, offers a good one-volume account of the sub campaigns in the Pacific; the following chapter is taken from it.

* Maj. Frank Hough, *The Island War*, p. 260.

SUBMARINE VS. DESTROYER

by Adm. Harley Cope and Capt. Walter Karig

Destroyers are the prime enemy of submarines. One of their essential duties is to screen larger vessels from submarine attacks, wherefore they are of shallow draft; light, fast and agile; hard to hit with a torpedo and quickly maneuverable to avoid attack. They can "spin around on a dime." They all carry depth charges and the newest listening gear. At the beginning of the war there wasn't a Jap destroyer afloat that didn't consider herself more than a match for any number of submarines, and, by all the rules except the incalculable factor of human intelligence, they should have been. But this confidence began to ooze a bit after the hunted turned hunter and we started cutting them down.

Of fifty-two American subs lost during the war, Japanese surface forces definitely only accounted for sixteen. Counting all the "possibles," they certainly did not sink more than twenty-four, mines probably accounting for most of the balance. On the other side of the ledger, Japanese anti-submarine forces lost forty-two destroyers and approximately one hundred lesser escort vessels to our submarines. The light vessels of the Japanese Navy not only failed fully to protect the heavy ships and the convoys, but they themselves took disproportionate losses in their war with the submarines.

They were worthy adversaries. The Japanese ships were good, and their crews brave and well-trained, by Japanese standards. They just weren't smart enough. They fought an orthodox war, whereas the Americans used ingenuity and initiative. It was the old story of the Indian fighter versus the classically trained Redcoat.

The duty of the submarine was to slip past escorting destroyers and, undetected, get to the valuable tankers and cargo ships. Normally, a sub didn't even consider attacking a destroyer unless it was found alone, or the submarine was backed into a corner and had to fight her way out. There were a few cases when the submarine, having been balked in an effort to reach the convoy, picked off the destroyers just to get even, but this was very rare. A tanker sunk meant that more than one ship couldn't go to sea for lack of the fuel of which Japan had to import every drop. Better to save a torpedo for a second chance at an oiler or munitions ship than to sink an escort.

There came a time, though, when the old feeling about destroyers was reversed. By April, 1944, when Jap tankers were rarer than destroyers and the mobility of the Japanese fleet was threatened, the Joint Chiefs in Washington decreed that, to maintain this condition and aggravate it, submarines were to give enemy destroyers high priority. They were made number two on the list, right after the much sought-for but by now rarer tankers.

Only one Jap destroyer, the *Sagiri,* was sunk by subs in 1941, and she was torpedoed off Borneo by a Dutch submarine. It was not until February 8, 1942, that an American submarine started the ball rolling and then only out of necessity. The ancient S-37, commanded by Lieutenant John C. Dempsey, was completing an eventless daylight submerged patrol off eastern Borneo and was just preparing to surface for the night to charge batteries when several ships were sighted through the periscope. Gearing the S-37's croupy Diesels into high to wring out her full ten and a half knots, Dempsey followed in the darkness. It was almost eight o'clock, when he had drawn close enough to see that hopes were partially realized in that it really was a Japanese convoy, but a column formation of four enemy destroyers was interposed between the S-37 and the cargo ships. Breaking through this tight defense posed a problem for which there was no satisfactory answer. A run around end by the plodding S-boat was as out of the question as a Percheron coming from behind to win the Derby. After pondering the situation for a few minutes vainly hoping for an inspirational angle of attack on the convoy, Dempsey decided to take on all four destroyers!

Later submarines were equipped with from four to six tubes forward, and four aft. What Dempsey proposed to do was rather like hunting a herd of lions with a single-barreled shotgun.

With four targets and four torpedoes he simply parceled one out to each destroyer in the column. That he got one out of the four was almost a seagoing miracle.

The third destroyer in the column caught its torpedo in the solar plexus. The amidships section rose twenty feet above the bow and stern ends and the *Natushio* went down, first of the two score plus that finally fell to American submarines.

This attack brings into sharp focus the prewar concept of submarine attacks on destroyers. Dempsey wouldn't have considered using a single torpedo on any larger type ship, but a destroyer was not thought to be worth a full salvo. A submarine that had fired four torpedoes at a single destroyer then, even though sinking it, would have been more likely to receive censure for wastefulness than praise for sinking an enemy ship. In 1944, almost any sub would pick one ship and let fly a four-torpedo salvo if presented with the same target.

In 1941 an average of 1.8 torpedoes were fired at each destroyer target. In 1944 it was 3.3 per attack. Of course the scarcity of torpedoes in 1941, as compared to the unlimited number available in 1944, probably had considerable bearing on this trend.

The directive from the Commander in Chief for the subs to bear down on destroyers came long after Sam Dealey had given the *Harder* her baptism of blood and a reputation that made her name a most descriptive one. The short, cheerful, tooth-brush-mustached officer was the second of six submarine skippers to receive the Congressional Medal of Honor. The Service, the whole Naval Service, suffered one of its heaviest and most saddening losses when the *Harder* failed to return from her sixth patrol. The long string of vicious depth-charge attacks that had all but blasted the *Harder* out of the water during five previous patrols finally caught up with her off western Luzon.

Sam Dealey arrived at Pearl Harbor on May 23, 1943, to take the *Harder* out for his first war patrol in command. Optimistically maybe, realistically as it proved eventually, Rising Sun stencils had surreptitiously been taken aboard to ornament the conning tower with the symbols of her kills. She looked far too bare among the grizzled veterans that were returning to the Base with a broom at the yard-arm.

The operating area for her first patrol was in Empire waters south of Honshu. On the night of June 22, the *Harder* made her first tackle and brought down a large freighter. Three well-placed torpedoes insured the first Rising Sun a place on her conning tower. She also received her baptismal depth-charge attack, prolonged and savage.

Now the *Harder* was a veteran too! When she arrived at Midway on July 7, returning to Pearl Harbor, there was a new light in the eyes of every man aboard, and a new swagger and jauntiness in their walk. For there was more than one scalp depicted on the conning tower and one stood for the ex-seaplane tender *Sagara Maru*. Sam Dealey had become a "hot" skipper on his first patrol.

On August 24 *Harder* headed back to her old area south of Honshu on her second patrol, to take up where she had left off. The hunting was still good, and the stenciled flags now accounted for an additional four cargo ships and one tanker.

On October 30, 1943, she started her third patrol as a member of Commander Freddie Warder's (of *Seawolf* fame) pack, accompanied by the *Snook* and *Pargo*. The hunting this time was conducted in the Marianas area. On this cruise the *Harder*'s torpedoes bagged three big freighters, insuring that some 20,000 tons of stores and supplies would never reach their destination on Saipan except as litter on the beaches.

When she returned from this patrol the *Harder* was sent to the coast for a "face lifting" treatment during a month at the Mare Island Navy Yard, and a well-earned shore leave for the crew.

Early in March, 1944, she was back at Pearl Harbor, ready, as the skipper phrased it, to "ride the Pacific merry-go-round again." And on March 16 she took off for her new area of operations in the western Carolines, in the immediate vicinity of Woleai Island 500 miles west of Truk. It was there that she intercepted the new directive making enemy destroyers a primary target.

It may have been coincidence, but she had no sooner received the changed order of things than the *Harder* showed strict compliance by summarily removing a destroyer from the Imperial Navy. The target obligingly provided was the *Ikazuchi,* of the 1,850 ton *Fubuki* class.

To fit the *Harder* for her fifth and most memorable war patrol she was sent alongside the tender at Fremantle, Australia. In addition to the usual refurbishing there was always a little extra patching up required when this submarine hit port. She always seemed to undergo more than her share of depth-charge attacks.

The *Harder* left Fremantle on May 26, 1944. Her assigned area was in the Celebes Sea off the northeast coast of Borneo, in the Sulu Sea, and in addition to sinking ships, she had two other assignments. One was to remove some Intelligence operators from the northeast coast of Borneo. A couple of other subs had failed in their attempts to rescue them, but success was mandatory for the *Harder* because the increasingly desperate Japs were closing in on our people. Evidence of the mission's importance was the presence of the Australian Ace Commando, Major William Jinkins, loaned to give aid in this rescue attempt.

Their other assignment was extremely important too. The heavy naval forces of the Japanese were known to be concentrated at Tawi Tawi anchorage in the Sulu Archipelago (northeast of Borneo). When we delivered our first blow at the gates of what the Japs considered their inner defense line, the Marianas, our High Command expected the reaction at Tawi Tawi to resemble a disturbed hornets' nest. So the *Harder* and *Redfin* (Lieutenant Commander Marshall H. Austin) were sent to hang around that vicinity and catch the first movement of the enemy. They were given permission to do any damage they could but they were especially directed to find out in which direction the Japs would jump.

Captain Murray Tichenor, operations officer for Submarines Southwest Pacific, went along on the *Harder* as an observer. He wanted to see at first hand how practicable the operation orders were that he had been scribbling for the boats. It's sometimes difficult to understand every facet of an operation from a seat on the tender. Furthermore, he also wished to observe at first hand the conditions under which the subs operated. Finally, and perhaps compellingly, he loved the submarine service and when a man attains four stripes it is rare that he gets a chance to see the enemy through a periscope. He certainly got an eyeful on this trip. In fact, there were times when he even hinted that Sam Dealey was putting on a show for his special benefit.

After doing considerable broken field running through fleets of fishing boats the *Harder* arrived off Cape Mangkalibat, which thrusts from eastern Borneo into the Strait of Makassar, at dawn on June 5.

The skipper strongly suspected by their actions that some of the sailboats were a little out of character for fishing vessels. They behaved more like wolves in sheep's clothing—spotters for the Japs, but Dealey's tight schedule didn't permit time to prove it. Anyway, it didn't matter too much if the boats were on picket duty because the enemy already had the grimmest sort of evidence that United States subs continually haunted those waters. It wasn't their presence, which they were impotent to prevent, but catching them that bothered the Japs most.

Rain squalls are often a great nuisance and source of discomfort but those the *Harder* encountered this cruise were an undisguised blessing. They permitted her to arrive undetected at the southern entrance of Sibutu Passage. This is the channel that lies between Sibutu Island on Borneo's northeast coast, and Tawi Tawi, the Japanese anchorage between Borneo and the Philippines.

Inasmuch as this is the only deep-water channel between the Celebes and Sulu Seas, the Japs knew that our subs had to use the passage, and they had no intention of letting any go through.

The *Harder* waited until after darkness before giving the Japanese the opportunity to try and stop her. As the affair turned out, it would have been a lot cheaper for them if they had given the submarine a safe conduct passage—including personal escorts.

Just as the *Harder* was getting all wound up to start her dash the radar operator brought the proceedings to a halt by reporting that a convoy was barging down the pass.

"We're not in such a big hurry after all," grinned the skipper. "Besides, this is business that can't wait. The other job can, within reason."

Sam described this first encounter thus: "The moon was full, brilliant, and almost overhead during the latter part of the run, but was shielded intermittently by low cumulus clouds. Our intent was to dive ahead of the convoy and to maneuver into a position between the flank escorts and the tankers from which an almost simultaneous attack could be made on the destroyer and the three closely grouped ships of the convoy. This optimistic intention was later frustrated."

And for a very good reason. The moon suddenly broke through the clouds, floodlighted the surfaced sub and made all on deck feel as self-consciously prominent as Lady Godiva at a ball game. The nearest destroyer wasn't slow to take advantage.

"It was immediately apparent," said Sam Dealey, "that he was headed hellbent for the *Harder,* smoking heavily and showing a prominent bow wave."

Two choices remained. She could dive or—

"We turned tail toward the destroyer, made flank speed and hoped the Jap would get discouraged and return to his convoy but he had other intentions (none of them friendly). His speed increased to 24 knots and the range was gradually whittled down to 9,000 yards as he followed down our wake. (At 19 knots we left a wake that looked like a broad avenue for five miles astern.)

"It was painfully evident that our business with the convoy would have to wait until the destroyer was taken care of."

The *Harder* decided she had run far enough. Now, she

had only one thing in mind: Get that fellow! She submerged to periscope depth, twisted around to bring the stern tubes to bear, and waited for the destroyer, racing down her wake, to come within torpedo range. And at twenty-four knots it couldn't take long! The Japanese was steering a straight course, charging after the sub which he apparently thought was still fleeing on the surface. It was a poor guess.

"At a range of 1,150 yards," related the skipper, "we sent a triple dose of torpex (referring to the war-head explosive) toward the Jap. The first shot missed ahead, the second and third shots were observed to hit near the bow and under the bridge respectively. The target was immediately enveloped in flame and smoke, the tail rose straight in the air, a half a dozen of his depth charges going off.

"Surfaced at 1,000 yards distant, watched the destroyer go under, and headed back toward the spot where it had been. One Franklin buoy (or one of similar design) burned lonesomely over a large oil slick—but there was no ship and there were no survivors to be seen. The last moments of the destroyer were observed by the commanding officer, most of the fire control party, by Captain Tichenor and the bridge lookouts."

Japanese records indicate that this was the destroyer *Minatsuki*.

The first pressing problem had been disposed of handily. Now to take the convoy under consideration. Full speed ahead on four engines! "From here," observed the skipper, "it would be a race to see who could get to Tarakan first."

But another destroyer popped into sight to offer strenuous opposition to any attempted liberties with the three precious tankers. Again the *Harder* prepared to square away for a passage at arms, but this time the target was wide awake and watchful. When the submarine let fly with her punch, the destroyer neatly sidestepped and countered savagely with heavy depth charges that battered and buffeted the *Harder* for the next hour and a half. As Sam Dealey admitted, "That fellow was on their varsity!"

When the weary destroyer drew away from her rather

groggy opponent, the *Harder* took cognizance of the time element that had inexorably crept into the problem. It was too late to try for another pass at the fast-stepping convoy, so the submarine headed for Sibutu and rescue for the trapped observation party.

At dawn the *Harder* sighted what was believed to be the mast of a ship, and the submarine slithered down for an attack position from well below the surface—just in case a plane happened to be sitting around overhead. After an hour and a half Sam figured that it was about time to take a look at the traffic and tried to come up to periscope depth. Then the most sickening sensation a submariner can feel, more dismaying than the jolt of depth charges, jarred all hands—the grate of the keel on a submerged obstacle. No one had suspected that the heavy set of the uncharted current during the night had taken them near the reef on which they were now in danger of being hung. Dealey gave the immediate order to blow main ballast tanks, then backed full speed and miraculously managed to clear the reef without apparent damage. But all hands sprouted goose bumps at the thought of what might have happened, if the skipper hadn't had the hunch to plane up for a look-see when he did. The Jap base was much too close for any Americans to be stranded on a reef, if they were lucky enough to get that much fresh air before extinction.

But the target? To top it all off, the "ship" was still where it had first been seen, and where it still is—a small island!

Shortly before noon the *Harder* submerged again to wait out an aircraft contact when a destroyer suddenly loomed up on the periscope, coming at a fast clip and only about 4,000 yards away. No one suggested that this might be an island when the *Harder* turned toward her. A minute later the two killers were headed for each other and closing fast. The Jap had seen the periscope. That was made as plain by his belligerent approach as if he had flown a flag hoist.

"Stood by with four tubes forward to fire down his throat, if necessary," related Sam in his war diary later. "At that stage there wasn't much choice. Angle on the bow changed from zero to 10 degrees starboard, then quickly back to 15 degrees port." The situation was growing more tense every second. What would the destroyer do next? If he would only stay on a steady course for just a few minutes! At this rate it looked as though it might surely have to be a head-on "down the throat" shot, with the target practically crawling over the submarine the next moment.

At a range of 650 yards the angle on the bow had opened to 20 degrees port. The skipper filled his lungs to expel a sigh of relief, and then the destroyer perversely but cannily began to swing back. Sam Dealey, his forehead bathed in sweat, waited no longer; he couldn't, unless he wanted the fellow coming through his conning tower.

"Fired one-two-three in rapid succession. Number four wasn't necessary. Fifteen seconds after the first shot was fired it struck the destroyer squarely amidships. Number two hit just aft—number three missed ahead. Ordered right full rudder and ahead full to get clear. At range of 300 yards we were rocked by a terrific explosion believed to have been the destroyer magazine. Less than one minute after the first hit, and nine minutes after it was sighted, the destroyer (later identified as the *Hayananmi*) sank tail first, observed by the Commanding Officer, Executive Officer, and, of course, Captain Tichenor."

But a lot of other equally interested persons had seen it go down. Sound reported fast screws racing up from all directions. So the sub went deep and philosophically rigged for depth charging, while the yeoman broke out the forms on which to record each explosion.

They weren't long in coming—and continued for two gruelling hours.

At 3:30 that afternoon the *Harder* had crawled from under and was again at periscope depth, tubes reloaded, looking for trouble. Two *Fubuki*-class destroyers came steaming up—and the *Harder* prepared to make someone pay for the depth-charge drubbing, but at 4,000 yards the destroyers suddenly wheeled about and quit the neighborhood.

However, it was still a busy area. Later in the afternoon an investigating committee of six destroyers headed for the submarine.

"Looked as though the *Harder* had worn out her welcome here," observed Sam. "We felt as if we had a monopoly on the whole Pacific war this date. (Such popularity must be preserved.)" The temptation was to further deplete the Imperial Navy's dwindling forces but the skipper—

"Made a quick review of the whole picture and decided that discretion here was definitely the better part of valor. The battery was low, air in the boat was none too good, the crew was fatigued, and our navigational position in a narrow strait, with strong and variable currents, was not well known. I really believe that we might have gotten one or two of the enemy ships, but under the above listed conditions, a persistent and already humiliated enemy (after two sinkings within twenty-four hours just off a fleet base) would probably have developed an attack from which the *Harder* might not have pulled through. No apologies are made for my withdrawal. The gamble would have been taken at too great a risk."

The skipper having made his decision, the *Harder* began evading to the north to lose the destroyers and get on with her assigned task. The navigator was unable to fix the ship's position due to a "fuzzy" horizon, but it appeared they were headed up the center of Sibutu Passage. A tiny blip suddenly blossomed on the radar screen, dead ahead at 1,500 yards. It was sighted immediately from the bridge by moonlight, a small boat by all appearances. At 1,200 yards it was discovered to be a low rock pinnacle sticking straight up out of the sea, with white foam breaking around it. Dealey ordered full right rudder, and "within 400 yards of grounding on this pinnacle as we reversed course," he noted in his diary. "Special credit is due Wilbur Lee Clark RT (radio technician) 3c, USNR, for his alert watchstanding. He undoubtedly prevented a grounding which might well have been disastrous."

The navigator was able to check his position a little later on Sibutu Island light and by midnight the submarine was heading north again. At ten o'clock on the morning of

June 8 the *Harder* was submerged off the northeast tip of Borneo below Cape Unsang. She was two days late for the rendezvous; Sam apologetically explained later that the compulsory sinking of two destroyers had delayed them.

Late that night the submarine crept in to keep her rendezvous with the Intelligence operators. With nothing to break the stillness of the night except the muffled paddling of the rubber boat, Major Jinkins pulled off his little miracle and got the operators aboard safely. There was a silent hand shake and a low murmur of thanks before they disappeared down the hatch.

Sam lost no time clearing the neighborhood. The Japs had been ready to spring their trap on the operators at dawn, and when it became obvious that the prey had escaped, they wouldn't have any trouble guessing how it had been managed. Sam wanted deep water under him before the investigating planes inevitably arrived.

At 5:32 a.m. the expected snooper came diving in. The Japs hadn't waited until dawn to find out that the agents they had hunted so long and persistently had been snatched away.

"Bridge lookout sighted float-type plane—close," related the skipper. "Made quick dive. Bomb exploded as we passed 75 feet—also close! The sub was thoroughly shaken and resulted in an early and prompt reveille for all hands, but no damage of a serious nature was sustained."

The new passengers were already getting a quick initiation into routine life aboard the *Harder*. One of them vowed later that if he had suspected what they were going to have to go through before he reached Australia nothing could have dragged him off Borneo. He would have insisted upon waiting for the next boat.

The skipper didn't doubt that the plane had sent a hurry call to the destroyers at Tawi Tawi. They could be expected to come swarming out in a few hours, looking for trouble—and the *Harder*. Conditions to receive them properly were not auspicious from the *Harder*'s point of view.

"The smooth glassy sea," explained Sam, "with aircraft overhead precluded a successful attack at periscope depth, so it was decided to swing to the northeast and not attempt a southward transit of Sibutu until nightfall. However, the longer we remained undetected, the more convinced that Jap aviator would be that his bomb hit the mark. Such an assumption wouldn't have been far wrong."

At 11:00 a.m. "sound picked up propeller noises of two destroyers approaching from the westward (direction of Tawi Tawi. The advance guard!). A periscope attack in the glassy sea against alerted destroyers with air support was not considered to be 'good ball.' Increased depth and rigged for silent running. Both destroyers passed overhead and nearby several times."

By early afternoon the searchers had been shaken off. Sam returned to periscope depth to find that the seas had picked up enough to ruffle the surface, so now they could make a periscope attack. He headed directly for the northern entrance to Sibutu, ready to do battle once more.

Soon after sunset the *Harder* was on the surface speeding down the pass. Radar picked up a few patrol vessels but they were far enough abaft the beam for the *Harder* to show them her heels. Nevertheless it indicated that the enemy was going to make his best attempt to prevent the submarine from going through.

At 9:00 p.m. the skipper recorded, "Entered northern bottleneck of Sibutu Passage with the Jap fleet base at Tawi Tawi just six miles away on port beam. Trouble was expected here and did we find it!"

Just a minute later radar reported a destroyer ahead. Sam saw it at the same time. It didn't worry him because by now he felt competent to handle the destroyer situation. Another was sighted almost immediately near the first, but Dealey still felt confident that he would be able to handle both of them.

The actions of the destroyers seemed to indicate that they were simply patrolling the narrows, and had no suspicion that a stranger was entering their midst. If they could just be kept in ignorance a few minutes longer! Sam picked out the logical one to "gun" first—the larger one.

"At 3,000 yards both destroyers zigged 30 degrees to their right (with the first presenting a 30 degree port track) and the picture became 'just what the doctor ordered.' At a range of 1,000 yards on the nearest target, both destroyers were overlapping, with a 100 degree track showing, so without further delay commenced firing the bow tubes. No. 1 appeared to pass just ahead of the first destroyer, No. 2 struck it near the bow, No. 3 hit just under the destroyer bridge, and No. 4 passed astern of the near target. The sub was swinging hard right to avoid hitting the first destroyer and fire was withheld on remaining tubes until a new setup could be put into the T.D.C. (target data computer) for an attack on the second destroyer. About 30 seconds after turning the second destroyer came into view just astern of what was left of the first one which was burning furiously. Just then No. 4 torpedo, which had passed astern of the first target, was heard and observed to hit the second target (no more torpedoes were needed for either).

"Meanwhile, a heavy explosion, believed to be caused by an exploding boiler on the first destroyer, went off and the sub (then about 400 yards away) was heeled over by the concussion. At almost the same time a blinding explosion took place on the second destroyer (probably the ammunition going off) and it took a quick nose dive. When last observed by the Commanding Officer and Executive Officer (and the eager Captain Tichenor, naturally) the tail of the second destroyer was straight in the air. And the first destroyer had disappeared."

The *Harder,* so far in her one-ship war, had whittled down Admiral Ozawa's badly needed light forces by four destroyers and the patrol wasn't even over.

The submarine surfaced to see the damage and to make a rapid shift to a more quiet neighborhood. Only a large cloud of steam and heavy vapor hung over the spot where the first destroyer had been. A lighted buoy marked the spot where the second ship had taken her last plunge.

At flank speed the *Harder* tore along to the south before the night flyers could arrive. Half an hour later she had to duck under for a while to let one go by, but she was soon up and off again.

At 11:05, however, things weren't so simple. "Sighted aircraft float-type plane, flying at height of 100 feet, coming in off our starboard quarter and almost on top of us. It is believed that he sighted us just as the rudder was shifted hard left. He whizzed by the starboard beam at a range of 100 yards! Submerged. First aerial bomb not so close, second aerial bomb damned close! Increased depth."

Then the bombs became more distant.

"Sound contact on approaching ship. Rigged for silent running. Remained deep for remainder of night to rest a weary crew."

At 0445, "Surfaced to change air in the boat before another all day dive, and to cram more 'amps' in the battery."

Before dawn she was once more submerged and heading for a point south of Tawi Tawi for her reconnoitering duty.

Destroyers were observed on apparently routine patrol but none came close to the lurking submarine. The passengers became wistful for the comparatively quiet life of dodging Jap patrols in the jungle.

At 5:00 p.m. the next afternoon, June 10, excitement surged through the *Harder* like a tidal wave when Sound reported a large movement of ships, light and heavy screws. The very thing they had come to witness! The passengers now began to ask, "Is this trip necessary?"

A quick periscope observation disclosed a large task force—three battleships, four or more cruisers, and six or eight destroyers. Float-type planes circled overhead. The first movement of Ozawa's force was coming out!

The skipper describes what happened: "Sea was glassy smooth and events which followed quickly showed that our periscope was sighted.

"While watching and identifying the nearest of the battleships (which was definitely of the *Musashi* class) it was suddenly enveloped in a heavy black smoke and Sound reported hearing three positive explosions. The first assumption (and hope still remained) was another of our subs had put three torpedoes in the battleship, but a reconstructed version of the affray shows that the following was more likely.

"Immediately after the smoke and explosions around the battleship, a destroyer, which until then had blended in with the big ship, headed directly for us belching black smoke. It is believed that one of the float-type planes had spotted our periscope and dropped a smoke float near it. Whereupon the battleship's escorting destroyer laid down a quick smoke screen between us and the battleship and dropped three 'scare' charges as he headed our way." But there was no guessing about the destroyer that was heading for the *Harder* with a bone in his teeth and fire in his eyes. "The sound man obtained a 'turn count' for 35 knots on the destroyer. His bow wave and rapidly closing range verified it!

"With the idea that we were now scheduled for another working over anyhow, it was decided to have a crack at the destroyer first. The bow was swung toward him for another 'down the throat' shot. (Maybe recent events have just gotten us too much in the habit of shooting destroyers anyhow?) At a range of 4,000 yards . . . the angle on the bow still zero and the destroyer echo ranging right on us steadily! The picture had reached the stage where we had to hit him or else."

When the range was 1,500 yards Sam calmly fired three torpedoes. With the destroyer knifing directly down on them the "fish" wouldn't have far to run—that is, to hit.

"Sound had now picked up other fast screws moving in from the starboard beam but this was no time to look; the *Harder* went deep.

"Fifty-five and sixty seconds respectively after the first shot, two torpedoes struck with a detonation that was far worse than depth charging. By this time we were just passing 80 feet and were soon beneath the destroyer. Then all Hell broke loose! It was not from his depth charges for if they had been dropped at that time this report would not have been completed, but a deafening series of progressive rumblings that seemed to blend with each other. Either his boilers or magazines, or both, had exploded and it's a lucky thing that ship explosions are vented upward and not down.

"The previously reported sound on the starboard beam was now reported moving in for his share of the fun and started laying his barrages as we were going deep. It is believed that they fell astern. They were loud and close and added their bit to the jolting around but none compared in intensity to the exploding destroyer we had just passed beneath.

"Other explosions, believed to be aerial bombs, began to land nearby, and all added up to make the most uncomfortable five minutes yet experienced during the *Harder*'s five war patrols. Something between twenty or thirty distinct depth charges or bombs were counted but no one was interested in numbers at the time."

Finally the *Harder* pulled clear of the bombed area and once more all hands, including the passengers, drew a deep breath. When they again raised their periscope in the darkness, a lone lighted buoy was burning forlornly over the spot where the attack had taken place. For the extraordinary exploit of sinking five destroyers in a matter of almost four days, Sam Dealey was awarded the Congressional Medal of Honor.

After surfacing, the *Harder* sent a contact report by radio announcing that the first of the heavy forces had left Tawi Tawi anchorage. At dawn she was back counting noses in the anchorage.

After a few days more the *Harder* returned to Australia to discharge her thankful passengers and to get a few more torpedoes so she could continue her patrol.

She never returned from the sixth patrol.

Philippine Victory

The next Marine beachhead was on Peleliu in the Palau Islands, a little more than 500 miles southeast of the Philippines. "In our hands, a pistol pointed at the enemy stronghold. In Jap hands, a potent threat to any invasion we might aim in that direction." *

As it happened, we were aiming an invasion in that direction. "MacArthur [had taken] a long hop up the northern New Guinea coast, landing on the 22nd of April to seize air strips at Hollandia and Aitape, by-passing Jap strongpoints at Wewak and Hansa Bay. . . . On the 30th of July, a week after the Marines had landed on Guam, MacArthur's troops seized Cape Sasanpor near the extreme western end of New Guinea.

"MacArthur's threat was aimed at the Philippines. A simultaneous seizure of Moratai by the Army and Peleliu by the Marine Corps on the 15th of September secured the gateway for his reconquest." **

On October 21, 1944, the 6th Army landed two corps under MacArthur on the beaches of Leyte Gulf; MacArthur had returned to the Philippines, after not quite three years. He could announce that Leyte was secured on December 26th; on January 9th, he invaded Luzon, reentering Manila on February 4, 1945. The worst threat to American recovery of the island had already been beaten off; one of the greatest naval engagements in world history, certainly the largest, had taken place on October 23rd to the 26th.

* Maj. Frank Hough, *The Island War*, p. 294.
** Maj. Frank Hough, *The Island War*, p. 212.

THE BATTLE FOR LEYTE GULF

by Hanson Baldwin

The greatest sea fight in history—perhaps the world's last great fleet action—broke the naval power of Japan and spelled the beginning of the end of the war in the Pacific. The Battle for Leyte Gulf, fought off the Philippine Archipelago, sprawled across an area of almost 500,000 square miles, about twice the size of Texas. Unlike most of the actions of World War II, it included every element of naval power from submarines to planes. It was as decisive as Salamis. It dwarfed the Battle of Jutland in distances, tonnages, casualties. But, unlike Jutland, there was no dispute about the outcome. After Leyte Gulf, the Japanese Fleet was finished. Yet it was a battle of controversy. . . .

The Empire was dying, and there were some who faced the fact. The long retreat was over, the great spaces of the Pacific had been bridged by the countless ships of the American "barbarians," and the enemy was knocking upon the inner strongholds of the Samurai. For Japan it was now the desperate gamble, the all-out stroke—to conquer or to die.

And so, the *Shō* ("To Conquer") plans were drawn; if the inner citadel—the Philippines, Formosa, the Ryukyus, the main islands—were penetrated by the U.S. Fleet all the remaining Japanese naval power that could steam or fly would be mobilized for a desperate assault.

From August 31 to September 24 the fast carriers supported by the battleships of Admiral William F. Halsey's Third Fleet had raked over Japanese bases from Mindanao to Luzon, and on the twenty-first while Radio Manila was playing "Music for Your Morning Moods," naval pilots combed Manila Bay. The bag throughout the islands was large, the enemy opposition was surprisingly feeble, and Admiral Halsey reported to Admiral Chester W. Nimitz, commander-in-chief, Pacific:

". . . no damage to our surface forces and nothing on the screen but Hedy Lamar."

The weak Japanese reaction led to a change in American strategy.[a] The planned capture of Yap and step-by-step moves to Mindanao in the southern Philippines and then northward were eliminated; the amphibious assault upon the island of Leyte in the central Philippines was advanced by two months to October 20, 1944. . . .

It started, according to plan. A great armada of more than 700 U.S. ships steamed into Leyte Gulf at dawn on the twentieth; a lone Jap plane braved the skies. Initial Japanese opposition was weak; the vast American armada —the greatest of the Pacific war, with some 151 LST's, 58 transports, 221 LCT's, 79 LCI's, and hundreds of other vessels, may have overawed the defenders. By the end of A plus 2—October 21—103,000 American troops had been landed on Leyte with few casualties, and only three warships had been damaged.

Four hours after the first landing on Leyte, General Douglas MacArthur waded ashore; later Colonel Carlos Romulo, the little Filipino, who was with him, was to quip:

"There was the tall MacArthur, with the waters reaching up to his knees, and behind him there was little Romulo, trying to keep his head above water."

In front of a Signal Corps microphone on the beach just won and beneath rain-dripping skies MacArthur recalled the bloody epic of Bataan:

"This is the Voice of Freedom, General MacArthur speaking. People of the Philippines: I have returned. . . ."

[a] This and succeeding letters and numerals refer to comments on this account by Admirals Kinkaid and Halsey, which are printed at the end of Mr. Baldwin's report.

But the Japs had not been fooled. At 0809, October 17, just nine minutes after U.S. Rangers had made preliminary landings on one of the smaller islands in the mouth of Leyte Gulf, Japanese forces had been alerted to carry out the *Shō* I plan. Admiral Soemu Toyoda, commander-in-chief of the Japanese Combined Fleet and leader of what he knew was a forlorn hope, had his last chance to "destroy the enemy who enjoys the luxury of material resources." From his headquarters at the Naval War College just outside Tokyo, he sent the word "To Conquer" to his widely scattered units.

The *Shō* plan was daring and desperate—fitted to the last months of an empire strained beyond its capabilities. The Japanese Fleet had not recovered from its cumulative losses, particularly from the heavy blow it had suffered four months earlier in the Battle of the Philippine Sea,[b] when Admiral Raymond W. Spruance, covering our Marianas landings, had destroyed more than 400 Japanese planes, sunk three Japanese carriers, and broken the back of Japanese naval aviation. In mid-October, when Halsey—in a preliminary to the Leyte Gulf landing—struck heavily at Formosa, Toyoda had utilized his land-based planes and had also thrown his hastily trained carrier replacement pilots into the fight. The gamble failed. But the "pathology of fear" and the curious propensity of the Japanese for transforming defeats into victories in their official reports magnified the normally highly inflated claims of enemy aviators; Tokyo declared the Third Fleet had "ceased to be an organized striking force."

An enemy plane dropped leaflets over recently captured Peleliu:

FOR RECKLESS YANKEE DOODLE:

Do you know about the naval battle done by the American 58th [*sic*] *Fleet at the sea near Taiwan* [*Formosa*] *and Philippine? Japanese powerful Air Force had sunk their 19 aeroplane carriers, 4 battleships, 10 several cruisers and destroyers, along with sending 1,261 ship aeroplanes into the sea. . . .*

Actually only two cruisers—*Canberra* and *Houston*—were damaged; less than 100 U.S. planes lost; the Japanese were to have a rude awakening as the great invasion[1] armada neared Leyte Gulf.

But for Toyoda, the Battle of the Philippine Sea and his futile gamble in defense of Formosa had left the Japanese Fleet naked to air attack. Toyoda had carriers,[c] but with few planes and half-trained pilots. *Shō* I, therefore, must be dependent upon stealth and cunning, night operations, and what air cover could be provided chiefly by land-based planes operating from Philippine bases and working in close conjunction with the fleet.

Toyoda also confronted another handicap—a fleet widely separated by distance. He exercised command—from his land headquarters—over a theoretically "Combined Fleet," but Vice-Admiral Jisaburo Ozawa, who flew his flag from carrier *Zuikaku,* and who commanded the crippled carriers and some cruisers and destroyers, was still based in the Inland Sea in Japanese home waters. The bulk of the fleet's heavy units—Vice-Admiral Takeo Kurita's First Diversion Attack Force, of battleships, cruisers, and destroyers—was based on Lingga Anchorage near Singapore, close to its fuel sources. The Japanese Fleet was divided in the face of a superior naval force; it could not be concentrated prior to battle.

These deficiencies, plus the geography of the Philippines, dictated the enemy plan, which was hastily modified at the last minute, partially because of the Japanese weaknesses in carrier aviation. Two principal straits—San Bernardino, north of the island of Samar; and Surigao, between Mindanao and Dinagat and Leyte and Panaon—lead from the South China Sea to Leyte Gulf, where the great armada of MacArthur was committed to the invasion. The Japanese ships based near Singapore—the so-called First Diversion Attack Force—were to steam north toward Leyte, with a stop at Brunei Bay, Borneo, to refuel. There the force would split; the Central Group, Vice-Admiral Takeo Kurita, flying his flag in the heavy cruiser *Atago,* with a total of five battleships, ten heavy cruisers, two light cruisers, and fifteen destroyers, would transit San Bernardino

Strait at night; the Southern Group, Vice-Admiral Shōji Nishimura,[2] with two battleships, one heavy cruiser, and four destroyers, was to be augmented at Surigao Strait by an ancillary force of three more cruisers and four destroyers under Vice-Admiral Kiyohide Shima, which was to steam through Formosa Strait, with a stop in the Pescadores, all the way from its bases in the home islands. All these forces were to strike the great American armada in Leyte Gulf almost simultaneously at dawn of the 25th of October and wreak havoc among the thin-skinned amphibious ships like a hawk among chickens.

But the key to the operation was the emasculated Japanese carriers, operating under Vice-Admiral Jisaburo Ozawa from their bases in Japan's Inland Sea. These ships —one heavy carrier and three light carriers, with less than 100 planes aboard—"all that remained of the enemy's once-great carrier forces"—were to steam south toward Luzon and to act as deliberate decoys or "lures" for Admiral Halsey's great Third Fleet, which was "covering" the amphibious invasion of Leyte. The northern decoy force was to be accompanied by two hermaphrodites—battleship-carriers, the *Ise* and *Hyuga,* with the after-turrets replaced by short flight decks, but with no planes, and by three cruisers and ten destroyers. Ozawa was to lure Halsey's Third Fleet to the north, away from Leyte, and open the way for Kurita and Nishimura to break into Leyte Gulf.

At the same time all three forces were to be aided—not with direct air cover, but by intensive attacks by Japanese land-based planes upon American carriers and shipping. As a last-minute "spur-of-the-moment" decision, the Japanese "Special Attack Groups" were activated, and the Kamikaze (Divine Wind) fliers commenced their suicidal attacks upon U.S. ships. As early as October 15, Rear Admiral Masabumi Arima, a subordinate naval air commander, flying from a Philippine field, had made a suicide dive and had "lit the fuse of the ardent wishes of his men."[d] All of these far-flung forces were under the common command of Admiral Toyoda far away in Tokyo.

Such was the desperate *Shō* I—perhaps the greatest

gamble, the most daring and unorthodox plan in the history of naval war.

It committed to action virtually all that was left of the operational forces—afloat and in the air—of Japan's Navy—four carriers, two battleship-carriers, seven battleships, nineteen cruisers, thirty-three destroyers, and perhaps 500 to 700 Japanese aircraft—mostly land-based.

But the opposing American forces were far more powerful. Like the Japanese forces which had no common commander closer than Tokyo, the U.S. Fleet operated under divided command. General MacArthur, as theater commander of the Southwest Pacific area, was in over-all charge of the Leyte invasion, and through Admiral Thomas C. Kinkaid, he commanded the Seventh Fleet, which was in direct charge of the amphibious operation. But Admiral Halsey's powerful covering force of the Third Fleet—the strongest fleet in the world—was not under MacArthur's command; it was a part of Admiral Chester W. Nimitz's Pacific Command forces, and Nimitz had his headquarters in Hawaii. And above Nimitz and MacArthur, the only unified command was in Washington.

The gun power of Kinkaid's Seventh Fleet was provided by six old battleships—five of them raised from the mud of Pearl Harbor, but he had sixteen escort carriers [3]—small, slow-speed vessels, converted from merchant hulls—eight cruisers and scores of destroyers and destroyer escorts, frigates, motor torpedo boats, and other types. Kinkaid's job was to provide shore bombardment and close air support for the Army and anti-submarine and air defense for the amphibious forces.

Halsey, with eight large attack carriers, eight light carriers, six fast new battleships, fifteen cruisers, and fifty-eight destroyers, was ordered to "cover and support forces of the Southwest Pacific [MacArthur's command] in order to assist in the seizure and occupation of objectives in the Central Philippines." [e] He was to destroy enemy naval and air forces threatening the invasion. He was to remain responsible to Admiral Nimitz, but "necessary measures for detailed coordination of operations between the . . . [Third

Fleet] . . . and . . . the [Seventh Fleet] will be arranged by their . . . commanders." [f]

It opened with first blood for the submarines. At dawn on October 23 the U.S. submarines *Darter* and *Dace*, patrolling Palawan Passage, intercepted Admiral Kurita, bound for his rendezvous with destiny. The *Darter* put five torpedoes into Kurita's flagship, heavy cruiser *Atago*, at 1,000 yards range; damaged the cruiser *Takao*. *Dace* [4] hit the cruiser *Maya* with four torpedoes. The *Atago* sank in nineteen minutes as Kurita shifted his flag to the destroyer *Kishinani* and later to the battleship *Yamato*. The *Maya* blew up and sank in four minutes; *Takao*—burning and low in the water—was sent back to Brunei, escorted by two destroyers. Kurita steamed on, shaken but implacable, toward San Bernardino Strait.

October 24 Aboard battleship *New Jersey*, flying "Bull" Halsey's flag, the plans are ready for this day as the sun quickly burns away the morning haze. In the carriers, bowing to the swell, the bull horns sound on the flight decks—"Pilots, man your planes."

At 6 a.m. the Third Fleet launches search planes to sweep a wide arc of sea covering the approaches to San Bernardino and Surigao straits. Submarine reports from *Darter*, *Dace*, and *Guitarro* have alerted the Americans—but not in time to halt the detachment of Third Fleet's largest task group—Task Group 38.1 commanded by Vice-Admiral John S. ("Slew") McCain with orders to retire to Ulithi for rest and supplies. The fleet's three other task groups are spread out over 300 miles of ocean to the east of the Philippines from central Luzon to southern Samar; one of them—to the north—has been tracked doggedly all night by enemy "snoopers." As the planes take off to search the reef-studded waters of the Sibuyan and Sulu seas and the approaches to San Bernardino and Surigao, Kinkaid's old battleships and little carriers off Leyte are supporting the "G.I.'s" ashore.

At 0746, Lieutenant (j.g.) Max Adams, flying a Helldiver above the magnificent volcanic crags, the palm-grown islands, and startling blue sea of the archipelago, reports a radar contact, and a few minutes later Admiral Kurita's First Diversion Attack Force lies spread out like toy ships upon a painted sea—the pagoda masts unmistakable in the sunlight.

The tension of action grips flag plot in the *New Jersey* as the contact report comes in; the radio crackles "Urgent" and "Top Secret" messages—to Washington, to Nimitz, to Kinkaid, to all task-group commanders. McCain, 600 miles to the eastward, enroute to Ulithi and rest, is recalled and Third Fleet is ordered to concentrate off San Bernardino to launch strikes against the enemy.

But at 8:20 far to the south, the southern arm of the Japanese pincer is sighted for the first time; Vice-Admiral Nishimura—with battleships *Fuso* and *Yamashiro,* heavy cruiser *Mogami,* and four destroyers—steaming toward Surigao. *Enterprise* search-attack planes attack [5] through heavy AA fire; *Fuso*'s catapult is hit, her planes destroyed, and a fire rages; a gun mount in destroyer *Shiguro* is knocked out—but Nishimura steams on to the east, his speed undiminished. And Halsey continues the concentration of his fleet near San Bernardino to strike the Japanese Central Force.

There has been no morning search to the north and northeast, and Ozawa's decoy carriers, steaming southward toward Luzon, are still undiscovered.

The *Shō* plan now moves toward its dramatic denouement. Japanese planes flying from Philippine bases commence the most furious assault since the landing upon the Seventh and Third Fleets. To the north off Luzon, carriers *Langley, Princeton, Essex,* and *Lexington* face the brunt of the winged fury. Seven Hellcats from the *Essex,* led by Commander David McCampbell, intercept sixty Japanese planes—half of them Zeke fighters—and after a melee of an hour and thirty-five minutes of combat the Americans knock down twenty-four Japs with no losses. *Princeton* claims thirty-four enemy from another large raid; the *Lexington*'s and *Langley*'s "fly-boys" are also busy; over the air come the exultant "Tally-hos," and "Splash one Betty—Splash two Zekes" of the pilots.

But the Japs draw blood. At about 0938, as Third Fleet

starts converging toward San Bernardino and the carriers prepare to launch deckloads to strike the enemy's center force, a Jap Judy dives unseen and unrecorded on the radar screen out of a low cloud. She drops a 550-pound bomb square on *Princeton*'s flight deck; the bomb penetrates to the hangar deck, ignites gasoline in six torpedo planes, starts raging fires. The fight to save her starts, but at 1002 a series of terrific explosions split open the flight deck like the rind of a dropped melon, throw the after plane elevator high into the air, and by 1020 *Princeton*'s fire mains have failed and she is dead in the water, with a 1,000-foot pall of smoke above her and hundreds of her crew in the water. The task group steams on southward to the San Bernardino rendezvous, while cruisers *Birmingham* and *Reno* and destroyers *Gatling, Irwin,* and *Cassin Young* hover about wounded *Princeton* in a day-long fight to save her.

But as *Princeton* flames and staggers, Kurita's Central Force of five battleships, accompanied by cruisers and destroyers, is running the gantlet. Carrier strikes start coming in against Japan's First Diversion Attack Force about 10:25 a.m., and the exultant U.S. pilots concentrate against targets none of them had ever seen before—the largest battleships in the world. *Yamato* and *Musashi*, long the mysterious focus of intelligence reports, lie beneath the wings of naval air power—their 69,500-ton bulk, 18-inch guns, 27.5-knot speed—dwarfing their sisters. *Musashi* is wounded early; oil smears trail on the blue water from her lacerated flank as a torpedo strikes home. But she is strong; her speed is undiminished. Not so *Myoko*'s. This heavy cruiser is badly hurt in the first attack; she drops to fifteen knots and is left astern to limp alone into port; Kurita has lost four out of the ten heavy cruisers that sortied so gallantly from Brunei.

But he has no respite. At three minutes past noon another strike comes out of the sun. The Jap AA fire blossoms in pink and purple bursts; even the battleships' main batteries are firing. Several American planes are hit; one goes down flaming—but *Musashi* takes two bombs and two torpedoes; she loses speed and drops back slowly out of formation.

An hour and a half later *Yamato* takes two hits forward of her Number 1 turret, which start a fire—but her thick hide minimizes damages; the fire is extinguished. But *Musashi* is now sore-wounded; she takes four bomb hits in this attack and three more torpedoes; her upper works are a shambles, her bow almost under water, her speed down first to sixteen and then to twelve knots.

But Kurita's slow agony drags on during this long and sunlit day. He hopes in vain for air cover. *Yamato* is hit again in the fourth attack and the older battleship *Nagato* damaged.

At six bells in the afternoon watch (3 p.m.) Kurita orders the limping *Musashi* to withdraw from the fight. But not in time.

The final and largest attack of the day seeks her out as she turns heavily to find sanctuary. In fifteen minutes *Musashi* receives the *coup de grâce*—ten more bombs, four more torpedoes; she's down to six knots now, her bow is under water, and she lists steeply to port—a dying gladiator.

Kurita is shaken. He has had no air cover; he has been subjected to intense attack; his original strength of five battleships, twelve cruisers, and fifteen destroyers has been reduced to four battleships, eight cruisers, and eleven destroyers; all of his remaining battleships have been damaged; fleet speed is limited to twenty-two knots. There is no sign that Ozawa's northern decoy force is succeeding in luring the Third Fleet away from San Bernardino. At 1530 Kurita reverses course and steams away toward the west. And American pilots report the "retreat" to Admiral Halsey aboard *New Jersey*. . . .

To Admiral Halsey there is "one piece missing in the puzzle—the [Japanese] carriers."

The northern task group of Third Fleet has been under attack by enemy carrier-type planes, which might have been land-based—but none of the sightings has reported enemy carriers. Where are they?

At 1405 (2:05 p.m.), as Kurita's central force is pounded in the Sibuyan Sea, *Lexington*'s planes take off to find out.[6] They are under orders to search to the north and northeast in the open seas untouched by the morning search.

The search planes fly through a cloud-speckled sky and intermittent rain squalls, leaving behind them a task group harassed by fierce, though intermittent Jap air attacks.

The flaming *Princeton,* billowing clouds of fire and smoke, is still afloat, with her covey of rescue ships around her. Despite intermittent explosions and singeing heat, cruisers *Birmingham* and *Reno,* destroyers *Morrison, Irwin,* and *Cassin Young* have clustered alongside, pouring water from their pumps on the blazing carrier. Submarine contacts and enemy air attacks interrupt the fire fighting; the rescue ships pull off. At 1523 (3:23 p.m.), about the time Kurita, 300 miles away, reverses course and heads to the westward in the Sibuyan Sea, cruiser *Birmingham* comes alongside *Princeton*'s blazing port side again. The cruiser's open decks are thick with men—fire fighters, line handlers, antiaircraft gunners, medical personnel, fire and rescue squads, watch-standers. There is fifty feet of open water between blazing *Princeton* and her salvor, *Birmingham;* a spring line is out forward between carrier and cruiser.

Suddenly a "tremendous blast" rips off Princeton's stern and flight deck; steel plates as big "as a house" fly through the air; jagged bits of steel, broken gun barrels, shrapnel, helmets, debris rake *Birmingham*'s bridge, upper works, and crowded decks like grapeshot; in a fraction of a second the cruiser is a charnel house, her decks literally flowing blood—229 dead, 420 mangled and wounded—the ship's superstructure sieved.

Aboard *Princeton* all the skeleton fire-fighting crew are wounded. Captain John M. Hoskins, who had been scheduled to take command of *Princeton* shortly and had remained aboard with the skipper he was relieving, puts a rope tourniquet around his leg, as his right foot hangs by a shred of flesh and tendon. The surviving medical officer cuts off the foot with a sheath knife, dusts the wound with sulfa powder, injects morphine. . . . Hoskins lives to become the Navy's first "peg-leg" admiral of modern times.

But still *Princeton* floats on even keel, flaming like a volcano, manned by a crew of bloody specters. . . .

At 1640 the search to the north pays off. U.S. planes sight Ozawa's decoy force of carriers. The contact reports electrify Third Fleet, but mislead it, too; Ozawa's northern group of ships, which were sighted about 130 miles east of the northern tip of Luzon, includes two hermaphrodite battleships but our fliers mistakenly report four.[7] Nor do our fliers know Ozawa's carriers are virtually without planes.

The contact reports decide *Princeton*'s fate; her weary crew of fire fighters are removed, the day-long struggle is ended, and at 4:49 *Reno* puts two torpedoes into the flaming hulk and the carrier blows up, breaks in two, and sinks. Mangled *Birmingham,* which lost far more men than the ship she was trying to save, steams with her dead and dying to Ulithi—out of the fight. . . .

Two hours later, near Sibuyan Island, the giant *Musashi,* pride of Kurita's Central Force, loses her long fight. Fatally wounded, she settles slowly deeper and deeper in the calm sea, and as the evening closes down, the greatest battleship in the world capsizes and takes with her to the depths half of her crew. But no American sees her passing. . . . And no American has seen Kurita, earlier in the afternoon, alter his course once more and at 1714 head once again with his battered but still powerful Central Force back toward San Bernardino Strait. . . .

At 1950, with the tropic dusk, "Bull" Halsey makes his decision and informs Kinkaid, commanding Seventh Fleet:

"Central force heavily damaged according to strike reports. Am proceeding north with three groups to attack carrier force at dawn."[8]

Third Fleet concentrates and steams hard to the north in what irreverent historians of the future are to call "Bull's Run." Night snoopers from *Independence* shadow the Jap northern force, and orders go to the carriers to launch planes at sunrise.[g] San Bernardino Strait is left uncovered—not even a submarine[h] patrols its waters; Kinkaid and

Seventh Fleet, protecting the Leyte invasion, believe it is barred by Halsey; Halsey, banking too heavily on exaggerated claims from his pilots,[i] thinks Kurita's central force has been stopped by the day's air attacks and the battered Jap survivors can be left safely to Kinkaid. On such misunderstandings rest the course of history and the fate of nations.[j]

Surigao Strait is dark under the loom of the land. Since the morning there have been no sightings of the Japanese southern force; even its exact composition is not known. But Kinkaid and the Seventh Fleet have no doubts; the Japs will try to break through this night. Kinkaid and Rear Admiral Jesse B. Oldendorf, his "O.T.C." (officer in tactical command) have made dispositions for a night surface battle. They have provided a suitable reception committee, including PT boats deep in the strait and covering its southern approaches, three destroyer squadrons near the center, and at the mouth—where the strait debouches into Leyte Gulf—six old battleships and eight cruisers.[9]

Into this trap the Japanese southern force blunders in two divisions—each independent of the other. Nishimura, with battleships *Fuso* and *Yamashiro,* cruiser *Mogami,* and four destroyers, lead the way. Cruising twenty miles behind Nishimura is Vice-Admiral Shima with three cruisers and four destroyers from Jap home bases. The two Jap forces attack piecemeal and uncoordinated; neither knows much of the other's plans. Shima and Nishimura were classmates at the Japanese Naval Academy; their careers have bred rivalry; Nishimura, formerly the senior, has been passed in the processes of promotion by Shima, who commands the smaller force but is now six months senior in rank to Nishimura. But Nishimura, a sea-going admiral, has seen more war. Neither seems anxious to serve with the other; there is no common command.

Radars on the PT boats pick up the enemy about 11 p.m. as "sheet lightning dim[s] the hazy blur of the setting moon and thunder echo[es] from the islands' hills."

Thirty-nine PT boats, motors muffled, head for Nishimura and attack in successive "waves" as the enemy ad-

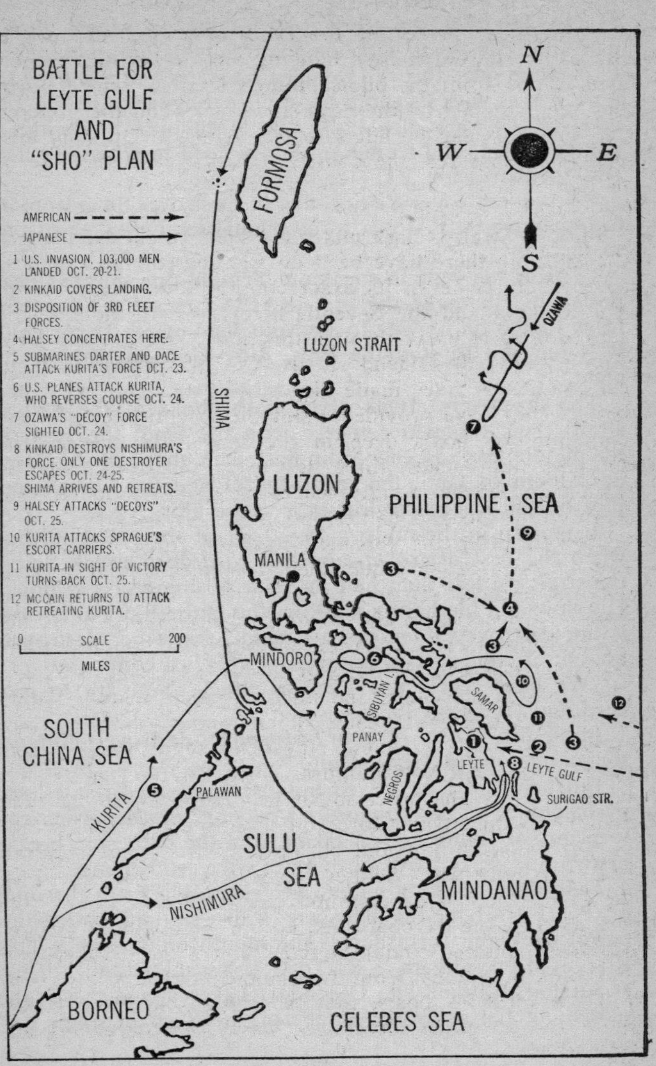

BATTLE FOR LEYTE GULF AND "SHO" PLAN
AMERICAN
JAPANESE
1 U.S. INVASION, 103,000 MEN LANDED OCT. 20-21.
2 KINKAID COVERS LANDING.
3 DISPOSITION OF 3RD FLEET FORCES.
4 HALSEY CONCENTRATES HERE.
5 SUBMARINES DARTER AND DACE ATTACK KURITA'S FORCE OCT. 23.
6 U.S. PLANES ATTACK KURITA, WHO REVERSES COURSE OCT. 24.
7 OZAWA'S "DECOY" FORCE SIGHTED OCT. 24.
8 KINKAID DESTROYS NISHIMURA'S FORCE. ONLY ONE DESTROYER ESCAPES OCT. 24-25. SHIMA ARRIVES AND RETREATS.
9 HALSEY ATTACKS "DECOYS" OCT. 25.
10 KURITA ATTACKS SPRAGUE'S ESCORT CARRIERS.
11 KURITA IN SIGHT OF VICTORY TURNS BACK OCT. 25.
12 MCCAIN RETURNS TO ATTACK RETREATING KURITA.
0 SCALE 200
MILES
N
W
E
S
FORMOSA
OZAWA
LUZON STRAIT
SHIMA
LUZON
PHILIPPINE SEA
MANILA
MINDORO
SIBUYAN I.
SAMAR
SOUTH CHINA SEA
PANAY
LEYTE
LEYTE GULF
SURIGAO STR.
NEGROS
PALAWAN
KURITA
SULU SEA
MINDANAO
NISHIMURA
BORNEO
CELEBES SEA

vances. But the Japs score first. Enemy destroyers illuminate the little boats with their searchlights long before the PT's reach good torpedo range; a hit starts a fire in *PT 152;* a near miss with its spout of water extinguishes it; *PT 130* and *PT 132* are also hit.[10] But Nishimura is identified; course, speed, and formation are radioed to Kinkaid's fleet and the harassing PT attacks continue.

Aboard destroyer *Remey,* flag of Destroyer Squadron 54, Commander R. P. Fiala turns on the loud-speaker to talk to the crew:

"This is the captain speaking. Tonight our ship has been designated to make the first torpedo run on the Jap task force that is on its way to stop our landings in Leyte Gulf. It is our job to stop the Japs. May God be with us tonight."

The destroyers attack along both flanks of the narrow strait; their silhouettes merge with the land; the Japs, in the middle, can scarcely distinguish dark shape of ship from dark loom of land; the radar fuzzes and the luminescent pips on the screen are lost in a vague blur.

It is deep in the mid-watch—0301 of the twenty-fifth—when the first destroyer-launched torpedoes streak across the strait. In less than half an hour Nishimura is crippled. His slow and lumbering flagship, the battleship *Yamashiro,* is hit; destroyer *Yamagumo* is sunk; two other destroyers are out of control. Nishimura issues his last command:

"We have received a torpedo attack. You are to proceed and attack all ships."

Battleship *Fuso,* cruiser *Mogami,* destroyer *Shigure* steam on toward Leyte Gulf.

But before 4 a.m. a tremendous eruption of flames and pyrotechnics marks *Yamashiro*'s passing; another American torpedo has found her magazine, and the battleship breaks in two and sinks, with Nishimura's flag still flying.

Fuso does not long outlive her sister. Up from the mud of Pearl Harbor, the avengers wait—six old battleships patrol back and forth across the mouth of the strait. This is an admiral's dream. Like Togo at Tsushima and Jellicoe at Jutland, Kinkaid and Oldendorf have capped the T; the remaining Jap ships are blundering head on in single column against a column of American ships at right angles to the Jap course. The concentrated broadsides of six battleships can be focused against the leading Jap, and only his forward turrets can bear against the Americans.

Climax of battle. As the last and heaviest destroyer attack goes home in answer to the command—"Get the big boys" —the battle line and the cruisers open up; the night is streaked with flare of crimson.

Fuso and *Mogami* flame and shudder as the "rain of shells" strikes home; *Fuso* soon drifts helplessly, racked by great explosions, wreathed in a fiery pall. She dies before the dawn, and *Mogami,* on fire, is finished later with the other cripples. Only destroyer *Shigure* escapes at thirty knots.

Into this mad melee, with the dying remnants of his classmate's fleet around him, steams Vice-Admiral Shima—"fat, dumb, and happy." He knows nothing of what has gone before; he has no cogent plan of battle. *Abukuma,* Shima's only light cruiser, is struck by a PT torpedo[11] even before she is deep in the strait; she is left behind, speed dwindling, as the two heavy cruisers and four destroyers steam onward toward the gun flashes on the horizon. About 4 a.m. Shima encounters destroyer *Shigure,* sole survivor of Nishimura's fleet, retiring down the strait.

Shigure tells Shima nothing of the debacle; she simply signals:

"I am the *Shigure;* I have rudder difficulties."

The rest is almost comic anticlimax. Shima pushes deeper into the strait, sees a group of dark shadows; fires torpedoes and manages an amazing collision between his flagship, the *Nachi,* and the burning stricken *Mogami,* which looms up flaming out of the dark waters of the strait like the Empire State Building. And that is all for futile Shima; discretion is the better part of valor; dying for the Emperor is forgotten and Shima reverses course and heads back into the Mindanao Sea and the obscurity of history.

The Battle of Surigao Strait ends with the dawn—debacle for the Japanese. One PT boat destroyed; one destroyer damaged for the Americans. The southern pincer toward Leyte Gulf is broken.[k]

October 25 Dawn of the twenty-fifth of October finds Admiral Ozawa with his decoy force[l] eastward of Cape Engano (fortuitous name: Engano is Spanish for "lure" or "hoax"), prepared to die for the Emperor. At 0712, when the first American planes appear from the southeast, Ozawa knows he has at last succeeded in his luring mission. The day before he has at times despaired; some seventy to eighty of his carrier planes—all he has save for a small combat air patrol—have joined Japanese land-based planes in attacks upon Halsey's northern task group. But his planes have not come back; many have been lost, others have flown on to Philippine bases. This day twenty aircraft—token remnants of Japan's once great flying fleets—are all that Ozawa commands. A few are in the air—to die quickly beneath American guns, as the first heavy attacks from Halsey's carriers come in.

The American carrier pilots have a field day; the air is full of the jabberwock of the fliers.

"Pick one out, boys, and let 'em have it."

The Jap formation throws up a beautiful carpet of antiaircraft fire; the colored bursts and tracers frame the sky-sea battle. The Japanese ships twist and turn, maneuver violently in eccentric patterns to avoid the bombs and torpedoes—but their time has come. Before 8:30, with the day still young, some 150 U.S. carrier planes have wrought havoc. Carrier *Chiyoda* is hit; carrier *Chitose*, billowing clouds of smoke and fatally hurt, is stopped and listing heavily; the light cruiser *Tama*, torpedoed, is limping astern; destroyer *Akitsuki* has blown up; light carrier *Zuiho* is hit, and Ozawa's flagship, the *Zuikaku*, has taken a torpedo aft, which has wrecked the steering engine; she is steered by hand.

A second strike at 10 cripples *Chiyoda*, which dies a slow death, to be finished off later by U.S. surface ships. In early afternoon a third strike sinks carrier *Zuikaku*, the last survivor of the Japanese attack upon Pearl Harbor. She rolls over slowly and sinks, "flying a battle flag of tremendous size." At 1527 carrier *Zuiho* "follows her down." The hermaphrodite battleships, with flight decks aft—*Hyuga* and *Ise*, "fattest of the remaining targets"—are bombed repeatedly, their bulges are perforated, their decks inundated with tons of water from near misses; *Ise*'s port catapult is hit—but they bear charmed lives. Admiral Ozawa, his flag transferred to cruiser *Oyodo*, his work of "luring" done, straggles northward with his cripples from the battle off Cape Engano. Throughout the day he is subject to incessant air attack, and in late afternoon and in the dark of the night of the twenty-fifth U.S. cruisers and destroyers, detached from the Third Fleet finish off the cripples.

The price of success for Admiral Ozawa's decoy force is high; all four carriers, one of his three cruisers, and two of his eight destroyers are gone. But he has accomplished his mission; Halsey has been lured, San Bernardino Strait is unguarded, and the hawk Kurita is down among the chickens.

Off Samar that morning of the twenty-fifth, the sea is calm at sunup, the wind gentle, the sky overcast with spotted cumulus; occasional rain squalls dapple the surface. Aboard the sixteen escort carriers of Seventh Fleet and their escorting "small boys" (destroyers and destroyer escorts) the dawn alert has ended. The early missions have taken off (though not the search planes for the northern sectors). Many of the carriers' planes are already over Leyte, supporting the ground troops—the combat air patrol and ASW patrols are launched, and on the bridge of carrier *Fanshaw Bay*, Rear Admiral C. A. F. Sprague is having a second cup of coffee.

The coming day will be busy; the little escort carriers have support missions to fly for the troops ashore on Leyte, air defense and anti-submarine patrols, and a large strike scheduled to mop up the cripples and fleeing remnants of the Japanese force defeated in the night surface battle of Surigao Strait. The escort-carrier groups are spread out off the east coast of the Philippines from Mindanao to Samar; Sprague's northern group of six escort carriers, three destroyers, and four destroyer escorts is steaming northward at fourteen knots fifty miles off Samar and halfway up the island's coast.

The escort carriers, designated CVE's in naval abbreviation, are tin-clads-unarmored, converted from merchant ship or tanker hulls, slow, carrying eighteen to thirty-six planes. They are known by many uncomplimentary descriptives—"baby flat-tops," "tomato cans," "jeep carriers," and new recruits "coming aboard for the first time were told by the old hands that CVE stood for Combustible, Vulnerable, Expendable!" Their maximum of eighteen knots speed (made all-out) is too slow to give them safety in flight; their thin skins and "pop-guns"—five-inchers and under—do not fit them for surface slugging; they are ships of limited utility—intended for air support of ground operations ashore, anti-submarine and air defense missions—never for fleet action.

Yet they are to fight this morning a battle of jeeps against giants.

Admiral Sprague has scarcely finished his coffee when a contact report comes over the squawk-box. An ASW pilot reports enemy battleships, cruisers, destroyers twenty miles away and closing fast.

". . . check that identification," the admiral says, thinking some green pilot has mistaken Halsey's fast battleships for the enemy.

The answer is sharp and brief, the tension obvious: "Identification confirmed," the pilot's voice comes strained through the static. "Ships have pagoda masts."

Almost simultaneously radiomen hear Japanese chatter over the air; the northern CVE group sees antiaircraft bursts blossoming in the air to the northwest; blips of unidentified ships appear on the radar screens, and before 7 a.m. a signalman with a long glass has picked up the many-storied superstructures and the typical pagoda masts of Japanese ships.

Disbelief, amazement, and consternation struggle for supremacy; the escort carriers, Admiral Kinkaid himself—in fact, most of the Seventh Fleet—had been convinced the Japanese center force was still west of the Philippines [12] and that, in any case, Halsey's fast battleships—now far away to the north with the carriers in the battle for Cape Engano—were guarding San Bernardino Strait. But Kurita has arrived. . . . And about all that stands between him and the transports, supply ships, and amphibious craft in Leyte Gulf and Army headquarters and supply dumps on the beach are the "baby flat-tops" and their accompanying "small boys."

There's no time for planning; within five minutes of visual sighting Japanese heavy stuff—18-inch shells from *Yamato,* sister ship of the foundered *Musashi*—are whistling overhead. Sprague, giving his orders over the voice radio, turns his ships to the east into the wind, steps up speed to maximum, orders all planes scrambled. By 7:05 a.m. escort carrier *White Plains,* launching aircraft as fast as she can get them off, is straddled several times, with red, yellow, green, and blue spouts of water from the dye-marked shells foaming across her bridge, shaking the ship violently, damaging the starboard engine room, smashing electrical circuits, and throwing a fighter plane out of its chocks on the flight deck.

White Plains makes smoke and the Japs shift fire to the *St. Lô,* which takes near misses and casualties from fragments. The "small boys" make smoke—and the carriers, their boiler casings panting from maximum effort—pour out viscous clouds of oily black smoke from their stacks, which veils the sea. . . . There is a moment of surcease; the planes are launched, most of them armed with small-size or anti-personnel or general-purpose bombs or depth charges—no good against armored ships. But there has been no time to rearm. . . .

The air waves sound alarm. Sprague broadcasts danger in plain language; at 0724 Admiral Kinkaid, aboard his flagship *Wasatch* in Leyte Gulf, hears the worst has happened; the Jap fleet is three hours' steaming from the beachhead; the little escort carriers may be wiped out. Just five minutes before, Kinkaid has learned that his assumption that a Third Fleet cork was in the bottle of San Bernardino Strait was incorrect; in answer to a radioed query sent at 0412 Halsey informs him that Task Force 34—modern fast battleships—is with Third Fleet's carriers off Cape Engano far to the north.

Kinkaid in "urgent and priority" messages asks for fast battleships, for carrier strikes, for immediate action. . . .

Even Admiral Nimitz, in far-off Hawaii, sends a message to Halsey:

"All the world wants to know where is Task Force 34 [13] [the fast battleships]?" [m]

But in Leyte Gulf and Surigao Strait the tocsin of alarm sounded via the radio waves puts Seventh Fleet—red-eyed [n] from days of shore bombardment and nights of battle—into frenetic action. Some of the old battleships and cruisers are recalled from Surigao Strait, formed into a task unit, and they prepare feverishly to ammunition and refuel. Seventh Fleet's heavy ships are in none too good shape for surface action; their ammunition is dangerously low from five days of shore bombardment, many of their armor-piercing projectiles were used in the night battle; destroyers are low on torpedoes, many ships short of fuel. . . .[o]

And in the battle off Samar, Sprague is fighting for his life.

Within twenty minutes, as the baby carriers steam to the east, launching planes, the range to the enemy has decreased to 25,000 yards—easy shooting for the big guns of the Japs, far beyond the effective reach of the American five-inchers. . . .

Destroyer *Johnston*, Commander Ernest E. Evans, commanding, sees her duty and does it. Without orders she dashes in at thirty knots to launch a spread of ten torpedoes against an enemy cruiser working up along a flank of the pounding carriers. She spouts smoke and fire as she charges—her five-inchers firing continuously as she closes the range. She escapes damage until she turns to retire; then a salvo of three 14-inchers, followed by three six-inch shells, hole her, wound her captain, wreck the steering engine, the after fire room and engine room, knock out her after guns and gyro compass, maim many of her crew and leave her limping at sixteen knots.

Sprague and his carriers, veiled in part by smoke, find brief sanctuary in a heavy rain squall; the curtain of water saves temporarily wounded *Johnston*. But well before 8 a.m. Kurita has sent some of his faster ships seaward to head off and flank the escort carriers; gradually Sprague turns southward, the enemy coming hard on both his flanks and astern. . . .

"Small boys, launch torpedo attack," Sprague orders over the TBS circuit (talk-between-ships voice radio).

Destroyers *Heermann* and *Hoel* and wounded *Johnston*, her torpedoes already expended but her guns speaking in support, answer the command—three destroyers in a daylight attack against [14] the heaviest ships of the Japanese fleet, three tin-clads against four battleships, eight cruisers, and eleven destroyers.

"Buck," Commander Amos T. Hathaway, skipper of the *Heermann*, remarks coolly to his officer of the deck: "Buck, what we need is a bugler to sound the charge."

Hoel and *Heermann*, followed by limping *Johnston*, sally forth to their naval immortality.

In and out of rain squalls, wreathed in the black and oily smoke from the stacks and the white chemical smoke from the smoke generators on the fantails, the destroyers charge, backing violently to avoid collisions, closing the range. They hear the "express-train" roar of the 14-inchers going over; they fire spreads at a heavy cruiser, rake the superstructure of a battleship with their five-inchers, launch their last torpedoes at 4,400 yards range. Then Hathaway of the *Heermann* walks calmly into his pilothouse, calls Admiral Sprague on the TBS, and reports:

"Exercise completed."

But the destroyers are finished. *Hoel* has lost her port engine; she is steered manually; her decks are a holocaust of blood and wreckage; fire control and power are off; No. 3 gun, wreathed in white-hot steam venting from the burst steam pipes, is inoperable; No. 5 is frozen in train by a near miss; half the barrel of No. 4 is blown off—but Nos. 1 and 2 guns continue to fire.

By 8:30 p.m. power is lost on the starboard engine; all engineering spaces are flooding; the ship slows to dead in the water and, burning furiously, is raked by enemy guns. At 0840, with a twenty-degree list, the order is given to "abandon ship." Fifteen minutes later she rolls on her port side and sinks stern first—holed repeatedly by scores of major-caliber shells.

In *Heermann*, the crimson dye from enemy shell splashes mixes with the blood of men to daub bridge and superstructure reddish hues. A shell strikes a bean locker and spreads a brown paste across the decks. *Heermann* takes hits, but, fishtailing and chasing salvos, she manages to live.

Not so, wounded *Johnston*. Spitting fire to the end, and virtually surrounded by the entire Jap fleet, she is overwhelmed under an avalanche of shells, to sink about an hour after *Hoel*.

The four smaller and slower destroyer escorts make the second torpedo attack. *Raymond* and *John C. Butler* live to tell about it; *Dennis* has her guns knocked out, but *Samuel B. Roberts*, deep in the smoke and framed by shell splashes, comes to her end in a mad melee. She is hit by many heavy-caliber projectiles, her speed reduced, and by 9 a.m. a salvo of 14-inch shells rips open her port side like a can opener, wrecks an engine room, starts raging fires. The *Roberts*, abaft her stack, looks like "an inert mass of battered metal"; she has no power; she is dead in the water.

But the crew of No. 2 gun load, ram, aim, and fire by hand. They know the chance they take; without compressed air to clear the bore of the burning bits of fragments from the previous charge, the silken powder bags may "cook off" and explode before the breach can be closed. But they fire six rounds, despite the risk. The seventh "cooks off" and kills instantly most of the gun crew; the breach is blown into a twisted inoperable mass of steel. But Gunner's Mate 3/c Paul Henry Carr, the gun captain—his body ripped open from neck to groin—still cradles the last 54-pound shell in his arms, and his last gasping words before he dies are pleas for aid to load the gun.

But smoke screens, rain squalls, and torpedo attacks have not saved the slow and lumbering baby flat-tops. Kurita has sent his cruisers curving seaward; slowly the fight swerves round from south to southwest; Sprague's carriers, strung out over miles of ocean, steam wounded toward Leyte Gulf, with the enemy destroyers coming hard on their landward flank, battleships astern and Jap cruisers to seaward.

The flat-tops dodge in and out of the 150-foot water-spouts from the major-caliber Japanese shells; they chase salvos and fire their five-inchers defiantly. *Fanshaw Bay* takes six hits from eight-inch shells, which wreck the catapult, knock holes in the hull, start fires. *Kalinin Bay* takes fifteen hits; *White Plains* is racked from stem to stern by straddles. But their thin skins save them; most of the huge armor-piercing projectiles pass clean through the unarmored carriers without exploding. *Gambier Bay*, trailing and on an exposed windward flank where the smoke screens do not shield her, takes a hit on the flight deck, a near miss close alongside, loses an engine, drops to eleven knots, then loses all power—and is doomed. For an hour, far behind the chase, she dies in agony, hit about once a minute by enemy fire. She sinks about 9 a.m., flaming brightly, gasoline exploding, a Jap cruiser still riddling her from only 2,000 yards away.

Well before 9:30 the chase which is drawing closer and closer to crowded Leyte Gulf, where frantic preparations are in progress, has enveloped the northern group of escort carriers; the central group is now under fire, and the sixteen jeep flat-tops have lost 105 planes.

". . . it seemed only a matter of time until the entire Northern Group would be wiped out and the Middle Group overtaken . . ."

Two destroyers, a destroyer escort, and a carrier are sunk or sinking; two carriers, a destroyer, and a destroyer escort are badly hurt.

Aboard *Kitkun Bay*, an officer quips:

"It won't be long now, boys; we're sucking 'em into 40-mm. range."

Suddenly at 0925, Vice-Admiral Kurita, with victory in his grasp, breaks off the action, turns his ships to the north, and ends the surface phase of the battle off Samar.

"Damn it," a sailor says. "They got away."

Kurita's action, inexplicable at the time, has some, though incomplete, justification. The charge of the American "small boys"—one of the most stirring episodes in the long history of naval war—and the desperate gallantry of the uncoordinated and improvised air strikes by the pilots of the escort carriers have had their effect. During the early action off Samar, U.S. carrier pilots—from the little CVE's—have harassed Kurita constantly, have shot down more than 100 enemy planes, dropped 191 tons of bombs and 83 torpedoes. The enemy ships have turned and maneuvered violently to avoid torpedoes. Effective smoke screens have confused the Japanese. The air attacks have been mounting in intensity and effectiveness as planes have been launched from the center and southern group of escort carriers and have been diverted from ground-support missions on Leyte to the new emergency. Pilots have strafed the Japanese ships recklessly, have dropped depth charges and anti-personnel bombs, have zoomed above Japanese mastheads with no ammunition and no weapons to win time and to divert and to distract.

The torpedo attacks by surface ships and aircraft had damaged enemy ships, and Kurita's fleet—composed of units now capable of widely differing speeds—is strung out over miles of ocean. Cruiser *Kumano*, torpedoed, is down to sixteen knots; cruisers *Chikuma* and *Chokai* are crippled; superstructures, charthouses, and communication equipment in other ships are damaged by five-inch shell fire and aircraft strafing; the Japs are shaken. Kurita, who has lost close tactical control of his command,[15] does not comprehend his closeness to victory; he thinks he has engaged some of the big, fast carriers of Third Fleet instead of merely the escort carriers of Seventh Fleet. Intercepted U.S. radio traffic convinces him—erroneously—that Leyte airstrips are operational.[p] He believes the rest of Halsey's powerful forces are nearby; he knows that Nishimura's southern pincer has been defeated in Surigao Strait; he has never received messages from Ozawa, far to the north, reporting the success of his decoy mission. So Kurita recalls his ships and assembles his scattered forces—and his chance has gone.

Admiral Sprague notes his thankful bewilderment: ". . . the failure of the enemy . . . to completely wipe out all vessels of this Task Unit can be attributed to our successful smoke screen, our torpedo counterattack . . . and the definite partiality of Almighty God."

The rest was anticlimax.

Kurita's irresolution was reinforced by mounting American attacks. Only two hours from the soft-skinned amphibious shipping in Leyte Gulf—his original goal—Kurita wasted time assembling his scattered forces and aiding cripples, and his fleet milled around in much the same waters, steering varying courses. *Suzuya,* cruiser, was fatally damaged by air attack, and at 10:30 a.m., two to three hours' flying time to the eastward, Admiral "Slew" McCain's Task Group 38.1 (which had been sent to Ulithi for rest, hastily recalled, and was steaming hard to the rescue) launched a strike. The bell has tolled for Kurita, and Japan's rising sun has passed the zenith. And far to the north, "Bull" Halsey, striking at Ozawa's decoy force, was alarmed at length by Kinkaid's frantic appeals for help; his fleet reversed course when within forty miles of decisive surface action, and Halsey detached some of his fast battleships to steam southward at high speed—but too late to intervene.[16]

The rest of that day, the twenty-fifth, and all of the next—the twenty-sixth—was mop-up and fierce stab, as the Japanese survivors fled and Jap land-based aircraft struck hard in angry futility. Japanese Kamikaze planes, attacking after the crescendo of battle, hit the escort carriers—damaged three and broke the back of *St. Lô,* which had survived the 18-inch guns of *Yamato.* But Kurita, who reached so closely to the verge of fame, paid heavily for the luxury of indecision. Air attacks struck him again and again during the afternoon of the twenty-fifth. Three of his damaged cruisers, crippled and on fire, had to be sunk. *Tone,* one of his two remaining heavy cruisers, was hit aft and damaged, and during the night of the twenty-fifth, as Kurita took his battered survivors back through San Bernardino Strait, U.S. surface forces caught and sank destroyer *Nowake.* At midnight of the twenty-fifth only one of Kurita's ships, a destroyer, was wholly undamaged.

On the twenty-sixth there was more slow dying as Halsey's and Kinkaid's fliers, augmented by some Army Air Force land-based bombers, chivvied and attacked the retreating Japs; and the First Diversion Attack Force, "which had already undergone more air attacks than any other force in naval history, once again braced itself for the final ordeal." Destroyer *Noshiro* was sunk; *Yamato,* with its gigantic but futile 18-inches, was hit twice and its superstructure sieved with splinters, and other cripples of the battle off Samar and the Battle of Surigao Strait, including cruiser *Abukuma* and destroyer *Hayashimo,* were finished off. And there still remained the gantlet of U.S. submarines. . . .

At 2130, October 28, "what remained of the Japanese Battle Fleet re-entered Brunei Bay."

The *Shō* plan—the great gamble—had failed completely. In the sprawling battle for Leyte Gulf, Japan had lost one large and three light aircraft carriers, three battleships, including one of the two largest warships in the world, six heavy cruisers, four light cruisers, and eleven destroyers; most of the rest of her engaged ships were damaged severely or lightly; hundreds of planes had been shot down, and between 7,475 and 10,000 Japanese seamen died. The Japanese Navy as a fighting fleet had ceased to exist; Leyte Gulf was a blow from which the enemy never recovered.

But for the United States it was, nevertheless, incomplete victory when we might have swept the boards. The penalty of divided command,[17] of failure to "fix definite areas of responsibility," and unwarranted assumptions by both Kinkaid and Halsey [q] led to the surprise of our jeep carriers and to the escape of Kurita with his battered survivors, including four battleships, and of Ozawa with ten of his original seventeen vessels. Admiral Halsey ran to the north, leaving behind a force (the Seventh Fleet) inadequate in strength and speed to insure Kurita's destruction, and then just at the time when he was about to destroy all of Ozawa's force, he turned about and ran to the south in answer to Kinkaid's urgent calls for help.[r] The Japanese "lure" worked, but the *Shō* plan, which depended funda-

mentally upon good communications, split-second co-ordination, and bold leadership, foundered in complete and fatal failure.

To the United States the cost of overwhelming victory was 2,803 lives, several hundred aircraft, one light carrier, two escort carriers, and the "small boys" who had helped turn the tide of battle—destroyers *Johnston* and *Hoel* and destroyer escort *Samuel B. Roberts*, fought by "well-trained crews in an inspired manner in accordance with the highest traditions of the Navy."

NOTES The battle for Leyte Gulf will be, forever, a source of some controversy, comparable to—though in no way as bitter as—the Sampson-Schley controversy after the Spanish-American War, or the Jellicoe-Beatty differences after Jutland. [18] Admiral Halsey and Admiral Kinkaid to this day believe their judgments were justified; each feels the other could—and should—have covered San Bernardino Strait.[s]

Leyte Gulf is a case history of the importance of communications to victory. Grossly inadequate communications made the co-ordination essential to Japanese success impossible; Kurita, for instance, never received Ozawa's messages. [19] But in the U.S. forces too many messages—and some messages improperly phrased [20]—led to the assumptions which made possible Kurita's surprise of Sprague's jeep carriers.

On October 24, while Third Fleet was launching its air attacks against Kurita, who was then in the Sibuyan Sea, Halsey sent out "a preparatory dispatch" [t] to his principal Third Fleet commanders designating four of his six fast battleships, with supporting units, as Task Force 34.[s] This task group was to be detached from the main fleet and used as a surface battle line against the Japanese surface ships if developments warranted. Halsey did not actually form this task force; he merely informed his own commanders that this was a "battle plan" to be executed when directed. However, Kinkaid, Nimitz and Vice-Admiral Marc A. Mitscher intercepted this message, though it was not

directed to any of them, and later in the battle—and partly because of subsequent messages—all misconstrued it.

When Halsey made his decision late in the evening of the twenty-fourth to steam north with all his available fleet and attack Ozawa, he informed Kinkaid that he was "proceeding north with three groups." Kinkaid, having intercepted the earlier message about Task Force 34, thought Halsey was taking his three carrier groups to the north and was leaving four of his six fast battleships to guard San Bernardino Strait. But Kinkaid, busy with preparations for the night action of Surigao Strait, did not specifically ask Halsey whether or not Task Force 34 was guarding San Bernardino Strait until 0412, October 25, and he did not get a negative reply from Halsey until just about the time Kurita burst out of the morning mists upon the surprised Sprague.

If Kinkaid had tried to clarify the situation earlier; if he had *not* intercepted the Task Force 34 message, or if Halsey had reported to him that he was "proceeding north with all my available forces," instead of "proceeding north with three groups," the surprise would not have occurred.[20]

There was one other factor that contributed to surprise. Kinkaid *did* send one or two aircraft to scout southward of San Bernardino Strait along the coast of Samar on the night of the twenty-fourth–twenty-fifth and the morning of the twenty-fifth. There was no report from the night search plane—a lumbering PBY "Black Cat," and the dawn search did not start until about the time Kurita's top hamper appeared over the horizon.[21] Halsey's fleet also sent out night "snoopers" and one report was received by Third Fleet on the night of the twenty-fourth indicating Kurita had turned east again toward San Bernardino.

The fact remains, however, that there had been no clear understanding, prior to the event, between Seventh and Third Fleets about San Bernardino Strait; the "coordination" required by Admiral Halsey's orders was defective, and he himself has written (in the *U.S. Naval Institute Pro-*

ceedings)[22] that Leyte Gulf "illustrates the necessity for a single naval command in a combat area responsible for and in full control of all combat units involved.[v]

"Division of operational control in a combat area leads at the least to confusion, lack of coordination, and overloaded communications (a fault which was pronounced during the battle on the American side), and could result in disaster."

In Third Fleet's after-action report of January 25, 1945, Admiral Halsey's reasoning which led him to take all of his available forces to the north in answer to Ozawa's "lure" is phrased as follows:

"Admiral Kinkaid appeared to have every advantage of position and power with which to cope with the Southern (Japanese) force. The Center force might plod on through San Bernardino Strait toward Leyte, but good damage assessment reports, carefully evaluated, convinced Commander Third Fleet, that even if Center Force did sortie from San Bernardino Strait, its fighting efficiency had been too greatly impaired to be able to win a decision against the Leyte forces (Seventh Fleet). The Northern force (Ozawa) was powerful, dangerous, undamaged, and as yet unhampered. Commander Third Fleet decided to (a) strike the Northern force suddenly and in full force; (b) keep all his forces concentrated; and (c) trust to his judgment as to the fatally weakened condition of the Center force—judgment which happily was vindicated by the Japs' inability to deal with the CVE's and small fry which stood toe-to-toe with them and stopped them in their tracks."[23]

Admiral Kinkaid's position, as stated in *Battle Report*, obviously does not agree completely with these conclusions:

". . . one must keep in mind the *missions* of the forces," Admiral Kinkaid is quoted. "The key to the Battle for Leyte Gulf lies in the missions of the two fleets.

"The mission must be clearly understood. The mission of the Seventh Fleet was to land and support the invasion force. My title was Commander of the Central Philippines Attack Force. Our job was to land troops and keep them ashore. The ships were armed accordingly with a very low percentage of armor-piercing projectiles.[w] The CVE's carried anti-personnel bombs instead of torpedoes and heavy bombs. We were not prepared to fight a naval action. . . .

"The only thing I can think of that I would have done differently if I had known Kurita was definitely coming through San Bernardino unopposed is that I would have moved the northern CVE group more to the south and I would have had a striking group from the escort carriers up looking for him at dawn.

"What mistakes were made during the battle were *not* due to lack of plans. Any errors made were errors of judgment, not errors of organization. The two areas coming together—the Central Pacific and the Southwest Pacific—posed a difficult problem of command, but one head would not have altered things." [24] [x]

Despite errors of omission and commission and initially exaggerated reports of damage by our fliers, Leyte Gulf was indubitably a major American victory. But the Japanese, who had a gambling chance—never of all-out victory—but at the best of causing the United States sufficient losses to extend the war, contributed to their own decisive defeat—by their communications failure,[y] their lack of air cover, the unco-ordinated nature of their air and surface operations, amazing deficiencies in timing, and the irresolution or blundering ineptitude of three of their four principal commanders. Only Admiral Ozawa, the "bait," really carried out his mission.

Luck, as well as judgment, obviously played a major part in the battle. But luck lay, in the final analysis, with the larger fleet and the more skilled commanders. The Japanese took their "eye off the ball," abandoned their fundamental objective—the thin-skinned amphibious shipping in Leyte Gulf—in the midst of battle, and thereby violated a cardinal military principle.

And the Americans—Third and Seventh Fleets—as Admiral Halsey radioed to Hawaii and Washington, broke "the back" of the Japanese Fleet "in the course of protecting our Leyte landings."

SPECIAL NOTES BY ADMIRAL THOMAS C. KINKAID, USN (RET.)

The notes are keyed to numerals or letters in text. Explanatory material in brackets inserted by author.

1. The invasion armada was "MacArthur's armada" in the sense that it came from his area, S.W.P.A. [Southwest Pacific Area], and might well be called the "great armada from Down Under" [or from MacArthur's area, or S.W. P.A.]. MacArthur derived his authority from the Combined Chiefs of Staff. He was designated "Supreme Commander" in S.W.P.A. and was specifically prohibited from taking personal command of any of his forces. He was required to exercise command through his three major commanders for land, sea, and air, Blamey [General Sir George Blamey, Australian Army general commanding land forces]; Kinkaid, and Kenney [General George C. Kenney, U.S. Army Air Forces, commanding air forces].

From the time we departed from ports in the Admiralties and New Guinea to invade the Philippines, I had direct command of the "armada," including the Army forces embarked, until I turned over command of the Army forces ashore in Leyte to Krueger [Lt. Gen. Walter Krueger, commanding Sixth Army]. MacArthur was present as a passenger in his capacity as Supreme Commander, Southwest Pacific Area. I exercised direct command, as witness the fact that I decided to go ahead with the operation without referring to MacArthur when Halsey sent a despatch, received when we were a few hours out from Hollandia, stating that he was concentrating his forces to attack the Japanese Fleet and would not be able to give the planned support to our landing at Leyte. When MacArthur joined our convoy, I sent him a bridge signal: "Welcome to our city." He replied with a gracious message referring to the fact that this was the first time he had sailed under my command and ending with: "Believe it or not we are on our way."

2. Nishimura was due in Leyte one hour before Kurita. He was ahead of schedule without reason—a serious error

in a coordinated effort. Kurita was late for good and sufficient reasons.

3. The Seventh Fleet had eighteen CVE's. Two had been sent to Halmahera for replacement planes and only sixteen were present during the action. The Seventh Fleet had a few PBY's, tender-based. Counting eighteen CVE's, the total number of [U.S.] carriers was thirty-four.

4. It is interesting that the *Darter* and *Dace* paced Kurita through the night in Palawan Passage and attacked at dawn—a good job. An extremely important fact, from the operations point of view, is that Kurita was separated from most of his communication personnel in the transfer from *Atago* to *Kishanani* to *Yamato*. Any naval commander will sympathize with him in that situation.

5. Only one strike was made on Nishimura and that only by small search-attack scouting groups. Davison [Rear Admiral Ralph E. Davison, commanding Task Group 38.4 of the Third Fleet] reported that the move to concentrate was taking him out of range of the enemy southern force, but Halsey continued the concentration. In the Seventh Fleet we felt well able to take care of the [enemy] southern force and had all day to make plans for its reception. I was not informed directly by Halsey that he was leaving Nishimura to me.

6. Halsey had ordered a morning search to northward by the northern group, but Jap attacks prevented it from getting off until the afternoon.

7. In the Seventh Fleet we had counted noses carefully and had come to the conclusion that only two BB's [battleships]—*Ise* and *Hyuga*—could be with Ozawa in the [enemy] northern force.

8. Halsey had four groups of carriers and had given preparatory orders to form TF [Task Force] 34. ". . . proceeding north with three groups" is phraseology which failed to give information of vital import not only to me and to Nimitz but to many others. Mitscher [Vice-Admiral

Marc A. Mitscher, commanding Task Force 38—the four carrier task groups and their supporting combat ships of the Third Fleet] actually sent instructions for the employment of the two BB's which were to stay with him, believing that TF 34 would be left behind to guard San Bernardino. It was impossible to believe anything else. The proposed composition of TF 34 was exactly correct in the circumstances.

Even though Halsey banked "too heavily" on the exaggerated claims of his pilots, he knew from the *Independence* night search planes that Kurita was headed for San Bernardino and he should have realized:

a. That the composition of the Seventh Fleet was designed to provide support for the amphibious landing and the troops ashore—not for major combat. Slow speed of the old battleships and a high proportion of high-capacity projectiles in their magazines made them an inadequate adversary for the Japanese central force, even if they had been available and were filled with fuel and ammunition.

b. That the Seventh Fleet would be engaged through the night with surface forces in Surigao Strait and, in any case, could not leave Leyte Gulf unguarded and take station off San Bernardino.

c. That the three CVE groups of the Seventh Fleet would be on station at daylight 25 Oct. carrying out their mission and would need cover.

d. That my destroyers would have expended their torpedoes in Surigao Strait and that the battleships would be low in AP ammunition and even in HC ammunition, having rendered gunfire support to forces ashore for several days.

9. Rarely has a commander had all day to stay quietly (except for the antics of Jap planes) in port and prepare without serious interruption for a night action. The tactical dispositions and plans of the Seventh Fleet were checked and counterchecked by all concerned.

10. I believe contact was made about 2215 [10:15 p.m.] a few miles south of Bohol Island. All three PT's of that

group were damaged by gunfire and unable to report the contact, but one of them (using his head) managed to make contact with the next PT group to eastward which sent through a message, which was received by Oldendorf [Rear Admiral J. B. Oldendorf, who was in tactical or direct command at Surigao Strait] about twenty-six minutes after midnight.

11. Fired by *PT 137*. The PT fired at a destroyer, missed, but hit and badly damaged the cruiser [*Abukuma*].

12. No, we did not think that the Jap central force was west of the Philippines, but we did think that TF 34 was guarding San Bernardino.

Also, it is of interest that in Leyte Gulf the temporary headquarters of the Army commanders were only a few yards from the water's edge and the beaches were piled high with food and supplies and ammunition for immediate use. Destruction of those supply dumps would have left our forces ashore without food and ammunition. Halsey has said that Kurita could only have "harassed" our forces in Leyte Gulf.

13. I think it should be pointed out that the first six words of Nimitz's despatch was "padding" [inserted by the communications officer for code security]. The despatch was first brought to me without padding, as it should have been. Later I was told of the "padding." [Halsey originally took this phrase, "All the world wants to know . . ." as tacit criticism of him and was irritated.]

14. The attack of the DD's [destroyers] and DE's [destroyer escorts] against the Jap heavy ships was the most courageous and also the most effective incident brought to my attention during the war.

15. Kurita committed a grave error in losing tactical control of his force. He had lost most of his communication personnel. He had been seriously damaged by torpedo hits from Seventh Fleet planes and surface ships and by bomb hits from Seventh Fleet planes, and the upper works of his

ships, charthouse, radio, etc., suffered from five-inch shellfire and from strafing. His ships sheered out of formation to dodge torpedo attacks, real or dummy, made by planes and escort vessels. Soon his individual units became widely separated, which he should not have permitted, and he could not see his forces, or the enemy's, because of the heavy smoke laid by the CVE's and their escorts. He was confused and his subordinates did not help him by reporting the nature of the enemy they were attacking. Ozawa had failed to inform him of his success in drawing Halsey away. Also, I have no doubt that Kurita was physically exhausted after three grueling days.

16. McCain sensed what was going on long before Halsey did and he launched his strike beyond range for a return flight—340 miles.

The following paragraphs constitute my analysis of what occurred:

Halsey had done exactly what the Japs wanted him to do. He had left San Bernardino unguarded, permitting Kurita to pass through the strait unopposed. Having taken all six of his BB's 300 miles to the north, when two would have been adequate and four were needed at San Bernardino, he belatedly at 11:15 turned south in response to my appeals and to the despatch from Nimitz, again taking all six BB's with him and leaving Mitscher without any. Mitscher urgently needed two BB's. By that time, 11:15, Mitscher's planes had developed Ozawa's force and the *Ise* and *Hyuga* were known to be with him, but Halsey took all six BB's south. Later Mitscher sent DuBose [Rear Admiral Laurence T. DuBose] to mop up the cripples (with four cruisers and twelve destroyers). Ozawa was informed of the actions of DuBose, and sent the *Ise* and *Hyuga* south to look for him. Fortunately the Jap BB's passed to eastward of our cruisers on their way south and again on their return course to northward.

Halsey informed me that he would arrive off San Bernardino at 0800 26 Oct. Too late! Later, at 1600 [4 p.m.], after fueling, he decided to speed up and took two of his fastest BB's, *Iowa* and *New Jersey*, with three cruisers and eight DD's, south at 28 knots. He missed Kurita entering the strait by two hours. Suppose he had intercepted him? Were two BB's enough?

Suppose Halsey had turned south at top speed immediately upon receipt of my first urgent message at 0825. He would have been about five hours closer to San Bernardino. Actually he steamed north for two and three quarters hours at 25 knots—69 miles—whereas if he had steamed south at 28 knots—77 miles—there would have been a total of 146 miles difference in his 11:15 position.

The net result of all of this was that the six strongest battleships in the world—except the *Yamato* and *Musashi*—steamed about 300 miles north and 300 miles south during the "greatest naval battle of the Second World War and the largest engagement ever fought upon the high seas"—and they did not fire a single shot. I can well imagine the feelings of my classmate, Lee [Rear Admiral Willis A. Lee, commanding the battleships of Third Fleet].

Even today Halsey believes it was not a mistake to take the whole Third Fleet north and he apparently overlooks the fact that the absence of TF 34 from San Bernardino Strait precluded the total destruction of Kurita's force on the spot, to say nothing of the loss of American lives and ships of the CVE force. The threat to our invasion of the Philippines seems not to have come to his mind. Halsey has stated that I should have sent CVE planes to scout the Sibuyan Sea and San Bernardino Strait during the night of 24-25 Oct. As is evident, I believed that TF 34 was guarding San Bernardino and that Lee was being kept informed by the night-flying planes from the *Independence*. Actually, I did order a search to the northward during the night by PBY's and a search toward San Bernardino at daylight by CVE planes, mostly out of curiosity to find out what was going on.

Even if I had known that San Bernardino was wide open, I did not have the force to meet Kurita. You have quoted me correctly from *Battle Report*. I would not have denuded Leyte Gulf of a defense force. I would have moved the CVE's clear of direct contact with Kurita's surface forces. And, of course, I would have sent planes from the CVE's to keep track of Kurita, although none were equipped or trained for night search.

In that case would Kurita have reached Leyte? It is interesting to speculate. It is very possible. His direct contact with the northern group of CVE's, though painful to us, delayed his progress, seriously damaged his forces, and so confused him that he turned back within two hours of his goal.

17. "Divided command" is, of course, not sound procedure. The hard, cold fact is, however, that despite the divided command both Halsey and I had what appeared to me to be clear-cut, definite missions. Had Halsey been mindful of his covering mission when Ozawa beckoned him to come north, he never would have left San Bernardino wide open. Also, he would have told me in a clearly worded despatch just what he was going to do about it.

The "unwarranted assumption" which you attribute to me probably refers to my assumption that TF 34 was guarding San Bernardino. Perhaps that was unwarranted, but, to my not unprejudiced mind, all logic seems to point the other way. Halsey's mission included covering our amphibious operation from interruption by the Japanese Fleet. His preparatory order to form TF 34, which I intercepted, set up a plan to guard San Bernardino against the passage of Kurita's forces which was perfect in concept and perfect in composition of the forces assigned to TF 34. I did not intercept further modifying messages regarding TF 34. Had I done so, I most certainly would not have remained silent.

It was inconceivable that Halsey could have scrapped a perfect plan. His message, "going north with three groups," meant to me that TF 34 plus a carrier group was being left behind—entirely sound. Not only did I and my staff believe it, and Nimitz and, presumably, his staff believe it, but Mitscher and his staff believed it also. As I have already pointed out, Mitscher actually gave orders for utilization of the two battleships which were to accompany him on the northern trek [four of the Third Fleet's six battleships were to have been left behind in TF 34 to guard San Bernardino; two were to have gone north with Mitscher's carriers after

Ozawa]. When Mitscher and his staff found out that TF 34 was not being left to guard the strait, his chief of staff—[Captain] Arleigh Burke, tried to get Mitscher to send a message to Halsey on the subject, but Mitscher declined on the ground that Halsey probably had information not known to him.

Later in your notes you point out that I did not specifically ask Halsey whether or not TF 34 was guarding San Bernardino until 0412, 25 Oct. That is correct. In the absence of information to the contrary from Halsey, anything else was unthinkable. Early in the morning of 25 Oct. a meeting of the staff was held in my cabin to check for errors of commission or of omission. It broke up about 0400 and my operations officer, Dick Cruzen [Captain Richard H. Cruzen], came back into the cabin and said, "Admiral, I can think of only one other thing. We have never directly asked Halsey if TF 34 is guarding San Bernardino." I told him to send the message.

18. The controversy has not been bitter for the simple and sole reason that I refused to take part in it. I have not publicly stated my side of the case but have kept quiet for ten years—not so Halsey. He has published several articles or interviews in addition to his book endeavoring to justify his actions at Leyte, sometimes at my expense.

19. I believe that the radio on Ozawa's flagship went out with the first bomb hit, but other ships could have sent a message to Kurita for him.

20. Only Halsey's strangely phrased message led to Kurita's surprise of Sprague's carriers.

In the early morning some important messages from me to Halsey were delayed in transmission and that should not have been.

21. Actually one or two PBY's took off from a tender in Surigao Strait to make the northern night search. They were ill equipped for that sort of mission. They had quite a hell of a time because every U.S. ship they came near fired at them. I imagine that their greatest concern was to avoid U.S. ships rather than to find Jap ships.

The dawn search ordered from the CVE's should have gotten off much earlier.

22. Halsey's writings in the *Naval Institute Proceedings* were subjective. If he had been mindful of his covering mission, and had no other distractions, the question of "a single naval command" would be purely academic.

23. Halsey's reasoning regarding the [enemy] center force falls short of the mark. His "careful evaluation" of the damage reports was not shared by everyone. Kurita's movements seemed to belie any such evaluation. We knew from our plot that Kurita was approaching San Bernardino at 22 knots. Some plodding! Halsey had a later report from the *Independence* plane which was not forwarded to me. Did he not plot Kurita's progress?

A count of noses by my staff showed that Ozawa's force could not have been as "powerful and dangerous" as Halsey seems to have thought. He took 119 ships north to deal with 19 ships in the [enemy] northern force. An intelligent *division* of his forces was in order. In setting up TF 34, he had actually made that intelligent division of forces but he failed to implement it.

Halsey's decisions (a) and (b) would have been sound if he had had no other obligations. His decision (c) can be described only as erroneous. I doubt if anyone will disagree with the statement that the only reason why Kurita did not reach Leyte Gulf, destroying the CVE's en route, was that he turned back when victory was within his grasp. His [Halsey's] judgment as to the "fatally weakened condition of the [enemy] center force" was definitely shown to be in error. Did his "judgment which was happily vindicated" include a forecast that Kurita would break off the action? If so, his crystal ball was certainly in fine working order. Does anyone believe in the "Japs' *inability* to deal with the CVE's and small fry"? They did not deal with them as they could have, but is that "inability"?

24. I am quoted correctly, but I did not have an opportunity to edit my remarks. In the last line "one head would

not have altered things" might have been reworded because it meant that "one head would not have produced a better end result if both Halsey and I had carried out our specific missions."

SPECIAL NOTES BY FLEET ADMIRAL WILLIAM F. HALSEY, USN (RET.)

a. I do not remember what Radio Manila was playing. They were usually sending out lying propaganda from "Tokyo Rose" or some other renegade Japanese Nisei. We used Radio Manila as an alarm clock. As soon as we heard the air-raid alarm, we knew our pilots had been sighted.

The change in the American strategy was the direct result of a recommendation sent by me. I recommended that the taking of Yap and Palau be eliminated and that a landing be made in the central Philippines instead of Mindanao. I had once previously recommended that the seizure of Palau be dropped. Admiral Nimitz approved my recommendation, except that about Palau, and immediately forwarded it to the Combined Chiefs of Staff, then sitting in Quebec. General Sutherland, in Hollandia, General MacArthur's chief of staff, in MacArthur's temporary absence, approved the landing in the central Philippines instead of Mindanao. The Combined Chiefs of Staff approved, and it received almost immediate approval from President Roosevelt and Prime Minister Churchill. It was fortunate that the Quebec Conference was on at that time.

The 1st Marine Division had heavy losses on Peleliu (in the Palau group), in many ways comparable to Tarawa. One combat team from the Army 81st (Wildcat) Division also received many losses in the fighting on Peleliu, where they so ably assisted. We constructed airfields on Anguar, captured by the 81st Army Division, and on Peleliu Island, and a partial naval base in Kossol Roads. Kossol Roads was not occupied by the Japanese and we merely had to make arrangement for its defense from the Japanese on Babelthuap Island, the largest island of the Palau archipelago. I mention these actions and this timing to show that this was not a "Monday quarterback" estimate of the situation on my part. Ulithi was not recommended to be dropped, as I always considered this a necessity as a fleet anchorage. It was occupied without opposition. Peleliu, Anguar, and Kossol Roads were a great convenience, but I thought then, and I think now, not a necessity for the further campaign in the Pacific.

The beginning of the end of the war in the Pacific was evident before the Battle of Leyte Gulf. When our fleet obtained freedom of movement, practically anywhere in the Pacific, the Japanese were doomed to defeat.

The *Shō* plan was just another of the many plans the Japs devised. They all failed.

Toyoda had carriers, but with few planes and half-trained pilots. Now that it is the Monday after the Saturday game, everyone seemed to know this excepting my staff and me. We bore the responsibility. If the rest of the Navy did not then know it, we, in the Third Fleet, were thoroughly cognizant that the carrier had replaced the battleship, and was potentially the strongest and most dangerous naval weapon our opponents possessed. We had been fighting the Japs for several years. We did not know how many planes the Japs had, but we could not take a chance. We knew the *Princeton* had been attacked and it was reported they were carrier planes. As we stood northward on the morning of the twenty-sixth, we had a large "bogie" on our screen. We naturally thought they were carrier planes heading toward the Japanese carriers. They finally went off our screen heading toward Luzon. We had been "shuttle-bombed" many times by the Nips, and only once off Guadalcanal had succeeded in reversing this process.

My decision to go north was not based on pilots' reports solely. A possible battle with the Japanese Fleet had long been a matter of discussion and study by us. We had played it frequently on a game board constructed on the deck of the flag quarters. We had long since decided the carriers were potentially the most dangerous ships the Japs had, not only to ourselves, but to MacArthur and the Pacific campaign. We named them our primary targets. We knew Kurita's ships had suffered damage from our attacks, particularly to their upper works and probably to their fire-control instruments. This was borne out by their poor shooting against the baby carriers.

b. The "Turkey Shoot" in the Marianas (the Battle of the Philippine Sea) was a magnificent show. That it alone broke the back of Japanese naval aviation, despite its great success, I seriously doubt. I cannot and will not forget the wonderful American pilots in the South Pacific and Southwest Pacific who had knocked out so many Japanese naval air groups and squadrons based on Rabaul. This statement is based on Japanese answers to American interrogations after the war. The fliers who accomplished this were from the U.S. Army Air Force, U.S. Naval and Marine Aviation, the R.N.Z.A.F. and the R.A.A.F. The Japs made their usual mistake of feeding in these groups piecemeal and were thoroughly knocked out.

c. The Japanese Navy had a number of carriers nearing completion in the Inland Sea. I have a fairly good-sized circular plaque, presented to me after the war. In the middle is a U.S. ensign—around the U.S. ensign and near the periphery are the silhouettes of various Japanese ships representing carriers, battleships, a heavy cruiser, light cruisers, and submarines. On the periphery it bears the inscription: "Plaque made of metal obtained from these vessels sunk by U.S. Carrier planes, July 1945 at Kure Naval Base, Kure, Japan." The names and numbers are interesting. CV-ASO, CV-AMAGI, CVE-RYUHO, BB-ISE, BB-HYUGA, BB-HARUNA, CA-SETTSU, CL-TONE, CL-OYADA (fleet flagship), CL-AOBA, CL-IZUMA, CL-AWATE and 5 SS. (CV large carrier, CVE small or jeep carrier, BB battleship, CA heavy cruiser, CL light cruiser, and SS submarines.)

We had orders to get rid of the Japanese Navy so that they could not interfere with the Russians if they decided to invade Japan. I sometimes wonder, in view of present-day events! Of course these ships were sitting ducks, and even high-altitude bombing, with some luck, might have hit them.

There is one Japanese cruiser that I would have felt sorry

for, if I could have felt sorry for a Japanese man-of-war in those days. She had escaped from the Battle of Leyte Gulf, sorely wounded. The Japs had brought her into a bay or cove on the west side of Luzon, and heavily camouflaged her and made her almost invisible. They were working night and day to make her seaworthy to return her to the home land. In the meantime, our fliers were combing every nook and corner, looking for Jap ships. As one of our last flights was about to return, a lucky photograph was taken of this hideout. Our photographic interpreters made out this cruiser. A heavy strike was made on her the first thing next morning, and that was curtains for this cruiser.

d. A "Betty" tried to land among our parked planes on the *Enterprise* during our attack on the Marshall and Gilbert Islands on 1 Feb. 1942 (Eastern Time). Thanks to the masterly ship handling by then Captain, now Admiral (Retired), George D. Murray, U.S. Navy, the "Betty" was forced into a slip while coming up "the groove" and did only minor damage. The "Betty" hit the edge of the flight deck, broke her back, and went over the side. She was undoubtedly on fire when she hit us. She cut off a gasoline riser aft and set it on fire. She cut off another gasoline riser forward, but no fire resulted, and cut off the tail of one of our SBD planes. The fire from the gasoline riser was soon under control, and I remember no further damage, except some slight and easily repairable damage to the flight deck. This was my first encounter with a Kamikaze plane; I saw many later. I doubt if this Japanese even knew he was a Kamikaze. She had dropped all her bombs and fortunately, for us, missed the *Enterprise*. His intentions were very clear. He knew his plane was doomed, and determined to do us as much damage as possible. He tried to land among some thirty-five or forty of our planes, lately returned from a strike, refueling and awaiting the return of all planes for respotting. The quick thinking of the ship's captain prevented what might have been a catastrophe. I do not mean to detract from Rear Admiral Masabumi Arima's very brave, but very foolhardy, suicide dive. Apparently we fought to live, the Japanese to die.

e. My orders went further than the quoted "to cover and support forces in the Southwest Pacific, in order to assist in the seizure and occupation of objectives in the Central Philippines." This is being written from memory without the advantage of notes, so my overriding orders can only be vaguely quoted. They were that, other conditions notwithstanding, the destruction of the Japanese Fleet was my paramount objective.

f. "Necessary measures for detailed coordination of operations between the [Third Fleet] and the [Seventh Fleet] will be arranged by their commanders." These are just so many words and nothing more. They were impossible of accomplishment. Kinkaid and I had not seen each other since we met in Hollandia, just after the plans for the invasion of the Philippines had been changed. Some key members of my staff and I had flown from Saipan to Hollandia to discuss preliminary arrangements with Kinkaid and his staff and MacArthur's staff. Both Kinkaid and I had been too busily occupied to confer during the Philippine invasion. This illustrates, as nothing else can, the importance of a unified command in the combat zone. Had Kinkaid or I been in Supreme Command at the time of the Battle of Leyte Gulf, I am sure it would have been fought differently. Whether for better or for worse can never be answered.

g. Night snoopers not only scouted the northern force but also the Sibuyan Sea and made reports of Kurita turning once again to the eastward—heading toward San Bernardino Strait. A report of this was directed sent to Kinkaid around 2100 or 2130 that night.

h. I had no operational control of submarines, except those specifically assigned to us for some operation. I had no submarines assigned to me at that time.

i. I never thought Kurita's force had been stopped by the day's air attacks. I had received and directed transmittal of a report that his force was again heading toward San Bernardino Strait. I did not bank too heavily on so-called exaggerated claims from pilots. We had rather good evaluation of pilots' reports at this time. I did think Kurita had been rather badly mauled by our pilots, particularly in their upper works and that their fire control would be poor. Their poor shooting against the CVE's, destroyers, and destroyer escorts the next day tended to corroborate this. I did not expect them to be opposed by CVE's, destroyers, and destroyer escorts. Their thin skins probably saved them somewhat. After the Battle of Guadalcanal, in which Rear Admiral Callaghan and Rear Admiral Scott lost their lives, there were some thin-skinned ships that were holed by heavy-armor piercing shells with little damage. I remember one destroyer, I have forgotten her name, that I inspected later. As I remember it, she had fourteen 14-inch hits from a Jap battleship. Her commanding officer was Commander Coward. Never did a man have a name so inappropriate to fit with his actions in battle.

j. I object to the statement "that on such misunderstandings rest the course of history and the fate of nations." I had no misunderstandings, with the possible exception (if true) that the Jap carriers had no planes. I knew what I was doing at all times, and deliberately took the risks, in order to get rid of the Jap carriers. My estimate that the Seventh Fleet could take care of Kurita's battered forces was amply justified even against the CVE's and small fry during the action of Oct. 26. These brave American ships put up a fight that will be an epic for all time. My hat is off to them.

k. The battle of Surigao Strait, with Admiral Oldendorf in tactical command, was beautifully conceived and executed. Never has a T been so efficiently capped, and never has a force been so completely defeated and demoralized as was the Jap Surigao force.

l. I am still far from sure that Ozawa's force was intended solely as a lure. The Japs had continuously lied during the war, even to each other. Why believe them implicitly as soon as the war ends? They had plenty of time, before reciting them, to make their stories fit their needs. Despite their "banzai" charges, their "Kamikaze" planes, their "foolish bombs" (men-driven), their one- and two-man submarines, built for the purpose of sacrificing their crew, and the many other foolish things they did, it is still difficult for me to believe that they would deliberately use their potentially most dangerous ships as deliberate sacrifices. This is partially borne out by reports from Americans who interviewed Admiral Kurita after the war. When asked why he turned away from Leyte Gulf, he stated that he intended to join forces with Ozawa and attack the Third Fleet.

m. Admiral Nimitz's despatch to me was "Where is Task Force 34?" The despatch as quoted is a gross violation of security regulations. [This despatch has been quoted in its entirety in numerous previous publications.]

n. I note the Seventh Fleet is described as red-eyed from days of shore bombardment and nights of battle. My fleet had been fighting almost continually since early September. When we finally reached Ulithi in late September, for rest and replenishment, we were chased out by a typhoon after a one-night stand. We were almost continually in combat, until some time after the Battle of Leyte Gulf. I wonder what color my splendid pilots' eyes were? I do not know, but I do know they were approaching a stage of exhaustion that kept me on edge. I dared not let up on the Japs when we were running them ragged. This goes for all my officers and men, manning battle stations, above and below decks. It was an almost unendurable strain. We fought no battle for Cape Engano—we fought to do away with the Jap carriers.

o. I knew what force Kinkaid had and believed them capable of taking on Kurita's damaged force. I did not know of Kinkaid's ammunition situation in his old battleships. I have since been told that one of these battleships in the Surigao Strait action did not fire a single shot from her main battery.

In moving north, I took a calculated risk. I figured then, and still believe, that if Kurita had arrived at Leyte Gulf he could make nothing but a "hit-and-run bombardment." While in command of the South Pacific, my forces in Guadalcanal had many times been bombarded by Japanese battleships, cruisers, and destroyers. The forces ashore caught unmerciful hell, but these bombardments served to delay us no more than a short time. Shipping put to sea, usually only partly unloaded, and moved away from the bombardment area. The troops ashore had to take it in such dugouts as they had. On most occasions I had no heavy fighting ships to oppose them, and they bombarded at their leisure. On one occasion PT boats drove them away. On another, Dan Callaghan and Norm Scott (both rear admirals) made the supreme sacrifice, but with their few ships, cruisers, anti-aircraft vessels and destroyers, they routed the Japanese forces consisting of battleships, cruisers, and destroyers. Their supreme sacrifice was not in vain. As a direct result of this action, the Japanese lost the battleship *Hiyei*—left a derelict and sunk by our planes the next day. During one of their last bombardments, we had been able to fool them and got two of our new battleships near Savo Island, the *South Dakota* and the *Washington*, under command of Rear Admiral, later Vice-Admiral, W. A. Lee, Jr., USN. As a result of the night action that followed, the Japs lost various destroyers and one battleship. She was sunk that night.

p. A statement is made that Kurita's intercepted radio traffic convinced him, erroneously, that Leyte airstrips were operational. This was not entirely erroneous. Admiral McCain flew his planes off at such a distance that it was impossible for them to return to their mother carriers. They were directed to land on Leyte airstrips. They did, and for a few days thereafter they operated from these fields until I was directed to return them to Ulithi. This was done, via Palau to Ulithi. Incidentally, I do not remember seeing a report of the damage McCain's fliers inflicted on Kurita's force. It must have been not inconsiderable.

q. I do not fully understand what the author means by unwarranted assumptions by me. Possibly that I placed too much credence in the pilots' reports; I do not believe that I did. These reports were carefully evaluated, and after due consideration a calculated risk was taken. My estimate that the Seventh Fleet could take care of Kurita's battered forces was amply justified. "The proof of the pudding is in the eating." Remember this estimate was "Saturday quarterbacking" and not "Monday quarterbacking."

r. I am in agreement that I made a mistake in bowing to pressure and turning south. I consider this the gravest error I committed during the Battle of Leyte Gulf.

s. I have never stated, to my knowledge and remembrance, that Kinkaid could and should have covered San Bernardino Strait. I have stated that I felt that Kinkaid's force could have taken care of Kurita's battered force, and furthermore, that Kurita was only capable of a hit-and-run attack if he entered Leyte Gulf. Such an attack, by my experience in the South Pacific, would have little effect on the troops ashore and could cause only a slight delay in the over-all picture.

t. I did not send a preparatory despatch, but instead a "Battle Plan" addressed only to the Third Fleet. To insure that the Third Fleet did not misunderstand, I sent a further message saying this plan would not be executed until directed by me. As Commander Task Force 38, Vice-Admiral Mitscher should have received both messages.

u. The statement that, had I sent a despatch to Kinkaid that I was "proceeding north with all my available forces" instead of "proceeding north with three groups," the surprise would not have occurred is purely academic. I did not know that he had intercepted my battle plan and believed it had been executed. A carrier task group was well defined, and every naval commander in the area knew its composition. My despatch was a correct one. I had notified all interested parties when Admiral McCain's Carrier Task Group started for Ulithi. I am sure no one misconstrued that message.

v. I have explained before that orders requiring "coordination" were mere words and meant nothing. I still stand by what I have written about Leyte Gulf, that "it illustrates the necessity for a single naval command in a combat area, responsible for, and in full control of, all combat units involved."

w. I knew nothing of how the Seventh Fleet was armed. At that time I believe we were rearming the Third Fleet under way. I gave no thought to the Seventh Fleet's armament of shells.

x. I am in agreement with Admiral Kinkaid when he says any errors made were errors of judgment. I am in complete disagreement when he states, "The two areas coming together—the Central Pacific and the Southwest Pacific—posed a difficult problem of command, but one head would not have altered things." As I have previously stated, "had either Admiral Kinkaid or I been in supreme command, the battle would have been fought quite differently."

y. There is only one word to describe the communications on the American side during this battle, and that word is rotten. We sent in a long report describing the deficiencies and interference we encountered, also a recommendation for drastic changes. As I remember, our combat circuit was filled with long and relatively unimportant intelligence summaries that could and should have been deferred. Most of these were not Navy reports. As a consequence, there were long and intolerable delays in getting urgent messages through. This should never be permitted again.

These comments have been written almost entirely from memory and without the advantage of any notes or reports. I hope I am not trusting my memory too far; ten and a half years is a long time.

Japan's Doorstep

The Japanese Navy was destroyed. Adm. Ozawa admitted that, after this battle, their surface forces were strictly "auxiliary"; from now on, the war was carried on only by the land forces, land-based air power and special Kamikaze attacks.

But the U.S. Navy's job didn't end here; during 1945 there would be fierce fighting in the waters around Okinawa, primarily against the Kamikaze planes.

The naval war might be in its last stage, but some of the worst fighting was still to come. There was still Okinawa to be taken; and, before that, the Marines were to be tested once again—this time in the crucible of Iwo Jima, about eight hundred miles from Tokyo. Iwo was within P-51 range of Japan; as an American base, it could provide Japan-bound bombers with fighter escort to the target and back.

"The bulk of the defenses in central Iwo were strictly man-made. Except for Mount Suribachi and the rugged northern third of the island, the terrain provided few naturally strong positions. . . . The land, however, lent itself readily to preparation. The beaches and most of the soil consisted of a curious loose volcanic ash, variously described as a coarse sand and a fine gravel.

"Tunnels ran clear under the airfields, connecting positions hundreds of yards apart. One, explored for 800 yards, contained two battalion command posts, complete with electric lights and hooked up with all sectors by means of an elaborate communications system.

"The strange ash combined with cement to make a concrete of very superior quality, and this was everywhere. Artillery, mortars, anti-tank guns reposed in emplacements with reinforced walls four to eight feet thick, from which they were trundled out for firing through armor-plate doors or on rails, or were fired through fixed ports barely above ground level. Entire hills were hollowed out, to be reconstructed from within.

"Iwo had been pounded intermittently from the air ever since our capture of bases in the Marianas, and from the sea on several occasions. In anticipation of a 20 January D-Day, American air power began what was to prove a record softening-up, Army, Navy and Marine Corps flyers working the island over in turn and in conjunction. For a while the most noticeable effect of this was increased resistance. Time after time the airfields were reported neutralized, only to have the next day's flight met by swarming enemy fighters and anti-aircraft fire of increased volume and accuracy. Involvement of the fleet in the Philippines necessitated postponing the landing until 3 February—but the air assault continued. It continued following the final postponement, until 19 February, by which time it had been sustained at full pitch for seventy-two days.

"H-Hour was set for 0900, 19 February.

"Everything seemed to work splendidly during that first hour. Resistance was scattered and sporadic, rated as slight to moderate. It began to look as though at last the long-sought-for result had been achieved: the neutralization of a fortified island by naval gunfire.

"But if the Japanese were giving little trouble at this particular stage, nature was giving plenty. The amphtracks hit the beach, only to find themselves in trouble immediately. Assault troops leaped to the ground to carry their rush forward—to find themselves up to their calves, or deeper, in that strange, loose volcanic ash which comprised the greater part of Iwo's soil. . . . Amphtracks, lurching and staggering across the beach, brought up short before a high terrace of the same material varying from five to eighteen feet, unscalable in most places because it afforded no traction. The forward rush of troops became a grim plodding. . . .

"Then all hell began to break loose. From Suribachi to the south, and the tangle of ridges to the north, artillery and mortars of all shapes and sizes commenced pounding the beach area and the water immediately offshore which the landing craft must traverse. That these weapons had been carefully ranged in beforehand for this particular purpose was all too apparent. The fire was deadly.

"The infantry, which had driven two hundred to three hundred yards inland with no great difficulty, found themselves suddenly pinned down. Harmless-appearing sand hummocks spat automatic weapons fire from narrow apertures only a few inches above ground level. Underground pillboxes and blockhouses, these proved to be reinforced concrete sunk deep in the shifting sand. The successive terraces leading up to the central table-land were studded with them. Tanks, lumbering up from the beach with great difficulty, ran into the fire of those deadly Japanese 47-mm. guns. Land mines were everywhere. The grim aspect of Iwo Jima, which during the next three weeks was to make the bloodiest operation ever handled by the Marine Corps, had begun in earnest.

"The final breakthrough to Iwo's northeastern shore occurred early in the afternoon of D-plus eighteen (9 March), and it was the 3rd Division, in the center, which achieved it. Other divisions, claiming that the 3rd consisted of a pack of glory hunters, pointed out that in their hurry to be first they had by-passed many unconquered strongpoints which remained to plague them from the rear. Which was true, except that the same applied in varying degree to virtually every unit on the island. With the enemy dug so deeply into ridges and the sides of ravines, in caves connected by tortuous underground passageways, it was a literal impossibility to seal them all up during the initial advance." *

The following selection deals with this very problem; it is taken from "U.S. Marines on Iwo Jima," a report compiled by five Marine Corps Combat Correspondents.

IWO: JUNGLE OF STONE

by Marine Combat Writers **

The northern half of Iwo, beyond the Japs' cross-island defenses, was a desolate, broken area of smoking sulphuric sand and barren, jagged ridges. The tall masses of rock sprawled and tumbled without pattern, where a series of earthquakes had once pushed up millions of tons of volcanic stone and left them lying in craggy heights and bare, sharp-edged spines several hundred yards long.

The looming rocks and narrow chasms added new terrors to the advancing Marines. It was like going through a miniature Grand Canyon, with Japs hidden in hundreds of caves

* Maj. Frank Hough, *The Island War*, pp. 331, 337-39, 350.

** Capt. Raymond Henri, 1st Lt. Jim Lucas, T/Sgt. David Dempsey, T/Sgt. W. Keyes Beech, T/Sgt. Alvin Josephy, Jr.

and pillboxes among the rocks and boulders. Moreover, the ridges, which often rose to the height of three-story houses, were undermined and laced like other parts of the island with interconnecting tunnels in which the Japs could hide. The rocks could be painfully and methodically cleared of Japs again and again, but always the enemy managed to reappear from inner caverns and recesses to harass our rear.

The fighting from approximately D plus 16 to D plus 25, around one such ridge that lay in the 3rd Division's zone of action near the third airfield, was typical of the struggles waged for all of them—struggles characterized not only by close-in, bitter combat, but also by a seemingly endless series of tragic episodes and unexpected deaths.

We first saw this particular ridge during one of the many battles that had flamed among its peaks and gullies. Its tall, twisting mass—running almost ten city blocks in length—looked as if it had been hit by many heavy explosions. The rocks and boulders had tumbled down the ridge's slopes in chaotic landslides. You had to look closely to distinguish the black mouths of cave entrances and the carefully camouflaged pillbox positions that lay among the debris.

White clouds from American smoke grenades made the scene unearthly. It blew like steam across the ridge's stone walls. Three American tanks lay 50 yards away, firing their 75s point-blank at a concrete pillbox perched near the ridge's summit. The Marines attacking the ridge crawled among the stones and sandy shellholes, peering through the smoke for enemy movements.

A flamethrowing team, guarded by two automatic riflemen, worked its way cautiously up to an already-blackened hole. The air was filled with the noise of exploding grenades and with the smell of cordite and dead bodies.

The smoke blew away from one section of the section of the rocks. The exposed stones and caves looked like an ogre's face, showing broken black and brown teeth, ready to snap at the Marines attacking it. From behind one of the "teeth"—a black hole in the wall—a Nambu machine gun chattered. A Marine rifleman, caught upright, scrambled toward the protection of a boulder. He stopped abruptly, reached for his throat and fell to his his knees. The machine gun kept chattering. The Marine screamed and slowly dropped to his full length.

It was ironic that at the time this ridge of death was almost a mile behind our front lines. Elements of the 9th and 21st Marines had first seized it several days before and, thinking it secured, had gone on. When we had passed it earlier in the morning, on our way toward the front, it had still been peaceful and quiet. A radio jeep had been parked in the open, its driver unconcernedly eating a can of rations. The only other Marines in sight had been a group of engineers, probing on their hands and knees for mines and joking about the hot sand burning through the knees of their pants.

None of us suspected that there were still Japs in the desertlike area. The ridge had had its day already, and we assumed that its story was over. The Marines who had originally taken it on D plus 16 had clambered across it, first knocking out its gun positions with mortars, bazookas and tank fire, in the usual way, and then poking into every hole for surviving enemy. Some of the holes needed treatment with hand grenades and flamethrowers, while others were sealed with demolitions. But there had been little trouble, and soon the ridge had become quiet. The lines had gone on. Platoons had moved ahead, fighting through the lost world of the sulphur area, up to the third airfield. Support elements had followed, pausing near the ridge, then flowing on toward the northern end of the island. Finally an aid station had arrived and set up among the tumbled boulders. And that was when the fireworks, which we were now witnessing, had begun.

The ridge, like all the others on Iwo, had been thoroughly integrated into the Jap scheme of defenses. Fifteen-centimeter guns had sat on top of the humps commanding the view in all directions. They had been shattered by our naval and aerial bombardments. From the ridge's sides, antitank guns, mortars and machine guns had poked out at the dreary landscape. Their scores of hiding places ranged from small concrete pillboxes, set into the rock, to narrow cave entranceways, camouflaged with stones, sand and sticks.

The entrances led into the network of tunnels and caverns. They ran all through the ridge and allowed the defenders to dart its length, from hole to hole, without being seen.

The Marine aid station had set up in a small amphitheater formed by the rocks at one end of the ridge. A smashed Jap antiaircraft gun loomed overhead, its long pocked barrel pointing into the sky.

The corpsmen had been too busy to notice the rocks. A battle was in progress 1,500 yards ahead, and the stretcher bearers were bringing back a stream of wounded. They set the litters down tenderly and went back for more wounded. The doctors and corpsmen worked silently over the torn and bleeding men.

A heavy Jap machine gun had suddenly rattled from the side of the ridge, just as a man carrying a crate of ammunition was passing by. He dropped his load of mortar shells, looked startled, and crumpled in a heap in the sand. A group of Marines, idling across the open space, hit the dirt and wriggled behind rocks. Two automatic riflemen, attached to a rifle company in reserve, peeked over the lip of the shellhole in which they had been resting. They tried to see where the bullets were coming from. They spotted an opening in the rocks and fired at it. The Jap machine gun ceased rattling. The two Marines cautiously clambered out of the shellhole and crawled toward the ridge. Other Marines, sensing a fight, waved to each other and began to close in. They covered each other with carbines and rifles and edged slowly toward the rocky hole.

A blaze of enemy small-arms fire came from at least five different parts of the ridge. Three Marines toppled over and the others dived for cover. The bullets whistled past the men in the aid station. The corpsmen looked up bewildered, then dropped to their hands and knees and went on working over the wounded.

The Marines in front of the ridge huddled behind rocks and waited. A step into the open meant death or injury. They studied the wounded men lying out in the open and tried to figure how to pull them to shelter. Finally a little corporal from New York City licked his lips and handed his rifle to the man next to him.

"Here goes," he said. He crawled out to the wounded man lying nearest to him.

He had almost reached him when there was another burst of fire and he stiffened. The injured man was also hit. His body jerked and quivered. Blood flowed from underneath the corporal's head. Both men had been instantly killed.

One of the corpsmen, a lanky fellow from Texas, left the aid station and came around the ridge to see what all the shooting was about.

"Get down," a Marine yelled at him. The corpsman dropped behind a rock and pushed his helmet back on his head. His eyes were bloodshot and glassy from lack of sleep.

"Hey," he called, "knock it off. This here's a hospital."

The Marines didn't appreciate the humor. They pointed down the road behind him. The corpsman turned. There were four stretcher bearers stumbling along the road with a wounded man, hurrying to the aid station.

The corpsman cupped his hands over his mouth to try to warn the stretcher bearers. There was too much noise. They couldn't hear him. The Japs began to fire at them. They ran faster. The corpsman wanted to run out and knock them flat, but something held him spellbound.

A bullet hit one of the stretcher bearers in the leg. He looked around wildly and crashed to the ground. The stretcher spilled on top of him. The men in front tripped as they tried to hold on to the stretcher. The Japs kept shooting into the group. The bullets peppered the sand around them. The wounded stretcher bearer jumped up again and grabbed his end of the litter. He started to drag the stretcher along, but dropped it. The man on the stretcher hung half over it. His head and shoulders dragged along the ground.

The other men half-crawled and half-ran with the stretcher until they reached the rocks. The wounded stretcher bearer loped after them. When he reached the shelter, he fell again. It was a miracle that he had been able to stay on his feet. The bullet had laid open his calf as if it had been hit by a meat cleaver. The man on the stretcher was stone dead. One of the bullets from the ridge had hit him in the skull.

No one knew how many Japs were in the ridge or where they had come from, or when. A supply captain, coming up from the rear, saw what was going on and radioed for tanks and demolitions men. More Marines from neighboring units gathered. They inspected the ridge from safety points behind some rocks.

When the tanks arrived, the Marines had started the step-by-step of again cleaning out the ridge. The dangerous and tedious work that had originally been done on D plus 16 by the front-line troops had to be repeated. The Marines threw smoke bombs and phosphorous grenades against the rocks and moved in with bazookas and automatic weapons. When the smoke drifted away, they had to shoot fast, or a Jap would catch them from one of the many holes. The tanks hurled their 75s at every position their gunners could locate. Engineers tried to fling dynamite charges into the caves.

Despite their preponderance of weapons, the Marines found that there were too many holes. They would attack one only to be shot at from another one half a dozen feet away. Moreover, the ridge was not a straight wall but, in many places, curved like an S. Entranceways protected each other, so that Marines would be hit in the back from holes guarding the one they were assaulting. The interconnecting tunnels inside the ridge also allowed the Japs to play deadly tag with the Marines. They would shoot out of one hole. But by the time Marines got close enough to that hole, the Japs had left it and were shooting from another one twenty yards away and higher up in the wall. The Marines had to post guards at every hole they could see in order to attack any of them. The tunnel also curved and twisted inside the ridge. The Japs could escape the straight trajectory weapons and grenades thrown into the cave entrances, merely by running back into the interior.

Finally flamethrowers were called. They threw long jets of flaming liquid into the holes and along the curving walls of the tunnels. The roaring flames did the trick. The Marines heard the Japs howling. A few rushed out of the caves on fire. The Marines shot them or knocked them down and beat out the flames and took them prisoners. When the Marines began to hear muffled explosions inside the caves, they guessed that some of the Japs were blowing themselves up with hand grenades.

The scene became wild and terrible. More Japs rushed screaming from the caves. They tumbled over the rocks, their clothes and bodies burning fiercely. Soon the flame-throwers paused. A Marine lifted himself cautiously into view. There were no shots from the caves. A Jap with his clothes in rags hunched himself out of one hole, his arms upraised. The Marines stood up behind the rocks and waved to him to come out. The Jap indicated that there were more who would like to surrender. The Marines motioned him to tell them to come out.

Almost forty scared and beaten men emerged from different holes. Some of them had round pudding faces. They grinned nervously and said they were Koreans. They had been forced by the Japs to stay in the caves. They said that everyone else in the caves had either been burned to death or had committed suicide.

The Marines sent them to the rear. Then they groped cautiously among the rocks from hole to hole, examining each entranceway. Dead bodies, some hit by bullets and grenade fragments, some burned into frightful black lumps, lay in the holes. The smell was overwhelming and men turned away in disgust.

The battle of the ridge seemed over. An officer made a note to bring up demolition crews as soon as they could be spared by the front-line companies. They would seal up the holes in this troublesome ridge. The Marines gathered their casualties and drifted away. The tanks shifted into reverse and backed out. Peacefulness settled once more over the area.

But it was not for long. The sudden death, which we had come on, was to strike again from the ridge, this time bitterly close.

That same day, several hours later, Sergeant Reid Chamberlain (El Cajon, Calif.) came up to the aid station. He was on his way to a front-line company. Chamberlain was a prominent figure in the Marine Corps. He had served with General MacArthur on Bataan and Corregidor early in the war. He had escaped from Corregidor to help organize Filipino guerrilla bands. He had stayed in the Philippines a year and a half and had been commissioned a lieutenant in the U.S. Army. Finally he had returned to America and been awarded the Distinguished Service Cross. Then he had resigned his Army commission, re-enlisted as a sergeant in the Marines, and had come overseas again. He was now a battalion runner with the 21st Regiment. He was short and handsome and wore a brown mustache. Despite the publicity that had been given to his exploits as a guerrilla leader in the Philippines, he had stayed modest and unassuming and was one of the most popular men in the outfit.

A small group of us accompanied Chamberlain to the front-line company. We began to cross the clearing which we thought had been rid of Jap sniper fire. To escape occasional mortar shells that were dropping in the open, we clung perhaps too closely to the rocky walls of the ridge. We were picking our way among the stones and the burned Jap bodies when three shots rang out from the hillside. We scattered and tried to run behind some boulders. Chamberlain drew his pistol and looked frantically around. There was another shot. We heard a thud. We thought the bullet had struck the curving side of the ridge.

When we reached safe spots, we paused and looked back. Our hearts beat wildly. Chamberlain was nowhere in sight. An ambulance driver and an automatic rifleman were crouched behind nearby rocks, their teeth clenched, their hands gripping their weapons. They were trying to find the hole from which the shots had come. We called Chamberlain but received no answer. Slowly we tried to edge back. Rifle shots cracked at us from several holes, and we ducked again.

The long, rocky ridge was once more alive with enemy. Again Marines began to gather, coming up cautiously to help us. They dashed from rock to rock and slid among the boulders, trying to seek cover from the many caves that looked out at us. We told them about Chamberlain, lying somewhere among the rocks. We formed a team quickly and began crawling forward. When the Japs fired at us again, the men covering us saw where the shots were coming from. They sent a stream of automatic fire at the holes and "buttoned up" the Japs. One burly sergeant stood straight up without a helmet on and, gritting his teeth, fired his carbine from his hip, moving directly at a hole as he fired. The jeep ambulance driver finally reached Chamberlain's body and lifted his head. A trickle of blood flowed from behind his ear. His eyes were open, but he was dead.

There is nothing you can say or do when a good friend is suddenly killed in battle. You feel stunned, angry, sad and somewhat frustrated. We could have fired point-blank the rest of the day at those holes. The Japs would only have laughed at us. In an instant they had claimed one of our best men. Chamberlain's wonderful war record had ended abruptly. After so many heroic deeds, it seemed an added tragedy that he was killed while doing nothing but walking. There was nothing anybody could do about it.

We crawled back and sent for flamethrowers, only to find that we couldn't get any more that day. They were all busy up front. Meanwhile, an outfit of the 9th Marines was moving up and pitching its bivouac on top of the ridge, which had become silent again. We hunted up the commanding officer and told him there were still Japs inside the hill. We related to him all that had happened at the ridge that day. He listened concernedly but decided it was too late in the afternoon to try to root out the Japs still in the caves. He posted guards behind the rocks facing the ridge and gave them orders to keep all straggling Marines away from the holes.

Another combat correspondent, Technical Sergeant Francis Barr (Dallas, Texas), had come up with the new outfit and was digging in for the night. What happened that night was later revealed by Barr.

According to him, as soon as it got dark the Japs tried to come out of their holes. The Marine guards saw them slithering out among the rocks and opened fire, killing some and driving the others back in. The Japs screamed and cursed when they realized they were trapped. Some of them committed suicide inside their holes.

Corporal H. E. Duke (Cheyenne, Wyo.) heard the muffled sounds of hand grenades exploding underneath him in the ridge. He had been sitting in a blackout tent, making out some operational reports on a typewriter. He looked at his watch. It was just before midnight.

Suddenly there was a terrific explosion that rocked the whole hill. A huge boulder flew through the tent and smashed Duke's typewriter into smithereens. Outside, Corporal Vincent M. Langa (Cleveland, Ohio) was blown out of his foxhole 20 feet into the air. Private John F. Muralt (Minneapolis, Minn.), a chaplain's assistant, was buried, as the explosion sent slides of hot sand into his hole.

A flash of flame shot into the air and there was a series of rumbles and more explosions. The ridge quivered and shook. Rocks, dirt and hunks of concrete showered among the dug-in Marines. Platoon Sergeant Rudolph Rott (Wonewoc, Wis.) thought the whole ridge was on fire.

By the light of the flames, the men dug each other out and scrambled down the ridge to safety. Stones cascaded after them in landslides that sealed up half the holes in the ridge's wall. The men took up positions behind the rocks and waited for the Japs to come out. Platoon Sergeant Waldo D. Humphrey (Kansas City, Kans.) saw two of them sitting among the stones in a dazed condition. They were carrying anti-personnel mines around their waists. He killed them as they tried to get up. Another man struggling down the slope saw other Japs trying to rush out from the holes, only to be buried in landslides. Their arms and legs protruded from the dirt and rocks. A group of five Japs, running along the wall of the ridge, were spotted by the light of the flames, and instantly killed.

"They looked like little devils running through Hell," a corporal said later on. "All they needed were pitchforks."

Slowly the Marines realized what had happened. The Japs had blown themselves up and, with them, the whole ridge. When dawn came, the Marines discovered that they had suffered only one serious casualty. Many men, like Private Muralt, had been completely buried by the rocks and sulphur ashes, but companions had dug them out before they had smothered. Scouts who poked into some of the remaining holes found that the Japs had used land mines and 125-pound aerial bombs to blow up the hill. They also discovered empty canteens on some of the torn Japanese bodies, indicating that the men who had tried to come out earlier in the night had probably been after water.

It was almost impossible and certainly foolhardy to try to trace the winding tunnels to their sources. The Marines instead decided to blow up all the holes still unsealed and trap whatever Japs might still be alive in the ridge's inner recesses.

It was a long and tedious job. The demolitions men worked all day, placing charges in the mouths of more than forty caves. When they were blown up, it was almost impossible to know whether tiny holes and cracks had not been left among the tumbled rocks through which hiding Japs could still fire. By nightfall, everyone felt a sense of frustration and further trouble. An officer in charge of a group of the engineers shook his head and said, "We ought to put up a sign here, 'Pass at your own risk.' "

The sign was not put up. If it had been, it would have made some of the men laugh. But the terrible ridge was still nothing to laugh at. It was still "hot." A supply unit for a 3rd Division regiment was the next outfit to run into the death that lurked among its rocks.

When the supply unit moved up, the area again looked secure. The unit pitched tents and galleys, built ration piles, parked jeeps and trailers and nonchalantly went about its business of shuttling hot food, ammunition and water to the battalions ahead.

Someone told the new arrivals about the ridge. But they looked at its silent, strewn rocks and shrugged. The fighting was now more than a mile ahead. A sniper or two this far back couldn't cause trouble.

But this time it wasn't a sniper.

A jeep and trailer, setting off one afternoon with hot coffee and doughnuts for the front lines, was fired at. The driver didn't wait to find out what kind of weapon was shooting at him. He knew it was something big. He stepped on the gas and raced out of the area. On the way back he was shot at again. Jeep ambulance drivers and other supply men reported similar attacks on them. Finally a tank, lumbering over the road, was hit. The crew jumped out and hid behind some rocks.

After a while, they came back and reported that an antitank gun was somewhere among the debris of the ridge. Some of the members of the supply unit armed themselves with rifles and carbines and went to have a look. A shower of small-arms bullets from the ridge drove them back.

They sent for help to an engineering outfit, but were told that demolitions men could not be spared at the moment. The drivers who had to take that road, moving back and forth to the front, called the route "Suicide Run." Every time they approached the rocks they stepped hard on the gas and raced past them as fast as they could go. The antitank gun hurled shells at them each time, but fortunately there were no hits. Finally, a tank was sent up. It waited behind some rocks till the Jap gun fired and showed its position. Then the tank blasted at it with its 75. In a few moments the Jap position was a pile of smoking rubble. Automatic riflemen who moved in to catch enemy survivors found the troublesome weapon to be a 47-mm. antitank gun. The Japs had kept it concealed during all the previous fighting around the ridge.

It would seem as if that might have ended the story of the ridge. But it didn't. As the battle for Iwo reached its conclusion in the northern cliffs, Jap riflemen and machine gunners continued to hang on inside the tunnels back here and fire out at passersby whenever a good shot was presented. The area soon became full of Marines. Rear camps pitched among the rocky heights dotting the landscape. And with the concentration of men to shoot at, the Japs meted out sudden death and injury to scores of unsuspecting Americans.

A wireman, stringing a telephone line between rear command posts, was shot through the head. Two cooks were winged in the arms. A whole mortar platoon was pinned down in its holes by a Jap machine gunner. A barber and an officer who was having his hair cut were sent running by a burst of rifle shots.

Whenever the Marines could spot exact positions from which Japs were firing, they attempted to knock them out. With automatic rifles and bazookas, they crept among the rocks and blasted at the small holes. Then they threw dynamite charges into the slits and hoped they would do the trick.

It was an almost hopeless task. The Marines soon realized that there was only one way to eliminate the Japs. That was to wait until they came out. And come out they eventually did, for food and water. One night near the end of the campaign five enemy emerged and crept up to a regimental headquarters unit. Automatic riflemen, in a circle of foxholes around the bivouac area, saw the Japs in the moonlight and opened fire. They killed all five.

In the same way, other Japanese stragglers were eliminated, one by one, group by group. But on D plus 25, the day the Marines overran the last bit of Iwo Jima and the island was declared secured, death was still coming from the ridge. A Jap sniper that day shot a passing corpsman through the ear.

We never knew just how many Japs were in that ridge or where they kept coming from. Some thought that the Japs moved around at night from one part of the island to the other, looking for water, and that at dawn they disappeared into the nearest ridges. Other men thought the Japs moved from ridge to ridge through underground tunnels. Only if we were someday to tear away from the sides of the ridges the tumbling rocks and debris which now cover the many holes would we ever be able to trace to their sources the tunnels that fill their dreadful interiors.

To Tokyo Bay

More than 4,500 Marines were killed on Iwo, and 16,000 wounded. Was the sacrifice worthwhile? One can make out a fair case for it. More than 800 B-29's—coming back to the Marianas after encountering enemy fire and engine failure over Japan—used the island for emergency landings after it was secured; their 9,000 crew members might otherwise have been lost.

On April 1, 1945, less than a week after Iwo had seen its last organized attack by the Japanese, the 10th Army, consisting of the 1st and 6th Marine Divisions, and the 7th and 96th Army Infantry Divisions, all under Gen. S. B. Buckner, landed on Okinawa in the Ryukyu Islands—last stop before the home islands of Japan. This campaign spanned three months, and war with the tenacious Japanese soldier was as grueling as ever; the U.S. casualty list was more than 12,500 killed, and 36,600 wounded.

But the Japanese army was decimated, the navy practically nonexistent, and the Jap air force had lost the stunning total of more than 7,800 planes from U.S. ground and naval efforts around Okinawa.

But heavy losses couldn't break the spirit of the Japanese; neither could the collapse of their German partner, leaving them to face the combined might of the Allied forces alone. They refused an unconditional surrender ultimatum issued, in July 1945, by the Allied heads of state at Potsdam. This refusal decided President Truman (with the assent of Prime Minister Churchill and both their staffs) to drop the newly-tested atomic bomb. It was hoped that this new weapon might avert a far greater bloodbath—the invasion of the Japanese home islands.

Thousands of leaflets were dropped in all major Japanese cities urging the population to evacuate. Then the first bomb was dropped on Hiroshima on August 6th; a second, August 9th, on Nagasaki. The terrifying power of this weapon did what years of defeat hadn't been able to accomplish. It broke the will of Japan's military leaders. The civilians took over, and Japan accepted the terms of the Potsdam ultimatum on

August 14th; a formal surrender was signed aboard the battleship *Missouri* on September 2nd.

When the islands of Japan were secured at last, there would be no bloody mopping up of survivors resisting to the bitter end, no last-minute Banzai charges—the fighting was really over.

Allied victory in the Pacific had been swift, compared to the long war predicted in early 1942; in those days the Japanese, whirlwind conquerors of East Asia and the Indies, seemed invincible. How had they lost it all? And how had we won? According to S. E. Morison, the chief reasons were:

"First, by stupid strategy on the part of the Japanese—the Pearl Harbor attack, 'Victory Disease,' and their complete lack of knowledge of or interest in defensive strategy.

"Second, by excessive Japanese inferiority in war production.

"Third, by intelligent strategic planning on the part of Adm. King, Adm. Nimitz, Gen. MacArthur and their staffs, as coordinated by the Joint Chiefs of Staff. After the initial defeats at Pearl Harbor, Wake Island, and the Philippines, they did not make a single major error.

"Fourth, by the superb fighting qualities of the American and Australian soldiers, marines, bluejackets, and aviators." *

No reader of the reports of fighting men in the Pacific can fail to agree with the last point. The war in the Pacific was above all a war of individual fighting men, and they wrote a record of heroism and endurance which deserves to last as long as the great ocean itself.

* S. E. Morison, *Strategy and Compromise*, p. 118.

DATE DUE

927791			
JAN 08 1998			
DEC 29 1997			